The Advance of Christianity Through the Centuries, Vol. VIII
General Editor: PROFESSOR F. F. BRUCE, M.A., D.D.

THE LIGHT OF THE NATIONS

THE LIGHT OF THE NATIONS

*Evangelical Renewal and Advance
in the Nineteenth Century*

by

J. EDWIN ORR

*Th.D., D.Phil. (Oxon),
F.R.Hist.S., M.Am.Hist.A.*

Wipf & Stock
PUBLISHERS
Eugene, Oregon

Wipf and Stock Publishers
199 W 8th Ave, Suite 3
Eugene, OR 97401

The Light of the Nations
Evangelical Renewal and Advance in the Nineteenth Century
By Orr, J. Edwin
Copyright©1965 Paternoster
ISBN: 1-59752-699-1
Publication date 6/2/2006
Previously published by The Paternoster Press, 1965

This Edition reprinted by Wipf and Stock Publishers
by arrangement with Paternoster

Paternoster
9 Holdom Avenue
Bletchley
Milton Keyes, MK1 1QR
PATERNOSTER Great Britain

EDITOR'S PREFACE

SOME MEN READ HISTORY, SOME WRITE IT, AND OTHERS MAKE it. So far as the history of religious revivals is concerned, the author of this book belongs to all three categories. When I first met him—thirty years ago, in Vienna—he was actively promoting the cause of religious revival; he is still at it today. The story of the Lord's dealings with him over the years has recently been told by Bishop Appasamy in *Write the Vision!* (London, 1965).

A word should be added on the relation between the present book and the author's standard works on *The Second Evangelical Awakening in Britain* (London, 1949) and *The Second Evangelical Awakening in America* (London, 1953), which represent the material of a thesis for which he received his Oxford doctorate in philosophy, and on the parallel movement in North America. Whereas they involved intensive research, the research involved in this work has rather been extensive, and since it is a work of interpretation, secondary as well as primary sources are cited.

The story told in the following pages is one without which a series purporting to cover the history of the Church would be incomplete, and it is difficult to think of any writer so well qualified to tell it as Dr. Orr. His world-wide experience as well as his specialist study entitles him to speak with exceptional authority on evangelical renewal and advance.

F. F. B.

CONTENTS

7

CHAPTER I

REVOLUTIONARY PRELUDE

THE REVOLUTIONS OF THE LATE EIGHTEENTH CENTURY USH-
ered in a nineteenth century of unparalleled opportunity and
advance in the expansion of the Christian Church, an epoch
rightly named by Latourette "The Great Century."[1]
In delimiting the century of advance, one need not measure an
exact hundred years from New Year's Day, 1800, until New Year's
Eve, 1900, but rather from the conclusion of the Napoleonic Wars
in 1815 to the outbreak of World War I in 1914, a period often
called *Pax Britannica*. And the revolutionary four decades which
preceded the *Pax Britannica* may be considered as a prelude.

There were two momentous revolutions in the concluding
quarter of the eighteenth century, the American Revolution and
the French Revolution. Both revolutions professed to oppose
tyranny and promote liberty and justice. But the mainsprings of
the revolutions were of different origin, for, whereas the French
Revolution seemed to explode from the igniting of an anti-
religious atmosphere,[2] the American revolution seemed to develop
from forces unleashed by the evangelical awakenings of the middle
quarters of the eighteenth century. Democratic liberty and equality
in America were traceable to evangelical sources.[3]

The nation of Great Britain, on the threshold of its Second
Empire,[4] stood in strategic apposition to these two dynamic
revolutions. For about twenty years, sometimes alone and sometimes in alliance with other nations, British sea-power was employed to curb the excesses of the belligerent French Revolution
which threatened to establish a greater tyranny than the one it had
overthrown;[5] and, for a century, British sea-power served to promote the interests of democratic liberty that had triumphed in
the American Revolution.[6]

What effect did the evangelical message have upon the social

[1] Latourette, K. S., *A History of the Expansion of Christianity*, Vols. IV, V, and VI.
[2] Bready, J. W., *This Freedom—Whence?* p. 342; cf. Aulard, *Christianity and the French Revolution.*
[3] Gewehr, W. M., *The Great Awakening in Virginia*, pp. 187 ff.; cf. Sweet, W. W., *Revivalism in America*, p. 22.
[4] Harlow, V. T., *The Founding of the Second British Empire, passim.*
[5] Brown, P. A., *The French Revolution in English History, passim.*
[6] Thomas, D. Y., *One Hundred Years of the Monroe Doctrine, passim.*

9

and political liberties of mankind? The liberating forces set in motion by the great Reformation and subsequent Revivals in English-speaking countries accelerated evolution towards government of the people, for the people, by the people. A violent revolution instead occurred in France, where the Reformation had barely failed. Freedom, whether revolutionary or evolutionary, was long delayed in other parts of Christendom untouched or unmoved by the Reformation. While the anti-clerical French and the pro-Protestant countries made steady progress, Russia remained autocratic, the glory of Spain declined, the energy of Portugal dwindled away, and Italy remained in political chaos until the middle of the nineteenth century; while dicatatorship flourished in each of these countries as well as Germany even in the twentieth century.

While the Great Awakening in the American Colonies made its lasting impact in the realm of political and religious liberty, a lasting impact of the Evangelical Revival in the United Kingdom was felt in the realm of social and industrial freedom. The flowering of both political and religious liberty in the first American Republic affected the politico-religious evolution of the Second British Empire, more particularly Canada, Australia, New Zealand and South Africa. The flowering of social and industrial freedom in Britain affected the social and industrial welfare of the United States in turn. Each was the laboratory of the other.

How extensive was the Evangelical Revival in Britain? Long before the eighteenth century had closed, Wesley surveyed what God had wrought:[1]

> This revival of religion has spread to such a degree as neither we nor our fathers had known. . . . There is scarce a considerable town in the kingdom where some have not been made witnesses of it. . . . In what age has such a number of sinners been recovered from the error of their ways?

Evangelical Revival of necessity begins with the Church rather than the State, and in its effect upon the social welfare there is a time-lag often as long as the lifetime of its converts.

The effect of the Evangelical Revival upon the social structure of Britain was summarized by the famous French historian, Halévy, thus:[2]

> . . . Evangelical religion was the moral cement of English society. It was the influence of the Evangelicals which invested the British aristocracy with an almost stoic dignity, restrained the plutocrats who had newly risen from the masses from vulgar ostentation and debauchery, and placed over the proletariat a select body of workmen

[1] Wesley, John, *Works*, Vol. VII, p. 425.
[2] Halévy, E., *History of the English People, 1830–1841*, p. 166.

enamoured of virtue and capable of self-restraint. Evangelicalism was thus the conservative force which restored in England the balance momentarily destroyed by the explosion of the revolutionary forces.

It was in Great Britain that the movement for the emancipation of the slaves began. It was also in Britain that the trade union movement began its work of uplifting the living standards of labour. It was there that John Howard and Elizabeth Fry and others began their work of prison reform. It was there that Shaftesbury began his deliverance of industrial slaves. And all these movements were felt in the United States and other democracies.

In the United States, the Baptists proved to be the main pioneers of political and religious liberty.[1] In Britain, the pioneering of social and industrial freedom fell to the Evangelical Anglicans in both the Methodist societies and in the parish churches.[2] John Wesley's social conscience was well-known. He provided encouragement not only for his own Methodists, but also for ardent Anglicans in the Church such as Wilberforce and John Howard.

Arthur Skevington Wood stresses the point that the message of the Evangelical Revival of the eighteenth century aimed at expounding the plain truth for plain people.[3] There were but few volumes of systematic theology or speculative philosophy published by the evangelical leaders. Almost all of their contributions were written as homiletic and devotional literature. They spoke and wrote with the major object of reaching the masses, and were content to leave apologetics to others called to the work of the defence of the gospel. Critical historians often deplore the inadequacy of theology in revival movements, and not only in the eighteenth century.

The preaching of the Revivalists was biblical. When a Bishop of London warned his diocese against the "new gospel" being preached by Whitefield, the latter sadly replied that he admitted that his message sounded like a new gospel to many hearers, but that it was actually the old gospel of salvation by grace.[4]

Great as were the changes in the English-speaking world in the realm of political, social and industrial activity, they were not quite so noticeable as the changes in the churches.

In New England, Congregationalism was well revived by the Great Awakening. The Log College evangelists of Pennsylvania helped transform a formal Presbyterianism. In the Middle and the Southern Colonies, the Baptists were converted from a tiny min-

---

[1] Sweet, W. W., *Revivalism in America*, pp. 42–43.
[2] Trevelyan, G. M., *English Social History*, p. 495; cf. Young and Ashton, *British Social Work*, p. 41.
[3] Wood, A. S., *The Inextinguishable Blaze*, p. 223.
[4] Whitefield, G., *Works*, Vol. IV, p. 15.

ority to a dynamic denomination. The Methodists in both the United States and in Britain became a major force in the evangelization of their nations. Whitefield's Scottish colleagues enjoyed a season of renewal in the Kirk. In England, the greatest lasting impact of the Revival was seen in the transformation of life of thousands of English clergy, who in a couple of generations transformed the Church of England.[1] Baptist and Congregational denominations rapidly became sturdy minorities. The preaching places of Dissenters, including Methodists, in Britain increased thirty-fold in a couple of generations.

The historian Lecky declared that the English clergy who were moved by the Evangelical Revival[2]

. . . gradually changed the whole spirit of the English Church. They infused into it a new fire and passion of devotion, kindled a spirit of fervent philanthropy, raised the standard of clerical duty, and completely altered the whole tone and tendency of preaching of ministers.

For the greater part of the fruit of the Revival, it is necessary to look to the nineteenth century, in which new movements were raised up and in which fresh awakenings occurred. It is significant that most of the results of the Evangelical Revival cited by historians occurred at the beginning of the nineteenth century. Some organizations were produced by later revivals and some helped much to produce such revivals.

It must never be forgotten that Evangelical Christianity at the beginning of the nineteenth century influenced a tiny part of the land area and population of the world.[3] It had major force in the United Kingdom and in Scandinavia and a great influence in the Netherlands and Switzerland. It shared the German States with Roman Catholicism, and was a minor force in Hungary, the same in France, and almost non-existent in Italy, Spain and Portugal and the rest of Europe.

In the Americas, there were vigorous bodies of Evangelical Christians in the coastal states between the Alleghenies and the Atlantic, a few settlers in the Ohio Valley and none at all in the West,[4] while Mexico, Central and South America had only a handful of Evangelical Christians that belonged to the trading and diplomatic colonies.

The Muslim countries scarcely knew what an Evangelical Christian was, while Africa was an unexplored continent, with a handful of Evangelicals at the Cape of Good Hope. Christianity in India was represented by an ancient communion in the South

[1] Binns, L. E., *The Evangelical Movement in the English Church, passim.*
[2] Lecky, W. E. H., *A History of England in the Eighteenth Century,* Vol. II, p. 627.
[3] Cf. Latourette, K. S., *op. cit.,* Vol. VI, introduction.
[4] Sweet, W. W., *Story of Religion in America,* p. 205.

and a scattering of aliens. There was but a handful of Evangelicals in China and the rest of Asia. Australia was unoccupied, and the islands of the Pacific were the haunts of cannibals. Such was the unoccupied world of Wesley's day. The few missionary agencies of the Protestant Churches were sent to reach Protestant colonists, their servants, and occasionally their neighbours.

And how was Evangelical Christianity equipped for the task? Throughout the major part of the eighteenth century, Evangelical Christianity operated without Bible Societies; its denominations, whether Anglican, Baptist, Congregational, Lutheran, Methodist, Presbyterian or Reformed, operated without missionary societies; its youth enjoyed no Sunday Schools for teaching the rudiments of the Christian faith.

Evangelical Christianity during the eighteenth century lacked the multiple agencies of inter-denominational co-operation which flourished in the latter half of the nineteenth century—such missionary organizations as the China Inland Mission and all the "faith" missionary societies; Home Missions of the various denominations; City Missions; the Salvation Army; agencies for the conversion of children and organizations for the rehabilitation of the lost and straying.

What was it that raised up these manifold agencies of evangelization and social reform? The eighteenth-century Revival had run its course. Where did the dynamic originate, the dynamic which produced the Christian action of the nineteenth century? As in the eighteenth century, the dynamic came from successive new movements of evangelical revival.[1] Yet before the nineteenth century with all its achievements began, there was a desperate death of spiritual life in the areas so recently blessed in revival.

[1] Cf. Latourette, *op. cit.*, Vol. VI, p. 35.

CHAPTER II

DARK BEFORE THE DAWN

ARTHUR SKEVINGTON WOOD, IN HIS VOLUME ON THE EIGHTEENTH century, *The Inextinguishable Blaze*, has summarized the desperate conditions typical of English-speaking Christendom in the sentence: "Nothing less than a revival could effectively deal with the situation."[1]

It is significant that the same sentence might have been applied to conditions at the *end* of the eighteenth century, despite the achievements of the Great Awakenings which had swept every part of Protestantism. And this was most clearly seen in the United States, where the Revivals had been most effective in transforming the national life.

The reaction against the evangelicalism of the Great Awakening took the form of popular deism, which captured the American mentality late in the eighteenth century.[2] For the origin of this deism, it is necessary to view England a century earlier.

In the heyday of the Puritans, Lord Herbert of Cherbury (1583–1648) presented a case for deism in five points—recognizing the existence of a personal God, the Creator and Ruler of all; the obligation of divine worship; the necessity of ethical conduct; the resolution of repentance of sins; and the assurance of divine rewards or punishments, both here and hereafter.[3]

The "father of deism" was followed by other writers who, between 1700 and 1750, conducted their campaign against orthodoxy. Eighteenth-century deism was best presented in England by John Toland and Matthew Tindal, who pleaded a case for natural religion as opposed to revealed truth.[4] They enlisted a following, and before long, the deistic propaganda had shaken the authority of Scripture in the minds of men, hamstringing the work of the churches.

The main result of the attack and defence was to lower the general tone of religious feeling, without destroying respect for the estab-

[1] Wood, A. S., *The Inextinguishable Blaze*, p. 25.
[2] Beardsley, F. G., *A History of American Revivals*, pp. 77 ff.
[3] Newman, A. H., *Manual of Church History*, Vol. II, p. 365; cf. Orr, John, *English Deism, passim.*
[4] *Vide* Toland, J., *Christianity Not Mysterious*, and Tindal, M., *Christianity as Old as Creation.*

lished creeds; to make men unwilling to ask awkward questions, and to compound with their consciences by not making arrogant assumptions; and, generally to bring about comfortable compromise which held together till Wesley, from one side, and Paine, from another, forced more serious thoughts upon the age.[1]

English deism was counter-attacked by clever Christian apologists, such as Bishops Butler and Berkeley.[2] Attacked on both sides by critics, the deism of the period gave way to the scepticism of David Hume and the rationalism of Thomas Paine which replaced eighteenth-century deism among the educated classes of Great Britain and America respectively.[3] Another century passed before this rationalism became atheistic.

Trevelyan, in his *English Social History*, specified the year 1776 in retrospect as the low-water mark in the ebb-tide of infidelity and of laxity of doctrine in England.[4] It was also a significant date in American history, the date of the Declaration of Independence. And Tom Paine, a champion of American independence and advocate of French revolution, popularized rationalistic deism as the proper doctrine for the emerging democracies.[5] Paine's writings were immensely popular and masses of restless people took hold of his ideas, abandoning orthodox Christianity.

It must be stated that deistic rationalism did not deny God or worship or Christian ethics. It made superfluous all that is contained in the expression "Christian experience" by removing God from needy humanity. In this sense, deistic rationalism provided a serious counterthrust to the workings of the eighteenth-century Revival and its personalized religion. This proved true in both Britain and America.

The noble figure of Thomas Jefferson, father of the American republic, lent much aid to the rapid spread of rationalistic deism in the newly independent United States. Jefferson was a deist,[6] with a reverent attitude towards religion, and he claimed to be a Christian "in the sense that Jesus wished anyone to be," though he did not make it clear how he knew what Jesus Christ wished in this regard. In fact, Jefferson compiled from the New Testament those sayings and doings of Jesus which met his approval, leaving aside every trace of the supernatural and every claim to Deity.[7]

In events, it so happened that the objects of patriotic American deists and patriotic American evangelicals coincided, and their efforts together so moved public opinion that the Revolution was possible and successful. If the matter had rested there, there would

---

[1] Stephen, Sir Leslie, *English Thought in the Eighteenth Century*, Vol. I, pp. 272–273.
[2] Trevelyan, G. M., *English Social History*, p. 354.
[3] *Ibid.*, p. 355.   [4] *Loc. cit.*   [5] *Loc. cit.*
[6] Beardsley, F. G., *op. cit.*, p. 80.
[7] The writer has seen this work in the Library of Congress in Washington.

have been little clash between this gentle deism of Jefferson and the positive evangelicalism of the recently revived Churches.

But an alliance between the American republic and the revolutionary republic of France, moved by a more violent form of insurrection, brought a flood of infidelity to the United States which the moderates were unable to control.[1] Gentlemen like Jefferson with inherited Christian ethics but without dynamic faith appeared to be powerless in the communicating of their ideals to the masses.

In the wake of the American Revolution came a disastrous setback for evangelical Christianity.[2] Revolution had not been a unanimous uprising of oppressed people, but rather a civil war, with a third or more of the population supporting active revolutionaries, a third loyalist, and the rest undecided, as usual in democracies. Christians too were divided in this issue. The Anglicans and Methodists were considered by revolutionaries as royalist in sympathy, the Congregationalists, Presbyterians and Baptists anti-royalist.[3]

Inevitably, republicanism in the new nation showed hospitality to the work of noted infidels and political radicals, the French revolutionists capturing the place of evangelical moderates so completely that Yale College was overrun with ungodly sceptics and rowdies, while Princeton fared no better, there being one year no more than two students who professed religion, and five or six who scrupled the use of profane language in common conversation, and sometimes profanity was of a very shocking kind.[4]

The Transylvania University, a Presbyterian foundation in Kentucky, passed under the control of infidels,[5] as did many other colleges.[6] George Washington, Patrick Henry, John Adams and kindred spirits were much opposed to the new ideas, but other national figures were not, for Thomas Jefferson was a deist, Henry Dearborn an unbeliever, and General Charles Lee a violent opponent of Christianity.[7]

The post-Revolution period was one of massive emigration west of the Appalachian Mountains to the opened frontier.[8] Uprooted people abandoned the restraints of settled society, drunkenness and violence abounding.[9]

---

[1] Thompson, C. L., *Times of Refreshing*, p. 68.
[2] Sweet, W. W., *Revivalism in America*, p. 117.
[3] Sweet, W. W., *Story of Religion in America*, ch. xii, "The War of Independence."
[4] Strickland, W., *The Great American Revival*, p. 33; cf. Beecher, Lyman, *Reminiscences*.
[5] Beardsley, F. G., *op. cit.*, p. 78.
[6] Cf. Sonne, N. H., *Liberal Kentucky*, 1780–1828, p. 287.
[7] Beardsley, F. G., *op. cit.*, p. 80.
[8] Sweet, W. W., *op. cit.*, pp. 206 ff.
[9] *Ibid.*, p. 225.

It was obvious that American Christianity had declined, for morals were bankrupt, and infidel clubs abounded, with their usual accompaniment of sex orgies—so that the national existence was itself seriously jeopardized, thought some.

It was no wonder a friend wrote to Washington in the year 1796:

> Our affairs seem to lead to some crisis, some revolution; something that I can not foresee or conjecture. I am more uneasy than during the war.

And George Washington replied:

> Your sentiment . . . accords with mine. What will be is beyond my foresight.[1]

The concern of statesmen became the alarm of churchmen, for the churches were emptying fast. Dark days clouded the end of the eighteenth century. Its middle fifty years had been a jubilee of expansion of the Church throughout American territory, but the final twenty-five years were as distressing as the first twenty-five.

In New England, where occurred a reaction against certain features of the Great Awakening, the people inclined towards formalism and against evangelism as they grew wealthier. Deism soon became a powerful ally of anti-evangelicalism. Unitarianism and Universalism, aided by the decline of orthodox Christianity, began to make great progress in the struggle for the control of the churches of New England.[2] In few decades, Unitarians gained control of many strategic and influential Congregational churches, splitting the denomination irreparably. The Universalists and Unitarians continued their drift from evangelical Christianity towards humanism.

Across the Atlantic, in Northern Ireland the revolt against orthodoxy manifested itself in an upsurge of Arianism among Irish Presbyterians,[3] resulting in a bitter controversy which was not resolved until Dr. Henry Cooke took up the sore challenge and rallied the forces of evangelical Calvinism against the Unitarians within Ulster Presbyterianism,[4] forcing the separation of the Unitarian denomination as the Non-Subscribing Presbyterian Church. The Unitarian rebellion constituted the greatest threat to orthodoxy in the history of Ireland.

Before the end of the eighteenth century, the religious life of Scotland showed a marked decline. Not only Arianism and Deism wrought a deadening work, but even greater havoc was wrought by lay-patronage, in which a patron without spiritual insight was

[1] Strickland, W., *op. cit.*, p. 40.
[2] Sweet, W. W., *op. cit.*, pp. 241–242.
[3] Reid, J. S., *History of the Presbyterian Church in Ireland*, Vol. III, p. 460.
[4] *Ibid.*, Vol. III, p. 415.

free to inflict an unspiritual minister upon a church.[1] The General Assembly protested year by year against the infringement of the rights of the local congregations, which were forced to accept an unwanted minister or to retreat from their beloved kirk and build themselves a chapel. Soon a greater and greater number of parochial ministers in the General Assembly were found to be indifferent to evangelical religion, and the condition of Scotland at the close of the century was sunken low in spiritual lethargy. The party accepting the abuse of patronage named itself the party of the Moderates.[2]

John Locke's volume *The Reasonableness of Christianity*, which circulated at the beginning of the eighteenth century, became the starting point[3] of two movements—English Deism, promoted by Toland and Tindal, and Latitudinarianism, which set the prevalent tone of the Church of England for several generations and contested the ground with Methodism and the Evangelicals.

As the gentler deism of Lord Herbert gave way to the scepticism of Hume and Gibbon, its appeal was limited to a highly educated audience. It was said that infidelity, like hair-powder for wigs, could be worn only by the aristocracy. The middle classes were actively or passively orthodox, the lower classes largely ignorant.[4] Even the aristocrats found it difficult to share dogmas or the lack of them with the mob which was busy guillotining their Gallic brethren.

But it was easy to slide from Latitudinarianism into Unitarianism, as the English Presbyterians largely did. It became fashionable to preach morality, with a little dogma apologetically attached.

That scepticism did not wreak quite so much havoc in England as in its neighbours upon the Continent is perhaps due to two factors: the deep and lasting work of the Methodist Revival and the failure of Napoleon to invade England. Fear of Napoleon brought about distrust of the infidelity that marked the French revolutionary movement and alienated all classes of British people.[5]

In France, one of the unhappy by-products of the Roman Catholic persecution of the Huguenots was the fact that hundreds of thousands of the best educated people, compelled to violate their consciences to conform outwardly to a religion that their souls abominated, laid themselves and their children open to scepticism and infidelity.[6]

Much of the free-thinking which preceded the French Revolution was derived from perjuring Huguenots, whose antagonism

---

[1] Trevelyan, *op. cit.*, p. 461.
[2] *Ibid.*, p. 459.   [3] *Ibid.*, p. 354.   [4] *Ibid.*, p. 355.   [5] *Ibid.*, p. 468.
[6] Newman, A. H., *op. cit.*, Vol. II, p. 487.

to forced religion was intensified by the fact that it was a Roman Catholicism of the poorest spiritual type that had triumphed, one of shameless immorality among the clergy and of limitless arrogance among the bishops.[1] When the revolution came, the people of France revolted against French Christianity.

Rousseau propounded his deism, but Voltaire preached scepticism, finding no antagonists like Butler and Berkeley to contradict him.[2] Voltaire denounced as *L'Infâme* the whole system of an unbearable ecclesiastico-political oppression, and produced a volcanic heat underground.[3]

When the explosion of the French Revolution scattered its fire all over Europe, the enfeebled Christian countries nearby were unable to offer resistance. And the fire inside France was so intense that nominal Protestants as well as the Roman Catholics embraced the new infidelity, so apostatizing. In Britain, fear of the excesses of the French Revolution made people pray.

In 1706, in neighbouring Germany, Christian Wolff was appointed professor of natural philosophy at the University of Halle.[4] Becoming very popular as a lecturer, he exercised far-reaching influence once he had committed himself to the proposition that all doctrines of the Christian faith are either capable of demonstration or else unworthy of credence. His activities were next transferred to Marburg; and by 1740 his teaching dominated religious thought in much of Germany.[5]

Frederick the Great, thoroughly sympathizing with such religious free-thinking, recalled the aged philosopher to Halle, and introduced into Prussia a degree of religious toleration till then unknown. He abetted the work of the leaders of the Enlightenment which, while it aided science and philosophy, denied the supernatural in things religious. Great as were the achievements of the Enlightenment in things cultural, they did not help forward the cause of the gospel of Christ.[6]

When the explosion of the French Revolution occurred, the German States lacked the moral power to resist and were overrun. Even neutral Switzerland was greatly influenced by French and German scepticism from the middle of the eighteenth century onwards, and religious conditions there became almost as deplorable. The Netherlands, which also had felt the influence of English deism and French scepticism, suffered evangelical eclipse. The judgment of the historian Latourette in the matter is

---

[1] *Ibid.*
[2] Trevelyan, G. M., *op. cit.*, p. 354.
[3] Newman, A. H., *op. cit.*, Vol. II, p. 492.
[4] Wolff, Chr., *Eigene Lebensbeschreibung, passim.*
[5] Newman, A. H., *op. cit.*, pp. 532 ff.
[6] *Ibid.*, p. 534.

thought-provoking:[1] "Again it looked as though Christianity were a waning influence, about to be ushered out of the affairs of men." In Spain and Portugal, vigour had already been lost, and the militant Order of the Society of Jesus had been dissolved.[2] Rationalism in Protestant thought had numbed conviction and cooled enthusiasm. One of the immediate results of the French Revolution and the Napoleonic Wars was injury to churches.

That all this evil should befall Christendom one short generation after the most glorious revival of elementary Christianity confounds the unbeliever more than the Christian, who has learned to look for the opposition of the Adversary after a victory.

Thus, at the end of the eighteenth century, in America and in Europe, through a rationalism that denied the reality of Christian experience, the old Christian faith faced a new threat to its existence.

The new rationalism—like evangelicalism—claimed to be vitally interested in the welfare of man, equally ready to grant him liberty, equality and fraternity. Its greatest lack lay in its inability to satisfy him in the things of the spirit. It offered bread, but forgot that man could not live by bread alone. Its appeals were heeded, and the multitudes turned away from things of the spirit. Evangelical Christians knew that they faced defeat. They began to pray the prayers of desperate men.

[1] Latourette, K. S., *A History of the Expansion of Christianity*, Vol. III, p. 454.
[2] *Ibid.*, p. 455.

CHAPTER III

RISING TIDE IN AMERICA

THE LAST DECADE BEFORE THE TURN OF THE CENTURY BEGAN in discouragement. Bishop Madison in the diocese of Virginia shared the conviction of Chief Justice Marshall, a devout layman, that the church was too far gone ever to be revived, while Bishop Provoost of New York felt that the situation was hopeless, and simply ceased functioning.[1] General Assembly in the Presbyterian Church officially deplored the dereliction of religious principles, the prevailing impiety and the corruption of public morals.[2] Baptists admitted a very wintry season in which the love of many had grown cold, while members were being lost to the Methodists alone at the rate of four thousand a year.[3]

In despair or hope or both, Isaac Backus (who was converted in 1741 during the Great Awakening), Stephen Gano and a score of New England pastors posted a call for a nation-wide "Concert of Prayer".[4] They were desperate men engaged in sincere intercession for many months and years.[5]

At that time, the colleges in the longest settled parts of the country were hotbeds of infidelity and immorality. Interest in things spiritual had ebbed away. When the tide turned, it did so imperceptibly at first in scarcely noticeable gatherings of just a handful of students for prayer.

In Hampden-Sydney College in Virginia, a few students, without one professing Christian among them, attempted to conduct a prayer meeting, of which one of the novices reported:[6]

We tried to pray, but such prayer I never heard the like of. We tried to sing, but it was in the most suppressed manner, for we feared the other students.

The ungodly students created a disturbance, and the President of the College came to investigate. He rebuked the rowdies and invited the intercessors to his study for prayer.[7] Within a short

---

[1] Sweet, W. W., *Story of Religion in America*, p. 224.
[2] *Ibid.*   [3] *Ibid.*
[4] Halliday, S. B., *The Church in America and Its Baptisms of Fire*, p. 386.
[5] Strickland, W., *The Great American Revival*, pp. 44 ff.
[6] Lacy, B. R., *Revivals in the Midst of the Years*, pp. 68 ff.
[7] Thompson, C. L., *Times of Refreshing*, p. 79.

space of time, more than half the number of students professed conversion in a movement which stirred the local churches too.

When the brilliant Timothy Dwight, grandson of Jonathan Edwards, came to the presidency of Yale College in 1795, he invited his students to attack freely the truth of the Scriptures, and he answered them in a series of pungent sermons in chapel. Among his topics were "The Nature and Danger of Infidel Philosophy," and "Is the Bible the Word of God?" Then he proceeded to grapple with the problems of materialism and deism in his direct exposition of theology.[1]

This provoked such interest in religion that in 1802, one-third of the total student body made public profession of conversion in a revival that moved the halls of ivy. In succeeding years, the student revivals at Yale were repeated.[2]

On a summer afternoon in 1806, five students of Williams College[3] were driven from a grove of maples where they were accustomed to meet for prayer. They sheltered from the thunderstorm under a haystack, and there prayed about a plan to reach the unevangelized heathen for Christ.[4]

The thunderstorm was of short duration, and the sun broke through the clouds as the light of a clear purpose broke upon their souls. Samuel J. Mills gave the decisive word:

"We can do it, if we will!"[5]

These students organized a society, youthful in spirit and habit, for they met in secret and in cipher recorded their minutes! They found no less than a score of students with the burden.

Four years later, at Andover Seminary, the students still carried the burden. Mills and his three closest friends went to the parlour of an interested professor to meet half a dozen ministers of their denomination.[6]

The counsels of their senior brethren were divided. Some thought the proposition a premature one; others felt that it smacked of infatuation; others that it would be too expensive; but after one minister observed that they had better not try to stop God, a majority gave the younger brethren their blessing.

Out of the Haystack Compact grew the whole modern American missionary movement. Out of the college awakenings came other blessings.

Thus began the movement in American schools of higher

---

[1] Sweet, W. W., op. cit., p. 226.
[2] Strickland, W., op. cit., p. 133 ff.; cf. Schaff-Herzog Encyclopedia on "Revivals."
[3] Strickland, W., op. cit., p. 138, Williams College.
[4] Shedd, C. P., Two Centuries of Student Christian Movements, pp. 51–52.
[5] Halliday, S. B., op. cit., pp. 515 ff.
[6] Ibid.

learning. There followed revivals of religion in Andover, Princeton, Washington and Amherst and other university colleges,[1] producing not only the modern American missionary movement but a generation of evangelistic ministers to serve the opening western states.[2]

In not one of these eastern college awakenings was there any extravagance reported. Revivals began quietly and continued without fanaticism of any kind. There was undoubtedly an appeal to the hearts of the students, but first their minds and consciences were moved.

The spread of infidelity was effectively halted and out of the movement came not only the home and foreign missionary societies, but also the foundation of numerous academies and colleges, theological seminaries, religious societies and philanthropic organizations.[3]

Latourette has pointed out that of one hundred and eighty denominational colleges in existence in 1860, four-fifths were founded and maintained by the evangelistic denominations.[4] The schools themselves were evangelistic communities, led by teachers with strong religious convictions, so it is not surprising that religious revivals again and again broke out in American colleges.

The turn of the century awakenings in schools of higher learning were related to simultaneous revivals among the illiterate of the frontiers.

When the first census of the United States was taken in 1790, it revealed that the bulk of the population resided in settlements scattered along the eastern seaboard from Maine to Georgia, about four million people in round numbers. There was an overflow of United Empire Loyalists to Nova Scotia and New Brunswick in Canada.

In Nova Scotia and neighbouring provinces, an awakening was manifest as early as 1776.[5] This movement began among the Congregationalists, but the greatest harvest was reaped by Baptists in the Maritime Provinces. Within a few years, there were revival movements also among the Methodists recently arrived from England.

At the turn of the century, southwards from Maine to Connecticut, throughout New York and Pennsylvania, and in each of the states of the Old South, powerful awakenings were manifested, in

[1] Strickland, W., *op. cit.*, pp. 139 ff.
[2] Tewkesbury, D. G., *The Founding of American Colleges and Universities*, pp. 1–5.
[3] Sweet, W. W., *op. cit.*, p. 226.
[4] Latourette, K. S., *A History of the Expansion of Christianity*, Vol. IV, p. 221.
[5] Armstrong, M. W., *The Great Awakening in Nova Scotia*, pp. 61–107; cf. Walsh, H. H., *The Christian Church in Canada*, p. 134.

every case spreading from the coasts to the far western reaches of
the Atlantic States.[1]

The turn of the century witnessed enormous movements of
population from the eastern states of America into the great
valleys on the western side of the Allegheny Mountains. Within
a single generation from the adoption of the Constitution, when
the nation's boundaries met the Mississippi, people poured over
the mountains into the empty territories and eleven new states
were admitted to the Union. Soon the state of Ohio had passed
all but four of the original states in population.

Of all the great Protestant denominations, the Presbyterians
were the best placed to supply the West with settlers.[2] The last
great wave of overseas emigration before the Revolution had been
the so-called Scotch-Irish, actually Ulstermen emigrating from
Ireland's northern province on account of injustices they had
suffered there at the hands of a short-sighted British government.
They were a rugged lot, veterans of the fighting against the
rebellious Irish clans in Ulster and pioneers of the dangerous
American frontier. A Scotch-Irish Presbyterian elder in kirk
session once prayed: "Grant, O Lord, that I may always be right,
for Thou knowest, Lord, that I am hard to turn." In 1802, the
Synod of Kentucky was set up, with three presbyteries.[3] These
Scotch-Irish led the wave of settlement westwards, but not all of
them, or even a majority of them continued to be Presbyterian,
for reasons of evangelism.

The typical Baptist preacher upon the frontier was a settler who
worked on his land six days a week, except for time off to conduct
funerals and prayer meetings.[4] He was generally without much
formal education, for, in contrast to Presbyterian opinion, there
was much prejudice against either educated or salaried ministers
among Baptists. Members of Baptist congregations often made
gifts in kind to the farmer among them who devoted his time to
ministry, and his position was recognized by licence to preach,
then by ordination as pastor.

The Methodists were best equipped to meet the challenge of
frontier conditions.[5] All the Methodist preachers in early days
were itinerants, moving from place to place within the wider
reaches of a circuit. The circuit riders appointed local men as their
class leaders, and quarterly conferences recognized any of talent
by making them licensed exhorters, from which they proceeded
to regular lay preaching or ordination as ministers. Like the
Baptists, they were men of limited education.[6]

[1] Beardsley, F. G., *A History of American Revivals*, pp. 84 ff.
[2] Sweet, W. W., *op. cit.*, p. 208.
[3] *Ibid.*, p. 210.   [4] *Ibid.*, p. 217.   [5] *Ibid.*, p. 218.   [6] *Ibid.*, p. 219.

It is noteworthy that the privileged churches, the Anglicans and the Congregationalists, failed to meet the challenge of the westward movement of population.[1] Not until 1835 was a bishop consecrated for the oversight of the vast western area. And the Congregationalists thought the West of so little importance that they made a comity arrangement with the Presbyterians, accepting the limited territory east of the Hudson and surrendering the vast West.

Encouraging as were the revivals in the eastern states, it was in the trans-Allegheny West that the phenomena beyond description were witnessed. In Logan County in Kentucky existed such a nest of escaped murderers, counterfeiters, highwaymen and horse thieves that it was known as "Rogues' Harbour."[2] To such a place came the Reverend James McGready, of Scotch-Irish stock and of frontier upbringing. McGready was so ugly in physical appearance as to attract the attention of the general public.[3]

For a number of years, McGready preached his powerful message. Others of Methodist and Baptist affiliation followed his example, until in the summer of 1800 following a solemn covenant of prayer, the most extraordinary manifestations of conviction of sin were witnessed.[4]

Interest had been building up for many months. Such crowds were in attendance that no church-buildings could contain them, so meetings were held in the open-air; and, as there were too few dwelling-houses around, great multitudes camped for days to listen to the preaching.

The movement spread to other counties nearby. At Cane Ridge, in Bourbon County, a communion service was held in August of 1801. The ministry lasted several days and was attended by crowds estimated between ten and twenty-five thousand. An eye-witness[5] reported that he

> attended with eighteen Presbyterian ministers and Baptist and Methodist preachers I do not know how many, all being either preaching or exhorting the distressed with more harmony than could be expected. . . .
> . . . The governor of our state was with us, and encouraging the work. . . .
> . . . The whole people were serious, all the conversation being of a religious nature or calling in question the divinity of the work.
> . . . The whole number brought to the ground under conviction was about a thousand.

The Kentucky awakenings spread to Tennessee and the Western

---

[1] *Ibid.*, p. 221.　　[2] *Ibid.*, p. 225.
[3] Johnson, C. A., *Frontier Camp Meeting*, pp. 32–38.
[4] Sweet, W. W., *op. cit.*, p. 227; cf. Johnson, *loc. cit.*
[5] Sweet, W. W., *op. cit.*, p. 228.

Carolinas and Georgia, and north into the Ohio Territory.[1] The movement increased; upon occasion, thirty or forty thousand gathered, addressed by Baptist, Methodist or Presbyterian preachers in different parts of the camp without clashing. These pioneer settlers were illiterate people, and as a result extraordinary emotional excesses were indulged, fainting and convulsions, prostrations and jerking—despite which untold good was done.[2]

The Methodist Bishop Francis Asbury stated in his Journal for 1811 that the number of camp meetings had increased to four hundred that year.[3] The influence of the western camp meetings upon society was both good and bad, with the good pre-dominating. A religious awe seemed to pervade the country, and profane expression was seldom ever heard. Drunkards, swearers, liars and the quarrelsome were remarkably reformed.[4]

Though the revival was largely Presbyterian in its beginnings, Baptists and Methodists reaped the largest benefits.[5] In Kentucky alone, associations of Baptists added ten thousand members in two years. The Western Conference of the Methodists added six thousand. But the movement led to schism in the Cumberland Presbytery, which in an attempt to meet the demand for ministers began to license and ordain candidates lacking the educational and theological qualifications of their denomination.[6]

The frontier revivals were also felt in Upper Canada or Ontario. The main vehicle of revival in the early years of the nineteenth century was Methodist local preaching.[7] The Baptists gained flocks of converts from the revival and planted new churches in Ontario.[8]

The camp meeting became a feature of North American life. The Baptists and Methodists used the great summer gatherings as evangelistic and devotional rallies. Throughout the winters, they assimilated the converts in their usual manner, through class meetings and the weekly worship services.[9] In due course, as settlement literacy increased, the excesses of the camp meetings dwindled away, though traces of extravagance are found to this day among the hill-billies of Kentucky and Tennessee.[10]

Between these two very different movements of evangelical revival, the college awakenings and the frontier revivals, there

[1] Cleveland, C. C., *The Great Revival in the West*, pp. 62 ff.
[2] Sweet, W. W., op. cit., p. 230.   [3] *Ibid.*, p. 229.
[4] Cleveland, C. C., *op. cit.*, pp. 128 ff.
[5] Sweet, W. W., *op. cit.*, p. 231.   [6] *Ibid.*, p. 232.
[7] Bangs, N., *A History of the Methodist Episcopal Church*, Vol. II, pp. 98-101.
[8] Walsh, H. H., *op. cit.*, p. 134.
[9] Sweet, W. W., *Revivalism in America*, p. 133.
[10] Torbet, R. G., *A Short History of the Baptists* (p. 317), claimed that the Baptists in Kentucky were not subject to the physical excesses so common among Presbyterians and Methodists.

was much inter-play. The college awakenings provided a flood of dedicated scholars for the uncouth western settlements, and converts among the roughest pioneers were encouraged to prepare for their western ministry in eastern schools. Between them, a host of new schools and colleges were founded in the newly settled parts of the country. The revival also equipped American evangelists who extended its influence for a lifetime. There were examples in every denomination.

John Peck was converted during a revival in Connecticut, and entered the Baptist ministry in 1812, becoming the home missionary of his own denomination, evangelizing the frontier districts of the Ohio and Mississippi valleys.[1] His ministry lasted forty-five years, and his labours produced a strong Baptist cause through the Middle West. Peck was one of many Baptist evangelists giving a lifetime to wholesome evangelism.[2]

Asahel Nettleton was born in Connecticut in 1783. In 1801, he was converted in local revival meetings in his Congregational parish.[3] Soon he felt called to the foreign mission field but instead became engrossed in revival work at home. For ten years, commencing 1812, his labours were in demand throughout New England. More than two thousand people were converted in Saratoga, New York State, in a time of blessing in 1819. Later, Nettleton's health broke down under the strain, but he continued warm in heart towards revival ministry until his demise in 1844. He employed no special means in his ministry, relying simply upon the preaching of the Word.[4]

Peter Cartwright, a convert of the Revival of 1800, became a Methodist exhorter in Kentucky, extending his evangelistic enterprise all across the expanding West and throughout his sixty-five years of extraordinary circuit-riding ministry.[5] Cartwright became a church-planter as well as an evangelist, building Methodist churches.[6]

As early as the seventeenth century, attempts had been made to reach the Red Indians with the gospel. Roger Williams had preached to the New England Narragansetts, but despaired of winning any converts among them. The Mayhews had been more successful, as was John Eliot.[7]

David Brainerd (1718–47) had been touched by the Great Awakening to minister to the Indians of the near-western frontier:

[1] Vedder, H. C., *Short History of the Baptists*, pp. 325 ff.
[2] Babcock, R., *Memoir of John Mason Peck, passim.*
[3] Thompson, C. L., *op. cit.*, pp. 92 ff.
[4] Nettleton, A., *Memoir of Asahel Nettleton, passim.*
[5] Latourette, K. S., *op. cit.*, Vol. IV, p. 189.
[6] Strickland, W., *Autobiography of Peter Cartwright.*
[7] Sweet, W. W., *Story of Religion in America*, pp. 156 ff.

his work in New Jersey was remarkably successful, but Brainerd died a young man, leaving his diary as an inspiration to aspiring missionaries for generations to come.[1]

In the eighteenth century, missionary efforts continued among the Indian tribes of the frontier. Kirkland, another convert of the Great Awakening, reached the Oneidas successfully.[2] The Quakers were concerned about the evangelization of the Indians of Pennsylvania.[3] The Moravians took an interest in many Indian tribes.

In the nineteenth century, the missionary impulse of the opening decades was felt. Cherokee missions were particularly effective,[4] even though they and other civilized tribes were deported west of the Mississippi. A Cherokee Baptist initiated the evangelization of the Kiowas.

The effect of steady ministry prevailed over the sporadic abuses and injustice inflicted by unregenerate white men. The Methodists and the Baptists extended their work and other denominations followed the Indians to the Pacific.

The war of 1812 interrupted national life for a few years, chiefly in the Middle Atlantic states. The next decade saw another wave of evangelism and revival, greater than ever before. Everywhere there were additions to the churches.

The effect of the Second Great Awakening upon American denominations is seen in a comparison of census figures.[5] The Methodists, who had been the smallest of the denominations at the winning of independence, were at mid-nineteenth century the largest, with 1,324,000 members; the Baptists, who had ranked third, were second with 815,000; the Presbyterians, who had ranked second, were now third, with 487,000; the Congregationalists, who had ranked first, were now listed fourth with 197,000; while the Lutherans and Disciples and Anglicans followed with 163,000, 118,000 and 90,000 respectively, the last-named being now seventh where they had ranked fourth in number. There were two factors, apparently, in success: the denominations which increased most rapidly were those which were most evangelistic in word and action, and most suited to democratic government. The Methodists and Baptists enlisted their membership from the unchurched masses.

The lasting effects of the early nineteenth-century Awakening provide a chapter's material in themselves. The American Evangelicals very readily adopted the ideas of their trans-atlantic brethren and promoted them with enthusiasm.

[1] Edwards, J., *Memoirs of David Brainerd, passim.*
[2] Sweet, W. W., *op. cit.*, p. 162.
[3] Kelsey, R. W., *Friends and the Indians, passim.*
[4] Hamilton, J. T., *History of the Moravian Church*, p. 365.
[5] Sweet, W. W., *op. cit.*, p. 221.

CHAPTER IV

RISING TIDE IN EUROPE

JOSHUA MARSDEN, A BRITISH METHODIST MINISTER WHO LAboured in Nova Scotia for many years, paid a visit in 1802 to the United States and reported:[1]

> I cannot contemplate without astonishment the great work that God has performed in the United States. It is here we see Methodism in its grandest form. . . . In England, Methodism is like a river calmly gliding on; here it is a torrent, rushing along and sweeping all away in its course.

Descriptions of the great camp meetings were circulated among British Methodists. They made a deep impression upon the mind of Hugh Bourne, a zealous young Methodist who was converted at the turn of the century and who participated in an unusual "outpouring of the Spirit" in 1804 at the village of Harriseahead.[2]

An American Methodist named Lorenzo Dow visited Great Britain and Ireland in 1805 to tell his British confrères of his experiences in the camp-meeting movements in the United States. He remained preaching for two years.[3] Dow in 1807 preached in the Burslem area and so met Hugh Bourne and his friends. It is not surprising that these Englishmen were much impressed to adopt the camp-meeting type of evangelism.

After Lorenzo Dow had sailed for America, Hugh Bourne and his friends decided to meet on the slopes of a local hill, Mow Cop[4], for a day's praying, announcing the meeting for six o'clock in the morning of May 31st—with a typical British proviso that there would be no gathering if the weather were inclement.

Prayer meetings went on all day, but as the numbers attending increased to many thousands, a considerable contingent of unconverted drawn by curiosity appeared and came under conviction of sin. From six o'clock in the evening, people began to depart, leaving counsellors dealing with the many inquirers.[5]

[1] Farndale, W. E., *The Secret of Mow Cop*, p. 26.
[2] *Ibid.*, pp. 15-19.
[3] Sellers, C. C., *Lorenzo Dow*, pp. 101 ff.
[4] Farndale, W. E., *op. cit.*, pp. 29-30.
[5] *Ibid.*, pp. 30-31.

The Mow Cop rally could scarcely be called a camp meeting. No one was engaged in camping. It resembled more the great open-air meetings on the Braes of Cambuslang when George Whitefield addressed the Scottish multitudes.

In July, 1807, the Methodist Conference held in Liverpool announced that it was their judgment that, even supposing camp meetings were allowable in America, they were highly improper in England and likely to be productive of considerable mischief. The Conference disclaimed any connexion with them.[1]

Hugh Bourne was dismayed by the objections of the Conference. He remembered the Anglican affirmation that General Councils "may err and sometimes have erred," and he remembered that Wesley himself in the Conference of 1744 had urged his Methodists to engage even more in field preaching. And he was convinced that an objection to "American" camp meetings did not apply to what he had in mind; so he obtained a civil licence to preach and another to use the grounds chosen for the purpose, and he defied his superiors by holding open-air preaching at the Norton-on-Moors fair.[2] Within a year, Hugh Bourne was expelled from the Methodist society.[3] He and his associates continued feeding converts into the Methodist societies, till they were refused. The new body operated without a name until 1812, when they adopted a phrase of Wesley's to call themselves a Society of Primitive Methodists.

The Primitive Methodists promoted field-preaching in the summer months in Britain, and attracted vast crowds at Mow Cop, Nottingham Forest and other suitable rallying points throughout the country, with many conversions.[4]

The Primitive Methodists not only renewed the aggressive evangelism of Wesley's day but developed a strong social conscience, contributing much spiritual strength to the trade unions in their struggle to better the lot of the labouring man in England.[5] The work grew rapidly. Within half a century, the Primitive Methodists had a total membership of 150,000 and as many more Sunday School children—approximately half the totals of the Methodist body that expelled them.

The greatest single convert of the "Ranters," as the Primitive Methodists were derisively designated, was not added to the ranks of Wesley's followers at all but to the sister Baptist denomination. Charles Haddon Spurgeon, born in the village of Kelvedon in Essex in 1834,[6] converted at mid-century in a little Primitive Methodist chapel, became one of the greatest preachers of all time,

[1] *Ibid.*, p. 33.   [2] *Ibid.*, pp. 34 ff.   [3] *Ibid.*, pp. 37–38.   [4] *Ibid.*, pp. 48 ff.
[5] Young and Ashton, *British Social Work in the Nineteenth Century*, p. 35.
[6] Fullerton, W. Y., *C. H. Spurgeon: A Biography*.

whose spoken sermons were heard by multiplied thousands and printed sermons read by the millions.

The spirit of revival abroad in Britain in the early nineteenth century affected the Dissenting denominations and produced some great men of God. It also affected the Establishment. Despite the success of Whitefield and Wesley and many ardent Anglican Evangelical clergymen still in the Mother Church, no Evangelical bishop served until Henry Ryder was consecrated as the Bishop of Gloucester in the year of Waterloo.[1]

Revival in the Church of England flowed in a different channel than that in the Free Churches. Evangelical clergy began to have second thoughts about the results of field-preaching and ministry in unconsecrated places, feeling that such a policy when applied to a national parish system would in fact result in schism.[2] They therefore began to devote their energies to the indoctrination of a body of clergy who would carry evangelical ideas into their parish pulpits and parsonages.

Charles Simeon was ordained in 1782. He had been strongly influenced by the evangelical vicar of Huddersfield, Henry Venn. Simeon preached at a farm house to a great crowd of people and was encouraged by the response, but satisfaction turned to dismay when his mentor wrote him a kindly letter deploring the irregularity.

Simeon moved to Cambridge, became Fellow of King's College and Vicar of Holy Trinity.[3] He not only preached an evangelistic message in Cambridge and round about, but devoted his life to combining the fervour of evangelism with the regular discipline of the Church. In this he made a profound impression upon the younger clergy in training at Cambridge, and soon the Simeonite clergymen became a dominant force in English life.[4] Had it not been for Simeon, the Evangelicals might have abandoned the Church of England for the easier method of an itinerant ministry.

Across the Irish Sea, the Church of Ireland thrived on Evangelicalism, continuing thus during the rest of the century.[5] But Presbyterians were in dire straits due not only to the Arian revolt in the manses, but also to Presbyterian involvement in the 1793 Rebellion, in which United Irishmen were executed or fled to America. Turning then to the comforts of faith, they founded the Evangelical Society of Ulster, and an increase of Bible reading and

---

[1] Davies, G. C. B., *The First Evangelical Bishop.*
[2] Trevelyan, G. M., *English Social History*, p. 510.
[3] Carus, W., *The Life of Charles Simeon, passim.*
[4] Binns, L. E., *The Evangelical Movement in the English Church*, pp. 37 ff.
[5] Phillips, W. A., *History of the Church of Ireland*, Vol. III, *passim.*

evangelical religion resulted.[1] From the main body, the Unitarians withdrew.[2]

Wales was known as the land of revivals, and the records tend to confirm the claim. From the year 1735 onwards, Wales had been the scene of an awakening in some locality or other.[3] Revival begets revival, for once a people has known the extraordinary outpouring of the Spirit of God, they are satisfied with nothing else. The greatest of human efforts in evangelism leave unsatisfied the oldsters with memories, while the youngsters live in expectation of another visitation. It is a living hope that awaits an answer.

There were many local revivals in Wales in the last quarter of the eighteenth century, and as many outstanding men of God traced their spiritual birth to such awakenings, among them Robert Roberts of Clynnog, Ebenezer Morris of Twrgwyn and John Elias of Anglesey, who were converted in awakenings at Brynengan (1785), Trecastle (1786), and Bala (1791) respectively.[4] The results were felt for a lifetime.

Llangeitho, where that greatest of all Welsh preachers, Daniel Rowland, held forth and saw extraordinary revival in the days of Wesley, again witnessed an awakening in the year 1781 under the preaching of the great pulpiteer.[5]

At the end of 1790, shortly after the death of Rowland, another great awakening occurred, being simultaneous with a great revival at Bala under the ministry of the Reverend Thomas Charles, who reported:[6]

> there was nothing to be heard from one end of the town to the other but the cries and groans of people in distress of soul. And the same very night, a spirit of deep conviction and serious concern fell upon whole congregations. In the course of the following week we had nothing but prayer meetings, and general concern about eternal things swallowed up all other concerns.

Before the turn of the century,[7] places in the shires of Cardigan, Carmarthen, Pembroke and Carnarvon and the island of Anglesey experienced awakenings. An awakening began in Aberystwyth in 1805, at which crowds of 20,000 gathered, and it was marked by an extraordinary movement among children and youth;[8] several other revival movements began in Sunday Schools.[9]

[1] Reid, J. S., *History of the Presbyterian Church in Ireland*, pp. 415 ff.
[2] *Ibid.*, p. 464.
[3] Evans, Eifion, *When He Is Come*, p. 11.
[4] *Ibid.*
[5] Hughes, John, *Methodistiaeth Cymru*, Vol. II, p. 17.
[6] Jenkins, D. E., *Life of Thomas Charles of Bala*, Vol. II, p. 89 ff.
[7] Evans, Eifion, *op. cit.*, p. 14.
[8] Jenkins, D. E., *op. cit.*, Vol. III, p. 114, quoting *The Evangelical Magazine*.
[9] Hughes, John, *op. cit.*, Vol. I, p. 346.

Yet another awakening began at Llangeitho in the 1810s, described as "the quiet revival" on account of the absence of the Welsh phenomenon of *moliannu* or praising.[1] In 1817, there was an unusual awakening at Beddgelert, considered the most powerful in Wales since the beginning of the Methodist Revival.[2] Thousands were added to the churches in North Wales thereby.

Some of these awakenings originated with the Calvinistic Methodists (now called Presbyterians) but the Baptists and the Congregationalists also shared richly in them. In five years, beginning 1816, Baptists received more than 8,000 members.

At the turn of the century in Scotland, there were many signs of an evangelical awakening. During the early 1800s, evangelical revivals broke out simultaneously in districts far apart in Scotland. These revivals helped counteract an unbelief that kept the gospel from the people by dominating the theological schools and deadening the pulpit ministry. Not only through the revivals was Moderatism overcome, but in district after district, immorality, drunkenness and profanity dwindled to the disappearing point.

Participating in many of the Scottish revivals were the brothers James and Robert Haldane,[3] who belonged to a wealthy and well-connected family and who had served with distinction in the Royal Navy.[4] These able evangelicals formed a society for the evangelization of the rural areas of Scotland. They sustained themselves in their evangelism, travelling in their own carriages, with a supply of tracts printed by themselves.

They preached in churches wherever invited, in hired halls, or in the open air. This ministry attracted extraordinary attention and the results were lasting, inside and outside the Churches. An outraged Assembly of the Church of Scotland passed acts against "vagrant teachers and Sunday Schools, irreligion and anarchy," and the lesser Presbyterian bodies condemned free-lance work. But this did not deter the brothers Haldane from continuing their itinerant ministry in Scotland.

In the midsummer of 1797, for example, the evangelist James Haldane visited Caithness, the most northerly mainland county of Scotland.[5] He commenced preaching to three hundred people in Thurso, the audience seemingly unconcerned, but by the following Sabbath the attendance had grown to seventeen hundred and attention was rapt. On the next Sunday, Haldane preached twice to about three thousand people, and continued preaching twice

---

[1] Evans, Eifion, *op. cit.*, p. 15.
[2] Hughes, Henry, *Diwygiadau Crefyddol Cymru*, p. 352.
[3] Haldane, A., *Lives of Robert Haldane and James Alexander Haldane*, *passim*.
[4] The Haldanes were nephews of Admiral Lord Duncan, British war hero.
[5] Haldane, A., *op. cit.*, pp. 144 ff.

B

daily until the end of September, when his daily audiences numbering four thousand people astounded observers in the little community.[1]

On October 1st, James Haldane preached to a congregation of twenty-five hundred people in the morning and four thousand in the afternoon in Wick. The parish minister was present in the evening, and Haldane created a sensation by attacking the minister's teaching. He continued ministering for ten days in Wick.[2]

In the counties of Ross, Inverness, Moray and Nairn, the awakenings of 1800 onwards were due largely to the labours of a famous Highland gospel preacher, the Reverend John MacDonald of Ferintosh.[3] Awakenings spread to Inverness and Tarbat, and in Tain where MacDonald first preached in Gaelic to a silent multitude, until, upon his evangelistic invitation, silent weepers began to sob and cry so that the preacher's voice was drowned, forcing him to pause and announce the singing of a psalm. Many young people were converted.

James Haldane[4] visited the island of Arran in 1800 and sowed the seed of a revival which broke out in 1804. In 1811, under the guidance of a man of God named McBride, there were prayer days set aside for fasting and intercession, continuing for as long as a year. The first signs of anything unusual was public crying out under conviction of sin. Then the awakening became general. Three hundred people were converted in that parish and several of them became outstanding Presbyterian ministers in the Church of Scotland.

In 1800, James Haldane and John Campbell[5] visited Campbeltown on the peninsula of Kintyre where the majority of the ministers were anti-evangelical, being Moderates or Socinians. The laymen preached on the slopes of a hill to about a thousand people in the morning and fifteen hundred in the evening. Evangelists in later years found a group of three hundred or more converts.

The Protestant Reformation had not moved the island of Skye, and the islanders at the end of the eighteenth century practised a religion made up of elements of Druidism, Romanism, and the Reformed faith. Superstition and drunkenness were all too common. The ministers of Skye in 1800 were unspiritual men. One later converted, the Reverend Roderick MacLeod, recalled that his first presbyterial act after his ordination was to assist his fellow-presbyters to bed in a helpless state of intoxication.[6]

[1] Ibid.   [2] Ibid.
[3] MacRae, A., Revivals in the Highlands and Islands, pp. 95 ff.
[4] Haldane, A., op. cit., pp. 251 ff.
[5] Ibid., p. 264.
[6] MacRae, A., op. cit., pp. 66 ff.

In 1805, a spiritually-enlightened blind man commenced what was reported to be the first prayer meeting in the history of Skye.[1] In 1812, a remarkable revival of religion began. There were conversions among the ministers; MacLeod, one of them, found not only his Sabbath but his weekday services crowded with seekers.[2] A similar awakening began on the island of Lewis in 1820,[3] under Alexander MacLeod.[4] Such was the ignorance of the people that an elder in the first prayer meeting prayed that a ship might be wrecked on the coast. But, year by year, the spiritual tide rose till, after eight years, a crowd of nine thousand people gathered for communion. After that event, people were converted week by week. The awakening spread to Harris, south of Lewis on the same island.[5]

In 1800, an awakening began in Perthshire, commencing in a parish where the minister was himself unconverted.[6] Among the many converts were the parents of Dr. Alexander Duff, one of Scotland's greatest missionaries of all time.[7] At the time, there were revivals in many parts of Perthshire and round about.

Records of the Scottish Awakening are scarce.[8] Some movements were due to the influence of the Haldane organization, but others were quite independent of it. There is every evidence of the awakening being a general and spontaneous one in the Highlands and Lowlands.

The power of the Scottish Revival of the early nineteenth century was carried to the Continent recently freed from the tyranny of Napoleon but still dominated by sceptical thinkers everywhere. In 1816, in Geneva, Robert Haldane began his lecturing to any students willing to listen to him.[9] He hired a room and used an interpreter as well. His method was simple: if students asked him a question, simple or complex, he replied directly, "What does the Scripture say?" This was so very different to the method of Reformed professors in sceptical Geneva that students flocked to hear the Scot who "knew his Bible like Calvin."

Before long, the wrath of the professors and clergy was incurred. Nevertheless, the ministry of Robert Haldane provoked a thorough revival of evangelical Christianity in the Swiss city.[10] Lasting value in his choice converts was seen in the lives of Merle d'Aubigné, Louis Gaussen, César Malan, Henri Pyt and Charles Rieu, outstanding scholars as well as ardent evangelicals.

[1] *Ibid.* [2] *Ibid.* [3] *Ibid.*, p. 80. [4] *Ibid.*, pp. 81 ff.
[5] *Ibid.*, p. 91. [6] *Ibid.*, pp. 131 ff. [7] *Ibid.*, p. 133.
[8] Mackay, J., *The Church in the Highlands*, pp. 243 ff.
[9] Haldane, A., *op. cit.*, pp. 375 ff.
[10] Bost, Ami, *L'Histoire du Réveil Religieux des Eglises Protestantes de la Suisse et de la France, passim.*

The awakening spread to the neighbouring old-Huguenot parts of France, carried there both by Haldane and by immediate converts.[1] Among the products of the Revival in France (*Le Réveil*) at this time were Ami Bost, Adolphe Monod, Felix Neff and Napoleon Roussel, who made a lasting imprint, not only upon France but upon Europe for a lifetime. The Awakening spread through the Reformed Churches of the Low Countries.

Britain and Prussia had been the two major Protestant powers confronting the dynamic push of Napoleonic France. Great Britain successfully resisted Napoleon, but Prussia, fighting bravely, was overrun. Fear of Napoleon had turned the people of Britain towards God; the misfortunes of Germany likewise had a quickening effect.[2]

Following the defeat of Napoleon at Waterloo, there was much rejoicing in Germany over the providential deliverance from the foreign yoke. In the north-western territories, between 1814 and 1836, there arose a movement which was Wesleyan in type; it was led by Krummacher, Hofäcker, Volkening, von Kottwitz and others; it moved many of both upper and lower classes to seek personal salvation and offer vital service to the nation.[3] The years after 1814 evidence a slow renewal of the indigenous Pietism.

In the north-eastern territories, the movement took a different form. Beginning 1810, it sparked a movement of evangelical zeal and philanthropy among the upper classes, influencing Frederick William IV of Prussia and outstanding leaders. It resulted in many missions to reach peasants and labourers—a missionary movement rather than a spontaneous awakening of the masses of the people.[4] It fell short of its English-speaking counterparts in effecting the reform of a nation, though it seemed to be an extension of the same, postponed by the Napoleonic Wars.

The distinguished German historian, Paulus Scharpff of Frankfort, has devoted many pages to the rise of "Die erste deutsche Erweckung im 19. Jahrhundert,"[5] and traced it to a revival of Pietism[6] as well as an invasion of Wesleyanism.

In 1793, Professor Hermann August Niemeyer published in Halle a two-volume biography of the English John Wesley. Two years later, Johannes Burkardt published a two-volume history of the Methodist Movement in England. Other volumes by noteworthy German writers followed.[7]

The Wesleyan influence was strong in the new German move-

[1] Haldane, A., *op. cit.*, pp. 411 ff.
[2] Scharpff, P., *Geschichte der Evangelisation*, pp. 121 ff.
[3] Summary received from Professor Scharpff prior to the publication of the work cited.
[4] *Ibid.*   [5] *Ibid.*, pp. 121 ff.   [6] *Ibid.*, p. 128.   [7] *Ibid.*, p. 131.

ment. Added to the Pietism of the national churches, it provoked many ministers to action. There were Awakenings in West Germany,[1] South Germany,[2] North Germany[3] and East Germany[4] and campaigns of evangelism in Bavaria, Baden, Württemberg, Hesse, and other parts.[5]

The intimate relations between Great Britain and the German States at the time were reflected in intimate relations between British and German Christians. Every British innovation, whether in the founding of missionary societies or of Bible societies, was duplicated in Germany.

The Awakening in Germany lasted for a whole generation. The leaders raised up in the revival extended its work throughout their homeland and exported it through dedicated missionaries to the far corners of the earth. Often the latter served as members of British societies.

Norway, scarcely moved by the Reformation and lightly touched by Pietism, enjoyed a vital revival towards the end of the eighteenth century.

Hans Nielsen Hauge was born in 1771 in a Norwegian peasant home.[6] He was converted to God in 1796. His experience was ecstatic:[7]

My soul was that instant so uplifted to God that I was no longer conscious of myself.

Hauge heard a voice telling him, "You shall confess My name before men." At first he talked to individuals, but within a year, he obeyed a call of the Spirit to preach, urging the people to repent of their sins, warning them against the prevalent rationalism of the revolutionary period.[8]

Hauge for eight years travelled up and down a country as noted for its roughness as for its beauty. He preached two to four times a day. His great activities did not please the state clergy; he was arrested ten times upon charges of breaking the Conventicle Act and of vagrancy. At that time, four of the five bishops in the country were known as rationalists.[9]

Hauge was imprisoned in 1804, and was not finally released till 1814, giving the last decade of his life to the ministry. Within his lifetime arose a vast multitude of lay preachers. Hauge died in 1824, but his work was carried on. His followers were known as 'readers," committed to preaching a thorough conversion and to teaching a genuine holiness of living.[10]

[1] *Ibid.*, pp. 154 ff. [2] *Ibid.*, p. 132 ff. [3] *Ibid.*, pp. 167 ff.
[4] *Ibid.*, pp. 178 ff. [5] *Ibid.*, pp. 137–148.
[6] Shaw, J. M., *Pulpit Under the Sky, passim.*
[7] Molland, E., *Church Life in Norway*, pp. 73 ff.
[8] *Ibid.* [9] *Ibid.* [10] *Ibid.*

Despite his persecution by the state church, Hans Nielsen Hauge urged his followers to stay in its fellowship, which they largely did. Out of the fertile soil of Haugeanism grew societies for home and foreign missions.[1] Hans Nielsen Hauge was a man of genius. The nation-wide revival that stemmed from his conversion to God was unique in the history of Norway. More than any other, he helped unite the common folk in a national and spiritual consciousness which prepared them for national responsibility soon to come as Norway emerged from a centuries-long eclipse.[2]

Denmark, closest to Germany, was affected less by Anglo-Saxon evangelicalism and more by the German Enlightenment. Nevertheless, a series of evangelical awakenings began and gave rise to missionary enterprises at home and overseas.[3] These awakenings coincided with a golden age of Danish culture.[4] Churchmen were revived. There were itinerant ministers and "readers" in Denmark, some suffering imprisonment.

From 1820 onwards, a dynamic and brilliant Lutheran clergyman, N. F. S. Grundtvig,[5] directed a national church movement which stressed the sacramentarian rather than the evangelistic way of life, and with this the revival-minded people clashed on occasion. Both movements helped a Church of Denmark struggling against invasions of scepticism and rationalism coming from the German schools of philosophy.

The Reformation in Sweden had been initiated by members of the upper classes and was largely doctrinal and ecclesiastical, reaching Sweden by way of Germany, as did Pietism a century later. But in the nineteenth century, an Anglo-Saxon influence began to eclipse the German lastingly.

The influence of the Great Awakening and the Evangelical Revival in America and Britain had begun to stir up Swedish Lutherans. Two Scots,[6] John Paterson and Ebenezer Henderson, crossed to Sweden and engaged in Bible distribution with Stockholm and Göteborg as their headquarters. In 1809, they founded a Bible and Tract company, *Evangeliska Sällskapet*.

At the turn of the century, Henrik Schartau[7] began his work of reviving the churches, and at the time of the intrepid Scots colporteurs, J. O. Hoof[7] pioneered a *kyrklig västgota väckelse*—a church-based revival in Western Gotland. In Sweden, there were

---

[1] Landmark, N., *Det Norske Missionselskap, passim*.
[2] Shaw, J. M., *op. cit.*
[3] Bundgaard, Nils, *Det Danske Missionselskabs Historie, passim*.
[4] Koch, H., *Danmarks Kirke gjennem Tiderne*, p. 129.
[5] Koch, H., *Grundtvig* (translated by Llewellyn Jones).
[6] Westin, Gunnar, *Den Kristna Friförsamlingen i Norden*, p. 24.
[7] Holmqvist, H., *Från Romantiken till Första Världs kriget* (Swedish Church History), p. 39.

other itinerant parish priests preaching in popular style, such as Per Nyman and Peter Lorenz Sellergren.[1]

There were "readers" also in Sweden.[2] Their followers formed conventicles. Some groups were quiet students of the Bible, but others indulged in abnormal religious frenzy, sometimes called "the preaching sickness" and very similar to the manifestations of American frontier revivals of preceding decades. Even so, moral reformation effected thereby was undeniable.

At the turn of the century, Finland had been wasted by war and was a picture of stupor and indifference. A barren moralism took the place of a vivid faith; but in the time of need, God in mercy sent a powerful awakening.

Strong similarity existed between Awakening in Finland and the Hauge Revival in Norway.[3] In 1777, Paavo Ruotsalainen was born and he was converted to God after a three years' struggle.[4] He did not know the writings of Martin Luther, which were translated into Finnish much later.

Throughout the eighteenth century, Finland had shared in the religious life of Sweden, but in 1808 the country became a grand duchy of the Russian Empire. In the turmoil of the change, Paavo Ruotsalainen began preaching as a prophet to the Finnish people and a great revival began.[5]

In 1820, two young Lutheran priests were converted, Jonas Lagus and Nils Gustav Malmberg. A great awakening in western Finland developed.[6]

In spite of the Russian annexation of Finland, the country continued to be Lutheran, and shared in the movements which were stirring the neighbouring country of Sweden. Although the means of communication between the two communities was the Swedish language, spoken by a minority of cultured Finns, the evangelical awakening did much to develop the indigenous Finnish culture and to revive the Finnish language.

[1] *Ibid.*
[2] Stephenson, G., *The Religious Aspects of Swedish Immigration*, pp. 31 ff.
[3] Professor O. Hallesby, introduction to *De Vakte*, by Juhani Aho, in Norwegian.
[4] Rosenqvist, G. O., *Finlands Kyrka*, p. 8 ff.
[5] Nyman, H., *Paavo Ruotsalainen, passim.*
[6] Aho, Juhani, *De Vakte, passim.*

CHAPTER V

AGENCIES OF MISSION

LATOURETTE, IN HIS CONSIDERATION OF THE GREAT CENTURY and the movements within Christianity through which the expansion of the faith had been chiefly accomplished, first noted the "revivals" which were particularly effective in the United States and the United Kingdom, and second, the organizations in large part growing out of them.[1]

It was in Great Britain that the first of these organizations had their beginning.[2] Reasons for prior British leadership included the effect of the Evangelical Revival on the thinking of Christians and the effect of the industrial revolution on the income of the people. With their desire to serve, the people were given the wherewithal to serve.

In 1784, a Baptist pastor named John Sutcliffe, who had been stirred by the reports of the Great Awakening in America, called upon Northamptonshire Baptist churches to pray for an outpouring of the Spirit. According to Dr. Ernest A. Payne,[3] it was these prayer meetings as much as any other influence which prepared the little group of ministers for the venture into missions.

The Anglican missionary statesman, Eugene Stock, selected the year 1786 as the "wonderful year" in the development of missionary passion.[4] In that year, William Wilberforce resolved to live for God's glory and his fellow-creatures' good. This and every other manifestation of the concern cited by Stock was due to the obvious influence of the Evangelical Revival.[5]

William Carey in 1786 first suggested to the Baptist ministers at Northampton that they must consider their responsibilities to the heathen. At Nottingham, on 30th May, 1792, William Carey preached a missionary sermon to his associated Baptist ministers, urging them to "Expect great things from God. Attempt great things for God."[6] Within six months, at a specially convened meeting of the association, what was soon to be called the Baptist Missionary Society was organized.

[1] Latourette, K. S., *A History of the Expansion of Christianity*, Vol. IV., pp. 34–35.
[2] *Ibid.*, Vol. IV, pp. 65–66.
[3] Payne, E. A., *The Church Awakes*, p. 31.
[4] Stock, E., *The History of the Church Missionary Society*, p. 57.
[5] *Ibid.* [6] Carey, S. Pearce, *William Carey*, p. 83.

The founding of the Baptist Missionary Society is generally regarded as the inception of modern Protestant missionary enterprise. There were endeavours to evangelize the non-Christian world before 1792, but they were limited in scope or in objective. The Northamptonshire shoemaker in retrospect appears to have been the first Anglo-Saxon Evangelical either in Britain or America to propose that Christians undertake to carry the gospel to the world's unevangelized millions. A real enthusiast for geography and linguistics, he cobbled shoes, taught school, and preached good news.[1] Carey not only promoted but pioneered in missions. And he not only urged Baptists, but all Christians to recognize their responsibility for carrying the good news to every creature.[2]

It was in 1786 that Thomas Coke established officially a Methodist mission to the West Indies.[3] In 1790, the British Methodist Conference set up a committee of management for this work and in successive steps committed itself to the official formation of the Wesleyan Methodist Missionary Society in 1817–18.[4]

Thomas Haweis, an Anglican evangelical, led the way in proposing the formation of the London Missionary Society—as an interdenominational organization—in 1795.[5] In 1796, the missionary ship Duff sailed for the South Seas and so began the ministry of this remarkable society, which drew its support more and more from churches within the Congregational Union.

In 1795, the Eclectic Society of Evangelical clergymen discussed a suggestion that the Church of England should attempt a mission to the non-Christian world. Out of Charles Simeon's idea[6] came the Church Missionary Society, founded in 1799 as a society for missions to Africa and the East. Strange to relate, the first missionaries of the Church Missionary Society were Germans trained in a missionary school in Berlin.

In 1796, the Scottish Missionary Society and the Glasgow Missionary Society were formed but that year the General Assembly of the Church of Scotland rejected a proposal to begin missionary enterprises; in 1824, it reversed itself and sent out Alexander Duff to India.[7]

In 1787, an appeal was made from Wales for more Bibles in the Cymric tongue. When little Mary Jones tramped fifty miles over

[1] Vedder, H. C., Short History of the Baptists, pp. 250 ff.
[2] Carey, W., An Enquiry into the Obligations of Christians (1792).
[3] Birtwhistle, A., The Proceedings of the Wesley Historical Society, Vol. XXX, pp. 25–29.
[4] Findlay and Holdsworth, History of the Wesleyan Methodist Missionary Society, Vol. I, p. 72.
[5] Lovett, R., The History of the London Missionary Society, Vol. I, p. 5.
[6] Carus, W., The Life of Charles Simeon, p. 229.
[7] Mackichan, D., The Missionary Ideal in the Scottish Churches, pp. 74, 112 ff.

the Welsh hills with her six years' savings only to find that the last copy of the Welsh Scriptures had been sold, Thomas Charles of Bala took up the matter with the Society for Promoting Christian Knowledge, and, failing, suggested to the Religious Tract Society that a Bible Society be formed.[1] The outcome was the foundation of the British and Foreign Bible Society in 1804. It was inter-denominational in character, dedicated to the dissemination of the Scriptures without note or comment at home or abroad. Its officers were largely members of the "Clapham Sect," making clear its debt to the Evangelical Revival.[2] The American Bible Society was formed in 1816 to combine the efforts of several associations.[3]

In 1799 through the urging of George Burder, a Congregational minister influenced by George Whitefield, the Religious Tract Society came into existence, dedicated to a diffusion of evangelical literature.[4] It was supported both by Church of England and Free Church people.

During the eighteenth century, there were many isolated attempts to evangelize children. In the year 1780, Robert Raikes of Gloucester organized a Sunday School to give religious and moral instruction to the children of the poor. It was found that the children needed to learn to read before anything else could be done.[5] As the standard of education among the children of the poor was raised, the Sunday School movement more and more devoted its energies to religious instruction. So in 1803, the inter-denominational Sunday School Union was formed. The American Sunday School Union was formed in 1824, aimed at establishing a Sunday School in every place in the country where there was sufficient population.[6]

The American Tract Society was founded in 1825 with the object of providing the religiously destitute with Christian literature.[7]

During the eighteenth century, there were sporadic American Protestant endeavours to evangelize the American Indians and Negroes. In the last decade of the century, some missionary societies extending this programme were begun.[8] But no organization, other than Moravian work, existed before 1800 for spreading Christianity outside North America.

---

[1] Balleine, G. R., *History of the Evangelical Party*, p. 133.
[2] Canton, W., *A History of the British and Foreign Bible Society*, Vol. I, pp. 1 ff.
[3] Dwight, H. O., *Centennial History of the American Bible Society*, Vol. I, pp. 7 ff.
[4] Jones, W., *A Jubilee Memorial of the Religious Tract Society*, pp. 12 ff.
[5] Rice, E. W., *The Sunday School Movement*, pp. 21 ff.
[6] Brown, A. A., *History of Religious Education*, p. 166; cf. J. O. Oliphant in *Church History*, Vol. VII, p. 133.
[7] American Tract Society, *Annual Report, 1826*.
[8] Latourette, K. S., *A History of the Expansion of Christianity*, Vol. IV, pp. 313 ff., 333 ff.

The awakenings in the American colleges at the turn of the century had a profound effect. At Andover Theological Seminary, a group of eager candidates—among whom were Samuel J. Mills and Adoniram Judson—committed themselves to work for the evangelization of the heathen, so they decided to bring the matter formally to the attention of the Congregational Church authority which, in 1810, organized the American Board of Commissioners for Foreign Missions.[1]

On the voyage to India, Judson and his bride, knowing that they would encounter William Carey, began to study the subject of believers' baptism. The Judsons and Luther Rice decided to embrace the Baptist viewpoint, and Rice returned to ask the support of American Baptists, who in 1814 formed the American Baptist Foreign Missionary Society as a general missionary convention of the denomination in the United States. Forced out of India by the antagonistic East India Company, the Judsons went to Burma and wrought a mighty work.[2]

In 1819, the Methodist Episcopal Church of the United States of America formed its missionary society.[3] The foreign missionary programme of the Protestant Episcopal Church was begun two years later.[4] The Presbyterians, divided by schism, took longer to commence an official missionary society, their Board of Foreign Missions being created in 1837.[5] That same year, the missionary society of the Evangelical Lutheran Church in the United States was formed.[6]

Throughout the nineteenth century, to meet the needs of a population increasing by seventy million, American Protestants organized home missions to settlers, to Negroes slave and free, and to Indians. Latourette has stated that the turn of the century revivals had an even greater effect than the earlier Great Awakening.[7] These second series of revivals motivated and manned the modern missionary movement.

The first of the modern European missionary societies was begun in 1797 in Rotterdam in the Netherlands in connexion with the new London Missionary Society.[8] Its chief founder was Jan Theodor van der Kemp, who became a pioneer in South Africa. The Netherlands Missionary Society drew its chief support from the Dutch Reformed Church, and until the

---

[1] Tracy, J., *History of the American Board*, pp. 24 ff.
[2] Wayland, F., *Memoir of Adoniram Judson, passim*.
[3] Reid, J. M., *Missions and Missionary Society of the Methodist Episcopal Church*, Vol. I, p. 17.
[4] Emery, J. C., *A Century of Endeavor*, pp. 29 ff.
[5] Brown, A. J., *One Hundred Years*, pp. 21 ff.
[6] Drach, G., *Our Church Abroad* (E.L.C.), p. 23.
[7] Latourette, K. S., *op. cit.*, Vol. IV, pp. 34–35.
[8] Kruijf, E. F., *Geschiedenis van het Nederlandsche Zendinggenootschap, passim*.

middle of the nineteenth century was the only Dutch missionary society.

Despite decline, the old tradition of Pietism in Germany remained and revival came again in the nineteenth century. A missionary school founded[1] in 1800 by Johann Jänicke prepared workers for the Netherlands Missionary Society, the Church Missionary Society and the London Missionary Society, serving fields in Asia and Africa.[2]

In 1815, the Basel Mission was founded, with support from Switzerland and Germany, and in 1828, the Rhenish Missionary Society was created. In 1836, the Evangelical Lutheran Mission was founded, moving its headquarters later to Leipzig. The same year saw the formation of the North German Missionary Society. The Berlin Mission was founded in 1824.[3]

The Danish Missionary Society was formed in 1821, beginning its ministry in Greenland before extending to areas beyond the sovereignty of the Danish crown.[4] In 1835, the Swedish Missionary Society was founded,[5] and, in 1842, the Norwegian Missionary Society,[6] all of evangelical impulse.

Latin American countries had been closed to Protestant missionary endeavour for centuries by the governments of Spain and Portugal. With the coming of independence to these countries, the doors were unbarred but not opened.

In the 1820s, the British and Foreign Bible Society distributed several thousand Testaments all over Latin America.[7] Their Scottish agent, James Thomson, was so successful that he was made an honorary citizen of both Argentina and Chile. The American Bible Society followed its partner, but it was not until the second half of the nineteenth century that Protestant penetration of Latin America really began.

Individuals rather than societies had concern. Allen Gardiner,[8] like the Haldanes, had risen to rank in the Royal Navy in the Napoleonic wars, and like them also had experienced a thorough evangelical conversion. In 1838 and 1839, he explored the possibility of missions to the pagan Indians of Argentina and Chile. He tried hard to enter Patagonia in 1845, but failed; he visited Bolivia in 1847, and failed again. His attempts to reach the savage inhabitants of Tierra del Fuego failed in 1848 and 1850, Gardiner and his six companions dying of exposure and starvation in 1851.

---

[1] Scharpff, P., *Geschichte der Evangelisation*, p. 94.
[2] Warneck, G., *Geschichte der Protestantischen Missionen*, pp. 140 ff.
[3] *Ibid.*, pp. 141 ff.
[4] Bungaard, N., *Danske Missionselskabs Historie*, pp. 7 ff.
[5] Sundkler, B., *Svenska Missionssälskapet*, pp. 7 ff.
[6] Landmark, N., *Norske Missionselskapet*, pp. 3 ff.
[7] Canton, W., *op. cit.*, Vol. II, pp. 83–84.
[8] Marsh and Stirling, *Story of Capt. Allen Gardiner*.

The publication of Gardiner's tragic diary stirred many Anglican Evangelicals to an interest in South America, the South American Missionary Society later entering the field.[1]

And what of home missions? The Awakening gave birth to a flock of societies in each nation. David Nasmith was born in Glasgow in 1799. He had an early religious experience, becoming an ardent Christian worker at the age of fourteen. He was turned down as a missionary candidate for Africa in 1817, but in 1826 he founded the Glasgow City Mission, in 1828 the Dublin City Mission, in 1830 the New York City Mission[2] and others in the United States and Canada; while in 1832, he founded the London City Mission which within two years had more than sixty workers.[1] These were interdenominational endeavours.

So also were the first societies to particular groups. Efforts were made in the 1810s and '20s to improve the moral and social conditions that seamen encountered at sea and in port, by 1830 the American Seamen's Friend Society reporting eight churches, seventeen boarding-houses, eight pastors and a chaplain overseas.[3] Seamen's missions were established in various countries and by various denominations, but the impulse came in the Awakening.

It was Theodor Fliedner, an Evangelical in a parish at Kaiserswerth, who instituted the use of deaconesses and soon organized his Society of deaconesses as well as other enterprises. In the next decade, J. H. Wichern organized the Inner Mission from which stemmed work for infants and cripples, rescue homes, and hospitals.[4]

The world-wide Young Men's Christian Associations stemmed directly from the Awakening. In 1837, a young Englishman, George Williams, experienced an evangelical conversion.[5] Shortly afterwards, he was greatly impressed through the reading of Finney's Lectures on *Revivals of Religion* and to *Professing Christians*. In 1841, he moved to London, where he found the working conditions among white-collar workers in stores and shops deplorable, so he and another convert began to evangelize their friends and workmates.[6] In 1844, they founded the Drapers' Evangelical Association, later renamed as the Young Men's Christian Association. Its first president was the Earl of Shaftesbury, and like him and its founder, the Y.M.C.A. was zealously evangelistic.[7]

[1] Despard, G. P., *Hope Deferred, Not Lost, passim.*
[2] Bready, J. W., *England Before and After Wesley*, pp. 408–409.
[3] American Seamen's Friend, *Annual Report, 1830.*
[4] Heuss, T., *Friedrich Naumann, passim.*
[5] Hodder-Williams, J. E., *Life of Sir George Williams.*
[6] Bready, J. W., *op. cit.*, pp. 289 ff.   [7] *Ibid.*

Organization of the Young Women's Christian Associations followed later. Both Associations received a mighty impulse from the Awakenings that occurred in America and Britain in 1858–59. The Awakenings of the nineteenth century had revitalized Protestantism, adding vision to a faith already transformed. Stated Dr. Latourette:[1]

> This Protestantism was characterized by an abounding vitality and a daring unequalled in Christian history. Through it for the first time plans were seriously elaborated for bringing the Christian message to all men and to make the life of all mankind conform to Christian principles.

[1] Latourette, K. S., *op. cit.*, Vol. IV, p. 44.

CHAPTER VI

DYNAMICS OF MISSION

IN THE SIXTEENTH, SEVENTEENTH AND EIGHTEENTH CENTURIES, the islands of the Pacific had been disclosed to European knowledge through great voyages of Spanish, Dutch and British navigators. It was in the latter part of the eighteenth century that the epic voyages of Captain James Cook made the South Sea Islands a subject of fascination and curiosity to the English-speaking world.[1]

At the time of the early nineteenth century Revivals, very little of the world was open to the Protestant missionary. An intransigent Roman Catholicism jealously held the door closed to the Latin American countries. Islamic ecclesiastical authorities barred the door of Muslim countries. The whole continent of Africa was *terra incognita*, except for the southern tip and certain enclaves. The vast empire of China was also closed, and it was by no means easy to gain a foothold in India. From the first, the revived evangelicals looked to the islands of the Pacific for an opportunity to convert the heathen[2]—as heathen truly they were.

The romantic idea of "ports of paradise" was contradicted by the facts of life as it was lived in the South Seas before the coming of Christianity. Life was cheap and wars were bloody. Infanticide, widow murder and cannibalism were common.[3]

William Carey dreamed at first of going to Tahiti to evangelize the islanders.[4] Before 1790, Haweis had attempted to send missionaries to the South Pacific. When the London Missionary Society debated, Haweis as a director argued that China and Japan were practically sealed off against Christianity, with India and the Muslim countries almost as difficult to enter, therefore the islands of the South Seas might offer a better opportunity.[5] A converted seafarer, James Wilson, volunteered to take the mission ship *Duff* to the South Pacific, and a party of thirty missionaries sailed in August, 1796.[6]

The enterprise proved much more difficult than its directors

[1] *Vide* Kitson, A., *James Cook, the Navigator.*
[2] Lovett, R., *The History of the London Missionary Society*, Vol. I, pp. 117–122.
[3] Ellis, W., *Polynesian Researches*, Vol. I, pp. 248 ff.
[4] Carey, S. Pearce, *William Carey*, pp. 39 and 53.
[5] Lovett, *loc. cit.*   [6] *Ibid.*, Vol. I, pp. 122 ff.

had anticipated, and by 1800 the mission project in Tahiti had dwindled away to a handful.[1] The Tahitian kings, however, were kindly disposed to the missionaries even though holding on to their ancient superstitions. In 1815, Pomare II toured his island kingdom and urged his people to accept Christianity.[2]

The Christianity popularized by this mass movement was rather superficial, but the leaders of the mission set about deepening the Christian commitment by erecting churches, teaching young people, translating the Scriptures, introducing a European system of law, and evangelizing others of the Society Islands. The London missionaries reached other island groups in Polynesia, often helped by the evidence of Tahitian reformation.[3]

The student awakening in New England had an indirect impact upon Hawaii, then a Polynesian kingdom in the Pacific. A Hawaiian youth named Opukahaia (or Henry Obookiah) found his way to Yale, attracting the attention of Samuel J. Mills,[4] the student evangelist and missionary zealot. In 1818, Opukahaia died,[5] but a year later a party of missionaries, challenged by his untimely death, sailed for Hawaii. They expected to find much drunkenness and prostitution among the natives aided and abetted by the lawless European and American whalers who frequented those parts, not to mention gross idolatry and taboos. They arrived in 1820 to learn that native movements had succeeded in destroying much idolatry and in discouraging pagan taboos, movements due to an awakened native interest in Christianity.[6]

King Kamehameha I had united the islands by force of arms.[7] His successor granted permission to the missionaries to land and to carry on their work. They made remarkable progress in their first decade, winning converts in the royal family and among the chiefs, instituting public services of worship, influencing native legislation in favour of morality, educating thousands of children in schools and defying opposition from foreigners who preferred a lack of moral control—a very different picture to that painted by novelists. By 1836, they had seventeen churches and a sixth of the population was enrolled in mission schools.[8]

Then followed the movement designated "The Great Awakening" by the American missionaries, for in 1837, a work of peculiar power began at Hilo in Hawaii and continued five years.[9] A total of 7,557 converts were received into one church, 1,705 of them in

[1] *Ibid.*   [2] *Ibid.*, pp. 208 ff.
[3] Ellis, *op. cit.*, Vol. II, pp. 167 ff.
[4] Spring, G., *Memoirs of the Rev. Samuel J. Mills*, pp. 47 ff.
[5] Dwight, E. W., *Memoirs of Henry Obookiah*, *passim.*
[6] Bingham, H., *A Residence of Twenty-one Years in the Sandwich Islands*, pp. 57 ff.
[7] *Vide* Ellis, W., *op. cit.*, Vol. IV.
[8] Anderson, R., *History of the Hawaiian Mission*, pp. 48 ff.
[9] Gulick, O. H., *The Pilgrims of Hawaii*, pp. 315 ff.

one day, under the ministry of zealous Titus Coan, who won 13,000 in all before 1870.

The awakening spread all over the Islands of Hawaii, Oahu, Maui, and to lesser communities, attracting congregations averaging between two thousand and six thousand. Between 1837 and 1842, more than twenty-seven thousand converts after thorough probation were received into the membership, about one-fifth of the population of the islands. In 1843 alone, 5,296 were admitted.[1] There were 19,679 church members in good standing twenty years later, in spite of the decline in numbers of the Polynesian population due to epidemics of alien diseases. The nation, regarded as Christianized, was granted a Bill of Rights by King Kamehameha III in 1839.[2]

The influx of non-Christian stock from the Orient changed the Christian and Polynesian majority into a minority, which through its own Hawaiian Evangelical Association[3] began to win the newcomers, often of Buddhist faith. Meanwhile, the sons of early missionaries played an unusual part in the affairs of Hawaii—kingdom, republic, territory and state of the United States.

Christian work on the Australian Continent took the form of a home mission rather than a foreign mission. The first chaplain sent out with the unwilling settlers to Botany Bay was Richard Johnson,[4] an ardent evangelical who owed his post to the interest of Wilberforce and others of the "Clapham Sect." Six years later, in 1793, Samuel Marsden[5] was appointed assistant to Johnson. He too was an ardent evangelical, with not only a burden for evangelism but also for the welfare of the convicts and the aborigines.

As the Church of England followed the English settlers, so the Church of Scotland followed the Scots. Methodism entered Australia in a typical and spontaneous fashion. Congregationalists and Baptists made small beginnings.

A most significant factor in the evangelizing of Australia was the comparative absence of the revival tradition. There are few records of any spiritual awakenings among the inhabitants. One reason undoubtedly was the antipathy which the "convicts" in some penal settlements felt towards the authorities which had sent them there for often trifling offences—they resented any compulsory religion instituted by the authorities.[6] Another lay in the fact that the evangelical strain in Anglican ministry was evenly matched by the newer High Church influence,[7] and, for a while,

[1] Brain, B. M., *The Transformation of Hawaii*, pp. 113 ff.   [2] *Ibid.*
[3] Anderson, R., *History of the Sandwich Islands*, pp. 315 ff.
[4] Bonwick, J., *Australia's First Preacher, the Rev. Richard Johnson, passim.*
[5] Elder, J. R., *Letters and Journals of Samuel Marsden.*
[6] *Vide* O'Brien, F., *The Foundation of Australia.*
[7] Micklem, P. A., *Australia's First Bishop, passim.*

Presbyterians also were distracted by loyalties to the Moderate and Evangelical parties in Scotland at Disruption.[1]

At the beginning of the nineteenth century, there were about quarter of a million aborigines in the whole of Australia.[2] Their whole culture was far removed from that of Europeans, Asians or Africans, and this made them hard to reach.

As early as 1825, the Church Missionary Society started an auxiliary which endeavoured to reach the aborigines.[3] The other denominations followed the Anglicans, but not only did they have to contend with the cruelty of some of the settlers towards the blacks, but also the rapid decline of the race itself, reduced to a fifth of its numbers within a century.

The Netherlands Missionary Society began to evangelize the outlying portions of Indonesia away from the Muslim heartland of Java.[4] In 1815, Joseph Carel Kam arrived and became the apostle to the Moluccas.[5] In 1822, the Dutch missionaries entered Minahassa, north-eastern Celebes, and in a remarkable work of evangelism made it a Christian country within fifty years.[6] In 1834, two missionaries of the American Board entered the island of Sumatra but were killed and eaten by the Bataks.[7] The Netherlands East India Company appeared to be more interested in the exploitation of the Indies than the transformation of the people. Nevertheless, the evangelization of parts of the Indies proceeded apace, helped by the influence of Christianity in Dutch colonial policy following the religious revivals of the 1830s in Holland.[8]

A first contact with the Polynesian Maoris of New Zealand was made by Samuel Marsden and missionaries of the Church Missionary Society.[9] On Christmas Day, 1814, at the Bay of Islands, Samuel Marsden conducted the first Christian service in New Zealand. He was then fifty years of age, and the visit to New Zealand represented twenty years of contacts with the Maoris through his work in New South Wales.

The first baptism of a Maori was that of a chief in 1825. By 1837, when Marsden paid his last visit, there were a couple of hundred church communicants and a couple of thousand attending public worship, served by more than thirty-five missionaries and fifty schools.[10]

Marsden was also responsible in part for the commencement of a Methodist mission to Maori New Zealand. He urged Samuel

[1] Cameron, J., *Centenary History of the Presbyterian Church in New South Wales.*
[2] Thomas, N. W., *The Natives of Australia.*
[3] Pitts, H., *The Australian Aboriginal and the Christian Church*, p. 98.
[4] Rauws, J., *The Netherlands Indies*, p. 51 ff.   [5] *Ibid.*   [6] *Ibid.*
[7] Strong, W. E., *The Story of the American Board*, pp. 116–118.
[8] *International Review of Missions*, Vol. XXIII, p. 211.
[9] McNab, R., *From Tasman to Marsden*, pp. 86 ff.
[10] Elder, J. R., *op. cit.*

Leigh, a pioneer Methodist in Australia, to visit New Zealand.[1]
In 1830, the first Methodist convert was baptized.

By 1840, when the treaty of Waitanga brought the Maoris under
the protection of Queen Victoria, the old pagan practices were
dying in many tribes, slavery was dwindling, polygamy, infanticide and suicide, like cannibalism, were becoming rare.

A steady stream of immigrants from Britain settled in the lovely
land. Despite the efforts of missionaries and officials, wars raged
between Maori and pakeha while contacts in peacetime brought
demoralization of the Polynesian folk.

In 1834, the island kingdom of Tonga (which was being evangelized by the Wesleyans) was moved by a great awakening
beginning on Yavau, spreading to the other islands.[2] It was
marked by an intense conviction of sin, weeping, public confession of sins and joyous conversions. This Polynesian kingdom
rapidly became Christian.

The gospel was carried to Polynesian Samoa from Tonga, and
after 1835 a great awakening[3] occurred; its converts multiplied
and recurrent revivals followed, Methodists rising from two to
thirteen thousand members in two years or less.

The Fiji Islands were populated mainly by a Melanesian folk.
War between tribes and villages was common and life was cheap.
Widows were strangled on the death of their husbands; sick and
old people were killed and cannibalism was practised. Religion
was gross superstition.[4]

The great awakening in Tonga aroused both native teachers
and resident missionaries to extend the Methodist mission to Fiji.
In spite of wars and opposition, Christianity gained ground. From
time to time, there were general revivals marked by deep emotion
and conviction of sin, followed by conversions.[5] In 1854, Thak-
ombau the king openly espoused the Christian faith, perhaps
because of an appeal of the Christian king, George of Tonga.
Cannibalism came to an end, as also did widow strangling, and
tribal warfare ceased. The Fijian people were rapidly evangelized.

One of the most difficult missionary projects was the opening
of the New Hebrides. Tribal war, cannibalism, and the killing of
widows prevailed. The people were regarded as lower in savagery
than other Pacific groups. Island population was mainly Melanesian. The intrepid pioneer, John Williams of the London Missionary Society, put three Samoans ashore on Tanna, but he himself

[1] Strachan, A., *Life of the Rev. Samuel Leigh*, pp. 82 ff.
[2] Findlay and Holdsworth, *History of the Wesleyan Methodist Missionary Society*,
Vol. II, pp. 287 ff.
[3] *Ibid.*, Vol. III, 339; cf. Lovett, *op. cit.*, Vol. I, pp. 379 ff.
[4] Thomson, B., *The Fijians*, pp. 85 ff.
[5] Townsend, Workman and Eayrs, *New History of Methodism*, Vol. II, p. 300.

was martyred on Erromanga.[1] Samoan teachers on Futuna were murdered. Other Samoans and Rarotongans took up the challenge along with the missionaries, and slowly the islands were won to the Christian faith.[2]

It should be remembered that the condition of the islanders before the arrival of the Christian missions was deplorable, sexual immorality and cannibalism, murder and robbery and the like being rampant, often exacerbated by traders and beach-combers. Often within a generation pioneer missionaries and their converts changed a whole society into a God-fearing, sober community. The two most potent forces in the evangelizing of the islands of the Pacific were Methodism and Congregationalism.[3] Both denominations stressed the conversion of the individual and admitted him to church membership only after a strict probation; yet their greatest triumphs resulted from mass movements which nevertheless held to the strict standards of individual conversion prevailing in all the historic evangelical revivals.[4]

The average English-speaking person, even the scholar, is often surprised at the inclusion of the great island of Madagascar in association with Indonesia and the islands of the Pacific. In actual fact, the people of Madagascar are more closely related to these areas in the east than to Africa in the west. The Malagasy are related in race and language to the Malay-Polynesian group and African, Arab and Indian blood is a minority strain. The island is twice the size of Britain.

The highland kingdom of Imèrina held political supremacy in the nineteenth century. Its people, the Hòva, were intelligent and energetic, skilled in certain crafts and keen in trading. In 1817, the British governor of nearby Mauritius entered into an agreement with Radàma I to supply money and other equipment in return for suppression of the slave trade.[5] In 1820, David Jones of the London Missionary Society reached Antanànarìvo, sought the permission of the king to remain, opened a school, and began a work of evangelization.[6]

From these beginnings, the London Missionary Society extended its work. In 1830, the complete New Testament was printed in the native tongue, and in 1836 the whole Bible. A church was formed. But in 1836, violent persecution under Queen Rànavàlona compelled the missionaries to abandon their two

[1] Prout, E., Memoirs of the Rev. John Williams, pp. 565 ff.
[2] Turner, G., Nineteen Years in Polynesia, pp. 365 ff.
[3] Latourette, K. S., op. cit., Vol. V, p. 259.
[4] Ibid.
[5] Ellis, W., History of Madagascar, Vol. II, pp. 193 ff.
[6] Lovett, R., op. cit., Vol. I, pp. 676 ff.

hundred converts to the fury of their persecutors.[1] Twenty-five years later, missionaries returned to find the converts grown to twenty thousand.

The foregoing survey of the evangelization of the islands of the South Seas in the early part of the nineteenth century noted significant factors.

The first is that evangelical revival provides the initial dynamic for missionary enterprise. The missions mainly concerned with the winning of the island populations to Christian faith were those receiving their impulse from eighteenth-century revivals and their personnel from early nineteenth-century movements.

The second is that wherever there occurred evangelism of an extraordinary kind, resulting in the winning of a whole people, it occurred by means of the same kind of awakenings in native communities as those experienced in the sending countries, with the same kind of preaching, the same kind of conviction, the same kind of repentance and the same kind of confession, followed by the same kind of conversion.

These two factors, noticeable in the pioneer evangelization of the early nineteenth century, are even more striking in the latter half of the century, following the great awakenings of 1858–1859, which provided impulse and personnel for another great movement of advance.

And the best evangelized areas of the world today are precisely those which were moved by these evangelical awakenings. Where decline has occurred in any of them, it is always due to the abandonment of evangelical principle or method.

[1] Ellis, W., *The Martyr Church*, pp. 59 ff.

CHAPTER VII

FINNEYAN FORMULA

T HE YEARS BETWEEN 1792 AND 1842 WERE SAID TO BE YEARS of continuous revival in the United States. The fifty-year period divides itself neatly into two parts, separated by the decade of the War of 1812.

The first period of revival, the Second Great Awakening in churches and colleges in the east and in churches and camp-meetings in the west, was a general awakening, producing many young leaders but dominated by no one leader.[1]

The second period of revival, from about 1822 until 1842, raised up Charles Grandison Finney,[2] who continued to dominate the field of evangelism in North America throughout the middle third of the nineteenth century, just as the figure of D. L. Moody dominated its final third.

Between 1822 and 1842, revivals occurred in the churches of almost all the denominations. Of the movement of 1830-31, Dr. Lyman Beecher some time afterwards gave his opinion:[3]

> That was the greatest work of God and the greatest revival of religion that the world has ever seen, in so short a time. One hundred thousand were reported as having connected themselves with churches as a result of that great revival. This is unparalleled in the history of the church.

The American Methodists were in the forefront of the continuing revivals.[4] In 1822, there were more than a thousand camp-meetings in which the Methodists participated. In 1839-40, the Methodist Episcopal Church alone received more than 154,000 additions.[5] The Methodists in their handling of converts were very thorough. Bishop Asbury told his Methodist preachers: "We must attend to camp-meetings; they make our harvest time."[6] The harvest was followed by as much work as that which preceded sowing. Of it, the church historian, William Warren Sweet, had declared: "There has been entirely too much stress placed upon

[1] Beardsley, F. G., *History of American Revivals*, p. 85.
[2] Wright, G. F., *Charles Grandison Finney, passim.*
[3] Quoted in Finney, *Revivals of Religion*, p. 30 n.
[4] Sweet, W. W., *Revivalism in America*, p. 129.
[5] *Western Christian Advocate*, Cincinnati, 10-iii-58.
[6] Sweet, W. W., *op. cit.*, p. 131.

the emotional excesses of camp meetings and all too little upon the routine work of the frontier churches and preachers."[1] The influence of evangelists of the First and Second Great Awakenings in America had been limited to English-speaking settlers by reason of language. It was not until the emergence of German-speaking revivalists in the 1800s that revival movements appeared among Germans.

In 1800, Jacob Albright, a Pennsylvanian of Lutheran background, began to organize class-meetings along Methodist lines which became the Evangelical Church.[2] In the same year, Philip Otterbein, a German-born missionary of Reformed Church background, formed the United Brethren in a Methodist pattern.[3] A century later, the two united as the Evangelical United Brethren.

The Second Great Awakening brought about a new major denomination, the Disciples of Christ.[4] Thomas Campbell, minister of a Presbyterian church in the North of Ireland, left his home to seek better health in America, arrived in 1807 in Philadelphia and was appointed to Western Pennsylvania where his deep spirituality and his unusual abilities provided him with a widening ministry and a growing influence.

Thomas Campbell possessed a truly catholic spirit, welcoming at the Lord's Table various believers who did not adhere to the Presbyterian organization to which he belonged. For this, he was censured and criticized so severely that he resigned from his affiliation.

Thomas Campbell convened a meeting of his friends and proposed a return to the teachings of the Word as a basis of truest unity. He held forth a maxim: "Where the Scriptures speak, we speak; and where the Scriptures are silent, we are silent." After discussion, it was decided to form "The Christian Association of Washington," a society to promote Christian unity and a pure evangelical reformation.

Thomas Campbell began to minister at large. Alexander Campbell,[5] son of Thomas Campbell, had previously crossed to Scotland to study for the ministry of the Seceding Presbyterians. In Glasgow, he had come under the influence of the brothers Haldane in whose ministry was blended revivalism and evangelism. The Haldanes were both of them congregational rather than presbyterial in church polity. Alexander Campbell found that he had lost confidence in his own denomination. The younger Campbell took

---

[1] *Ibid.*, p. 132.
[2] Yeakel, R., *Jacob Albright and his Co-Laborers*.
[3] Drury, A. W., *History of the United Brethren*.
[4] Garrison, W. E., *Religion Follows the Frontier: A History of the Disciples of Christ*, pp. 70 ff.
[5] Richardson, R., *Memoirs of Alexander Campbell*.

ship for America. On the road from New York to Western Pennsylvania, father and son met, each ignorant of the other's secession from Secession principles.[1] The Christian Association made overtures to the Synod of Pittsburgh for recognition, which was refused.[2] The members adopted baptism by immersion, which led to temporary association with the Baptists of that neighbourhood.[3] Both a Presbyterian movement, under Barton W. Stone,[4] and a Methodist movement under James O'Kelly,[5] merged with the new fellowship of churches. In intention, the rank and file of the movement set out to unite divided Christians by restoring the churches to apostolic purity. They stressed a baptism "unto remission of sins" and practised a wide open communion, so in due course this Restoration Movement separated from Baptists also.[6] Alexander Campbell became the leader of the denomination, which within a century passed the million mark in membership.

The majority body of the Disciples of Christ continued in the Campbell tradition of Christian reunion on the basis of New Testament practice. A more radical wing developed an antagonistic attitude towards other Christian denominations.

The Baptists in the early 1800s had carried on their revival ministry by means of farmer-preachers of little education.[7] In the 1820s, the whole of the country including the frontier was covered by a network of Baptist Associations made up of local churches acting in voluntary co-operation. In 1832, the American Baptist Home Mission Society was formed.[8]

The Presbyterians were divided as a result of the Second Great Awakening, but it was a division over manifestations and methods, and both sides continued to advance the cause of evangelism and spiritual awakening in agreement with their type of theology.[9]

The same controversies over manifestations and methods and the doctrine of the sovereignty of God raged among the Congregationalists, who nevertheless continued active support of revival and evangelism.[10] Outstanding among them stood Dr. Lyman Beecher, who influenced many lives.

The evangelism of Anglicans, Lutherans and Reformed differed in degree rather than in kind from the more evangelical denominations. The Anglican Evangelicals, for example, "were more careful than others to guard against emotional extravagance," and so

---

[1] Garrison, W., *op. cit.* [2] *Ibid.*, p. 98. [3] *Ibid.*, pp. 106 ff.
[4] *Ibid.*, p. 150. [5] *Ibid.*, p. 61. [6] *Ibid.*, p. 144.
[7] Sweet, W. W., *Revivalism in America*, pp. 128–129.
[8] Vedder, H. C., *Short History of the Baptists*, p. 327.
[9] Sweet, *op. cit.*, pp. 124–125.
[10] *Ibid.*, p. 120.

seldom took part in united campaigns.[1] Anglicans in America had begun to divide into Anglo-Catholic and Evangelical sides, while Lutherans[2] had begun to divide along lines of confessional orthodoxy and tolerant evangelism.

It has been pointed out by Latourette that the Canadian settlements experienced no such explosive religious revivals as known in United States.[3] Canada did not experience anything resembling the great movements which began in Britain, nor did any Great Awakening, or series of revivals on the frontier or in the colleges ever originate on Canadian soil—with the possible exception of the Hamilton Revival of 1857 which commenced the Awakening of 1858–59 around the world.[4] Yet each of the revival movements which moved the United States had its effects upon Canada.

Between the Atlantic Provinces of Canada and the rich lands of Ontario lay the block of French-speaking *habitants* in Quebec. Hence Maritime Protestants tended to look south to New England, and Ontarians to the Great Lakes and the Ohio. Between the Ontario farmlands and the Canadian west lay the Laurentian Shield of rocky wilderness.[5] The settlers in the Canadian prairies at first tended to look south, to the Middle Western States. Canada was not a geographical unity.

French Canada, experiencing a strengthening of religious loyalty through national feeling, was unaffected by the evangelical awakenings which moved United States and other parts of Canada.

In 1823, Samuel Codner and others touched by the Evangelical Revival formed an Anglican society for service in Newfoundland.[6] Presbyterians developed an interest in the Maritimes.[7]

After the resentment felt in the War of 1812, the influence of American evangelism in revival movements was again seen in Ontario.[8] For fully twenty years, the dominant forces in Canadian religious activity were American-related. After 1832, the numbers of native-born Canadians and British settlers increased, so Canadian religious life began to take on a more British flavour. The Baptists in the Maritimes[9] and the Methodists in Ontario[10] developed ties with their British brethren and the links with the United States weakened in inverse proportions.

[1] Manross, W. W., *The Episcopal Church in the United States, 1800–1840*, pp. 104–105.
[2] Wentz, A. R., *Lutheranism in America*, pp. 89 ff.
[3] Latourette, K. S., *History of the Expansion of Christianity*, Vol. V, p. 7.
[4] *Vide* Orr, J. Edwin, *The Second Evangelical Awakening in America*, pp. 23 ff.
[5] Latourette, K. S., *loc. cit.*
[6] Mullins, J. D., *Our Beginnings*, pp. 1–12.
[7] Balfour, R. G., *Presbyterianism in the Colonies*, pp. 17 ff.
[8] Sanderson, J. E., *First Century of Methodism in Canada*, Vol. I, p. 97.
[9] Bill, I. E., *Fifty Years with the Baptist Ministers and Churches of the Maritime Provinces*, p. 122; cf. Fitch, E. R., *The Baptists of Canada*, pp. 86–87.
[10] Cornish, G. H., *Cyclopedia of Methodism in Canada*, pp. 15 ff.

The frontier-type revival and evangelism had a lasting effect upon the social structure of the Canadian nation. It was an understandable British reaction to American revolution to distrust the political and religious forms of democracy. The anti-American, pro-British leaders therefore tried to establish tight little oligarchies, many working for an establishment of the Church of England. The "Family Compact" type of society thrived. Baptists, Methodists and Presbyterians fiercely resisted, among them Egerton Ryerson,[1] an ardent Methodist who emerged as a powerful influence in the shaping of Canadian democracy. The cause was successful, for in due course the various denominations in Canada accepted the principle of self-support, and those which had enjoyed state establishment or bounty in the Old Country were content to operate without it.

It was in the country south of Lake Ontario that the greatest evangelist of the nineteenth century—with the possible exception of Moody—arose to harness the movement of evangelism. Charles G. Finney was born in Connecticut in 1792, a year after John Wesley died in England.[2] His family moving farther west, Finney studied law in western New York.[3] He began to read the Bible with reference to the Mosaic legal code, and from this interest his familiarity with the Scriptures grew until he was convinced of the authority of the Word. Finney was converted, not through evangelistic witness, but by private study of the Scripture and prayer.[4] His conversion caused a great stir in his community, for he was already (at 29 years of age) a brilliant fellow, a splendid pagan, impressive in personality, and proudly conscious of his intellectual as well as his physical superiority.

Self-taught, but well-disciplined in theology, Finney rebelled against the rigid Calvinism of his Presbyterian fellows, yet he was ordained by a lenient presbytery in western New York.[5] To the end of his days, he pursued his own way in theology, and adopted methods of evangelism which brought him into conflict with many of the leaders of the Calvinistic churches.

In 1824, Charles Finney conducted a series of meetings at Evans Mills in Oneida County, New York State.[6] He preached faithfully, but after a score of sermons, there were no decisions. The evangelist told his audience that he would preach to them no longer unless some received Christ as Saviour. Still none responded, so Finney said: "You have rejected Christ and His gospel. You may

[1] Sissons, C. B., *Egerton Ryerson, His Life and Letters*, Vol. I, *passim*.
[2] Finney, C. G., *Memoirs of Charles G. Finney*, p. 4.
[3] *Ibid.*, p. 5.   [4] *Ibid.*, pp. 12–20.
[5] Sweet, W. W., *Revivalism in America*, p. 135.
[6] Finney, C. G., *op. cit.*, pp. 62 ff.

remember as long as you live that you have publicly committed yourself against the Saviour."[1]

A packed church heard him preach what was announced to be his last sermon. The evangelist took for granted that the audience was committed against the Lord, and preached accordingly. He asked for no reversal of their decision. During the night, scores tried to contact him, but he was nowhere to be found. A great concern developed among the unconverted, bringing such a response that almost every one was converted, including a number of atheists. Such was the beginning of Finney's extraordinary ministry, and an unusual power remained with him the rest of his life.

One of Finney's earlier campaigns was held in the town of Antwerp.[2] Unaware that the place was so wicked that it had been nicknamed "Sodom," or that there was one godly intercessor therein who was derisively called "Lot," Finney preached on the text: "Up, get you out of this city, for the Lord will destroy the city." The congregation thought that Finney had become facetiously offensive, but anger turned to conviction and conviction brought numerous conversions. His fame spread along with his extending ministry.

Finney's labours in the local awakenings in western New York reached a climax at Rochester where one-tenth of the city's ten thousand people were converted, and twelve hundred members in that year 1830 joined the churches there.[3] Soon the impulse of the awakening was widely felt in a general movement throughout the States, with a hundred thousand joining the churches in 1831.[4]

Finney became a national figure and was soon invited to conduct revival meetings in Boston, New York, Philadelphia and the larger cities. His "new measures" aroused opposition, among them his use of the "anxious seat," a bench or a pew reserved for inquirers.[5] His theology moved away from the Presbyterian-Congregationalist brand of Calvinism and approximated a middle course between Arminius and Calvin, between a Methodist and a Baptist viewpoint. Later in life, Finney developed a strong doctrine of Perfection.[6]

In 1836, Finney became professor of theology at Oberlin College.[7] During this period, he held preaching missions in many states, and visited England besides, holding an unusual series of meetings in Whitefield's old Tabernacle. Finney became president of Oberlin College in 1851, an office he held until 1866.

Finney's career was one of the most unusual in the history of

[1] *Ibid.*, p. 63.   [2] *Ibid.*, pp. 98 ff.   [3] *Ibid.*, pp. 284 ff.   [4] *Ibid.*, p. 300.
[5] Sweet, W. W., *loc. cit.*
[6] Sweet, *Story of Religion in America*, pp. 283-284.
[7] Beardsley, F. G., *op. cit.*, p. 146.

evangelism. Reacting against a kind of fatalism in his own denomination, Finney deplored the notion that sinners should continue under conviction of sin until God should deign to grant them repentance: rather he felt that they should by an act of the will surrender to God. It was this emphasis upon immediate decision and his preaching of "whosever will" which had made a powerful effect.[1]

As a gospel tactician, Finney was second to none. As a strategist his practice was better than his theory. Finney went to the extreme of stating that revivals of religion were nothing more or less than a result of the right use of the appropriate means.[2] Finney's expectancy of revival in his ministry, a ministry obviously empowered by the Holy Spirit, was justified by the results almost everywhere evidenced in his labours.

But his theory of revivals encouraged a brash school of revivalists and evangelists who thought that they could promote genuine revival by the use of means chosen by themselves.[3] The use of means was patently successful in the case of so many other Spirit-filled men. In the case of the less spiritual promoters, the theory gave rise to a brand of promotional evangelism, one full of sensationalism and commercialism,[4] a scandal of American religious life in the low period between the Moody-Torrey-Chapman campaigns and the campaigns of Billy Graham.

Despite these objections, one may designate Charles Grandison Finney as the most brilliant evangelist of the nineteenth century.

An honest and earnest New England farmer, a Baptist named William Miller, whose zeal had made him leader of many evangelists preaching a doctine of the Second Coming of Christ, fixed the date of that event as 21st March, 1843.[5]

In 1831, Miller began an ambitious mission to warn the American people of the approaching end of all things. Within a decade he had gathered a following of between 100,000 and 1,000,000 people still in the membership of the various churches.

Alas, the many who camped in the open fields or climbed the hilltops to await the Coming of the Lord in white garments at dawn were disappointed. Miller assured them that the Coming might occur any day within a year, but 21st March, 1844, came and went also, likewise 22nd October.[6]

Multitudes were disappointed and embittered, for many had sold their possessions. A nucleus of believers formed an Advent

[1] *Ibid.*, pp. 148–149.
[2] Finney, C. G., *Lectures on Revivals of Religion*, p. 5.
[3] McLoughlin, W. G., *Modern Revivalism*, p. 132.
[4] *Ibid.*, pp. 447–450.
[5] Sweet, W. W., *op. cit.*, pp. 277 ff.   [6] *Ibid.*

Association from which the Seventh-Day Adventists[1] separated in 1846, diverging from other Evangelicals on the Seventh-Day, the Immortality of the Soul, and—devising a new doctrine to cover the fiasco of 1844—the Investigative Judgment of Saints, asserting that Christ had already come secretly. Ellen G. White, their reputed prophetess, was rejected by other Evangelicals as heretical.

By means of excellent medical missions, the Seventh-Day Adventists established a world-wide fellowship, a million in a hundred years or so.

There were other evangelists of the Revival of Finney's days who were effective in Britain as well as the United States. James Caughey,[2] of the Troy Conference in New York State, was moved in the times of revival in 1840 to give himself to the work of an evangelist.

His first two campaigns were in Canada, in Montreal and Quebec, where five hundred people professed conversion.[3] Many years later, he also conducted services in Toronto and London.

Caughey became a great man of prayer and a very definite preacher of scriptural doctrine. In early 1841, he crossed to Ireland and began his ministry in Dublin, where he preached 129 times and turned over seven hundred converts to the care of the churches.[4]

In Liverpool, Caughey preached 120 times and more than 1,200 converts were reported. A like number professed conversion in Sheffield, and in Nottingham an even greater number. He preached in many of Britain's cities and towns.[5]

From 1841 until 1848, Caughey laboured in the United Kingdom, with 22,000 people professing conversion to God. One of those greatly moved was a young man in Nottingham, William Booth, who immediately took to street preaching.[6]

From 1848 onwards, James Caughey preached in the United States and Canada, fruitful revivals following his ministry, although without as many visible results as in the British Isles.[7]

Meanwhile, local awakenings continued to be reported in Wales, the land of revivals. North in Denbighshire, there was a revival in 1821,[8] followed by another in Anglesey in 1822.[9] South

---

[1] Olsen, M. E., *History of the Origin and Progress of Seventh-Day Adventists, passim.*
[2] Beardsley, F. G., *op. cit.*, p. 202.
[3] Halliday, S. B., *The Church in America and Its Baptisms of Fire*, pp. 605-606.
[4] *Ibid.*; cf. Caughey, J., *Methodism in Earnest.*
[5] *Ibid.*; cf. Caughey, J., *Showers of Blessing.*
[6] Beardsley, F. G., *loc. cit.*
[7] Halliday, S. B., *loc. cit.*
[8] Hughes, John, *Methodistiaeth Cymru*, Vol. III, p. 154.
[9] Hughes, Henry, *Diwygiadau Crefyddol Cymru*, p. 293.

in Carmarthenshire, an awakening occurred in 1828 which spread throughout the counties of South Wales, and added thousands to the churches.[1]

In 1832, there was another revival in North Wales, in Caernarvonshire.[2] In 1840, more than two thousand were added to the churches of Merionethshire in a movement which affected North Wales and areas to the north and south. Charles Finney's *Lectures on Revival* had been studied by the promoters of this work, and both prayer and preaching services were organized, to the sorrow of Calvinists who disapproved the "use of means." This 1840 Awakening was quiet and solemn and lacked the usual emotional disturbances. Very few of the converts fell away.

In 1849, a great cholera epidemic afflicted South Wales, and several thousand people were converted in a few months.[3] Local awakenings were becoming fewer towards the mid-century and a generation of great preachers converted in the earlier movements was dying off. There was a noticeable decline in evangelical religion in the 1850s, with ministers who remembered better things discussing "The Inefficiency of the Ministry," "The Ungodliness of the Present Generation," and "Worldliness in relation to Religion."[4]

In 1839, William Chalmers Burns (later the famous pioneer in China) told a congregation in Kilsyth of the mighty movement of God in that place a century previous. So great was their hunger for God that the rehearsing of the story produced the same intense conviction of sin as before, and many were the conversions.[5]

In the next month, August, Burns proceeded to Dundee to supply for his friend, the saintly Robert Murray McCheyne, telling his church of what had happened in Kilsyth. The whole city of Dundee was moved by the praying and preaching.

W. C. Burns was asked by interested clergy[6] to minister in neighbouring counties, and in so many places there were revivals brought about by his preaching of the love of Christ in dying for sinners. It was chiefly during prayer times that lasting transformations of life were made.

From 1839 to 1843, the Scottish Highlands were moved by a general awakening which also affected the English-speaking Lowlands greatly. In Oban, there occurred such a movement in 1841 that people from the countryside flocked to the meetings, walking as many as twelve miles.[7] A second wave of blessing visited the

[1] Evans, Eifion, *When He is Come*, p. 18 (30,000).
[2] Hughes, John, *op. cit.*, Vol. III, p. 152.
[3] Evans, Eifion, *op. cit.*, p. 19.   [4] *Ibid.*, p. 22.
[5] Shearer, J., *Old Time Revivals*, pp. 66 ff.
[6] Bonar, A., *Memoir of Robert Murray McCheyne*, p. 25.
[7] MacRae, A., *Revival in the Highlands and Islands*, pp. 53 ff.

places that had been moved thirty years before. Again the islands were the scenes of religious revival, including some that had not experienced earlier awakenings. The spiritual folk in cities and towns were being girded for a national emergency.

In the 1840s, there was a renewed awakening all over Norway. At the beginning of the century, there had been only one non-rationalist bishop in Norway, Johan Nordal Brun of Bergen. A grandson, Pastor Lyder Brun of Bergen, faced a crisis of the spiritual life in the '40s, and emerged as a great revival preacher in Bergen and the weatern parts of Norway.[1]

In the same decade, a Lutheran pastor, Gustav Adolf Lammers, led a great revival in Skien in South Norway in 1848, but his convictions led him to secede from the State Church.[2] For a while, it seemed as if the movement would progress more outside the Establishment, but it proved not so.

The State Church movement in the awakening was led by a professor of theology in Oslo, the Charles Simeon of Norway, Professor Gisle Johnson, under whose inspiration there was an outstanding revival from 1851 onwards.[3]

The Norwegian Missionary Society had been founded in the revival decade of the 1840s, and in 1853, a year marked by a cholera epidemic, the first Home Mission (*Indremisjon*)[4] was begun. Both were voluntary societies with the Church of Norway. The *Indremisjon* continued to be a bulwark of Evangelicalism in Norway, with its own *Bedehuser* (Prayer Halls) alongside parish churches where more formal worship was held. Its relationship to the State Church compared with that of Methodist societies before secession.

A British chaplain, George Scott, started in 1830 a ministry that had a profound effect on the religious life of Sweden.[5] Born in Edinburgh, he was Wesleyan in preaching but an interdenominationalist in practice. He awakened a religious zeal among the humble classes, influenced men of importance, organized missionary societies, published newspapers, and helped to deliver the Swedish people from the curse of brandy.

In 1837, George Scott founded the Bethlehem Church in Stockholm, for a hundred years known as an evangelical citadel.[6] Scott had no desire to commence a work in any kind of opposition to the Church of Sweden. His grandest passion was to strengthen the

[1] Molland, E., *Church Life in Norway, 1800–1950*, pp. 35 ff.
[2] Westin, Gunnar, *Den Kristna Friförsamling i Norden*, p. 256.
[3] Ousland, G., *En Kirkehovding: Professor Gisle Johnson, passim*.
[4] Molland, *op. cit.*
[5] Westin, Gunnar, *George Scott och Hans Verksamhet i Sverige, passim*.
[6] Westin, Gunnar, *Den Kristna Friförsamling i Norden*, p. 26.

cause that remained. In 1842, he was driven out by persecution but those whom he had influenced continued the work of revival and evangelism, Carl Olof Rosenius of Stockholm (converted at the age of 15 in 1836) becoming heir to his ministry.[1] Two students of the University of Uppsala—Rosenius and Anders Wilberg—became leaders of the evangelical movement in Sweden.[2] Later the movement split in two, one section becoming Baptist and following Anders, the other founding the Evangelical National Foundation, known in Swedish as *Evangeliska Fosterlands Stiftelsen*,[3] led by Rosenius. Rosenius, not a Pietest, edited a magazine titled *Pietisten*. He was free of any trace of the fanaticism that marred other revivals.

About the same time, an effective preacher of law and grace named Laestadius arose,[4] and his followers multiplied from northern Sweden into the neighbouring parts of Norway and Finland. It was a more exotic movement, inclined to extravagance and separatism,[5] and it continued as the Laestadian movement generation after generation.

The two Lutheran pastors, Jonas Lagus and Nils Gustav Malmberg, became the leaders of a fruitful awakening in western Finland, the great *Österbottenväckelse*,[6] which remained effective in Finland during the 1830s and 1840s.

Meanwhile, the awakening of French-speaking, Reformed Churches continued to spread, reaching Holland (and still called *Reveil*) in 1830. Many people were awakened. In the decade 1840–50 came a greater awakening, enlisting abler men. A Jewish convert, Da Costa, was called the prophet of the Revival, Beets the preacher, Heldring the philanthropist and Prinsterer the statesman. Evangelism at home and abroad increased.[7]

The Awakening in the Netherlands was fully matched by the continuing revival in the German states, including Austria and Switzerland. In the year 1828, Samuel Heinrich Frölich was converted in Switzerland.[8] In Zürich, a couple of young Hungarians heard Frölich preach and, changed in heart, returned to Budapest to commence the ministry which resulted in the emergence of the Hungarian denomination, the Nazarenes.

---

[1] Stephenson, G., *The Religious Aspects of Swedish Immigration*, pp. 38 ff.
[2] Westin, Gunnar, *op. cit.*
[3] Stephenson, G., *op. cit.*, p. 45; cf. Gidland, M., *Kyrka och Väckelse*, 1840–80, p. 344.
[4] Stephenson, G., *op. cit.*, p. 28.
[5] Wordsworth, J., *National Church of Sweden*, pp. 370–371.
[6] Rosenqvist, G. O., *Finlands Kyrka*, pp. 17–22; cf. Åho, Juhani, *De Vakte* (in Norwegian).
[7] Kluit, M. E., *Het Reveil in Nederland*, *passim*.
[8] Broadbent, E. H., *The Pilgrim Church*, pp. 329 ff.

In 1788, large colonies of Mennonites settled in the "black earth" region of Russia, with other German farmers.[1] It was agreed that they would be free to practise their own religion, but it was forbidden to proselytize Russians. There was a gradual deterioration of the spiritual life.

In 1818, Edvard Hugo Otto Wüst was born and in 1845 he was converted in Württemberg. He was called to a Pietist church that served the German settlers at Neuhoffnung in South Russia. Nearby,[2] Mennonites attended his preaching and soon were awakened from formality. The great revival that followed exhibited elements of extravagance and resulted in dividing the Mennonites into opposing camps, the new body calling itself the Mennonite Brethren. In die course, the older body also was awakened and the differences softened; but an unplanned effect was a missionary zeal to win their Russian neighbours to vital faith in Christ.[3]

The German Mennonites and Pietists in the revival called their devotional meetings *Stunden*. The converted Russians in turn were called the Stundists. The great movement (still within the Orthodox Church) was helped by a great increase in Bible circulation due to the labour of the Scot, James Melville—known as Vassily Ivanovich[4]—the agent of the British and Foreign Bible Society who was encouraged by the Czar Alexander I to found a short-lived Russian Bible Society. State and Church drove the Stundists out.

[1] Smith, H., *The Story of the Mennonites*, pp. 384 ff.
[2] Smith, H., *op. cit.*, p. 429; cf. Broadbent.
[3] Broadbent, E. H., *op. cit.*   [4] *Ibid.*, p. 314.

a

CHAPTER VIII

EVANGELIZATION OF THE NEGRO

E VANGELIZATION OF THE NEGRO RACE IN MODERN TIMES began in the eighteenth century among the slaves of the American plantations.[1] In the years between the Declaration of Independence of the United States and the Proclamation of Emancipation, many Christian slave-owners provided both religious worship and education for their households. At first, the Negro slaves worshipped with their masters in recognized sections of the same churches, but, as Christianity gained ground, the Negroes preferred to organize their own churches[2] in which members with a generally lower grade of education could minister in clerical and in lay capacities. A Negro Baptist church was formed in South Carolina just before the Revolution.[3]

The fact that more than 90 per cent of all Negro church members[4] in the United States have belonged to Baptist or Methodist congregations demonstrated how effective and widespread was the evangelism of these two denominations after the First and Second Great Awakenings, especially the latter. Before long, the greatest work of evangelizing the Negroes in the United States was being done by Negro Christians themselves, with white American Christians initiating enterprises or educating the leadership.

Among Negro converts, there were laxities of behaviour in certain respects—for example, in the married relationship.[5] Slavery often broke up families, causing a disregard of the sanctity of marriage. Some Negroes brought superstitions into their Christianity, but probably no more so than converts in early days of the evangelization of pagan Europe.

The impact of an evangelical faith upon both masters and slaves was definite. Negro spiritual songs expressed the longing of slaves to be free, and, by the same evangelical conviction, many

---

[1] Gewehr, W. M., *Great Awakening in Virginia*, pp. 235 ff.
[2] Mays and Nicholson, *Negroes' Church*, pp. 22-27, 279.
[3] Townsend, L., *South Carolina Baptists*, p. 259.
[4] U.S. Census 1926, 95%—10% more than the figures for 1860, in DuBois, *The Negro Church*, p. 29.
[5] Latourette, K. S., *A History of the Expansion of Christianity*, Vol. IV, p. 343.

of the dominant race longed to free them.[1] Kenneth Scott Latourette made this careful observation:[2]

> It is highly significant that fresh religious awakenings with their renewed emphasis upon putting into practice the ideals of the New Testament usually gave rise to attempts to free the slaves.

Latourette cited several pages of quotations to prove his contention. It is true that several denominations split over the slavery issue, the abolition of slavery being too strong a medicine for sick brethren involved in southern plantation society. Yet Christian idealism made possible not only the Emancipation Proclamation of 1863 but also the Thirteenth Amendment of 1865, writing an end of slavery into the Constitution. A majority of the nation forced its idealism upon a minority, which alas included many unconvinced Christians.

There were opportunities to evangelize Negro folk elsewhere. First among these lay in certain of the West Indies under the control of Denmark, Britain, and the Netherlands. The population of these colonies was predominantly Negro, living in a cultural environment very different from that of the Negro minority in the United States, therefore less assimilated to European culture.

At the beginning of the nineteenth century, the morale of the Church of England in Jamaica was low.[3] The British settlers in the tropics had a reputation for indulgence in drunkenness and profligate living, and there was little spiritual uplift offered to the black proletariat. The Church Missionary Society under evangelical impulse sent out teachers and catechists to help the newly consecrated Bishop of Jamaica, arriving in the second quarter of the century.[4]

Fifty years before Emancipation, a Negro preacher named George Lisle from the United States had begun to preach to people of his own race, gathering converts into Baptist churches.[5] This evangelist and his associates were of high moral character, though illiterate and naïve.

In 1814, missionaries of the Baptist Missionary Society began arriving in the island to assist Lisle and his colleagues.[6] The missionaries were ardent advocates of Emancipation, hence they underwent persecution from the plantation owners, several being arrested and their chapels burned.[7]

[1] Gewehr, W. M., *op. cit.*, chapter x.
[2] Latourette, K. S., *op. cit.*, p. 346.
[3] Ellis, J. B., *The Diocese of Jamaica*, pp. 53 ff.   [4] *Ibid.*, pp. 49, 66.
[5] Payne, E. A., *Freedom in Jamaica*, pp. 17–18.
[6] *Ibid.*, p. 19.   [7] *Ibid.*, pp. 27 ff.

With the coming of Emancipation, the Baptist membership rose from about ten thousand in 1830 to more than twenty-five thousand in 1840.[1] In 1842, the Jamaica Baptist Association voted to become self-supporting and formed a Baptist Missionary Society to evangelize the other West Indies.[2] In 1843, Jamaican Negroes began to participate in the work of evangelizing Africa with their parent society in England.[3]

Violence also met the operation of the English Methodist Mission,[4] which, like the Baptist cause, passed the ten thousand mark in membership in 1830. Methodist membership declined from 1840 till 1860 however, partly because of divisions in British Methodism and partly because of economic distress on the island.[5] The Presbyterian work in Jamaica was of much smaller proportions than either the Methodist or Baptist. Various other Protestant denominations followed.

In 1836, the Society for the Propagation of the Gospel was assisting Anglican work in Trinidad and, after Emancipation, the Church Missionary Society sent missionaries and teachers.[6] Ill-will discouraged Methodists and Congregationalists. Methodists who tried to effect a foothold on the island of Barbados, an Anglican stronghold, were subjected to violence.[7] Methodism spread widely throughout the islands and had more than sixty thousand adherents less than a decade after the general Emancipation took effect.[8]

Much the same pattern of missionary penetration prevailed in the Guianas and in British Honduras, though in Dutch Surinam, Protestant societies with the larger followings were Dutch Reformed, Lutheran and Moravian.[9]

The Bantu tribes, of Negro-Hamitic origins, were beginning to cross the Zambesi when the first European settlers arrived at the Cape of Good Hope, a thousand miles south.

At the southern tip of Africa, at the beginning of the nineteenth century, the British took over a Dutch colony of more than twenty thousand of European blood, together with their Hottentot and mixed-blood adherents.[10]

In the first quarter of the nineteenth century, the Dutch Reformed settlers in South Africa were suffering from a dearth of

[1] Cf. Linton, J. H., *Memoir of William Knibb*, p. 358.
[2] Payne, E. A., *op. cit.*, pp. 69-70.   [3] *Ibid.*, pp. 72 ff.
[4] Findlay and Holdsworth, *History of the Wesleyan Methodist Missionary Society*, Vol. II, pp. 63 ff.
[5] *Ibid.*, Vol. II, p. 365.
[6] Stock, E., *The History of the Church Missionary Society*, Vol. I, p. 346.
[7] Latourette, K. S., *op. cit.*, Vol. V, p. 60.
[8] Walker, F. D., *The Call of the West Indies*, pp. 89 ff.
[9] Latourette, K. S., *op. cit.*, Vol. IV, p. 66.
[10] DuPlessis, J., *Life of Andrew Murray, passim.*

clergy. The Revivals had already moved Scotland, but not Holland, so a Governor of the Cape succeeded in persuading a number of Scottish ministers to emigrate to the colony to minister to its Dutch-speaking people.[1] Among these Scots came the elder Andrew Murray, who not only quickly identified himself with his adopted people but prayed earnestly for an evangelical revival in South African churches.[2] Andrew Murray, senior, sent his sons John and Andrew to study in Scotland, where they were deeply moved by the revival under W. C. Burns.[3] They decided to enter the ministry, and went to Utrecht University for their theological studies.[4] Their involvement in the Revival in Holland and Scotland had lasting results in South Africa.

The Dutch settlers before British annexation had begun to evangelize the Hottentots and other non-Europeans in their vicinity, on a master-servant relationship.[5] Other settlers followed.

British emigration to South Africa began in earnest with the 1820 Settlers in the eastern parts of the Cape Province. The High Church S.P.G. (Society for the Propagation of the Gospel) and S.P.C.K. (Society for the Promotion of Christian Knowledge) following them helped give Anglo-Catholicism strength in South Africa and Evangelicalism remained weak in Anglicanism.[6]

Methodism, like Presbyterianism, entered South Africa with the British troops.[7] The first Methodist minister, arriving in 1816, had much opposition to encounter, his chapel being burned by a regimental colonel. The Baptists commenced a work at Grahamstown among 1820 Settlers.

Before the start of the nineteenth century, the Moravians revived their abandoned mission to the Hottentots and began in 1818 to evangelize the Bantu in eastern Cape Colony. A Swede, Hans Peter Hallbeck, became bishop of the Moravians and the work went forward steadily.[8] Methodists began a missionary work among Bantu in 1823,[9] and maintained their leadership numerically.

In the 1830s, spiritual awakenings moved the European and non-European populations in the tiny dorps of South Africa, in Gnadendal in 1833,[10] and in Grahamstown in 1837,[11] and elsewhere.

[1] Ibid., p. 15.   [2] Ibid., pp. 27–28.   [3] Ibid., pp. 39 ff.   [4] Ibid., pp. 55 ff.
[5] DuPlessis, J., History of Christian Missions in South Africa, pp. 19 ff.
[6] Pascoe, C. F., Two Hundred Years of the S.P.G.; Allen and McClure, Two Hundred Years of the S.P.C.K.
[7] Whiteside, J., History of the Wesleyan Methodist Church in South Africa, pp. 35 ff.
[8] Anshelm, C., Bishop Hans Peter Hallbeck, passim.
[9] Shaw, W., Story of My Mission in S.E. Africa, pp. 337 ff.
[10] Hamilton, J. T., History of the Moravian Church, p. 378.
[11] Taylor, W., Christian Adventures in South Africa, p. 68.

At the turn of the century, Jan Theodor van der Kemp arrived at the Cape to represent the London Missionary Society.[1] He and his friends founded a mission for Hottentots in the eastern Cape Colony. His first wife having died in the Netherlands in a tragic accident, he married—not very happily—a girl of mixed blood,[2] as did some other missionaries.[3]

In 1820, a mature Scottish minister, John Philip, was appointed superintendent of London Missionary Society work in South Africa. For a full generation, he directed the work, embracing the viewpoint of the natives and exasperating the Afrikaner farmers by his advocacy of the rights of non-Europeans. He lived a stormy life.[4]

Robert Moffat, another Scot, devoted himself to evangelizing the Bantu tribes of Bechuanaland, winning a notorious chief to the faith. His main mission station was built at Kuruman.[5] A quarter of a century later, David Livingstone arrived in South Africa, yet another product of the Revival in Scotland. He married Moffat's daughter. He took his wife and children with him on dangerous journeys, but after losing his youngest child and almost losing all the others, he sent them home and pursued his extraordinary explorations all alone. His heroic exploits pointed the way to an evangelization of the interior later that century.[6]

Scotsmen were represented not only in the London Missionary Society, but also in national societies. Scottish Presbyterians contributed a major benefaction to the education of the Bantu, by founding the Lovedale Institution in 1841.[7]

The Anglicans were somewhat tardy in their outreach to the Bantu people, the colonial policy of a ministry chiefly to settlers absorbing their attention till the coming of Bishop Gray in 1847.[8]

In 1825, the American Board (Congregational)[9] entered Natal in 1835 to evangelize the Zulus. In 1829, the Paris Evangelical Missionary Society, a produce of the Revival in France, sent its first missionaries to South Africa; and in 1833 they entered Basutoland and founded an abiding work. Their greatest missioner was François Coillard, himself a revivalist, whose heart had been kindled by the ministry of Robert Haldane in France.[10]

---

[1] Lovett, R., *History of the London Missionary Society*, Vol. I, p. 481.
[2] Martin, A. D., *Doctor Vanderkemp, passim.*
[3] Lovett, R., *op. cit.*, Vol. I, pp. 534 ff. [4] *Ibid.*, pp. 539 ff.
[5] Moffat, J. S., *Lives of Robert and Mary Moffat;* cf. Northcott, C., *Robert Moffat, Pioneer in Africa.*
[6] *Vide* Campbell, R. J., *Livingstone, passim.*
[7] Shepherd, R. H. W., *Lovedale, South Africa, passim.*
[8] Pascoe, C. F., *op. cit.*, pp. 269–273.
[9] Strong, W. E., *Story of the American Board*, pp. 132 ff.
[10] Mackintosh, C. W., *Coillard of the Zambesi*, pp. 3 ff.

Another Revival-sparked Society, the Rhenish Mission, sent out its first missionaries to South African Hottentots and Bantu in 1829.[1] They were followed by its sister Berlin Missionary Society in 1834. Yet another missionary product of the Revival in Europe, begun through a revival in Hanover, 1848, was the Hermannsburg Mission.[2]

The Revival in Norway under Hans Nielsen Hauge led to the sending of Hans Schreuder and a Norwegian Mission to the Zulus of Natal, in the years following 1843.[3] Schreuder was a forerunner of several Scandinavian enterprises.

The South African pattern was repeated in West Africa, then called "the White Man's Grave."

Evangelical Anglicans of the "Clapham Sect" were instrumental in the foundation of Sierra Leone, as a refuge for freed Negro slaves. To Freetown, the Church Missionary Society sent a couple of German missionaries from the Berlin School in 1806.[4] Under Wilhelm Augustin Bernard Johnson, there occurred 1816–23 a remarkable mass movement of freed men to Christian faith.[5] In 1811, the British Methodists sent a mission to Sierra Leone,[6] followed by other Evangelicals.

Liberia, also a refuge for freed slaves, owed its inception to the Second Great Awakening.[7] In 1820, the first contingents of American Negroes began arriving. Two Negroes began the Baptist enterprise there in 1821, and in 1833 American Methodists sent their first overseas missionary.

The S.P.G. commenced a mission in Ghana (then the Gold Coast) in the middle of the eighteenth century but the work had lapsed several years before a contingent of Basel missionaries entered in 1828, only to find graves there.[8] Then Methodists arrived in 1834, and under Thomas Freeman, a mulatto, made striking advances.[9]

In the 1840s, the Church Missionary Society, the Methodists and the United Presbyterians of Scotland entered neighbouring Nigeria. They not only preached the Good News but combatted the killing of twin babies, the murder of old folk and other shocking customs. The Southern Baptists opened a mission to Nigeria in the next decade.[10]

Johann Ludwig Krapf of Württemberg was an obvious product

---

[1] DuPlessis, J., *op. cit.*, pp. 200 ff. [2] *Ibid.*, pp. 373 ff.
[3] Burgess, A., *Unkulunkulu in Zululand*, pp. 104 ff.
[4] Stock, E., *op. cit.*, Vol. I, pp. 81 ff.
[5] Thiessen, J. C., *Survey of World Missions*, p. 191.
[6] Findlay and Holdsworth, *op. cit.*, Vol. IV, pp. 73–117.
[7] *Vide* Spring, G., *Memoirs of the Rev. Samuel J. Mills.* (Mills died in action there.)
[8] Schlatter, W., *Geschichte der Basler Mission*, Vol. III.
[9] Walker, F. D., *Thomas Birch Freeman, passim.*
[10] Latourette, *op. cit.*, Vol. V, pp. 435 ff.

of the post-Napoleonic Revival in Germany.[1] He received his training at Basel and entered the service of the C.M.S. in Africa. After several attempts to enter closed doors, he moved southwards to Zanzibar and Mombasa to preach, becoming proficient in Swahili. Krapf dreamed of a chain of mission stations across the breadth of Africa. The fulfilment of such a dream awaited the coming of recruits from the next series of evangelical awakenings.

What of the remainder of Africa, south of the Sahara? It was indeed a Dark Continent. First European contacts with Black Africa had come through the nefarious Slave Trade, in which the professedly Christian nations followed the Arab example in abetting the raiding of innocent tribes for slaves.

In the early nineteenth century, this Slave Trade was suppressed, but settlements around the coasts begun for trading purposes continued. Explorers and missionaries began to traverse the Continent. Then followed the "Scramble for Africa" in which European nations carved up the Continent for themselves.

In many instances, missionaries preceded the flag; in others, they followed it. Their motives seldom coincided with that of the colonizers. In a majority of cases, their heroic sacrifices for the cause were humanitarian and spiritual. The Evangelical Awakenings provided the personnel.

[1] Claus, W., *Dr. Ludwig Krapf, passim.*

CHAPTER IX

FIELD OF RIVAL RELIGIONS

IN THE EARLY YEARS OF THE NINETEENTH CENTURY, THE EVAN-
gelical societies of the denominations awakened by the Revivals of the period sent out missionaries to the South Sea
Islanders and to Africans in their home continent and in tropical
America. They enjoyed a remarkable success among the former,
winning whole peoples to the gospel; and they made a fair beginning among the latter, laying the foundations of a work that made
Christianity within the century the dominant faith in many tribes
and nations.

In both cases, the evangelical missionaries were pitted against
the dark forces of primitive paganism which was scarcely able to
stand its ground against an enlightened religion.

It was a very different story when the eager emissaries of the
Evangelical Revivals tried to enter the homelands of rival reli-
gions—Islam in northern Africa and western Asia, Hinduism and
propinquent systems in India, and Buddhism and propinquent
faiths throughout the Orient. In these settings, New Testament
Christianity was to encounter communities of interest or systems
of philosophy that fiercely resisted the message of the gospel. The
command to go was followed by reconnaissance, raids, invasion
and sorties.

In the Maghreb, the block comprising three countries, Morocco,
Algeria, Tunisia and a few alien enclaves, the dominant foreign influence throughout the century was French. In the 1830s, Protestant care for French Reformed settlers in Algeria was begun,[1] while
the Church Mission to the Jews commenced a work in several cities
of the Maghreb. Muslims were virtually untouched.

In Egypt, the ancient Coptic Church survived, but it possessed
little evangelistic power while claiming a standard of morality
higher than that of the Muslims in marriage, but lower in social
drinking. The Church Missionary Society in its early revival
enthusiasm sent out missionaries to help the ancient church,
which, in the 1830s, received them cordially.[2] The Church Mission

---

[1] Cooksey, J. J., *Land of the Vanished Church*, p. 70; *vide* Davis, N., *Voice from
North Africa*, 1844.
[2] Stock, E., *The History of the Church Missionary Society*, Vol. I, pp. 222 ff.

to the Jews and the Church of Scotland opened work in the Jewish enclaves, but Muslims were virtually untouched. It was the same in Libya.

The Church Missionary Society also tried to enter into Ethiopia, in which the population was Hamitic or Negro, the prevailing religion Coptic or pagan. Little came of the venture.[1]

The Church Mission to the Jews opened work in Palestine in the 1820s, surprisingly resulting in the establishment of a Protestant Bishop in Jerusalem, nominated by the crowns of Prussia and Britain, afterwards becoming wholly English.[2] The Church Missionary Society followed in the 1850s and gathered a few congregations.[3]

In Syria, the Church Mission to the Jews[4] and the American Board commenced operations in the 1820s. The converts of the latter were made largely from other nominally Christian bodies.[5] This was also true of the work of the American Board in Turkey, where most of the converts were enlisted among Gregorian Armenians.[6] The Church Missionary Society appointed a gifted German, Karl Pfander, to work among Muslims, and he won both a few converts and a storm of persecution.[7] No other societies succeeded in a larger measure, either in Asia Minor or in Iraq, then Turkey's Mesopotamian provinces. Arabia remained a closed land for half a century.

Henry Martyn, a brilliant development of the Evangelical Revival in the Church of England, a protégé of Charles Simeon, visited Persia in 1811 and 1812 to complete a translation of the New Testament.[8] He debated with the Muslim scholars and won one Persian convert. Twenty years later, the American Board entered the country and majored on education and medical work without neglecting prayer for the kind of revival that they had known in the New England college towns.[9] They were successful in gaining converts among the ancient Nestorian Christians, creating the Assyrian Evangelical Church. Few converts were made from Islam.

Afghanistan remained a closed land for all of the nineteenth century and part of the following.

A more hopeful opportunity was afforded in India, where an extension of British commercial and imperial power opened a vast

[1] *Ibid.*, Vol. I, p. 353.   [2] *Ibid.*, Vol. III, pp. 276 ff.
[3] *Ibid.*, Vol. II, pp. 142 ff.   [4] Wolff, J., *Travels and Adventures*, pp. 168 ff.
[5] Anderson, R., *History of the Mission of the ABCFM to the Oriental Churches*, Vol. I, pp. 40 ff.
[6] Barton, J. L., *Daybreak in Turkey*, pp. 168 ff.
[7] Stock, E., *op. cit.*, Vol. II, pp. 150 ff.
[8] Smith, G., *Henry Martin*, pp. 340 ff.
[9] Anderson, R., *op. cit.*, Vol. I, pp. 163–223.

sub-continent to the preaching of the gospel. In its early days in the middle of the eighteenth century, the East India Company in general practised a religious neutrality, which towards the end of the century became a handicap to the missionaries.

The year 1793 marked a turning point in the evangelization of India. William Wilberforce as an Anglican Evangelical persuaded the House of Commons to make better provision for chaplains to the Protestant employees of the Company.[1] A number of chaplains were strong Evangelicals and were constrained to evangelize not only the Europeans but the Indian non-Christians.

There were many outstanding chaplains in the service of the East India Company during the first quarter of the nineteenth century, but the most remarkable was Henry Martyn. Martyn was born in Cornwall in 1781, and had a profound religious experience at Cambridge University at the turn of the century. He became a fellow of St. John's College and a curate to Charles Simeon in Holy Trinity Church. He was called to missions.[2]

In 1806, Henry Martyn arrived in India, noting in his diary: "Now let me burn out for God!" In six short years, his ambition was fulfilled, yet he became India's best remembered missionary. He was a manly disciple and a disciplined man, faithful in his duties as a chaplain, enthusiastic in his preaching to Hindus and Muslims, very brilliant in his work as a translator into Arabic, Persian and Urdu. He died on his way home.

In 1793 also William Carey arrived in India.[3] In spite of difficulties, the debts of a colleague and the insanity of his wife, the demands of his employment and the opposition of the authorities, Carey persisted, transferring his residence at the end of the century to Serampore, under the Danish flag. There he and Ward and Marshman set up a printing press, opened a school for the children of Europeans and preached to Indians. Their first convert was baptized in 1800.[4]

The energy of the Serampore missionaries was astounding. Not only did they translate the Scriptures into various Indian languages but they found time to experiment in the growing of sugar, coffee, cotton, cereals and fruit trees.

To India, the London Missionary Society sent Nathaniel Forsyth, and within five years, in 1813, a number of their missionaries were settled in the South.[5] In 1813, the American Board placed its missionaries in Bombay.[6] In 1813 also, the Anglican Evangelicals

---

[1] Hole, C., *Early History of the Church Missionary Society*, p. 20.
[2] Smith, G., *Henry Martyn, passim.*
[3] Carey, S. Pearce, *William Carey, passim.*
[4] *Vide* Marshman, J. C., *Life and Times of Carey, Marshman and Ward, passim.*
[5] Lovett, R., *History of the London Missionary Society*, Vol. II, pp. 18 ff.
[6] Strong, W. E., *Story of the American Board*, p. 18.

in England persuaded the Company to provide a bishop and archdeacons for the supervision of missionaries in territory controlled by the East India Company forces.

In the year 1813, a time of missionary push was evident in India. The main factors favouring the advance were the extension of the Company's rule in India, its change of attitude to missions, the conclusion of the Napoleonic Wars, and the increased interest of the British, American and European Protestants in missions reinforced by "the rising tide of religious revivals."[1]

During the decade following 1813, the Church Missionary Society sent twenty-six missionaries to India, eleven of them German Lutherans.[2] In 1816, the Society began a Mission of Help to the ancient Syrian Church of Kerala in the south. It enjoyed good relations with its hosts for a while; then tensions developed, resulting in a number of Syrian Christians entering the Anglican fold and later in withdrawal of the more evangelical into a new denomination, the Mar Thoma Church.[3] In Tirunelveli, there was a mass movement into the Tamil work of the Church Missionary Society.[4]

In 1830, Scottish Presbyterian missionaries arrived, their most noted leader being Alexander Duff, a product of the nineteenth-century revival in Scotland and a protégé of Thomas Chalmers.[5] Duff introduced far-reaching new methods in the missionary approach, developing Christian institutes of higher learning using English with great expectation of attracting young men of the higher castes desirous of a European education. The occasional converts of these colleges provided an educated leadership for the emerging Indian churches. Duff advocated schools for women.

Alexander Duff proved to be one of the most influential men to reach India. Not only did he leave his imprint upon the educational systems of India, including State schools, but he worked as an evangelist with a care for souls.[6]

Another famous Scottish missionary, John Wilson, arrived in India the same year as Duff under the sponsorship of the Scottish Missionary Society.[7] He too was a product of the Revival of the early 1800s, in the Scottish border country, and he too became a famous educator as well as an evangelist. He helped found the University of Bombaÿ. Stephen Hislop, another convert of the Revival in the border country, arrived in India in the 1840s and continued in educational work and evangelism in the Central

[1] Latourette, K. S., *A History of the Expansion of Christianity*, Vol. VI, p. 109.
[2] Pickett, J. W., *Christian Mass Movements in India*, pp. 39 ff.
[3] Cheriyan, P., *The Malabar Christians and the C.M.S.*
[4] Pickett, J. W., *loc. cit.*
[5] Smith, G., *Life of Alexander Duff, passim.*   [6] *Ibid.*
[7] Smith, G., *Life of John Wilson, passim.*

Provinces.[1] The Scots also founded a college in Madras. In the 1840s, the Irish Presbyterians began a work in Gujerat,[2] gathering their converts into villages. Welsh Presbyterians, hitherto working through the London Missionary Society, sent their own missionaries to the Khasi hill tribes of Assam in 1841, winning converts and founding churches.[3] In the 1840s, American Presbyterians entered[4] the Punjab, while John Scudder and missionaries of the Reformed denomination in America were gathering congregations at Arcot in the Madras area under the American Board of Missions.[5]

Anthony Norris Groves of the Open Brethren brought out a dozen missionaries to India in 1836.[6]

In 1821, the British General Baptists began their work in Orissa and a decade later General Baptists from the United States joined them.[7] In 1835, American Baptists entered both Assam and Andhra, Telugu country, to found the missions so signally successful in later years.[8]

In 1819, British Methodists in Madras formed a missionary society, ministering to the British soldiers and civilians and to Tamil Indians.[9] The work spread throughout the South.

In the second third of the century, American Lutherans entered India and operated a mission in Telugu country.[10] German Lutherans, through the Basel Mission, opened a work on the Kannara coast at Mangalore about the same time.[11] The Evangelical Lutheran Mission, later of Leipzig, entered India through Madras in 1840.[12]

By the mid-century, the number of Protestant Christian Indians had reached approximately a hundred thousand. The various missionary bodies managed to maintain a surprising measure of comity and co-operation. This they inherited in turn from the co-operation of revival evangelism.

The very rapid growth of the Christian Church in India in the first half of the nineteenth century was due not to the vigour of existing Christian communities but to the effects of the Awakenings in Protestant countries of Europe and America, the churches

[1] Smith, G., Stephen Hislop, Pioneer Missionary.
[2] Jeffrey, R., The Indian Mission of the Irish Presbyterian Church, pp. 29 ff., 131 ff.
[3] Morris, J. H., The Story of Our Foreign Mission, pp. 9 ff.
[4] Gordon, A., Our India Mission, pp. 17 ff.
[5] Chamberlain, Mrs., Fifty Years in Foreign Fields, pp. 24 ff.
[6] Groves, Mrs., Memoir of Anthony Norris Groves.
[7] Sutton, A., Orissa and Its Evangelization, pp. 101 ff.
[8] Sword, V. H., Baptists in Assam, pp. 41 ff; Clough, E. R., Social Christianity in the Orient, pp. 61 ff.
[9] Findley and Holdsworth, op. cit., Vol. V, pp. 176 ff.
[10] Drach and Kuder, The Telugu Mission of the Evangelical Lutheran Church, passim.
[11] Schlatter, W., Geschichte der Basler Mission, Vol. II, pp. 1 ff.
[12] Karsten, H., Geschichte der Leipziger Mission, Vol. I, pp. 66 ff.

taking advantage of the extension of British rule to evangelize a sub-continent.

The Baptist Missionary Society entered the island of Ceylon in 1812,[1] and the Methodists in 1814, alas without their leader, great-hearted Thomas Coke, who died during the voyage out.[2] In 1817, the Church Missionary Society sent four Evangelical Anglican clergymen to Ceylon,[3] and in 1815, the American Board started a mission to the Indian Tamils in the Jaffna area.[4]

Adoniram Judson, originally a missionary of the American Board but switched by convictions on baptism to the American Baptists, arrived in Rangoon in Burma in 1813. He and his wife went through many years' privation before baptizing their first convert in 1819.[5]

The outbreak of the Anglo-Burmese War in 1824 caused the imprisonment of Judson and in 1826, his wife Ann Haseltine died. In 1834, he completed his translation of the whole Bible into Burmese. He laid the foundation for a successful missionary enterprise.

George Boardman[6] arrived in Burma to assist Judson, and opened a station south of Moulmein where he baptized Ko Tha Byu, a Karen. Soon the Karen convert became a fiery evangelist and began preaching in the hills and mountains near and far to Karen villagers.[7] The Karens were a non-Buddhist people, ready for the gospel, and a mass movement followed the preaching with inevitable persecution from the Burmese until the annexation of Lower Burma by the British.

American Presbyterians entered Thailand in 1840 and won a few converts.[8] The evangelization of Thailand proved to be very slow, indeed. In Indo-China, among the Cambodians, Laos and Annamese, there was practically no contact on account of the colonial policy of the French.

In 1793, that significant year for missions to India, the Emperor of China forbade any teaching of the "English religion" in his wide domains.[9] In the meantime, as the new century began, several missionary bodies were engaged in promoting a translation of the Scriptures into Chinese.

[1] Ewing, J. A., *Lanka—The Baptist Mission in Ceylon*, pp. 16 ff.
[2] Findlay and Holdsworth, *op. cit.*, Vol. V, pp. 15 ff.
[3] Stock, E., *op. cit.*, Vol. I, pp. 216-217.
[4] Root, H. I., *A Century in Ceylon: History of the American Board*.
[5] Wayland, F., *Memoir of the Life and Labors of Adoniram Judson, passim*.
[6] King, A., *Memoir of George Dana Boardman*.
[7] Mason, F., *The Karen Apostle—Ko Tha Byu*.
[8] McFarland, G. B., *A Historical Sketch of the Protestant Mission in Siam*, pp. 35 ff.
[9] Latourette, K. S., *op. cit.*, Vol. VI, p. 295.

Then in 1807, Robert Morrison of the London Missionary Society arrived in Canton to begin a very restricted residence.[1] Within a year and a half of his arrival, he had mastered so much of the local Cantonese, the national Mandarin and the literary language of the Empire that he was appointed translator for the East India Company.

His first assistant, William Milne, arrived in 1813,[2] both men converts of the turn-of-century Evangelical Revival in Britain. In 1814, their first convert was baptized.

Karl Gützlaff, a graduate of Jänicke's school in Berlin, toured the coasts of China in the 1830s distributing literature.[3] In the 1830s, the American Board sent its first missionaries to China, as did the American Baptists. American Anglicans and Presbyterians followed, choosing only the port of Canton as a base of operations.[4]

The Anglo-Chinese War of 1839-42 opened up additional ports of China to the residence of foreigners. Out of the evil of opium importation came opportunities for the gospel.[5] Hong Kong was ceded to Great Britain, and missionaries went to live there, at Shanghai, and other ports.

Gützlaff gathered about him a staff of Chinese preachers and colporteurs who were reported to be distributing Scriptures and gathering converts in most of the Chinese provinces.[6] He was very discouraged to find that many of his agents were thoroughly dishonest double-crossers.

Society after society entered the Treaty ports of China, Shanghai becoming a strategic centre. In 1847, W. C. Burns, whose revival ministry in Scotland had affected not only the Scottish kirks but many who were to become missionaries, came himself out to China.[7] For more than six years, he laboured without a convert in Amoy. As soon as accessions to the church were made, he moved on as an evangelist to the other Treaty ports. He impressed many, both missionary and national, by his transparent saintliness.

At the middle of the nineteenth century, the missionary enterprise was confined to Hong Kong and the five Treaty ports around the coast. The Chinese maintained an almost unbroken front of resistance to the penetration of the hinterland. It could be said only that the evangelical forces had secured beach-heads for invasion.

[1] Lovett, R., op. cit., Vol. I, p. 104.
[2] Milne, W., Retrospect of the First Ten Years of the Protestant Mission to China.
[3] Kesson, J., The Cross and the Dragon, pp. 221 ff.
[4] Latourette, K. S., op. cit., pp. 300 ff.
[5] The missionaries opposed the Opium War; vide Bready, J. W., Lord Shaftesbury, pp. 342 ff.
[6] Latourette, K. S., op. cit., Vol. VI, pp. 304-305.
[7] Burns, I., Memoir of the Rev. W. C. Burns, passim.

A Hakka villager in South China named Hung Hsiu-Chuan came into touch with Christianity in the 1830s. He had strange visions of power, and out of his preaching came a new movement in the mountains of Kwangsi. In the 1840s, Hung renewed his contacts with Protestant missionaries, but in unknown ways, Hung converted his movement into an army and overran China from the south to the middle Yangtze, setting up a capital in Nanking.[1]

From 1856 to 1860, a second Anglo-Chinese War was raging, one in which France joined in. The terms of peace opened China further to trade and missionary penetration followed. It had been suggested that the Chinese guarantee protection for Chinese Christians as well as missionaries in the exercise of their religion. Shortly after, with foreign help, the Imperial Chinese armies were able to crush the Taiping Rebellion under Hung.[2] Although these political upheavals gave many missionary societies freedom to expand, they did not break uniform Chinese resistance to Christianity. Converts were comparatively few in number.

Though the intrepid Gützlaff[2] visited ports in Korea and Japan, both kingdoms remained tight-closed against the gospel until the second half of the nineteenth century.

In the main, the entrance to China was made by missionaries of societies brought into being by the nineteenth-century Evangelical Revivals.[4]

[1] Hail, W. J., *The Taiping Rebellion*.   [2] *Ibid*.
[3] Gützlaff, Karl, *Journal of Three Voyages*, pp. 357 ff.
[4] Latourette, K. S., *op. cit.*, Vol. VI, pp. 336.

CHAPTER X

SOCIAL IMPACT OF REVIVAL, I

"CHRISTIANITY," SAID WESLEY, "IS ESSENTIALLY A SOCIAL religion; to turn it into a solitary religion is indeed to destroy it."[1]
The seed of social and political reform was sown in eighteenth-century revivals.

It is clear that democracy did not spring out of the Reformation immediately, though it owed so much to the indirect effects of the two great Reformation doctrines: the rightful duty of free inquiry, which led to liberty; and the priesthood of all believers, which led to equality.[2]

Neither did democracy spring immediately out of the Puritan Commonwealths in England or New England, though American democracy owed much to the adoption of the congregational form[3] of church government and to the town meetings.

In Europe, Lutherans followed their founder in supporting princes; it was natural for Anglicans to support monarchy and aristocracy; and it was understandable for Presbyterian leaders to lend support to oligarchy, for John Calvin held a low opinion of the common people,[4] and considered a democracy as the "meanest form of government." In the American colonies, these denominations were influenced, more or less, by the democracy being practised in the evangelistic fellowships.

In the eighteenth-century revivals, churches of evangelical conviction gained rapidly as they influenced the American population towards the democratic ideal, for all their revivalists emphasized the doctrine that all men are equal in the sight of God, a conviction which inculcated a self-respect in humbler people everywhere.[5]

The itinerant evangelists sought to reach all classes of men: educated and ignorant, rich and poor, masters and slaves. They knew no social distinctions, for all were considered as sinners in need of a Saviour. The Awakenings were a great levelling force

[1] Wesley, John, *Works* (1872 Edition), Vol. V, p. 296.
[2] Gooch, G. P., *English Democratic Ideas of the Seventeenth Century.*
[3] Sweet, W. W., *Revivalism in America*, p. 22.
[4] *Vide* McGiffert, A. C., *Protestant Thought before Kant*, p. 59.
[5] Cf. Gewehr, *The Great Awakening in Virginia*, ch. viii, "Contributions to the Rise of Democracy."

81

in American life, for these revivalists sowed the seeds of true democracy more than any other group of men.[1] The common people looked for political leaders in their own ranks, as they were used to doing in the fastest-growing denominations, Baptist and Methodist.

It had been said that American democracy is based on an application of Baptist principles to secular politics, but that the federal system of the United States is borrowed from the Presbyterian system of courts and delegation of powers. One thing is very certain: it was the Baptists chiefly who pioneered liberty in America, who consistently stood for the democratic principle.[2] They remembered that Anglicans, Independents and Presbyterians as well as Roman Catholics had taken their turn in the saddle in the Mother Country, but always Baptists were the underdogs. Their sufferings made them see too clearly that Establishment was a root cause of their trouble: so they fought it wherever encountered.

In Britain, the Baptists were never strong enough to fight effectively for this principle. In America, sometimes they lost: but they finally won a victory which they shared with all comers, "Jews, Turks and Infidels as well as Christians."[3]

The sowing of the seed of social reform was carried on in the eighteenth century in Britain. There were two main periods of harvest in the century that followed, coinciding in their beginnings with early and middle nineteenth-century revivals around the world.

Europe and America were convulsed by war in the days of Napoleon, hence it was to be expected that the flowering of social reform would follow the coming of peace after Waterloo. Peace made possible the way for social improvement not only in Great Britain and parts of Europe but in United States also. The first period of impact came to an end about the time of the abortive revolutions of 1848 and the Crimean War and American Civil War; the second one commenced in the 1860s.

The first social impact of the awakenings of the nineteenth century was felt in the emancipation of the slaves, in the protection of prisoners, in the care of the sick and wounded, in the betterment of the standards of workers, in the defence of women and children and of helpless animals.

Thirteen years before the formation of the Abolition of Slavery Committee, John Wesley published his *Thoughts upon Slavery*,[4] a

---

[1] Sweet, W. W., *op. cit.*, p. 41.   [2] *Ibid.*, p. 42.
[3] Quoting the sentiments of Roger Williams from *The Bloudy Tenent of Persecution*.
[4] Wesley, John, *Thoughts upon Slavery*, 1774.

direct and penetrating argument against the inhuman traffic in human beings.

Can human law turn darkness into light or evil into good? Notwithstanding ten thousand laws, right is right and wrong is wrong still.

Wesley absolutely declared all slave-holding as inconsistent with any kind of natural justice, let alone Christian ethics. He declaimed that the whole business was hypocritically greedy, that slavery bred other vices. Men-buyers, he said, were no better than men-stealers. He denounced wealthy slave-merchants as the mainspring that put into motion the slave-captains, slave-owners, kidnappers and murderers.[1] These were strong words to use freely in 1774, when slaving itself was protected by law, when philosophers of old and statesmen of the time were quoted to justify the outrageous institution.

Slavery as such was not practised in Europe, but in the European colonies in the New World as well as in some Asian and African countries. In the nineteenth century, slavery was mainly practised in the plantation communities of the Southern States and the West Indies, as well as in the Ibero-American colonies. Yet the control of the machinery of slavery lay in the efficient shipping organizations of England, Old and New.

The pioneer advocates and engineers of the abolition of slavery within the British Empire were almost all the products of the Evangelical Revival. William Wilberforce and his colleagues were evangelicals, many of them the pillars of the then-derided, now-extolled Clapham Sect,[2] a group of Church of England Evangelicals and Free Church adherents with a greater concern for the souls and bodies of men than for current ecclesiastical strife. As the Abolition movement gained strength by spiritual persuasion, great men such as William Pitt, Edmund Burke and Charles James Fox, and others of that calibre, joined the evangelicals in their grand endeavour, as did liberals with inherited Christian ethics.[3]

From the time that Lord Mansfield declared in a famous case (1772) that any slave brought to England was automatically free,[4] agitation made progress, the Slave Trade being abolished in 1807 and Emancipation of the Slaves coming into law throughout the British Empire in 1834.[5] No less than 750,000 in the West Indies alone were proclaimed free men, their chapels being crowded at midnight July 31st, while the day of liberation, far from being one of bloodshed as predicted, became a day of order, reverence and

---

[1] *Ibid.*   [2] Colquhoun, J. C., *Wilberforce: His Friends and His Times, passim.*
[3] Trevelyan, G. M., *English Social History*, p. 495.
[4] *Vide* Bready, J. W., *This Freedom—Whence?* p. 44.
[5] Harris, J., *A Century of Emancipation*, pp. 3 ff.

rejoicing, the Negro having been prepared for his liberty through the influence of the evangelical missions. Parliament cheerfully paid twenty million pounds sterling to recompense the slave-owners.

It took another thirty years to bring about the Emancipation of the Slaves in the United States.

In the eighteenth century, in Pennsylvania the Quakers had decided early against slave-holding.[1] The first impulse in New England came from Samuel Hopkins, a successor to Jonathan Edwards in the Great Awakenings. Hopkins stressed that Christ had died for all men, Negroes and Indians as well as Europeans and Asians.[2]

The success in the nineteenth century of the British Emancipation dealt a staggering blow to the American institution of slavery, but it took more agitation by tender-conscienced Christians and yet another Evangelical Awakening before a majority of people were ready to abolish slavery.

Many anti-slavery advocates were among the early nineteenth-century revivalist leaders.[3] In Kentucky, Presbyterian evangelists proclaimed that slavery was repugnant to American ideals and to Christian teachings. The Baptists and the Methodists also espoused the cause of the slaves. The abolitionist William Lloyd Garrison in New England found his greatest supporters in Baptists and Methodists, and not in the Congregationalist and Unitarian majority as often supposed.[4]

The Finneyan Revivals had a powerful effect on anti-slavery agitation. When Lyman Beecher as president opened Lane Theological Seminary in 1832, a good number of the enrolled students were Finneyan converts and anti-slavery men.

Finney's solution to the slavery problem was simple and direct: convert the slaveowners! He made a practice of calling on hearers to repent of the sin of slave-holding, and many did. This movement, in some minds, was far more telling in effect than the political polemics of Garrison.[5]

Another evangelist, Henry Ward Beecher, put forth tremendous defiance of the Fugitive Slave Law of 1850, while his sister Harriet Beecher Stowe wrote one of the most effective novels of all time, *Uncle Tom's Cabin.*[6]

Among ardent evangelicals, there were two schools of anti-

---

[1] Jones, R., *Quakers in the American Colonies*, p. 397.
[2] Sweet, W. W., *The Story of Religion in America*, pp. 286–287; *vide* Works of Samuel Hopkins, Vol. II, pp. 549 ff.
[3] Sweet, W. W., *Revivalism in America*, pp. 155 ff.
[4] Barnes, G. H., *The Anti-Slavery Impulse*, pp. 90 ff.
[5] Sweet, W. W., *op. cit.*, pp. 157–159.
[6] Barnes, G. H., *op. cit.*, pp. 73, 231.

slavery propaganda, those who made a frontal attack upon the social evil, using every opportunity to preach against it; and those who made an indirect attack, using their talents to win to a vital Christian experience all sinners—hoping that the regenerate slave-owner might become more susceptible to humane entreaty.

Parliamentary legislation or executive action, said some, could not reach down to the root of a social evil, which, more entrenched than is personal sin, can be overcome only by the Spirit of God in a general revival of religion. So when localized and intermittent revivals gave way to a seemingly miraculous, nation-wide awakening, many evangelicals felt that the liberation of the slave was at hand. Alas, it came with a sacrifice of blood in the catastrophic Civil War, when the grapes of wrath were trampled out in 1861–65.

As with the slave, so with the poor prisoner. Already in the eighteenth century, a significant prison reform was under way. John Howard was one of the greatest products of the Evangelical Revival.[1] He was in turn influenced by Dissenting, Methodist and Anglican Evangelical Christianity. A prisoner of war of the French, he developed an interest in prison conditions in every part of the United Kingdom and in many countries of Europe, travelling fifty thousand miles in the prisoners' cause and spending £30,000 of his own fortune before contracting jail-fever in 1790 in Russia and dying far from home.

The conditions of life in prisons were at that time indescribably foul.[2] Old, decrepit buildings were commonly used as prisons; strait-jackets, irons and chains were added for security upon the slightest excuse. The prisons were dens of despair with disease, drunkenness, indecency and debauchery forced upon their inmates. Not only were vicious criminals so incarcerated but also first offenders, and even persons already declared not guilty of any crime.

John Howard received the official thanks of Britain's House of Commons.[3] He was recognized as the father of modern prison reform, inspiring others to take up the task only barely begun in his lifetime. Evangelicals took the lead, followed by the humanitarian rationalists who tackled the reform of the penal code itself.[4]

As early as a hundred years before the War of the American Revolution, the Quakers of New Jersey and Pennsylvania had revolted against a system of brutal and inhuman punishments that were inflicted on criminals outside prison walls. They instituted

[1] Field, J., *The Life of John Howard, passim.*
[2] Bready, J. W., *This Freedom—Whence?* pp. 246 ff.
[3] *Ibid.*   [4] *Ibid.*, pp. 251 ff.

punishment of a more humane sort within houses of correction, but the British Government of the time disallowed their effort.[1]

In the eighteenth century, an Italian Marquis of Beccaria had published a treatise on prisons and penology, translated into a score of western languages.[2] His ideas were welcomed in France by Voltaire and in England by Jeremy Bentham, another humanitarian freethinker. There was a noteworthy alliance between the freethinking party in England and the evangelical reformers.

The American Revolution occurred at a time when Howard was achieving reform in England. The new authorities permitted a return to older Pennsylvanian experiments.[3] The Quakers were timely in pioneering prison reform. They based new ideas on the conviction that prison was not a method of savage reprisal, but one of reform and rehabilitation. Therefore they sought to minimize the vicious effects of housing all criminals of all types together as companions in evil by providing every prisoner with a cell. The Quakers wished to encourage quiet reflection upon the results of evil-doing, a typical approach on their part. The method had its weaknesses.

Raikes, the founder of the Sunday Schools in Britain, was also active in the reform of prisons.[4] Stephen Grellet, a French émigré who became a busy worker in the Society of Friends, took up a concern for the relief of prisoners both in Great Britain and on the Continent.[5] He passed on his concern to a young lady, Elizabeth Gurney, who had become converted at the age of seventeen, a dedicated woman later known as Mrs. Elizabeth Fry.[6]

A young Quaker mother with eleven children, Elizabeth Fry became burdened for the women, desperate and depraved, whom she found in the notorious Newgate prison that Wesley had called the earthly equivalent of hell. Elizabeth Fry not only read the Scriptures and prayed with these unfortunates, but also opened successful prison schools for them. In 1817, Mrs. Fry founded a society for prison reform, dedicated to those principles now taken as elementary: separation of the sexes, classification of criminals, useful employment, secular education, and religious instruction, with a view to restoring prisoners to society as reformed and rehabilitated.

In 1840, Elizabeth Fry visited Germany to see the work of Theodor Fliedner in Kaiserwerth, a little town near Düsseldorf. It was a return visit. She was so lastingly impressed by what these

---

[1] *Encyclopedia Britannica*, 1960, article "Prisons."
[2] Farrer, J. A., *Crimes and Punishment* (English translation), Beccaria's *Dei Delitti e Delle Pene.*
[3] *Encyclopedia Britannica*, 1960, *loc. cit.*   [4] Field, J., *op. cit.*, p. 107.
[5] Stead, F. H., *The Story of Social Christianity*, Vol. II, p. 168.
[6] Whitney, J., *Elizabeth Fry, Quaker Heroine*, *passim*.

German evangelicals were accomplishing in care of the sick that she returned to England to found a school of nursing, using girls of humble origin.[1]

Theodor Fliedner was born in the first month of the year 1800, the son of a Lutheran pastor.[2] He had attended the Universities of Giessen and Göttingen but his faith was not deepened there.[3] A greater influence upon his life was the record of what August Francke had done at Halle.

In due course, Fliedner was called to the cure of Kaiserswerth, a Protestant parish in the midst of a Roman Catholic population.[4] A threat of foreclosure of a mortgage sent him off to Holland and Britain to collect funds.[5] It was in the latter place that the effect of the Revival dispelled finally any trace of rationalism in Fliedner's mind.[6]

> I learned to know a whole host of institutions that minister to the bodies and souls of men. I inspected their schools and prisons. I observed their homes for the poor and the sick and the orphaned. I studied their missionary societies and Bible societies and their societies for the improvement of prisons and so forth. And I particularly noted that practically all of these institutions and organizations were called into being by a living faith in Jesus Christ and that nothing but this vital faith sustains them.

In 1823, Fliedner had visited Elizabeth Fry in London. Upon his return to Germany, Fliedner requested his voluntary imprisonment, but was refused. In 1826, he organized a prison society, the first of a series of philanthropic institutions.

In 1833, Fliedner and his wife risked abuse[7] by offering the hospitality of their parsonage to a prostitute recently discharged from a prison. She was the first of 2,500 to be cared for within a century at Kaiserswerth alone, and there were a hundred other houses of rescue and rehabilitation established in Germany through Fliedner's action.

In 1836, Theodor Fliedner instituted an order of Protestant deaconesses, borrowing some of his ideas from Mennonite sisterhoods.[8] His premier deaconess was Gertrud Reichardt. The opposition accused Fliedner of "trying to make nuns of our Protestant girls."[9] He won valuable friends.

In 1840, King Frederick William IV of Prussia began to help Fliedner's projects. The residence of the deaconesses was named the Motherhouse. In 1842, Fliedner founded an orphanage. In 1848, he founded a home for the feeble-minded and the epileptic.

[1] Young and Ashton, *British Social Work in the Nineteenth Century*, p. 159.
[2] Fliedner, Th., *Aus meinem Leben, Erinnerungen und Erfahrungen, passim.*
[3] Wentz, A. B., *Fliedner, the Faithful*, p. 13.
[4] *Ibid.*, p. 21.   [5] *Ibid.*, p. 25.   [6] *Ibid.*, p. 29.
[7] *Ibid.*   [8] *Ibid.*, p. 43.   [9] *Ibid.*, p. 56.

To further these many enterprises, he printed a hundred thousand calendars annually.

His wife died, and, in 1843, Fliedner married again, this time a Huguenot girl. The idea of the deaconesses spread over Germany and to other countries, and, in a hundred years, produced a hundred Motherhouses and 35,000 sisters.[1] In 1849, Fliedner visited the United States and began an order of deaconesses.[2] He established a Motherhouse in Jerusalem, and promoted others in the Orient. His other enterprises were too numerous to chronicle. He died in 1864.

An English gentlewoman, Florence Nightingale, was much intrigued by a report of the ministry of Theodor Fliedner at Kaiserswerth, where the sick were lovingly cared for by German deaconesses.

Florence Nightingale[3] was the daughter of a Unitarian, but she herself became a confirmed Anglican. Early in her life, she came under a conviction of sin and so experienced a change of heart which led her into the service of the Lord in His healing ministry.[4] At the age of 17, she heard the voice of God calling her to His service.

It has been disputed whether Miss Nightingale was a Unitarian or a Trinitarian. In her later retrospective writings, far from theological in tone, she made allusion to the Trinity.[5] She was appreciative of the Roman Catholic Church, but that was on account of the provision made by the Church for dedicated women to enter full-time service in its orders of nuns, rather than because of theological convictions. Florence Nightingale summed up her position by saying that the spiritual religion of St. John's Gospel was enough for her.[6]

She took her training in nursing at the obscure village on the Rhine.[7] Looking back years later, she deplored the backwardness of the hospital but commended its tone as "excellent." She recalled that she never had met with a higher tone, or a purer devotion. She returned to London to apply the lessons learned in the same evangelical way. She awaited a further call from God.

It was noteworthy that the nurses at Fliedner's hospital were of peasant stock, as were Elizabeth Fry's in London, nursing being regarded as too low a calling for refined ladies.

In October 1854, Florence Nightingale and a company of thirty-eight nurses left for the theatre of war, where the wounded of the Crimean battles were dying like flies for lack of care.[8]

---

[1] *Ibid.*, p. 95. [2] *Ibid.*, p. 104.
[3] Cook, Sir Edward, *The Life of Florence Nightingale.*
[4] *Ibid.*, Vol. I, p. 49.   [5] *Ibid.*, Vol. II, p. 486.   [6] *Ibid.*, Vol. II, p. 366.
[7] *Ibid.*, Vol. I, pp. 108 ff.   [8] *Op. cit., passim.*

Hospitals were vast, dilapidated buildings without proper sanitation or even the conveniences for common decency. By superhuman efforts, the "Lady with the Lamp" brought some order out of chaos, and saved the lives of grateful multitudes of soldiers. Every night, she inspected the wards, becoming the idol of the troops and of their folks at home.[1]

Before she died at the age of ninety, the lady Florence Nightingale had revolutionized the life of the private soldier. She is generally regarded as the founder of modern nursing. Historians have conceded not only her training at a school born of evangelical revival, but her debt to Evangelicals for her lifelong simplicity of purpose.

Some secularists have contended that Florence Nightingale betrayed an anti-evangelical spirit by deriding prayer for the sick. This was a strange misrepresentation of fact. The attitude of the famous nurse was that of many modern Christian doctors. What was the good, she asked, to pray for deliverance from plague and pestilence as long as sewers ran into the Thames?[2]

The greatest reformer of all was the seventh Earl of Shaftesbury.[3] At the base of the Shaftesbury Memorial in the heart of Piccadilly Circus in London is carved a striking inscription composed by Gladstone:

> During a public life of half a century, Lord Shaftesbury devoted the influence of his station, the strong sympathies of his heart and the great power of his mind to honouring God by serving his fellowmen—an example to his order, a blessing to his people, and a name to be by them ever gratefully remembered.[4]

Standing in direct succession to the Clapham Sect, of the same aristocratic background and religious preference, a scholar of Oxford and a peer, Anthony Ashley Cooper became benefactor of the factory workers of industrial Britain.

His father, the sixth Earl, a hard-drinking and haughty relic of eighteenth-century deism, and his mother, a society worldling of the stock of Marlborough, had relinquished the boy to the care of a faithful Christian nursemaid, Maria Millis, who taught him to pray, and moulded his life and character by godly precept and righteous living in a difficult environment.[5]

England was the first of the countries of the world to become industrialized. The Industrial Revolution brought about a sorry exploitation of the toiling masses—an exploitation about which

---

[1] *Encyclopedia Britannica*, 1960, "Florence Nightingale."
[2] Cook, Sir Edward, *op. cit.*, Vol. I, p. 479.
[3] Bready, J. W., *Lord Shaftesbury and Social-Industrial Progress, passim.*
[4] Bready, J. W., *This Freedom—Whence?* pp. 261-262. [5] *Ibid.*, p. 262.

deism had little conscience. Lord Shaftesbury once described himself as "an Evangelical of the Evangelicals,"[1] and his spiritual experience led him into a crusade for human betterment which was an unparalleled demonstration of Christian love, rather than of class hatred, harnessed to the improvement of the lot of the working poor.

Before Lord Shaftesbury's reforms, workers were caught in a treadmill of competitive labour which served to keep them straining for sixteen hours a day. Shaftesbury and his friends put an end to that by legislation limiting the operation of the factories to ten hours a day, introducing a Saturday half-holiday, as well as abolishing all unnecessary Sunday labour.[2]

Shaftesbury's *Mines and Collieries Act* made impossible any further exploitation of women or children in coal mines where they had been used to drag coal in heavy wagons through darksome tunnels. His *Chimney Sweep Acts* prohibited the vile use of little boys to clean narrow chimneys of soot—many a child had suffocated in the task and others had been maimed therein. He also delivered children in the countryside from an agricultural exploitation as terrible as that of the factories.[3] Shaftesbury, by his *Lunacy Acts*, transformed the lot of the insane from that of abused prisoners to protected patients.

Shaftesbury promoted public parks, playing-fields, gymnasia, garden allotments, workmen's institutes, public libraries, night schools, choral and debating societies, and other self-help.[4]

Not only did Shaftesbury accomplish the work of ten men in social reform, but he also kept busy in evangelistic ministry, being president of the Ragged School Union, the World Y.M.C.A., the British and Foreign Bible Society, the Church Pastoral Aid Society, the Religious Tract Society and many others—so many, in fact, that at his memorial service in Westminster Abbey in 1885 no less than two hundred religious, social and philanthropic organizations were represented by officials, with all of which Lord Shaftesbury was more or less directly concerned.[5]

Even Kenneth Scott Latourette in his weighty volumes has confessed that there is not enough space to list more than a few of the reformers and reforms impelled by evangelical motivation.[6] Nine out of ten of Lord Shaftesbury's colleagues in social and industrial reform were as much products of Evangelicalism as the Earl himself.[7] A great cotton-mill owner, John Wood, provided most of the money needed for the Ten Hours' Crusade. Richard

[1] Hodder, E., *The Life and Work of the Seventh Earl of Shaftesbury*, Vol. III, p. 3.
[2] Bready, J. W., *op. cit.*, pp. 264–268.
[3] *Ibid.* [4] Hodder, E., *op. cit.* [5] *Ibid.*
[6] Latourette, K. S., *A History of the Expansion of Christianity*, Vol. IV, p. 155.
[7] Bready, J. W., *op. cit.*, p. 265.

Oastler, who did so much for factory children, was a Methodist lay preacher. Others associated in the work were active in the lay preaching of the gospel.[1] The Ten Hours' Act was the Magna Charta of the liberty of industrial workers, closing the factories at 6 p.m., keeping them closed for twelve hours, preventing labour from being robbed of evening and Sunday leisure. Working people were deeply grateful.[2]

It is significant that trade unionism grew during this period of social impact of the gospel. All of British Trade Unionism owed much to the six Dorchester labourers who were transported for seven years' servitude to the Australian penal colonies.[3] Their crime was that of forming an Agricultural Union to resist further depression of their wages as farm hands, wages already cut to a below-subsistence level of a shilling a day.[4] These labourers were guilty of no violence and no intimidation, not even a strike. In 1834, all six were dragged from their homes and given short shrift at a trial. On April 30th, thirty thousand men bearing thirty-three trade banners marched on Whitehall to petition the government against the harshness of their sentence.[5]

These Dorchester labourers, often called the "Tolpuddle martyrs," included three Methodist local preachers and two others who were active in the Tolpuddle Methodist Chapel. A sixth man professed no religious convictions, but was so impressed with the religious life of one of his companions, who slaved with him in a convict gang, that he became a Christian and a Sunday School superintendent in later life.[6] An aroused public opinion forced the early pardon of these working men and their transportation home. The trade union cause had won a round in its battle for working men's elementary rights. Christian leadership continued for a hundred years.

Prime Minister David Lloyd George paid an unusual tribute to evangelical influence in trade unions in these careful paragraphs:[7]

> The movement which improved the condition of the working classes, in wages, hours of labour, and otherwise, found most of its best officers and non-commissioned officers in men trained in institutions which were the result of Methodism. . . . John Wesley inaugurated a movement which gripped the soul of England, that deepened its spiritual instincts, trained them and uplifted them; the result is that when a great appeal is made to either England or America, there is always the response, and it is due to the great Religious Revival of the Eighteenth century.

[1] *Ibid.*   [2] *Ibid.*, p. 266.
[3] *Vide* Webb, S. and B., *History of Trade Unionism.*
[4] Bready, J. W., *op. cit.*, pp. 269.
[5]   *id.*, p. 271.   [6] *Ibid.*, p. 269.   [7] *Ibid.*, p. 275.

It was in the nineteenth century, largely, that the Wesleyan-Whitefield Revival bore the fruit cultivated by converts of later awakenings.

It cannot be denied that the influence of Great Britain upon the United States of America was a powerful force, especially in the realm of social progress. As Britain was first industrialized, the hitherto unknown problems of industrial life were therein first encountered and overcome.

The decades following 1830 in American life have been called by historians "The Sentimental Years,"[1] for it was a time when organized good works and betterment flourished as never before.[2] There was scarcely an object of benevolence that lacked a dedicated society or institution,[3] and all of the organizations (whether church related or not) were directly indebted to the Evangelical Awakening of the time[4].

In the United States, there were societies to promote education, to reform prisons, to stop prostitution, to colonize Africa with freed slaves, to advance the cause of peace, to provide social and spiritual amenities for sailors in port[5]—not to mention the multitude of home and foreign missionary societies, Bible and Tract societies, Sunday School associations, temperance clubs, and other organs of co-operative evangelism.

Reference has already been made to the great number of schools, high schools and colleges that were founded in the United States as a result of the Second Great Awakening in the churches and the colleges, which provided not only founders but teaching staff. Most of these denominational school and high school systems gave way to free public school programmes. Latourette declared with good reason:[6]

> Even more important, the initiative and the early leadership in the creation of the system of free public schools supported by the state came largely from those who seem to have caught their inspiration from the Protestant wing of Christianity.

Much the same was true of Great Britain and the parts of Europe influenced by the Revivals.

David Stow, influenced by the great evangelical leader Thomas Chalmers, inaugurated his model schools and teacher training colleges that set the pattern for Scotland's national education system.[7] There were similar evangelical influences at work in

[1] Branch, E. D., *The Sentimental Years*, 1836–1860.
[2] Sweet, W. W., *Revivalism in America*, p. 159.
[3] Barnes, G. H., *The Anti-Slavery Impulse*, pp. 18–28.
[4] Sweet, W. W., *op. cit.*, p. 159.   [5] *Ibid.*
[6] Latourette, K. S., *op. cit.*, Vol. IV, p. 416.
[7] Fleming, J. R., *History of the Church in Scotland*, p. 50.

Wales, Ireland and England. In England, there was both loss and gain in the denominational and religious squabbles over school promotion. Then the great network of voluntary schools gave way to a system of universal primary education.[1] In a similar manner, denominational schools were replaced in Scandinavia and the German States.

The Royal Society for the Prevention of Cruelty to Animals was founded in London in 1824, and became the largest as well as oldest society of its kind in the world.[2] Not only did it endeavour to stamp out cruelty, but it offered free veterinary service to as many as one quarter million mute creatures annually. It is not surprising to learn that the founder of the Society was an evangelical clergyman named Arthur Broome, and that Sir Thomas Fowell Buxton, the famous evangelical emancipator, chaired the first meeting assisted by Wilberforce and Mackintosh.

This was a fitting climax to the campaign by evangelicals against cruel sports, bull-baiting, cock-fighting and other matches that caused pain to animals. In the United States, the spread of camp-meeting evangelism ended brutal sports, in Britain "humanitarianism and religiosity."[3]

Some pro-Evangelical historians have suggested that the working classes were captured by the forces of the Evangelical Revival.[4] In the United States, a little more than ten per cent were members of evangelical churches at the mid-century,[5] and in Great Britain, church attendance was as low as ten per cent in the great manufacturing towns and London.[6]

This invalidates the claims of anti-Evangelical sociologists that the Evangelical Revival had made the masses so obsessed with the life to come that they accepted social conditions that would have caused revolutions in other European countries.[7] A majority of the working classes were uninfluenced by Evangelicism.[8] From the Evangelical minority came most of the reformers of the social order.[9]

[1] Trevelyan, G. M., *op. cit.*, pp. 580 ff.
[2] Fairholme and Pain, *A Century of Work for Animals, passim.*
[3] Trevelyan, G. M., *op. cit.*, p. 504.
[4] *Vide*, J. L. & Barbara Hammond, *The Town Labourer, 1760–1832.*
[5] Cf. Baird, Robert, *The State and Prospects of Religion in America.*
[6] Inglis, K. S., *Churches and the Working Classes*, p. 2.
[7] *Vide*, Sargant, W., *Battle for the Mind*, p. 201.
[8] Engels, F., *The Condition of the Working Class in England in 1844*, London, 1892.
[9] Cf. Letourette, K. S., *op. cit.*, Vol. IV, p. 155.

CHAPTER XI

DISSENSION AND DECLINE

THE FIRST THIRD OF THE NINETEENTH CENTURY HAD SEEN the rise of the Anglican Evangelicals to a position of great influence. At the turn of the century, they had numbered (according to the statesman, W. E. Gladstone) no more than one in twenty of the clergy.[1] Yet Canon Overton, a High Church historian, summed up their record thus:

> It would be no exaggeration to say that morally and spiritually, the dominant religious power both inside and outside the Church of England at the close of the eighteenth century was that which had been evoked by the Evangelical Revival.[2]

In the second third of the nineteenth century, Evangelicalism in the Church of England met a rival in the battle for influence. The Evangelical Revival with its great increase of religious life and its drive for reform shocked and alarmed a great number of refined and scholarly churchmen. As the years of the nineteenth century rolled by, the Evangelical Party not only actively co-operated with dissenters in philanthropic and missionary enterprises, but favoured religious freedom more and more, aided and abetted by Roman Catholics, Jews and many Broad Church leaders. The High Churchmen took fright.

In 1833, some Oxford "Friends of the Church" began to publish a series of "Tracts for the Times" regarding church history and doctrine.[3] In 1834, seven thousand clergy addressed the Archbishop of Canterbury, deploring reckless changes and promising hearty co-operation in reviving much ancient discipline of the English Church.

The best-known figures in this Tractarian, High Church movement were John Keble, John Henry Newman, R. H. Froude, and E. B. Pusey. Their Tracts seemed to suggest a return to not only pre-Revival and pre-Puritan beliefs and practices but to pre-Reformation positions.[4] In 1841, John Henry Newman published Tract 90, aimed at proving that the Thirty-Nine Articles of the

[1] Simon, J. S., *The Revival of Religion in the Eighteenth Century*, p. 282.
[2] Overton, J. H., *The Evangelical Revival in the Eighteenth Century*, p. 161.
[3] *Vide* Brilioth, Y., *The Anglican Revival, passim.*
[4] Church, R. W., *The Oxford Movement, passim.*

Church of England are capable of being interpreted in accordance with the Roman view of the sacraments.[1] It caused an uproar. As a logical conclusion to his convictions, Newman abandoned the Church of England, and entered the Church of Rome, followed by a large number of the ablest and most zealous members of the High Church Party.

The effect of Newman's conversion to Rome was felt in the revival of the Roman Catholic mission in England. Pusey and Keble continued promoting the Anglo-Catholic cause in the Church of England.[2] Its zeal took the form of founding of brotherhoods and sisterhoods of medieval colour to help uplift the classes and the masses.

It has often been asked whether the Tractarian Movement could be considered as a Revival in a historic sense of the term.[3] Unlike the Evangelical Revivals before and after, the Tractarian action did not operate by the pentecostal method of extemporaneous prayer and decisive evangelism. It had its devotional drive but it was liturgical and sacramental. The eighteenth-century evangelical Revival had its greatest effect upon the masses, spontaneous and simultaneous. The Tractarian movement was a well-prepared campaign, with a very different evangelism than that of the historic Evangelical Awakenings, and it lacked the ecumenical brotherhood of the great Revivals.

By 1847, the Anglo-Catholic party was strong enough to challenge the institution of an ordinary Evangelical parson, G. C. Gorham, in his parish. The Privy Council found in favour of Gorham—the opposite decision would have made it utterly impossible for Evangelicals to remain in their Church of England parishes.[4] The Broad Church party entered into conflict with Anglo-Catholics over Hampden's "liberal lectures" in 1836.[5] The Broad Church party supported the Evangelicals against the Tractarians but differed from both in doctrine.

Thus it was that the members of the Church of England were becoming agitated in a politico-ecclesiastical commotion which was hurtful to the spread of the gospel among the masses.

The evangelical ecumenism of the nineteenth century produced an interesting development in its second quarter, from 1825 onwards.

Dr. Edward Cronin, a Roman Catholic dentist, professed an

---

[1] *Ibid.*, pp. 234 ff.   [2] Trevelyan, G. M., *English Social History*, p. 516.

[3] Historians have interpreted the Oxford Movement partly as an outgrowth of, and partly a protest against the Evangelical Revival; *vide* Latourette, *History of the Expansion of Christianity*, Vol. IV, p. 39.

[4] Balleine, G. R., *History of the Evangelical Party in the Church of England*, pp. 147 ff.

[5] Warre-Cornish, F., *The English Church in the Nineteenth Century*, pp. 252 ff.

evangelical conversion in Dublin[1] and had received a warm welcome from various Protestant bodies in that city. He was greatly disturbed when told that he must make a choice among them, something he was reluctant to do. He was told that the various Protestant bodies were as regiments in the army of the Lord, but this simile lost its appeal when he noticed that far too often they turned their weapons upon one another instead of against their common enemy.[2]

Cronin found a number of like-minded young believers in Dublin—Bellett, Darby, Hutchinson, Parnell (afterwards Lord Congleton), Stokes and Wilson.[3] His little group had begun "breaking of bread" on Sundays at a time that did not conflict with the regular worship of Protestant churches. The meetings begun in 1825 grew in numbers and influence as thoughtful men, dissatisfied with all denominationalism, joined the company. By far, the most brilliant accession was John Nelson Darby, an Anglican curate, whose voice became the most influential in the movement.[4]

The post-Napoleonic Revival in Germany had brought another leader into the movement later known as Christian Brethren, though miscalled the Plymouth Brethren.

George Müller was born in Prussia, in 1805.[5] At the age of 20, he was brought into touch with a vital gospel message at Halle, and was converted. Coming to England, he met with the Brethren. He married the sister of Anthony Norris Groves, a devoted Brethren missionary.[6] Müller became quite famous in connexion with Bristol, where he established the remarkable Orphans' Homes and where he had oversight of a Brethren assembly, Bethesda. And in connexion with the latter, he came into sharp conflict with Darby.

Darby had (rather unfairly) excommunicated an assembly of Brethren in Plymouth because of the alleged heresy of its leader, B. W. Newton.[7] Brethren from this excommunicated assembly moved to Bristol and sought fellowship with the Bethesda congregation, which, ascertaining that they repudiated the alleged heresies, received them. Darby demanded that Müller and Bethesda believers should excommunicate these brethren, and, when the demand was refused, he himself excommunicated Bethesda and all in fellowship with Bethesda.[8]

John Nelson Darby had discovered a principle of ecclesiastical

---

[1] Ironside, H. A., *Historical Sketch of the Brethren Movement*, p. 10.
[2] *Ibid.*   [3] *Ibid.*, pp. 12 ff.   [4] *Ibid.*, pp. 13–16.
[5] *Autobiography of George Müller; vide* Pierson, A. T., *George Müller of Bristol.*
[6] *Vide* Groves, Mrs., *Memoir of Anthony Norris Groves;* cf. also Lang, G. H., *Anthony Norris Groves: Saint and Pioneer.*
[7] Ironside, *op. cit.*, chs. iii and iv.   [8] *Ibid.*, ch. v.

fission which fragmentized the Brethren movement into pieces large and small and which destroyed the hope of gathering saints in New Testament fellowship. Darby thus begat Exclusive Brethrenism, in bewildering varieties mutually antagonistic and isolated.

The churches that followed George Müller became known as Open Brethren, maintaining an open fellowship more or less towards other Christians, though sometimes possessed of an exclusive spirit due to recurring legalism.

It appears to any neutral observer of Brethren divisions that the Open Brethren, the truly open, were the inheritors of Brethren first truths and practices. Not only were they loyal to the ideas that motivated the first meetings, but they were fully committed to their significant evangelical programme of evangelism and missions.[1] Their influence grew out of all proportion to their own numerical strength, and they influenced greatly even the Evangelical party within the Church of England, and parties in many denominations.

In practical matters, the Christian Brethren co-operated in assuredly evangelical enterprises, evangelism, revival, missions and philanthropy. The Brethren movement proved an abortive type of ecumenism. In the irony of history, Brethren doctrines (especially eschatology) have provided the main opposition in modern fundamentalism to twentieth-century Ecumenism. Unlike their contemporary movement, the Disciples of Christ, which apart from its radical wing maintained its early ecumenical zeal, the Brethren exercised a powerful influence against the ecclesiastical co-operation of Evangelical denominations. They consistently remained evangelical in doctrine.

At the time of the emergence of the Disciples of Christ in the United States and the Christian Brethren in Great Britain, a brilliant but erratic star arose in Scotland. Edward Irving was born in August 1792, the birth-year of Finney.[2] He was appointed assistant to the great Thomas Chalmers in Glasgow in 1819, but his preaching scarcely moved the congregation. He was more successful as a missionary among the poorer classes.

After an indifferent apprenticeship in the city, in 1822, Irving was called to minister in a Scots church in London. He became

---

[1] In this connection, the author wrote in 1942 to Dr. Elmer T. Clark regarding a statement in his worthy survey, *The Small Sects in America*, courteously contradicting his statement that the Brethren engaged in no missionary activity. He cited the facts regarding the large number of Brethren missionaries abroad. Dr. Clark replied, noting the objection. Several editions have since appeared without any correction of this unintentional but very unfair slight.

[2] Oliphant, Mrs., *Life of Edward Irving, passim*.

D

obsessed with the interpretation of apocalyptic prophecy, deciding the year 1830 to be a significant year in which an outpouring of the Spirit could be expected. In Clydeside there occurred a glosso-lalic manifestation, so a deputation from London went there to investigate. Soon tongues and prophecy appeared in Irving's church in Regent Square in London. It became a centre of controversy.[1]

Edward Irving died comparatively young in 1834. The Catholic Apostolic Church, which sought to revive the apostolate as well as gifts of the apostolic era, was his monument rather than his actual creation. The last of the Twelve Apostles died in 1901, after which the movement became moribund, though an offshoot, the New Apostolic Church, appointed additional apostles and spread into a number of countries of Europe and America, claiming 300,000 members.[2]

For half a century, Scotland had been swayed by a vested interest party named the Moderates, who made a mockery of vital religion by their concern for worldly success and patronage. Of course, they had little sympathy for the message and methods of the Evangelicals.

Between 1833 and 1843, a conflict developed between the Evangelicals and the Moderates over the question of the patron-age of parishes being in unspiritual hands. The Evangelical party in the Scottish capital was led by an indomitable parish minister, Andrew Thomson of St. George's Kirk,[3] a prince among debaters. An equally outstanding leader was Thomas Chalmers of Glasgow.[4] The Government in Westminster legally supported the patronage system. So Thomas Chalmers led the great majority of the Evan-gelicals out from the State Church, 474 seceding ministers and their lay elders forming the Free Church of Scotland even though it meant losing sanctuaries, manses and salaries.[5] All but one of the State Church's missionaries and most of its best scholars joined the Free Church. Within its first year, the Free Church erected about five hundred churches and supported its own min-istry and founded its own colleges, besides undertaking the support of each Church of Scotland missionary overseas. Free Church ministers also supported home missions, for Chalmers and his associates were not only evangelists but warm supporters of social reform.[6]

[1] Encyclopedia Britannica, 1960, "Edward Irving."
[2] Shaw, P. E., The Catholic Apostolic Church.
[3] Bayne, P., The Free Church of Scotland, ch. iv.
[4] Blaikie, W. G., Life of Thomas Chalmers, passim.
[5] Watt, H., Thomas Chalmers and the Disruption, passim.
[6] Fleming, J. R., The Church in Scotland, pp. 150 ff.

In Germany, the Prussian and associated state governments took advantage of the renewed zeal and unity of their peoples, following the end of the Napoleonic Wars, to unite Lutheran and Reformed in a single Evangelical but State controlled *Kirche*.[1]

Some who objected to the union upon theological grounds suffered persecution and decided under a pastor named Grabau to migrate to the American Middle West.[2] Another group, objecting to the easy going liberalism of the united *Kirche*, migrated to the area of St. Louis in Missouri and formed what became the Missouri Synod of the Lutheran Church.[3]

In Germany, the New Rationalists appeared at Tübingen University, their leading exponent being F. C. Baur, who, applying the Hegelian philosophy of history to the early Christian records, denied the apostolic authorship of the Gospels as well as the authenticity of many of the Epistles.[4] Lutheran High Churchmen arose to dispute the issue.

There was dissension also in Swiss Reformed circles, the Evangelicals of the Revival being caught between Rationalism and Erastianism. In the Netherlands, revivals of the post-Napoleonic period made many people dissatisfied with easy-going liberalism in the Reformed Church. From 1834 onwards, large numbers of people separated from the Reformed Church to create a new body, the Christian Reformed Church, but Dr. Abraham Kuyper stayed within the established church with hopes of leading it back to evangelical orthodoxy.[5]

Between 1845 and 1855, religious life in the United States of America was in decline. There were many reasons for the decline, political and social as well as religious.

The question of slavery was of paramount importance and men's passions and energies were being diverted into the channels of contention on either side of the controversy.[6]

Many people at the time lost faith in spiritual things because of the extremes of apocalyptists who followed William Miller and others in predicting Christ's return and reign in 1843 and in 1844. Public confidence became shaken as the excitement died down, some deluded victims becoming bitter infidels while others embraced materialism and quite a number were spoiled for Christian service. So widespread was the delusion that the churches became the subjects of ridicule and faith in religion was impaired.

---

[1] Newman, A. H., *Manual of Church History*, Vol. II, pp. 553 ff.
[2] Wentz, A. R., *The Lutheran Church in American History*, pp. 186–187.
[3] *Ibid.*, pp. 181–186.
[4] *Vide* Mackay, R. W., *The Tübingen School and Its Antecedents*.
[5] Winkel, W. F. A., *Leven en Arbeid van Dr. Kuyper*, *passim*.
[6] Beardsley, F. G., *A History of American Revivals*, pp. 213–214.

Between 1845 and 1855, there were several years in which the number of church accessions scarcely kept pace with severe losses due to a relenting discipline and a relentless death-rate. The tide that had flowed in so strongly was now ebbing out rapidly.

There were secular factors operating as well. Financial and commercial prosperity had had an adverse effect upon the American people of the mid-century. The zeal of the people was devoted to the accumulation of wealth, and other things (including religion) took a lesser place. Cheap and fertile land attracted multitudes of settlers, and the frontier was pushed farther and farther back. Cities and states were founded in rapid succession and the population in them increased at an astounding rate. Harvests were plenteous. Boom times caught the public fancy, and turned men's hearts from God.[1]

Secular and religious conditions combined to bring about a crash. The third great panic in American history swept the giddy structure of speculative wealth away. Thousands of merchants were forced to the wall as banks failed, and railroads went into bankruptcy. Factories were shut down and vast numbers thrown out of employment, New York City alone having 30,000 idle men.[2] In October 1857, the hearts of people were thoroughly weaned from speculation and uncertain gain, while hunger and despair stared them in the face.

There had been a commercial revulsion, quite as widespread and unexpected, in the year 1837. It was tenfold more disastrous, yet it produced then no unusual turning to religion, no revolution of the popular mind, no upheaving of foundations. The people as a whole were far more intent upon examining the political and the economic causes of their pecuniary pressure than searching for a spiritual explanation.[3] Now, in the United States and the world, distress preceded an awakening.

[1] *Ibid.*, p. 216.   [2] *Ibid.*, p. 217.
[3] Chambers, T. W., *The Noon Prayer Meeting*, p. 284.

CHAPTER XII

AMERICAN HOUR OF PRAYER

FOR THE BEGINNINGS OF THE RELIGIOUS REVIVAL SOON TO flood the United States, it is necessary to look beyond the borders of the Union. It was among the Ontarian Methodists that the first fruits of the 1858 revival occurred.[1] The Methodist *Christian Advocate and Journal* of New York carried on 5th November, 1857, a prominent headline "Revival Extraordinary" on its front page, with a sub-title declaring that from three to four hundred souls had been converted in a few days. A score had professed conversion the first day of the movement and, as the work steadily increased, public professions grew in number to forty-five daily, until a hundred people had been converted on the Sunday previous to the penning of the report. An enthusiastic correspondent stated:[2]

> The work is taking within its range persons of all classes. Men of low degree, and men of high estate for wealth and position: old men and maidens and even little children are seen humbly kneeling together pleading for grace. The mayor of the city, with other persons of like position, are not ashamed to be seen bowed at the altar of prayer beside the humble servant.

Somewhat significant it is that Hamilton's "gust of Divine power" reportedly sweeping throughout the entire community "took its rise in the rise of the laity" and was entirely spontaneous. This rise to leadership on the part of the laymen became typical of the great movement that followed. In fact, the Hamilton revival bore all the marks of the subsequent American revivals save one, the union prayer-meeting feature developed in New York City and popularized throughout the United States and Canada.

The account of this extraordinary revival of religion was read by hundreds of wistful pastors in the Methodist Episcopal Church, the largest and most evangelistic body of Americans at that time. The expectancy created by the Hamilton outbreak was recognized six months later in an article on the revival sweeping the

[1] Orr, J. Edwin, *The Second Evangelical Awakening in America*, pp. 21 ff.; cf. *The Revival*, London, 17th September, 1859.
[2] New York *Christian Advocate*, 5th November, 1857.

nation.[1] True spiritual awakenings are exceedingly infectious, and proximity in time and place adds to desire for similar blessing. The appearance of the account of the Hamilton revival in the *Christian Advocate* was followed by a steadily increasing number of paragraphs describing local revivals, a few in number in November, increasing in December, and a veritable flood in late winter and spring of the year 1858.

Among the signs of preparation of heart for an awakening was the calling of a convention under Presbyterian auspices at Pittsburgh on 1st December, 1857.[2] The gathering was largely attended by the ministers of the Synods of Pittsburgh, Allegheny, Wheeling and Ohio. The convention continued in session for three days, considering "the necessity of a general revival of religion" in all the churches represented and others as well. The agenda of the meetings set out the means, the encouragements, the hindrances, the demands of the times, the indications of divine providence, and everything relating to the momentous question of revival. It was a solemn, anxious, melting and encouraging time. Two hundred ministers and many laymen attended, spending much of the time in prayer. A committee was appointed to draw up an address to the churches, to be read from the pulpits by the pastors. It was also recommended that the official members of the respective churches be called together to discuss the convention agenda, and above all, that the people be called together to pray. As a result of this programme, many ministers of the Presbyterian denomination and others delivered messages on the first Sunday of the New Year (1858) on the subject of revival, and the first Thursday was observed as a day of humiliation, fasting and prayer. An intelligent and mighty impulse was felt. Shortly afterwards, a similar convention was called at Cincinnati.[3] There the convention became a great meeting of prayer, and churches participating were stirred.

On 1st July, 1857, a quiet and zealous business man named Jeremiah Lanphier took up an appointment as a City Missionary in down-town New York.[4] He had been born in 1809 in Coxsachie, New York, and had been converted in 1842 in the Broadway Tabernacle built by Charles G. Finney a decade earlier. A local journalist described Lanphier as "tall, with a pleasant face, an affectionate manner, and indomitable energy and perseverance; a good singer, gifted in prayer and exhortation, a welcome guest to any house, shrewd and endowed with much tact and common sense."

Lanphier was appointed by the North Church of the Dutch

[1] *Ibid.*, 13th May, 1858.   [2] *Presbyterian Magazine*, September, 1858.
[3] *Ibid.*   [4] Chambers, T. W., *The Noon Prayer Meeting*, pp. 3-34.

Reformed denomination. This church was suffering from deple-
tion of membership due to the removal of the population from
the down-town to the better residential quarters, and the new
City Missionary was engaged to make diligent visitation in the
immediate neighbourhood with a view to enlisting church attendance among the floating population of the lower city. The Dutch
Consistory felt that it had appointed an ideal layman for the task
in hand, and so it was.

Burdened so by the need, Jeremiah Lanphier decided to invite
others to join him in a noonday prayer-meeting, to be held on
Wednesdays once a week. He therefore distributed a handbill:[1]

How Often Shall I Pray?

As often as the language of prayer is in my heart; as often as I see
my need of help; as often as I feel the power of temptation; as often
as I am made sensible of any spiritual declension or feel the aggres-
sion of a worldly spirit.

In prayer we leave the business of time for that of eternity, and
intercourse with men for intercourse with God.

A day Prayer Meeting is held every Wednesday, from 12 to 1
o'clock, in the Consistory building in the rear of the North Dutch
Church, corner of Fulton and William Streets (entrance from Fulton
and Ann Streets).

This meeting is intended to give merchants, mechanics, clerks,
strangers and business men generally an opportunity to stop and call
upon God amid the perplexities incident to their respective avoca-
tions. It will continue for one hour; but it is also designed for those
who may find it inconvenient to remain more than five or ten
minutes, as well as for those who can spare the whole hour.

Accordingly at twelve noon, 23rd September, 1857[2] the door
was opened and the faithful Lanphier took his seat to await the
response to his invitation. . . . Five minutes went by. No one
appeared. The missionary paced the room in a conflict of fear and
faith. Ten minutes elapsed. Still no one came. Fifteen minutes
passed. Lanphier was yet alone. Twenty minutes; twenty-five;
thirty; and then at 12.30 p.m., a step was heard on the stairs, and
the first person appeared, then another, and another, and another,
until six people were present and the prayer meeting began. On
the following Wednesday, October 7th, there were forty intercessors.

Thus in the first week of October 1857, it was decided to hold
a meeting daily instead of weekly.[3] In the same week, the extraordinary revival of religion swept the city of Hamilton in faraway
Canada. In the second week of October, the great financial panic
of that year reached a crisis and prostrated business everywhere.

[1] *Ibid.*, p. 42. [2] *Ibid.*, p. 43. [3] *Ibid.*, p. 44.

It is impossible not to connect the three events, for in them was demonstrated the need of religious revival, the means by which to accomplish it, and the provision of divine grace to meet the situation.

Within six months, ten thousand business men were gathering daily for prayer in New York, and within two years, a million converts were added to the American churches.

At the turn of the New Year, 1858, New York had a population of eight hundred thousand that included neither the inhabitants of Brooklyn nor of the other Boroughs now in New York.[1] New York was by no means an irreligious city, for therein were church sittings for fully one quarter of the inhabitants and church attendance was fairy good.[2] Unlike the New York of the twentieth century, it was a predominantly evangelical Protestant city. There were 50 Protestant Episcopal churches, 41 Presbyterian, 34 Methodist, 29 Baptist, 23 Dutch Reformed, 7 Congregationalist, 7 Lutheran, 5 Reformed Presbyterian, 4 Associate Presbyterian, and 80 other churches.[3]

Notices of revivals of religion began to appear in the religious press at the beginning of the year. Meanwhile, the faithful Fulton Stret company was ever growing in strength, and prayers were being answered in "droppings and showers" of blessing.[4] The Gothic Church in Brooklyn reported seventy-five conversions in a local awakening in January. During the same month, a thorough revival moved the Hudson River town of Yonkers, when nearly ninety conversions occurred.[5] Over in New Jersey towns, unusual awakenings were beginning, and throughout the whole country was increasing an expectancy of a downpour of Divine blessing. As yet, the revival was in its preparatory stage, with the quickening quite obvious to the ministers of the various churches but unnoticed by the general public or secular press.

In the month of February, "showers of blessing" had increased so greatly that they had become a deluge. The secular press, noticing that something unprecedented was happening, began to give space to the news of revival. On 10th February, 1858, the New York *Daily Tribune* gave widespread publicity to the movement in an editorial:[6]

> Some two or three years ago, a daily prayer meeting was started in the lower portion of the city, which met from 12 to 1 o'clock p.m. with a view to giving merchants and merchants' clerks an oppor-

[1] U.S. Census figures, 1860, adjusted.
[2] Newcomb, H., *The Harvest and the Reapers*, p. 16.
[3] New York *Christian Advocate*, 13th May, 1858.
[4] Chambers, T. W., *op. cit.*, p. 69.
[5] New York *Christian Advocate*, 28th January, 1858.
[6] New York *Daily Tribune*, 10th February, 1858.

tunity of uniting in acknowledgment of their obligations to Divine grace and mercy.

A few months ago, after a long silence, this meeting was revived at the Consistory of North Dutch Church at the corner of Fulton and William Streets, and has been crowded every day since the commencement of the financial panic.

Another meeting has been established up town in Ninth Street Dutch Reformed Church and was opened yesterday at noon. Upwards of two hundred persons were present including several clergymen, and great interest prevailed.

We understand that arrangements are being made for the establishment of one or two additional meetings in the upper portion of the city, and soon the striking of the five bells at 12 o'clock will generally be known as the signal for the "Hour of Prayer." These meetings are non-denominational. The advancement of sectarian views is not tolerated in any form.

Indicating a move from prayer to evangelism, the same journal announced two weeks later that "Religious Inquiry Meetings" were being carried on daily in the Norfolk Street Church, of which Dr. Armitage was the pastor.[1] The hour was from 4 till 6 p.m., and the attendance was already noteworthy. The same journal reported that the Ninth Street Noonday Prayer Meeting had overflowed. Another nooday meeting was begun in Forsythe Street Methodist Church.

Prayer meetings multiplied. Meanwhile in the original meeting-place in Fulton Street, sponsors were trying to accommodate crowds by holding three simultaneous prayer meetings one above the other in rooms in the same building.[2] The seats were all filled, and the passages were so crowded that it was scarcely possible for people to pass in or out. Hundreds were unable to gain admission, and a demand arose for more meetings at noon. It was not surprising to note another item in the press:[3]

A business men's union prayer meeting is held daily from 12 to 1 o'clock in John Street Methodist Church, number 44 John Street, a few doors east of Broadway. This meeting is similar to the one held in Fulton Street. Owing to the overcrowded state of the rooms in that place and the manifest increasing interest, it has been thought best to open this place also.

Undoubtedly the greatest revival in New York's colourful history was sweeping the city, and it was of such an order to make the whole nation curious. There was no fanaticism, no hysteria, simply an incredible movement of the people to pray. The services were not given over to preaching. Instead anyone was free to pray!

[1] *Ibid.*, 24th February, 1858.
[2] Noble, W. F. P., *A Century of Gospel Work*, p. 419.
[3] New York *Daily Tribune*, 27th February, 1858.

In the capital, Washington,[1] the daily *National Intelligencer* noted that in New York "a religious interest has been growing in the midst of the rowdyism everywhere so long prevalent," and "Religious revivals were never more numerous or effective than at present."[2]

The churches began to feel the impact of the noonday meetings, which were largely laymen's voluntary efforts. A typical example of reaction in the churches may be seen in the fact that on March 14th (Sunday), the Thirteenth Presbyterian Church of New York City received 113 by profession of faith in Christ and 14 by letter. Of these professions, 26 were heads of families, 10 Sunday School teachers, and 62 Sunday School pupils. Of the total, 63 were between the ages of twelve and twenty, 50 over twenty, and 10 over forty years of age.[3]

On March 17th, Burton's Theatre in Chambers Street, was opened for noonday prayer meetings. These meetings were initiated by the merchants doing business in the neighbourhood of Chambers Street, and were continued by them at their own expense. Mr. Burton, owner of the theatre, was "perfectly willing" for them to operate religious services there, and himself expressed a desire to be prayed for. Half an hour before the time appointed for the service, the theatre was packed in every corner from the pit to the roof. By noon the entrances were so thronged that it required great exertions to get within hearing distance, and no amount of elbowing could force an entrance so far as to gain a sight of the stage! People clung to every projection along the walls, and they piled themselves upon the seats and crowded the stage beneath, above and behind the curtain. The street in front was crowded with vehicles and the excitement was tremendous. Nearly all assembled were business men, only two hundred being ladies and fifty clergymen. The Reverend Theodore S. Cuyler led the services that day.[4]

Three days later, the *New York Times* reported that Dr. Henry Ward Beecher led three thousand people in devotions in Burton's Theatre. During his remarks, he was interrupted by singing from an overflow meeting in the bar-room, whereupon he led the vast throng in thanksgiving that such a thing could take place.[5] A couple of days later, the *Herald* stated in a column titled "The Revivals" that Chauncey Schaffer had led a two-hour meeting in the same theatre.[6]

A two-column "write-up" on the front page gave a significant

[1] Washington *National Intelligencer*, 2nd March, 1858.
[2] *Ibid.*, 11th March, 1858.   [3] *Ibid.*, 23rd March, 1858.
[4] Conant, W. C., *Narratives of Remarkable Conversions*, p. 362.
[5] *New York Times*, 20th March, 1858.
[6] *New York Herald*, 22nd March, 1858.

review of the movement in New York City (Manhattan without Brooklyn). At least 6,110 people were in attendance at daily prayer meetings. A partial survey on March 26th showed:[1]

Fulton Street (Dutch Reformed)	300
John Street (Methodist Episcopal)	600
Burton's Theatre (Union)	1,200
Ninth Street (Dutch Reformed)	150
Church of the Puritans (Congregational)	125
Broome Street (Dutch Reformed)	300
Waverley Place (Y.M.C.A.)	200
Mercer Street (Union)	150
Madison Square (Presbyterian)	200
Trinity 34th Street (Methodist Episcopal)	250

The estimates were made by reporters using horse cabs to rush from place to place. Another dozen places were in their list, which was still very incomplete.

Meanwhile, the noonday prayer meetings had flowed over into week-night services in many of the churches, in which conversions were common. The most sensational conversion in March was that of Orville Gardner, a pugilist better known as Awful Gardner. Gardner's public testimony had greatest impact on a certain class of citizen. Before very long ten thousand New Yorkers had been converted to God and were in the care of the churches,[2] and in May a good authority gave the total for the city as fifty thousand converts.[3] The national press from coast to coast carried news of the great awakening in the metropolis, and citizens everywhere were challenged by the movement. The "showers of blessing" in New York had caused a flood which suddenly burst its bounds and swept over New England, engulfed the Ohio Valley cities and states, rolled over the newly settled West, lapped the edges of the mountains in the South, and covered the United States of America and Canada with divine favour.

The most publicized work of grace undoubtedly was the condition prevailing in the metropolis of New York, but the phenomenon of packed churches and startling conversions was noted everywhere inquiries could be made.

There seemed to be three streams of blessing flowing out from the Middle Atlantic States, one northwards to New England, another southwards as far as Texas, and a third westwards along the Ohio valley.

An observer in a leading secular newspaper stated it well when he wrote that "the Revivals, or Great Awakenings, continue to be

[1] *Ibid.*, 26th March, 1858.
[2] Shaw, J., *Twelve Years in America*, pp. 182–184.
[3] *Presbyterian Magazine*, June, 1858.

the leading topic of the day . . . from Texas in the South to the extreme of our Western boundaries and our Eastern limits; their influence is felt by every denomination."[1] Papers from Maine to Louisiana reflected his view.

Denominational organs confirmed the news of extraordinary happenings. As early as the beginning of February, "extensive revivals" prevailing in the Methodist Episcopal Church all over the country were reported to the denomination's own leading journal, which observed that its exchanges with its Methodist contemporaries in the Central, Pittsburgh, North-western, Western, and its own territories, told of a total of eight thousand people converted in Methodist meetings in one week.[2]

A Baptist journal attempted to keep abreast of the news of conversions reaching its offices, but its editor apparently gave up the task after listing seventeen thousand conversions reported to him by Baptist leaders in three weeks. These figures are exceedingly incomplete, and possess only an impressional value. They were reported thus:[3]

Maine	411	Ohio	1,148
New Hampshire	82	Indiana	737
Vermont	304	Illinois	1,146
Massachusetts	2,575	Michigan	604
Rhode Island	387	Wisconsin	278
Connecticut	795	Iowa	278
New York	2,386	Minnesota	388
Pennsylvania	1,746	Missouri	424
New Jersey	698	Tennessee	711
Delaware	40	Virginia	205
Maryland	9	Other States	177
D. of Columbia	21	Canada	287

It should be noticed that these figures were simply those reported to the editor by Baptists concerned, and do not represent total results in any state, even for Baptists, although it is probable that the details for states closer to New York were more accurate than those farther away.

There was another attempt at estimating the actual number of converts, again "exceedingly incomplete" and valuable only for the relative proportions in various states. In May 1858, an editor in New York collected interdenominational figures from as many sources as possible.[4] They showed that a total of 96,216 people had become converted to God in the few months passed, and

[1] Washington *National Intelligencer*, 20th March, 1858.
[2] New York *Christian Advocate*, 11th February, 1858.
[3] *New York Examiner*, quoted in Louisville *Daily Courier*, 30th March, 1858.
[4] New York *Christian Advocate*, 3rd June, 1858.

were considered very heartening. His smaller numbers from States of the Deep South or from California may be attributed to delay in transmission of information over great distances.

Maine	2,670	Illinois	10,460
New Hampshire	1,376	Wisconsin	1,467
Vermont	770	Minnesota	508
Massachusetts	6,254	Iowa	2,179
Rhode Island	1,331	Missouri	2,027
Connecticut	2,799	Kentucky	2,666
New York	16,674	Tennessee	1,666
New Jersey	6,035	Delaware	179
Pennyslvania	6,732	Maryland	1,806
Ohio	8,009	Virginia	1,005
Michigan	8,081	Deep South	1,494
Indiana	4,775	California	550

The influence of the awakening was felt everywhere in the nation. It first moved the great cities, but it also spread through every town and village and country hamlet, swamping school and college.[1] It affected all classes without respect to their condition. A divine influence seemed to pervade the land, and men's hearts were strangely warmed by a Power that was outpoured in unusual ways. There was no fanaticism. There was remarkable unanimity of approval among religious and secular observers alike, with scarcely one critical voice heard anywhere.[2] It seemed to many that the fruits of Pentecost had been repeated a thousandfold. At any rate, the number of conversions reported soon reached the total of fifty thousand weekly, a figure borne out by church statistics showing an average of ten thousand additions to church membership a week for a period of two years.

[1] Orr, J. Edwin, *op. cit.*, p. 33.
[2] *Ibid.*, cf. Smith, T. L., *Revivalism and Social Reform*, in which 1858 is designated *Annus Mirabilis*.

CHAPTER XIII

SOWING IN THE CITIES

THROUGHOUT THE 'FIFTIES, CHURCH ATTENDANCE IN NEW England had remained high, with fully one-quarter of the population attending church regularly and another quarter occasionally.[1] But New England had always been a fruitful ground for theological controversy, producing the most rigid conservatives and the most volatile radicals in America. Finney visited the city of Boston in the winter of 1856, and found that his vital evangel[2] was opposed strongly by various very orthodox theologians. Boston was the happy hunting-ground of controversialists, and a divisive spirit was prevalent in the churches.

A daily prayer meeting had been held in Boston for several years before the 1858 Awakening. An interest in religious revival continued to increase, so it was decided to commence a business men's prayer meeting in the Old South Church, which was convenient to the business centre of the city. To the surprise of the sponsor, a business man, the place was crowded the first day, and many could not get in at all.[3]

Early in March 1858, the secular press began to take notice of the revival, declaring that religious excitement was on the increase.[4] Finney, all the while, was holding forth in Park Street Church preaching on evangelistic topics.[5] By that time, the revival had swept the city, and had become (to quote Finney) "too general to keep any account at all of the number of converts, or to allow of any estimate being made that would approximate the truth."[6]

By middle March, the awakening in Boston, like its counterpart in New York City, became news to the whole nation. The Boston correspondent of a Washington paper wrote his editor that clearly the chief concern in many cities and towns of New England was religion.[7]

The meetings (he declared) were crowded and solemn, with the whole assembly sometimes in tears under the melting power of the Holy Spirit. A few days later, the same journal reported that

[1] Newcomb, H., *The Harvest and the Reapers*, p. 26.
[2] Finney, C. G., *Memoirs of the Rev. Charles G. Finney*, p. 442.
[3] *Ibid.*, p. 443. [4] Boston *Daily Transcript*, 5th March, 1858.
[5] *Ibid.*, 9th and 21st March, 1858. [6] Finney, C. G., *op. cit.*, pp. 443–444.
[7] Washington *National Intelligencer*, 20th March, 1858.

among other instances it was stated "that there are several New England towns in which not a single adult person can be found unconverted,"[1] a report which appeared in various publications, secular and religious. Typical of these prayer meetings in Boston was the notice:[2]

> On account of the crowd that daily throngs Father Mason's chapel in North Street, unable to gain admittance, Father Taylor has thrown open the Bethel in North Square, and a Prayer Meeting will be held daily in that place 12 to 1.

Professor Finney reported that daily prayer meetings in Park Street Church filled the church on every occasion announced; Mrs. Finney held Ladies' Prayer Meetings in the large vestry of the church, which become so crowded that the good women stood outside wherever possible to hear the proceedings.[3] South Baptist Church held a daily meeting from 8 a.m. till 9 a.m. The Old South Chapel organized two: from 8.30 a.m. till 9.30 and from 12 noon till 1 p.m. Salem Street Church also had a meeting at noon, while Park Street Church and Church Street Methodist both held meetings daily at 3 p.m. Tremont Temple had its daily prayer meeting from 4 p.m. until 5 p.m., and the Y.M.C.A. from 5.30 until 6.30 p.m.[4] Most Boston churches had evening meetings for pure evangelism. It is not surprising that Boston's 177,000 citizens seemed to be moved throughout.[5] All its classes were making inquiry everywhere, including large numbers of Unitarians, some of whose pastors organized daily prayer meetings.[6]

The movement in New England generally was even stronger than in the metropolis. The most numerous denomination reported 11,744 added on profession in the revival period;[7] and another had claimed 8,479 in a few months,[8] while two hundred and sixty smaller centres of population reported over ten thousand conversions in two months.[9] In Springfield in Massachusetts, inquiry meetings were held by nearly every pastor in the city. In New Bedford, one in twenty of the people made a profession of faith in a few months, and similar awakenings were reported in Lynn and Haverhill.[10] In the revival at Holliston, two hundred and fifty conversions occurred, a like number of additions being registered at Winchester. Unprecedented awakenings occurred at Lowell and Williamstown, and Orange, "a stronghold of error", was transformed by the movement. In Massachusetts, a total of

[1] *Ibid.*, 23rd March, 1858.   [2] Boston *Daily Transcript*, 26th March, 1858.
[3] Finney, C. G., *op. cit.*, p. 443.
[4] Conant, W. C., *Narratives of Remarkable Conversions*, p. 376.
[5] Finney, C. G., *op. cit.*, p. 443.   [6] Conant, W. C., *op. cit.*, p. 377.
[7] *Congregational Quarterly*, January, 1859.
[8] New York *Christian Advocate*, 15th July, 1858.
[9] Shaw, J., *Twelve Years in America*, pp. 182–184.
[10] Conant, W. C., *op. cit.*, p. 377.

one hundred and fifty towns were moved by this revival of religion, with five thousand conversions before the end of March.[1]

Great crowds in Portland, Maine, attended the morning, noon, afternoon, and evening meetings and the church bells daily summoned thousands to prayer.[2] An extensive revival arose in Bangor and the neighbouring towns; and in Biddeford, the movement was distinguished for the remarkable rapidity of the work of conversion, adults and heads of families being the outstanding fruit of the revival.[3] Large accessions were made to the churches of Saco, and one hundred and ten persons were converted at Deer Isle.

The city of Providence in Rhode Island had a time of religious interest never before known. Nearly every church was awakened, conversions becoming numerous. Morning prayer meetings overflowed, and other meetings were crowded, making a strong impression. It was noteworthy that there was no unhealthy excitement reported.[4] At Pawtucket, the revival increased until over a hundred people were professedly born again. At Warren, a single Baptist church experienced a wave of blessing that resulted in the conversion of more than one hundred people. Another thirty-six towns reported a thousand decisions made to receive Christ as Saviour.[5]

In the State of Connecticut, the revival swept the communities in an unprecedented way. One of the largest churches in New Haven was full to capacity for an 8 a.m. prayer meeting, repeating the achievement daily at 5 p.m.[6] Equally large prayer meetings were begun in Hartford and in New London. At Bethel, business was suspended for an hour every day between 4 and 5 p.m., and two hundred persons were reported converted in two months, three-quarters of whom joined the Congregational Church. In Connecticut also was reported a town where no unconverted adult could be found.[7] No fanaticism was reported anywhere.

In the neighbouring states of Vermont and New Hampshire,[8] revivals occurred in the Dartmouth College, and Brattleboro, Claremont, Northfield, St. Alban's, Burlington, Castleton, Middlesbury, Derby and Manchester, in each of which a daily prayer meeting had met with success. Two hundred conversions were reported from Dover and New Ipswich, and forty other New Hampshire towns reported four hundred and twenty-five as forty Vermont towns reported over six hundred conversions. Alone in Rutland, Vermont, two hundred people were led to decision for Christ, seventy in a single meeting.

[1] *Ibid.*, p. 429.   [2] *Ibid.*, p. 378.   [3] *Ibid.*, pp. 426–427.
[4] *Ibid.*, p. 379.   [5] *Ibid.*, p. 430.   [6] *Ibid.*, pp. 377–378.
[7] *Presbyterian Magazine*, June, 1858.   [8] Conant, W. C., *op. cit.*, pp. 379, 380.

Outstanding in the results of the revival in New England was the work among the Colleges. Yale experienced an awakening in which it was "impossible" to estimate the conversions,[1] and it was later claimed that forty-five seniors and sixty-two juniors, sixty sophomores and thirty-seven freshmen had professed a change of heart. Amherst's President reported that nearly all the students there had been converted.[2]

The State of New York was soon swept by a wave of religious interest comparable to the one being experienced in its greatest centre of population. Along the beautiful Hudson River, busy little towns and cities witnessed unusual happenings. At Hudson, the Dutch Reformed, Baptist, Methodist, and Presbyterian churches launched a daily prayer meeting as a union effort, the people coming "as doves to their windows" to throng the place beyond precedent.[3] At Yonkers, more than two hundred people were converted in a few weeks. The Washington Street Methodist Episcopal Church in Poughkeepsie, where meetings were held every day, found its altar-rails crowded with inquirers, and in three weeks of special meetings in all churches, three hundred people sought salvation. Peekskill, a reputedly wicked town, saw the same means used and the same results achieved. At Kingston, Ulster County, the union prayer meetings overflowed from one church to another.

Farther up the Hudson river at Troy, clerks, merchants, and professional men particularly showed an interest in their own spiritual welfare, hence meetings were held daily and nightly in the churches, which gained several hundred additions.[4] Catskill, formerly sunken in religious indifference, saw a revival commence through the conversion of a young Bible class attender; every other member became converted and 115 new members were soon afterwards received into church memberships.[5] Albany, capital city with 60,000 population, was the scene of unusual happenings. An early morning prayer meeting was initiated by State Legislators, who began with six participants in the rooms of the Court of Appeals opposite the Senate Chamber; soon afterwards the rooms were overflowing.[6] The noon prayer meetings attracted great crowds in Albany, as elsewhere. The Baptist pastor at Union Village baptized 111 converts and expected soon to baptize more, saying that he had never witnessed a revival of such extent where there was manifest so little mere sympathetic excitement. More than fifty of those baptized were heads of families between the ages of twenty-five and fifty, one being a man in his eighty-third

[1] New York *Christian Advocate*, 12th May, 1858.
[2] Washington *National Intelligencer*, 27th April, 1858.
[3] Conant, W. C., *op. cit.*, pp. 370-371.
[4] *Ibid.*, p. 370.   [5] *Ibid.*, p. 431.   [6] *Ibid.*, pp. 369-370.

year. A hundred and forty people "decided" in Olean; two hundred in Cold Spring.[1]

All this was accomplished without devices of any kind, other than the call to prayer. Typical of the revivals in New York State's little cities was a report from Salem, which stated:

> Without any alarming event, without any extraordinary preaching or any special effort or other means that might be supposed peculiarly adapted to interest the minds of people, there has within a short time past been, in several towns and villages in Washington and Warren Counties, and in towns and villages along the western parts of the State of Vermont, revival so extraordinary as to attract the attention of all classes of the community.
>
> In one town, over a hundred have been brought to conviction and conversion, and the glorious work is still going on; they expect the whole town will be converted—for this they pray. This work does not appear to be confined to the churches; hundreds are converted at prayer meetings, in private homes, in the workshops, and at their work in the fields. Men of fortune and fashion, lawyers, physicians and tradesmen and indeed all the classes, ages, and sexes, are the subjects.[2]

Farther west, along the strategic Mohawk river, similar revivals occurred in towns and villlages. In Schenectady, church bells sounded every evening, calling great crowds to meeting, filling each church.[3] Two popular prayer meetings held daily bore much fruit, and converts came into church fellowships with surprising rapidity. The ice on the Mohawk was broken for believers' baptism.[4] From the month of December onwards in Utica, the pastors of the evangelical churches united in union prayer meetings held in rotation in the various churches; the movement being so well supported that the early morning prayer service in a large church was filled with worshippers, some frequently having to stand.[5] Syracuse held its union services in Convention Hall. Geneva produced a revival of unusual stillness and solemnity, with numerous conversions and the usual prayer meetings, one church trebling its membership. Buffalo witnessed a powerful revival of religion. Examples could be multiplied, for two hundred towns reported six thousand specific cases of conversion.[6]

One of the first sections of the country to experience an awakening was the New Jersey area, which reported stirring revivals of religion as early as late October 1857. In Readington and Pennington, one hundred and twenty conversions occurred before the New Year, while blessing began in Newark in January with sixty additions in the Mount Lebanon Circuit. Orange Methodists

[1] *Ibid.*, p. 431.   [2] *Ibid.*, p. 432.   [3] *Ibid.*, p. 372.
[4] Washington *National Intelligencer*, 23rd March, 1858.
[5] Conant, W. C., *op. cit.*, pp. 371-372.   [6] *Ibid.*, pp. 431-432.

rejoiced in no less than one hundred and twenty-five additions in early February. Locality after locality experienced revival of religious interest.[1]

In the month of March, the awakening in New Jersey equalled anything known on the American continent. The city of Newark, population 70,000, witnessed startling evidences of the sweeping movement there. In a couple of months, 2,785 people professed conversion, averaging a hundred conversions in each reporting congregation. It became a common sight to see business houses closed, with a notice "will reopen at the close of the prayer-meeting" and the union meetings thus advertised were crowded to overflowing. Extra efforts were made to reach members of the Fire Department with the gospel, and on one occasion, nearly two thousand firemen attended one such meeting at the National Hotel in Market Street. Dr. Scott, a leading Newark pastor, testified that the revival was winning the most mature minds in the community, saying that, in his opinion, the most mature personalities in his congregation were the forty-five who had just united with it by profession of faith in Christ.[2]

Similar scenes of revival were witnessed in Paterson, New Jersey, where a successful union meeting was begun, as well as evening meetings, and all the churches reported accessions to membership. In Jersey City, large numbers professed conversions, and there a union meeting was held daily between 7 and 9 a.m. in the Lyceum on Grand Street. In New Brunswick, New Jersey, 177 joined the Methodist Church, 112 of whom were heads of families, including steamboat captains and pilots, and, in Trenton, the Methodists alone gained upwards of 1,700 additions. Sixty centres of revival in the State of New Jersey reported approximately six thousand conversions.[3] There was not a single instance of fanaticism reported.

Among the first attenders of the original Businessmen's Prayer-Meeting in New York City was a young man, not yet twenty-one years of age, hailing from Philadelphia. Upon his return to his home, he and some of his fellow Y.M.C.A. men approached the trustees of the Methodist Episcopal Church on Fourth Street below Arch Street, and requested the use of their lecture room for a similar meeting. The request was granted, and the first noon prayer meeting in Philadelphia was held in the Union Methodist Episcopal Church on 23rd November, 1857.[4]

For a long time, however, the response of Philadelphia's business men was disappointing, the average attendance being

[1] New York *Christian Advocate*, 22nd October, 1857; 24th December, 1857; 7th January, 1858; 18th February, 1858.
[2] Conant, W. C., *op. cit.*, p. 368.   [3] *Ibid.*, pp. 432–433.
[4] Noble, W. F., *op. cit.*, p. 420.

about a dozen men. But on February 3rd, the meeting was removed to a little ante-room in the spacious public hall owned by Dr. Jayne, popularly known as Jayne's Hall. Throughout February, increase in attendance was gradual; twenty, thirty, forty, fifty and then sixty attending.[1] The wave of revival reached the place in March.

At the first only the small room was occupied, with a few in attendance. Then it became overflowing, and the meeting removed to the main saloon, meetings starting there on March 10th. Twenty-five hundred seats were provided, and were filled to overflowing.[2] The sponsors next removed a partition from the main floor space and platform; next the floor, platform and lower gallery; then floor, platform, and both galleries filled; soon every nook and cranny in the place was full of worshipping people, fully six thousand gathering daily at noontime for prayer.[3]

In order to continue the work, which (as in New York) flooded the churches with inquirers and converts, a big canvas tent was bought for $2,000 and opened for religious services on 1st May, 1858. During the following four months, an aggregate of 150,000 people attended the ministry under canvas, many conversions resulting.[4] The churches in Philadelphia reported five thousand converts in the revival of religion.

It was impossible to keep record of all the Pennsylvanian towns and villages and country places that reported blessing, for even the most enthusiastic editors wearied of the task. West in Pittsburgh, two daily prayer meetings were begun to accommodate intercessors desiring to pray at noon between the hours of 11.30 and 12.30, about a thousand attending in these two places, and as many more in meetings elsewhere in the city. The churches of Pittsburgh reaped a harvest of additions from the movement.[5]

In Maryland, the revival began in December, when there were sixty conversions reported in Havre de Grace and over one hundred from the Monroe Circuit of Baltimore Conference, both instances among Methodists.[6] In the spring, a daily prayer meeting was begun by the Y.M.C.A. with encouraging attendances. Methodist journals continued to report great numbers of conversions from all around the State, and other denominations shared equally in the stirring.

In Washington, the nation's capital, five daily prayer meetings were started, commencing at 6.30 a.m., the Y.M.C.A. and churches sponsoring the efforts.[7] The *National Intelligencer* described the

[1] *Ibid.*   [2] *Ibid.*, p. 421.
[3] New York *Christian Advocate*, 6th May, 1858.
[4] Noble, W. F., *op. cit.*, p. 422.   [5] Conant, W. C., *op. cit.*, pp. 372–373.
[6] New York *Christian Advocate*, 24th December, 1857.
[7] Conant, W. C., *op. cit.*, p. 375.

meetings as "still and solemn,"[1] and on April 1st commented editorially that the religious excitement in the city was unabated, five thousand or so attending the prayer service in the Academy of Music Hall.

Writing of the Revival of 1858, no less a person than Charles G. Finney stated:[2]

> Slavery seemed to shut it out from the South. The people there were in such a state of irritation, of vexation, and of committal to their peculiar institution, which had come to be assailed on every side, that the Spirit of God seemed to be grieved away from them. There seemed to be no place for Him in the hearts of Southern people at that time.

Beardsley, a more recent historian, echoed Finney in sentiments,[3] also held by Northern historians. Both declaration and explanation became insecure in the light of research.

Bishop Candler, on the other hand, insisted that the results of the revival were "in proportion to the population, greater in the South than in any other section,"[4] and his clear accounts of the amazing revivals of religion in the Confederate Armies in the War between the States seem to give the lie to the contention that pro-slavery sentiment had in significant ways hindered revival in the South.[5]

The *Southern Presbyterian Review*, July 1859, countered the Northern claim strongly, saying then "it is not Northern, nor Southern, Eastern nor Western," and declaring that the Revival in the South had reached as far as the Florida reefs. There is good reason to believe that the revivals were as widespread in the South as in the North. Allowance should be made for the fact that the South possessed no great industrial cities like the Northern metropolitan areas, and that southern population was scattered over an agricultural countryside; hence, it was less spectacular down South, where newspapers could not immediately influence the crowded cities as up North.

A Northern authority testified,[6] nevertheless, that revivals of more or less power were sweeping Wilmington, Baltimore, Washington, Raleigh, Richmond, Charleston, Columbia, New Orleans, Savannah, Augusta, Mobile, Nashville, Memphis.

In Richmond, Virginia, a daily prayer meeting was commenced with success. In Lynchburg, in the same state, a revival of no mean dimensions converted many young men to the Christian

---

[1] Washington *National Intelligencer*, 25th March, 1858.
[2] Finney, C. G., *op. cit.*, p. 444.
[3] Beardsley, F. G., *A History of American Revivals*, pp. 227–228.
[4] Candler, W. A., *Great Revivals and the Great Republic*, p. 216.
[5] *Ibid.*, p. 225.   [6] *Presbyterian Magazine*, June, 1858.

faith.[1] In Mobile, Alabama, sermons were preached daily in the Catholic, Episcopal, Baptist, and Methodist churches, with "unusually numerous converts."[2] In April, when the secular press reported that the revival was declining in New York City, it assured its readers that the awakening was increasing in the Southern and Western States, where revivals had broken out in Nashville, Mobile, New Orleans, and Charleston, and was "by no means confined to the cities" of the Southland.[3]

With these facts in mind, it is quite easy to believe that the revival swept the South in spite of the slavery issue. Bishop Candler quoted the official statistics show that in 1858, 1859, and 1860, over one hundred thousand converts were added to the Methodist Episcopal Church South, adding that the equally large Baptist denomination shared similar blessing.[4] Finney's opinion, then, must be rejected.

[1] Conant, W. C., op. cit., p. 375.
[2] Washington National Intelligencer, 25th March, 185.
[3] Louisville Daily Courier, 17th April, 1858.
[4] Candler, W. A., op. cit., pp. 216–217.

CHAPTER XIV

REAPING ON THE PRAIRIES

EARLY IN THE YEAR 1858, THE WAVE OF REVIVAL PASSED OVER the crest of the Appalachian system of mountains, and poured down the Ohio valley following the line of settlements established by the pioneers. Within two months, four hundred and eighty towns had reported fifteen thousand conversions.[1] Prayer meetings multiplied.

The *Presbyterian Magazine* hastily announced that the entire western country was sharing in a great revival movement.[2] It added the details of great awakenings occurring in all the cities—in Cleveland, Cincinnati, Louisville, Indianapolis, Detroit, Chicago, St. Louis, and Dubuque, saying also that the cities, villages, and country places of Kentucky, Ohio, Michigan, Indiana, Illinois, Wisconsin, Missouri, and Iowa, were receiving revival increase. And the *Western Christian Advocate*, exulting in the spiritual winning of the West, described awakenings in Ohio, Illinois and Indiana, stating that forty-two Methodist clergy had reported 4,384 conversions in three months, 750 being in one place.[3]

In Wheeling, Virginia (later West Virginia and properly belonging to the Ohio Valley system), it was reported that the past winter (1857-8) would long be remembered for the revivals of religion. Methodist leaders declared that there had been nothing to equal the movement in strength, not even the glorious days of 1839-40 which added to the Methodist Episcopal Church 154,000 converts. In some neighbourhoods of West Virginia, almost the entire adult population had been brought under the influence of the awakening, many churches reporting one hundred to two hundred accessions.[4]

On the south bank of the Ohio river, Kentucky experienced an unprecedented stirring of religious interest. As in other cities farther east, the newspapers in Louisville began giving space to revival intelligence in March of 1858. The Louisville *Daily Courier* of March 6th noticed that the Brook Street Methodist Episcopal Church had received about a hundred new members,

[1] Shaw, J., *Twelve Years in America*, pp. 182–184.
[2] *Presbyterian Magazine*, June, 1858.
[3] Cincinnati *Western Christian Advocate*, 10th March, 1858.
[4] *Presbyterian Magazine*, June, 1858.

three-quarters of them by profession of new-found faith in Christ. Within a week, the revival had become the talk of the town, for the same journal announced that the churches of Louisville were open day and night caring for inquirers.[1]

Union prayer meetings were soon launched in Kentucky's big city, secular journalists observing that the meetings were growing in such interest that it was impossible for the Y.M.C.A. premises to accommodate the crowds, hence a move to the large Masonic Temple was announced, meetings to be held daily at 7.45 a.m., lasting until 9 a.m. The *Daily Courier* of March 27th announced in a column headed "The Religious Awakening" that long before the appointed hour of the meeting, the large hall of the Masonic Temple was overflowing with more than a thousand eager people in attendance. The meeting began with John Newton's hymn:

> Amazing grace! how sweet the sound
> That saved a wretch like me!
> I once was lost, but now am found;
> Was blind, but now I see.

The exuberance and concern of the meeting so infected the secular journalists that one might conclude that the press had been converted.

Two days later, the same journal declared that the previous day's meeting had broken all records, the largest crowd yet seen there being unable to find space in the Masonic Temple.[2] Meanwhile, the daily prayer meetings were increasing, their influence pervading the city, with over a thousand conversions resulting to the praise of God. The Religious Movement claimed a column in further issues of the newspaper, the last issue of March observing that the Masonic Temple had again been packed, while other prayer meetings had grown in catering for the overflowing crowds of people.

In early April, four popular prayer meetings attracted the crowds to the Masonic Temple, the Mechanics' Library, the Key Engine House, and the Relief Engine House. A reporter, on April 5th, stated that an "immense concourse" had entirely filled the Masonic Temple at an early hour, and the holding of an overflow meeting was necessary.[3] Next day, an editorial declared that there was no abatement of interest or diminution of attendance, observing that licentiousness had been restrained and that "drunkard-manufacturers" had become apprehensive of their trade prospects. The other prayer meetings grew and abounded, one starting in the Lafayette Engine House.

By April 8th, such had been the improvement in the city's

[1] Louisville *Daily Courier*, 6th March, 1858.
[2] *Ibid.*, 29th March, 1858.   [3] *Ibid.*, 5th April, 1858.

morals and such were the reports from the rest of Kentucky and the other States, that it was thought by the press that the millennium had arrived at last.[1] One writer stated his impression:

The Spirit of God seems to be brooding over our city, and to have produced an unusual degree of tenderness and solemnity in all classes. Never since our residence in the city have we seen so fair a prospect for a general and thorough work of grace as is now indicated.[2]

Revival had already commenced in Lexington, Covington, Frankfort, and other towns throughout the state. The Ohio river figured in two items of news. Under the heading "Add Colour to Revival," it was announced that eighteen coloured converts of the revival had been baptized in the river; and the *Daily Courier* was informed that on the steamer *Telegraph* of the Cincinnati and Louisville Mail Packet Line, religious revival was the universal topic on the voyage up river, a spontaneous and crowded prayer meeting having been held in the main saloon until a late hour.[3]

Across the river, in the State of Ohio, two hundred towns reported twelve thousand conversions in a couple of months.[4] In Cincinnati, the attendance at the daily prayer meetings became so large that the venue chosen was unable to accommodate the crowds, necessitating a move to the large First Presbyterian Church.[5] The *Daily Commercial* on April 2nd commented that the religious excitement in the city was unabated, and the churches were becoming more popular every day with citizens who were unaccustomed to means of grace.[6]

In Cleveland, in population forty thousand, the attendance at the early morning prayer meetings throughout the city churches was two thousand.[7] The whole community was stirred. The Plymouth Congregational Church held five meetings daily from six in the morning until nine at night. One thousand people were received into fellowships in a couple of months.[8] The Methodist Episcopal Church of Circleville, Ohio received two hundred and ten accessions, with others promised, while other churches in the same town were receiving thirties and forties.[9]

In Indiana, one hundred and fifty towns reported from four to five thousand converts in two months of revival.[10] Noonday prayer meetings were begun in Indianapolis, the State capital, and a religious interest pervaded the city.[11]

[1] *Ibid.*, 8th April, 1858.
[2] Conant, W. C., *Narratives of Remarkable Conversions*, p. 374.
[3] Louisville *Daily Courier*, 6th March, 1858.
[4] Conant, W. C., *op. cit.*, p. 433.
[5] *Ibid.*, p. 373.   [6] Cincinnati *Daily Commercial*, 2nd April, 1858.
[7] Conant, W. C., *loc. cit.*
[8] Washington *National Intelligencer*, 30th March, 1858.
[9] Conant, W. C., *op. cit.*, p. 433.   [10] *Ibid.*   [11] *Ibid.*, p. 373.

In Michigan, morning prayer meetings held in the downtown Baptist and Congregational places of worship in Detroit were crowded by business men of all denominations.[1] The Congress Street Methodist Episcopal Church reported over one hundred and forty conversions, and numerous inquirers and converts were reported in the other churches. In six Michigan towns, revivals with between fifteen hundred and two thousand conversions to God were recorded.

There was a striking instance of the power of prayer demonstrated in Kalamazoo in Michigan.[2] There the Episcopalians, Baptists, Methodists, Presbyterians and Congregationalists united in announcing a prayer meeting. The ecumenical effort was begun in fear and trembling, and many wondered if the public would consider attending.

At the very first meeting a request was read: "A praying wife requests the prayers of this meeting for her unconverted husband." All at once a burly man arose and said: "I am that man; I have a praying wife, and this request must be for me. I want you to pray for me!"

As soon as he was seated, another man arose, ignoring his predecessor, to say with tears: "I am that man; I have a praying wife. She prays for me. And now she asks you to pray for me. I am sure I am that man. I want you to pray for me!"

Five other convicted husbands requested prayer, and a spirit of conviction moved that assembly. Before long, there were between four and five hundred conversions in the town.

Farther west, an unusual interest manifested itself in St. Louis, Missouri, both in the churches and in the business circles of the city. The union prayer meetings were well attended by all classes of people, among whom great seriousness existed: and all the churches were crowded.[3] In St. Joseph, a great awakening began, the churches of the city uniting to carry on the work. Whole families were converted. Similar blessing was reported from St. Charles. A nephew of the renowned English Baptist minister Andrew Fuller, J. B. Fuller, a converted actor, produced great excitement in Missouri by his preaching. Fifty Missouri towns reported two thousand converts.[4]

A hundred and fifty towns in Illinois announced between three and four thousand conversions.[5] A thousand converts were registered in Wisconsin in the early part of 1858, and about the same number was reported from Minnesota Territory.[6] three hundred accessions being made by Minneapolis churches, while a private correspondent in nearby St. Paul wrote that "the good

[1] *Ibid.*, p. 374.   [2] Chambers, *The Noon Prayer Meeting*, pp. 196–197.
[3] Conant, W. C., *op. cit.*, p. 374.   [4] *Ibid.*, p. 434.   [5] *Ibid.*   [6] *Ibid.*

work of the Lord goes on. The interest is still on the increase. St. Paul never saw a time like the present. The Holy Spirit seems to pervade the entire community, in every department of business." In Iowa, the *Congregational Herald* observed that never before had such a general interest in religion existed in Dubuque. Sixty other towns sharing in the awakening reported fifteen hundred converts.

In autumn, 1856, a young man named Dwight Lyman Moody arrived in the budding metropolis of Chicago. The events of the next two years, as they transpired in the Illinois city, were destined to shape his life in a way that has received scant treatment at the hands of his biographers.

Chicago, built upon a mud-flat on the shores of Lake Michigan, had only thirty thousand citizens in 1850; but in 1860 it could boast of more than one hundred thousand inhabitants. It was a place combining a reputation for crime with a renown for Christian work.

Chicago was hit by the depression of 1857, but not as badly as were the eastern cities, for it was enjoying a local boom due to the opening-up of the Middle West. There were few signs of revival in 1857, but the turn of the year 1858 brought news of "a very interesting revival of religion" at the Wabash Avenue Methodist Episcopal Church.[1]

By the month of March the state of religion had become phenomenal.[2] Two hundred people had already been converted in four Methodist churches, and more than a hundred in as many Presbyterian churches, where 8 a.m. prayer meetings were in full swing daily. The Trinity Episcopal Church had a noonday prayer meeting, and the Dutch Reformed Church reported marked interest. First Baptist Church noted an increase, and in Tabernacle (Second) there had been fifty conversions in meetings begun before New Year. In many cases, the proportion of heads of families converted was noticeably high, up to 50 per cent. On March 13th, the Chicago *Daily Press* carried a column of news, entitled "Religious Awakening," with the editorial comment:

> In all these religious efforts there has been no appearance of excitement and no unusual means used; the movement has been quiet, deep and effective. The pastors of the churches have had very little assistance.

On March 19th, a proposal was made to organize a general prayer meeting of the union type, similar to New York and Philadelphia meetings.[3] Within a week, the press described it as "gaining strength daily," with upwards of twelve hundred per-

[1] Chicago *Daily Press*, 5th January, 1858.   [2] *Ibid.*, 13th March, 1858.
[3] *Ibid.*, 19th March, 1858.

sons present in the Metropolitan Hall, early morning prayer meetings increasing all the while.[1] On March 25th, the newspapers, in reporting which they called "unusual and almost unprecedented," reported that two thousand people now gathered daily at noon-time for prayer in Metropolitan Hall.[2]

A letter from Chicago, dated March 21st, thus described the situation:[3]

> The religious interest now existing in this city is very remarkable. More than 2,000 businessmen meet at the noon prayer meeting. The Metropolitan Hall is crowded to suffocation. The interest in the First Baptist Church is beyond anything ever known in this city, and exceeds anything I have ever seen in my life. Some who have come to the city on business have become so distressed about their condition as sinners before God, that they have entirely forgotten their business in the earnestness of their desire for salvation. I am amazed to see such evidences of God's grace and power manifested among men. I might add that the First Baptist Church has daily meetings from eight to nine in morning, twelve to one at noon, and at six-and-a-half o'clock in the evening. The church today has had an all day meeting.

At the end of that week, the press reported that nothing like the present general interest had ever occurred in the history of Chicago and it commented on the perfect union of all evangelical Christians.[4] A religious review of the week told of morning and noon-time meetings in churches of all denominations, with conversions daily. First Presbyterian Church reported seventy-five and St. John's Episcopal nearly forty added, while Union Park Baptist gave a week's increase as forty and Tabernacle Baptist twenty-four on the Lord's Day. The Negro community was strongly affected by the revival, and conversions were reported by the Baptist churches of Negro stock.

The coming of temptingly good weather in April brought about a slackening of attendance at the main meeting at Metropolitan Hall.[5] A thousand people were still regular supporters of prayer meetings, but the curious and spurious had now dropped off. By April 20th, the noonday meeting at Metropolitan Hall was transferred to the First Baptist Church.[6] The revival had begun to run in different channels, there being an increase in the evening meetings of an evangelistic nature, with a thousand conversions in all churches to date.

In May, the revival interest in the city gradually retired from the union meetings into the individual churches. The number of

[1] *Ibid.*, 24th March, 1858.   [2] *Ibid.*, 25th March, 1858.
[3] Conant, W. C., *op. cit.*, pp. 373–374.
[4] Chicago *Daily Press*, 27th March, 1858.
[5] *Ibid.*, 3rd April, 1858.   [6] *Ibid.*, 20th April, 1858.

prayer meetings increased, but not the attendance, 1,800 day-time and 5,000 at night. Large numbers joining the churches so constantly excited curiosity no more.[1]

A typical example of this trend reported that Dr. Hatfield (Presbyterian) had received eighty-two persons the previous Sabbath, more than a half being heads of families. The church, which had 177 members in 1856, now reported 508.

On May 24th, the Moderator of the Presbyterian General Assembly (meeting that year in Chicago) declared that they were witnessing "scenes of revival such as the Church of Christ had never enjoyed as richly before".[2]

During winter and spring D. L. Moody received his first great challenge to Christian work, writing to his mother in New England to tell of constant attendance at services and his delight at the results therein. It was during the hot summer of 1858 that Moody got together a class that he decided to teach, their first sessions being held on a Michigan beach.

[1] *Ibid.*, 4th May, 1858.   [2] *Ibid.*, 24th May, 1858.

CHAPTER XV

YEAR OF GRACE IN IRELAND

CONNEXIONS BETWEEN THE PEOPLE OF THE UNITED STATES and those of the United Kingdom have been always immediate, but most intimate has been the connexion between Ulster and the tens of thousands of Ulster-Americans. Understandably, the General Assembly of the Presbyterian Church in Ireland sent an official deputation of two of its most honoured members to visit North America.[1] Professor William Gibson, soon to be elected to highest office in the Assembly, and the Rev. Wm. McClure visited the centres of revival in North America, and the much-thrilled professor published his experiences in one city under the title *Pentecost, or the Work of God in Philadelphia.*

Throughout Ulster, reports of the American Revival tended greatly to quicken the minds both of pastors and people. Many sermons on Revival were preached and prayer meetings multiplied.[2]

The first prayer appeared to be one offered in Kells near Ballymena by a young man named McQuilkin who had been reading the testimony of George Müller, the man of faith, as well as hearing of the Revival in America. James McQuilkin said to himself: "Why may we not have such a blessed work here, seeing that God did such things for Mr. Müller simply in answer to prayer?"[3]

Out of this thought grew the Kells meeting of four young men for prayer for revival in Ulster. James McQuilkin and his prayer helpers held a meeting on 14th March, 1859, in the First Presbyterian Church in Ahoghill. Such large crowds attended that "it was deemed prudent to dismiss the meeting lest there be a fatal accident from a falling in of the galleries that threatened to give way under the alarming pressure." So a layman thereupon addressed 3,000 people outside in the chilling rain, where, moved by his fervour and apostolic language, hundreds fell on their knees in the mud of the streets.[4]

Three miles from Ahoghill is the prosperous market town of Ballymena, hub of mid-Antrim, and nearby is the parish of Con-

[1] *Minutes, General Assembly of the Presbyterian Church in Ireland,* Vol. II, p. 678.
[2] *Proceedings of the General Assembly on Revival.*
[3] Müller, *Autiography of George Müller,* pp. 448 ff.
[4] Adams, D., *The Revival at Ahoghill,* p. 7.

nor in which had begun the original prayer meeting. At that time, Ballymena had a population of 6,000, largely Presbyterian. The *Ballymena Observer* first noticed the Revival on 26th March, 1859, and within six months had chronicled the events of the Awakening and its "extensive social, moral and religious improvements" already effected among the people.[1]

The Rev. Samuel J. Moore noted several cases of deep conviction among his charges. Upon his return from a meeting of the Presbyterian Synod, he found the town in a great state of excitement, many families having neglected their night's sleep for two preceding nights. The awakening seen in Ahoghill had spread to Ballymena.[2]

A group of prepared young laymen devoted almost their entire time to giving spiritual and physical comfort to the scores of people in need of it. Prayer meetings were held at all hours of the day and night, and the evangelical churches were open for evening services, the Presbyterian, Episcopalian and Methodist ministers and people uniting in such efforts as well as in union prayer meetings. Eye-witnesses added their descriptions[3] of these extraordinary gatherings and results—such as one of about 5,000 people in a quarry.

In the month of May, the Awakening made its appearance in Belfast, a town of 120,000 people, one-third of whom were Roman Catholics. By the end of May, the *Belfast News Letter* was giving a half-column or a column of space to Revival news.[4] The outbreak of revival fervour in Belfast came through a visit of some of the "converts of Connor." It was in Berry Street Presbyterian Church that the greatest demonstration came. So many people lingered after the service that the Rev. Hugh Hanna reopened the church and took charge.[5] On the Sunday following, most of the evangelical churches of the town were utterly overcrowded by interested folk, and "the Revival" had full sway.

Dr. Knox, the bishop of the united dioceses of Down, Connor and Dromore, invited all his clergy to a breakfast in order to hear their opinion respecting the Revivals, which apparently had his careful support.[6] All at length agreed that it was a work of God, but there was difference of opinion among the clergy regarding "prostrations" of sinners coming under conviction, some regarding them as hysteria, others as a divine method of conviction. The Belfast Presbytery met and expressed its gratitude to God for the

[1] *The Ballymena Observer*, 17th September, 1859.
[2] Weir, J., *The Ulster Awakening*, p. 38.
[3] *The Revival*, 30th July, 1859.
[4] *Belfast News Letter*, 30th May, 1859.
[5] Gibson, W., *The Year of Grace*, pp. 66–67.
[6] *The Revival*, 6th August, 1859.

Revival, also urging caution regarding physical manifestations.[1]
Ministers of the Wesleyan, Congregationalist and Baptist churches
supported the work from the start.

With something approaching unanimity, the ministers of Belfast launched a united prayer meeting in the Music Hall, with the
Mayor in the chair. The building was crowded to excess. A week
later, the Bishop took the chair, assisted on the platform by 146
clergymen, including the Moderator of the Presbyterian General
Assembly and the President of the Wesleyan Methodist Conference, by Presbyterian and Methodist ministers, Episcopalian
clergy, by Baptists, Congregationalist, and even the noted Dr.
Montgomery of the Unitarian communion. As hundreds participated in overflow meetings, many thousands were turned away
from the large hall.[2]

By June most of the evangelical churches were open and
crowded for weekday services. Friends[3] of the Revival estimated
that 10,000 people were converted (only a small proportion of
them violently by prostration) in the weeks and months which
followed in Belfast. The Bishop declared in Trinity Church that
he was satisfied that the Revival was doing much good.

Another development in the Belfast Revival came with organiz-
ing mass open-air meetings for prayer in the beautiful Botanical
Gardens. At the end of June the first meeting attracted an assem-
blage never before seen in the north of Ireland. About 15,000
attended the first meeting over which the Presbyterian Moderator
presided, and "results exceeded anything hereto known."[4]

In July the labours of ministers, visitors and converts in Belfast
continued unabated in energy, zeal and success.[5] The Rev. H.
Grattan Guinness preached to at least 15,000 people in the open
air.[6] In August the churches of every denomination were crowded
to excess, and visiting ministers from all over the three united
kingdoms officiated in many pulpits. Another Botanic Gardens
prayer meeting, on August 16th, attracted 20,000, the proceedings
being undertaken by the Y.M.C.A.[7] In September the churches
remained crowded, without any signs of weariness on the part of
ministers or people, and in October the attendances were still "in
no wise abated" although the novelty had worn off. The October
meeting of the Maze Racecourse drew 500 people instead of the
customary 10,000. A large distillery, capable of turning out
1,000,000 gallons of whisky per annum, was put up at auction to

[1] Massie, J. W., *Revivals in Ireland*, p. 46.
[2] *Belfast News Letter*, 23rd June, 1859.
[3] Baillie, J., *The Revival*, "What I Saw in Ireland," p. 45.
[4] *Belfast News Letter*, 30th June, 1859.
[5] *Banner of Ulster*, 26th July, 1859.
[6] *The Freeman*, 10th August, 1859.   [7] *Banner of Ulster*, 20th August, 1859.

be sold or to be dismantled. The Belfast reports were confirmed by the Evangelical Alliance meeting there that year.[1]

Meanwhile the Ulster Revival began to spread into County Down. Writing from Holywood Palace, the Bishop notified his opposite number in the Presbyterian Church (Professor Gibson) that of 106 replies from clergy seventy-five gave gratifying testimony of the spiritual blessing.[2]

Townsfolk of Coleraine, in that part of County Derry close to the County Antrim Revival centres, witnessed some of the most amazing scenes in the whole movement in Ireland. A schoolboy, under deep conviction of sin, seemed so incapable of continuing his studies that the kindly teacher sent him home in the company of another boy, already converted. On the way home the two boys noticed an empty house and entered to pray.[3] At last the unhappy boy found peace, and returned immediately to the classroom to tell his teacher: "I am so happy: I have the Lord Jesus in my heart!" This innocent testimony had its effect on the class, and boy after boy slipped outside. The master, standing on something to look out of the window, observed the boys kneeling in prayer around the school-yard, each one apart. The master was overcome, so he asked the converted schoolboy to comfort them. Soon the whole school was in strange disorder, and the clergymen sent for remained all day dealing with seekers after peace—schoolboys, schoolgirls, teachers, parents and neighbours, the premises being thus occupied until eleven o'clock at night. These happenings stirred the whole district.[4]

On 7th June, 1859, an open-air meeting was held on Fair Hill to hear one or two of the converts. So many thousands attended that it was deemed advisable to divide the crowd into separate meetings, each addressed by an evangelical minister of one denomination or another. The people stood motionless until the very last moment, when an auditor cried in distress. Several others likewise became prostrated, bewildering the ministers, who, having had no similar experience previously, scarce knew how to help the distressed in soul and body. The clergymen spent all night in spiritual ministration, and, when the sun arose, the following day was spent in like manner. A union meeting was begun and attracted the crowds for many months.[5]

Dr. H. Grattan Guinness addressed more than 6,000 people in a single meeting in Coleraine.[6] In August the work progressed steadily, and in September the churches were as full as ever. By October there were very few cases of prostration, but the prayer

---

[1] *The Freeman*, 5th October, 1859.   [2] Gibson, W., *op. cit.*, p. 111.
[3] Arthur, W., *The Revival in Ballymena and Coleraine*, pp. 12 ff.
[4] *Vide* Carson, J. T., *God's River in Spate*, ch. ix–x.
[5] Gibson, W., *op. cit.*, p. 51.   [6] Weir, J., *op. cit.*, p. 73.

E

meetings continued as numerous and well attended as before. Said the *Coleraine Chronicle* in a leader, "No one can deny that a change for the better, which all must believe to be permanent, has taken place in the case of hosts of individuals."[1] In 1860 the Grand Jury of the Coleraine Quarter Sessions was informed by the presiding judge that, in His Worship's opinion, only the moral and religious movement of the previous summer accounted for the reduction of crime to almost negligible proportions, there having been only one case (of an unimportant character) to try.[2]

The Revival spread into the towns and villages of County Derry, and reached the historic city of Londonderry, where it appeared with great suddenness among all denominations. It began on June 12th through a visit of Ballymena converts, who moved many hearers to tears.[3] Further open-air meetings attracted up to 5,000 people. In County Tyrone, the Revival spread rapidly southwards.[4] The people of County Armagh experienced the movement in their towns and villages simultaneously with Tyrone, but later than Antrim, Down and the city of Belfast.

In the ecclesiastical capital of Ireland, the city of Armagh, there was the usual evidence of strange happenings. On Wednesday, 21st September, 1859, a prayer meeting for all Ireland was arranged.[5] People came from a hundred miles around, riding on roofs of railway carriages and stowing away in cattle-trucks and goods-vans. Scenes at Armagh were overpowering, for 20,000 people assembled in a large field, to be addressed (in part) by a distinguished Englishman, the Hon. and Rev. Baptist Noel. In October the local ministers reported that "a great and good work of conviction and conversion" was progressing.

County Fermanagh shared in the Revival, though rather belatedly. Unlike the other northern counties, Fermanagh possessed 38 per cent Episcopalians and only 6 per cent other Protestants, chiefly Methodists, while there were 56 per cent Roman Catholics in the county.

Outside the six northern counties the Revival movement was felt, but in a degree inversely proportionate to the Roman Catholic majority in each county as well as directly proportionate to the presence of Presbyterians, Methodists, Baptists, Congregationalists and Quakers among Protestants. This was specially true of the remaining three of the nine counties of Ulster—Donegal, Monaghan and Cavan.[6]

There was more encouragement around Dublin, which possessed a large Protestant population amounting to 22 per cent in

[1] Quoted in *The Revival*, 5th November, 1859.
[2] Gibson, W., *op. cit.*, pp. 55–56.   [3] Weir, J., *op. cit.*, p. 130.
[4] Gibson, W., *op. cit.*, pp. 155 ff.   [5] *The Revival*, 24th September, 1859.
[6] Orr, J. Edwin, *The Second Evangelical Awakening in Britain*, pp. 52–54.

the city itself, no less than 40 per cent in the suburbs around; and 20 per cent in the County of Dublin. When tidings of the Revival in Ulster reached the Irish capital many clergymen and ministers repaired thither. Among them was the Rev. J. Denham Smith of Kingstown (now named Dun Laoghaire, pronounced Dunleary), who was profoundly moved by what he saw.

In September 1859 Christians in Kingstown had a new spirit of prayer that became the forerunner of blessing, and in October and November there were inquiries after salvation in every meeting.[1] The union prayer meeting in Dublin was supported by members of all three major evangelical denominations.[2] The large Metropolitan Hall, seating about 3,000, was made the venue of special meetings, Spurgeon preaching five times in January 1860, and the Rev. Samuel J. Moore of Ballymena giving a discourse on the Revival in the North. In April, the Metropolitan Hall was opened on Tuesdays for free prayer, 3,000 attending with more than 100 inquirers in each of the first three meetings. In July an "increasing interest" was reported from the Metropolitan Hall, inquirers undiminished in numbers, Sunday open-air meetings attracting 3,000. Without a doubt, Protestant people were revived.

On the whole the Revival movement in the south and west of Ireland had none of the startling effects of the Ulster Awakening; nevertheless the work of grace among the isolated Protestant communities launched out many eager and faithful evangelists, clerical and lay, who laboured against overwhelming odds for the evangelization of their Roman Catholic fellow-countrymen.[3]

The Hon. and Rev. Baptist Noel told a conference of the Evangelical Alliance that he thought 100,000 converts in the Ulster Revival was probably under the mark.[4] In all Ireland, there were more. Thus it was that the movement, which originated in a prayer meeting of four young men in the village school-house of Kells in the parish of Connor in the county of Antrim, made greater impact spiritually on Ireland than anything else reported since the days of Saint Patrick. In 1959, the six major denominations in Ireland united in commemorating the centenary of the Revival.[5]

---

[1] Reid, W., *Authentic Records of Revival*, pp. 303 ff.
[2] *The Revival*, 4th February, 21st April, 26th May, 1859.
[3] Orr, J. Edwin, *op. cit.*, pp. 56–56.
[4] Morgan, G. E., *R. C. Morgan: His Life and Times*, p. 96.
[5] The author was the guest of a united committee representing a thousand churches in this commemoration. (Ed.)

CHAPTER XVI

WORK OF GOD IN SCOTLAND

A FTER A YEAR'S OBSERVATION OF THE AWAKENING, THE GEN-eral Assembly of the Church of Scotland, held in Edinburgh in May 1860, unanimously approved an Overture on Re-vivals of Religion:[1]

> General Assembly, taking into consideration the gratifying evidence manifested in many countries, and in various districts of our own land, of an increased anxiety about salvation and deepening interest in religious ordinances, followed in so many cases by fruits of holy living, desires to record its gratitude to Almighty God. . . .

In the same month, the General Assembly of the equally large Free Church of Scotland met in the same capital city and heard a moving address by the incoming Moderator, Dr. James Buchanan of Glasgow:[2]

> Two years ago, our Assembly was deeply stirred by the intelligence of what God was doing in the United States of America. One year ago, the impression was deepened . . . the pregnant cloud had swept onwards and was sending down upon Ireland a plenteous rain. This year, the same precious showers have been and are even now falling within the limits of our own beloved land.
>
> We, as a Church, accept the Revival as a great and blessed fact. Numerous and explicit testimonies from ministers and members alike bespeak the gracious influence upon the people. Whole con-gregations have been seen bending before it like a mighty rushing wind.

And in the same month of May the Synod of the United Presbyterian Church, the third largest church organization in Scotland:[3]

> resolved to recognize the hand of God in the measure of new life outpoured upon our churches, and appointed the second Sabbath of July as a special Day of Prayer for the Revival.

Thus the three main branches of the dominant Presbyterianism of Scotland, whose adherents formed 70 per cent of the total

[1] *Acts of the General Assembly of the Church of Scotland*, 26th May, 1860.
[2] *Proceedings and Debates of the General Assembly of the Free Church of Scotland*, 1860.
[3] *United Presbyterian Magazine*, Vol. IV, p. 326.

population, declared in no uncertain way that Scotland was experiencing a Revival of Religion as striking as the movement in neighbouring Ulster. And at that time there were three times as many Protestants as in Ulster, for Scotland's population approximated 3,000,000.

As in Ireland, many were the preparations for Awakening. Already the Christian life of Scotland was being quickened by evangelists, often drawn from the higher ranks of society. The news of the Revival of Religion in the United States provoked[1] much interest and not a few united prayer meetings, as in Edinburgh, Glasgow, and Aberdeen, where there was united intercession for an abundant outpouring of the Holy Spirit.

A measure of prayer in preparation of heart for Revival is indicated in the official report[2] of the United Presbyterian Church that one in every four of its 162,305 communicants was attending its regular prayer meetings, an average of some 40,549 at prayer in 1,205 regular meetings; with 129 new prayer meetings and an increase of 16,362 regular attenders developing in 1859.

The news of the religious awakening in Ulster quickened the interest of Scottish Christians already stirred by reports from America. The main development of the movement seemed to come from America via Ulster to Scotland. An observer (the Rev. Adam Blyth of Girvan) was later struck by the fact that the union prayer meeting in New York (itself a product of the American Awakening) had been requested to pray for the spiritual needs of Coleraine in Ulster. The union prayer meeting in Coleraine (a product of the resultant Revival in Ulster) in turn was asked to pray for the spiritual welfare of Port Glasgow on the Clyde which soon afterwards was in the throes of a Revival.[3]

Spiritual sympathy expressed in prayer knows no barriers of race or space. But that does not mean that racial affinity and geographical proximity played no part in the spread of the mid-nineteenth-century Awakening. The Scotch-Irish of America (Ulster emigrants) had played a leading part in the colonization of America and the establishment of the United States; it was to be expected that their kith and kin across the Atlantic in Ulster should have become the first community in Britain to be moved by the same sort of religious fervour. Likewise, the majority of Ulster Scots who built the prosperous communities of Northern Ireland were immigrants from south-western Scotland, chiefly from the shores of the Firth of Clyde: it was to be expected that the same Awakening would spread via their cousins across the North Channel from Galloway to Glasgow. Such was the case, for south-western Scotland in general, and Glasgow, its hub in

[1] *Ibid.*, p. 82.　　[2] *Ibid.*, p. 333.　　[3] *The Revival*, 27th August, 1859.

particular, were soon extraordinarily quickened in matters religious.

In the middle of August 1859, the Revival became news in Glasgow with all the suddenness of a summer thunderstorm.[1] Almost a column in a newspaper was devoted to a public meeting held in the City Hall, which crowded gathering was presided over by Bailie Playfair. Another newspaper reported a similar meeting to hear about the Revival in the Stockwell Free Church in the city, a meeting crowded to excess in which the interest was so deepened that great excitement and tears were in evidence. Four days later, at 6.30 p.m. on August 19th, a public meeting was held on Glasgow Green, and the *North British Daily Mail* reported that approximately 20,000 people were present, crushing to hear the speakers.

Religious writers were very little ahead of secular in recognizing the sudden outbreak of Revival in Glasgow. The *Scottish Guardian* of 2nd August, 1859, claimed that:

> The Holy Spirit has been manifesting His gracious power in a remarkable manner in this neighbourhood during the last few days. Our readers are aware that ever sunce the news of the Great Revival in America reached Scotland, prayer meetings for the special purpose of imploring a similar blessing have been held in Glasgow as well as in other places. The intelligence which has reached us recently leaves no room to doubt that these prayers have been heard.

The report referred to increased attendances at prayer meetings as well as increased numbers of conversions among those waiting behind for counsel by the ministers and workers present. Three weeks later the same weekly paper commented on the increased attendance at union prayer meetings.[2] As in America and in Ireland, the noon prayer meetings gave rise to prayer meetings and preaching services in the various evangelical churches on weeknights, and in these meetings there were scores of reported conversions.

After a year of the movement, Glasgow was still enjoying such "times of refreshing":[3]

> Every Sabbath evening service since the Bridegate Church was opened, the crowds around the stone pulpit have been increasing, until on Sabbath evening last, there could not have been fewer than 7,000 hearers, probably more. We say "hearers," for, notwithstanding the vastness of the congregation, voice of the preacher appeared to be perfectly audible at the furthest extremity.
>
> At the close of the open-air service, an invitation is given from the pulpit to all who wish to come to a decision in the matter of religion to attend the prayer meeting. . . . Within ten minutes the church is

[1] *North British Daily Mail*, 11th, 12th, 15th, 20th August, 1859.
[2] *Scottish Guardian*, 23rd August, 1859.   [3] *The Revival*, 25th August, 1860.

generally packed, and, being seated for 900, it will receive probably upwards of 1,100 when thus crowded.

About ten o'clock, the meeting was brought to a close, and those only were asked to remain who wished conversation with the minister and other friends. About 500 waited including, of course, the friends of those who were in distress. This meeting continued till 11.45 p.m.

Just as "approximately 20,000" had gathered on Glasgow Green at the start of the movement, a similar-sized crowd gathered on 6th September, 1860.[1] An adjoining theatre was opened for the inquirers. The outstanding speaker, whose powerful voice seemed to fill the Green, was a butcher named Robert Cunningham. So great was the interest and so heavy the work entailed that three visiting speakers, Gordon Forlong, Reginald Radcliffe and Richard Weaver, collapsed with fatigue.

The Awakening of 1859–60 permeated every corner of south-western Scotland down to the Vale of Dumfries and the borders of Cumberland.[2] The movement repeated the phenomena of the Ulster Awakening, but most reports noted seemed to stress the dispensability of "prostrations" and other physical phenomena, recognizing their value in first startling the observers, but relieved when they have way to quieter manifestations.

In the New Year of 1861, the second wave of revival blessing was felt in the Vale of Dumfries and in Glasgow.[3] The occasion was the visit of an American student of theology, Edward Payson Hammond, who was invited to conduct revival services in Annan on the Solway Firth. It was stated by the *Dumfries Standard* that the revival spirit reached a degree of intensity unparalleled in the religious history of the burgh. Hammond, his assistant Drysdale, four ministers and many helpers often had to help inquirers (as many as 500 at a time) until the early hours of the morning. The work among the children was noteworthy, and this factor shaped Hammond as a children's evangelist in future years. In Dumfries, a secular newspaper described the response as "marvellous." Payson Hammond carried the revival influence to Glasgow again, where such a work was wrought that a thanksgiving meeting attracted 12,000 to the City Hall, one-third of whom gained entrance.[4] The effect of Hammond's preaching was felt for many months, and permanent results were claimed by his gratified sponsors. The lasting result of his work was creation of interest in child conversion.

The Highland Revival, sweeping up the western islands and the northern highlands, jumped across the Pentland Firth to the

---

[1] *Ibid.*, 15th September, 1860.   [2] *Ibid.*, 14th January, 1860.
[3] Morgan, G. E., *R. C. Morgan*, p. 125.   [4] *Ibid.*

Orkney Islands, from which a Kirkwall gentleman reported: "There is a most marvellous, miraculous work of God's Spirit going on here. . . . I believe that the whole character of this end of the island is changed."[1] In 1860 there were eight special prayer meetings in the Shetlands, and the general interest grew until 1862, when Dr. Craig and Mr. John Fraser commenced an evangelistic campaign to which up to 1,200 people came, overcrowding the parish church night after night.[2] This work continued for many months into the spring of 1863, spreading from town to the rural districts.

In north-east Scotland, from the Moray Firth to the Firth of Tay, including the counties of Nairn, Moray, Banff, Aberdeen, Kincardine and Angus, the Awakening was felt immediately and intensely in 1859. Following the prayer movement in 1858, and limited Revival in early 1859, there were ambitious open-air services in the city of Aberdeen in the spring and summer of 1859.[3] In London, religious editors were credibly informed that there was scarcely a town or village between Inverness and Aberdeen that had not been moved by the quickening power of the Spirit.

As to the nature of these awakenings, the Rev. W. T. Ker of Deskford stated:

> It is indeed a most wondrous work of the Lord, and it is passing along this whole coast like a mighty wave, having assumed a character identical with that of the work in Ireland.[4]

Almost every parish in the county of Perth felt the quickening influences of the Spirit during the wonderful years of 1859–60. Wherever there was a living Christian community, the Revival was long prayed-for and its arrival hailed with gratification.[5] More than fifty pastors and lay workers addressed about 4,000 people between 11 a.m. and 6 p.m. on an occasion (22nd August, 1860) in which the sponsors declared that they "buried sectarianism in the South Inch of Perth that day, and saw no Christian weep over its grave." Church of Scotland, Church of England, United Presbyterian, Congregationalist and Baptist ministers participated. In the City Hall, 2,000 attended and simultaneously three churches were used that evening, many inquirers being dealt with by the pastors. Seven weeks later local ministers reported no abatement of movement, "all the country round on fire."

There was a remarkable outbreak of revival phenomena in Fifeshire, to the south of Dundee. An Army officer of high rank

---

[1] *The Revival*, 8th December, 1860.   [2] *Ibid.*, 27th November, 1862.
[3] *Ibid.*, 30th July, 6th August, 10th September, 1859.
[4] *Ibid.*, 3rd March, 1860.   [5] MacRae, A., *Revivals in the Highlands*, p. 145.

summed up his impressions of what he had seen in Cellardyke thus:[1]

> Those of you who are at ease have little conception of how terrifying a sight it is when the Holy Spirit is pleased to open a man's eyes to see the real state of his heart.
> Men who were thought to be, and who thought themselves to be good, religious people . . . have been led to search into the foundation on which they were resting, and have found all rotten, that they were self-satisfied, resting on their own goodness, and not upon Christ.
> Many turned from open sin to lives of holiness, some weeping for joy for sins forgiven.

The forerunner of the Edinburgh Revival was a united prayer meeting commenced in April 1858, when the news of the American Revival crossed the Atlantic, held every Monday for twenty-one months, becoming a daily prayer meeting in January 1860. In this meeting, Church of Scotland, Free Church and United Presbyterian ministers worked together in happy unity.[2]

In November, it was reported from Edinburgh that "a very general expectation of a manifest outpouring of the Holy Spirit exists."[3] The American revivalist, Professor Charles G. Finney, was in Edinburgh for a short visit at that date and his meetings were exceedingly well attended, producing many converts.[4] Strange things were already happening in the Carrubber's Close Mission (which had opened doors eighteen months before, ejecting an Atheist Club from the premises) where scores of people of all ages were being converted. Only two converts displayed physical manifestations. Before long, the influence of the work began to radiate in all directions, churches opening their doors to the converts.

By March 1860 the work of Revival was making progress in Edinburgh and the surrounding district, prayer meetings having been established in many towns and villages nearby, as well as in the city.[5] Evangelistic meetings began to attract huge crowds, with happy results. Radcliffe and Weaver, English evangelists, could not get a place large enough for their meetings. On one occasion, 1,800 people crowded the Richmond Place Chapel, whilst thousands packed a street outside. These evangelists had to walk on the shoulders of stalwart men in order to alternate in ministry inside and outside the chapel. Hundreds remained behind for conversation, even though the preaching had gone on intermittently from seven until eleven p.m.

[1] *The Revival*, 23rd June, 1860.
[2] *United Presbyterian Magazine*, Vol. IV, p. 82.
[3] *The Revival*, 15th October, 1859.   [4] *The Freeman*, 28th September, 1859.
[5] *Ibid.*, 11th January, 21st March, 1860.

In the Border Counties, south of Edinburgh,[1] the Awakening began with prayer meetings that were quickened by news brought by their ministers from northern Ireland and western Scotland. It continued effective for many years.

What began as a movement of prayer among Christians in Scotland continued as a remarkable movement for the evangelization of Scotland. Professor William G. McLoughlin of Brown University has affirmed (*Modern Revivalism*, p. 183 n.) that the Presbyterian churches soon dissociated themselves from this movement, as did the Anglicans. Authority was not cited. He explained to the author that he referred to the distaste that many parish ministers had for the itinerant revivalists and evangelists who followed the Awakening. The incoming Moderator of the Free Church Assembly (Dr. Candlish) in 1861 paid tribute to the quality of the work:[2] "Fathers and Brethren, I congratulate you on your meeting again in the midst of an outpouring of the Spirit of God, and a remarkable work of grace pervading the whole church and the whole land."

Five years after the initial outbreak of revival,[3] a typical Presbytery Report noted (summary ours):

(1) The Awakening had continued throughout the years, and was not so much a completed period of Revival but rather the beginning of a better state of things in the spread of vital religion.

(2) All classes were influenced, and only its earliest stages were accompanied by excitement.

(3) Agency was both lay and clerical, method both united prayer and expository preaching.

(4) Revival had resulted in the quickening of believers, increase of family religion, decrease of cases of discipline in all congregations since.

Special conversions of a remarkable character had stood the test of time, but it was difficult to state accurately what proportion of the total number of converts had been genuine, no attempt to count such conversions having been made.

A well-known evangelist was quoted as saying that thousands stood of the fruit of 1859–60, and many were going on well; and another added that in the first stages of revival there was a seeking of the evangelist, whereas later it became a seeking of the lost by the evangelist.

The United Presbyterian Church in Scotland reported that 477 of their congregations added 15,314 new members, presumably in the latter months of 1859.[4] Checking with Irish figures, it is

[1] Reid, W., *Authentic Records of Revival*, pp. 321 ff.
[2] *Proceedings and Debates in the General Assembly of the Free Church of Scotland*, 1861.
[3] *Ibid.*, 19th January, 1865.
[4] *United Presbyterian Magazine*, Vol. IV, p. 371.

found that both Scottish and Irish Presbyterian congregations gained 33 per cent.

The Revival, now *The Christian,* was the real day-to-day historian of the movement, and its trusted correspondents summed up in 1865 thus:[1]

> The wave of Divine blessing came to us apparently from Ireland four or five years ago. It struck first the west coast of Scotland, then spread over a great part of the country. It was a very blessed season, perhaps the most extensive in its operation that we have ever known amongst us. But it has, in a great measure, passed away. Still, fruit remains—living, active, consistent Christians who keep together, cherishing the memory of the time, blessing and praying for its return. . . . The number of students entering our divinity halls this season will be double or triple that of former years; this is the blessed fruit of the Revival. Such men are likely to be of the right stamp. . . .

It was to a revived, prepared Scottish Church that the greatest evangelist produced by the 1858–59 Revival came to Scotland. Dwight L. Moody found a well-ploughed field in which to sow seed and reap harvest fifteen years later.

[1] *The Revival,* 19th January, 1865.

CHAPTER XVII

TIME OF PRAISE IN WALES

HE 1859 REVIVAL IN WALES CAN BE TRACED TO THE IN-
fluence of the American Revival of 1858, but, unlike its
Scottish counterpart, it owed nothing to the influence of
the Ulster movement.[1] Indeed, there is evidence to suggest that
the outbreak of revival phenomena in Wales actually preceded
those experienced in Ulster.[2] Nevertheless pride of place must be
given to the Ulster movement on account of its influence upon the
remainder of the United Kingdom, for English and Scottish
religious life was comparatively uninfluenced by happenings in
Cymric-speaking Welsh churches. In fact, in the summer of 1859,
thousands of English Christians travelled through North Wales
to embark at Holyhead on their way to study the "work of grace"
in Ireland, without realizing that as profound an Awakening was
stirring the villages and towns passed by whose inhabitants spoke
the incomprehensible Welsh.[3]

The literature of the 1859 Revival in Wales is meagre, even in
the vernacular. Most of the Welsh accounts of the 1859 Revival
partake more of the nature of poetic raptures than of soberly-
stated facts. It would be well to begin instead with a statement by
a border-country Englishman, the Rev. John Venn, M.A., Prebendary of Hereford, read before the Evangelical Alliance
gathering in the autumn of 1860.[4] In it he claimed that almost
every county in the principality had been influenced by a more or
less remarkable work of grace. He endeavoured to assess the
lasting worth of the movement by giving details of great numbers already received into church membership by the various
authorities, and adding a proportionate number for additions in
the Established Church (his own denomination), Prebendary Venn
estimated that about 100,000 persons in all had been received into
full communion in the course of two years. Carefully, he was
willing to deduct 10 per cent or so to avoid going beyond the
truth, a deduction that could be ignored if one desired to estimate
the numbers of professed conversions rather than additions to

---

[1] Orr, J. Edwin, *The Second Evangelical Awakening in Britain*, p. 78; cf. Evans,
Eifion, *When He is Come*, reaching the same conclusion.
[2] Morgan, J. J., *The '59 Revival in Wales*, p. vi.
[3] *The Revival*, 24th November, 1860.   [4] Morgan, J. J., *op. cit.*, p. 462.

church membership, for it can be clearly demonstrated that great numbers of actual church members are professedly converted in every revival movement.

In his *History of Protestant Nonconformity in Wales*, published in 1861,[1] Thomas Rees stated the number of conversions in the Revival of Nonconformists alone as being between 85,000 and 95,000, adding that "the numerous converts with comparatively rare exceptions hold on remarkably well." Fifty years after the Revival a reliable authority declared upon the basis of additions to church membership that it could be "safely accepted that the whole harvest of the Revival in Wales did not fall short of a hundred thousand souls," the great majority of whom satisfied the test of time. Thus approximately a tenth of the population of Wales was permanently influenced by the Revival, there being about a million people in Wales in 1859.

"Before the '59 Revival," said Principal T. C. Edwards, D.D., of Bala, "the churches were withering away in our country; a wave of spiritual apathy and practical infidelity had spread over Wales."[2] In the year following the Revival, the number of criminal cases before the Welsh Courts decreased from 1,809 to 1,228.[3]

How did a revival so fraught with good originate? A Welsh lad named Humphrey Rowland Jones was born in North Cardiganshire about the year 1832.[4] Fifteen years later he became converted, and in 1854, he applied to the Wesleyan District Meeting (South Wales) for admission to the ministry. He was rejected, and emigrated to the United States to join his parents. The Methodist Episcopal Church ordained him there.[5] He became a revival preacher, travelling widely.

Caught up in the American Revival movement in 1857–58, he returned to his native Wales in the summer of 1858.[6] His evangelistic labours had a measure of success, but his success created unconcerned and good-natured scepticism in the mind of a neighbouring Calvinistic Methodist minister, David Morgan, who distrusted anything of American extraction or Wesleyan communication.

David Morgan himself had been awakened in a local revival in his native Cardiganshire in the year 1841.[7] His ministry was recognized in 1857, when he was ordained by the Trevine Association. For ten years he had prayed for an outpouring of the Divine Spirit. Hence, in spite of his deep prejudice, he went to hear young Humphrey Jones at a Wesleyan Chapel nearby, Ysbytty Ystwyth, and was deeply convicted by an address on the words: "Because

[1] *Ibid.*, p. vi.   [2] *Ibid.*, p. 3.   [3] *Ibid.*, p. vii.   [4] *Ibid.*, p. 2.
[5] Evans, Eifion, *When He is Come*, p. 39.
[6] Morgan, J. J., *op. cit.*, pp. 3 ff.   [7] *Ibid.*, p. 7.

thou art neither hot nor cold, I will spue thee out of my mouth."
David Morgan entered into experience of spiritual deepening a
few days later.[1]

In David Morgan's village, Ysbytty Ystwyth, the population
did not exceed 1,000, yet 200 adult converts had been won before
the end of 1858.[2] A feature of the Revival was *moliannu* or praising,
a peculiar form of worship described as a chorus of rapturous
praise from preacher and people in turn. In early 1859 David
Morgan began to visit neighbouring village churches. In Pont-
rhydfendigaid, more than half the population of 800 united themselves to the Calvinistic Methodists. An unordained Pontrhydfen-
digaid lad carried word to Tregaron, where the congregation burst
into praising and eighty-seven people were converted in the
service. By midsummer the whole county of Cardigan had been
pervaded with the most fervid religious feeling, and Calvinistic
Methodist converts alone numbered 9,000 in June, 15,000 in
August, in a population of 70,000.[3]

Every county in Wales experienced blessing.[4] Following the
week of prayer in January 1860, a second wave of revival swept
Wales, with greater strength in some places, and with the same
happy interdenominational unity.[5]

In Monmouthshire, culturally a Welsh county though a part of
England, the Revival movement may be traced to the Congregational Association meetings at Beaufort, June 29th and 30th, in
1859.[6]

Cardiff, the Welsh metropolis, shared in the evangelistic movements stirring England in the 1860s.[7] In 1862, in spring, Dr. and
Mrs. Walter Palmer (American evangelists) began to experience
stirring times in Cardiff. For thirty days "a remarkable work of
the Spirit" was acknowledged and felt throughout the town,
affecting public morals, bringing hundreds to the house of prayer,
so much so that an Anglican town councillor of long experience
testified that police cases were dwindling in number, a detective
adding "Cardiff has become a different place." Local ministers
supported the work well, and 800 people became inquirers in their
churches. The Palmers were followed by Richard Weaver, and
"half the people could not get in." The largest building in South
Wales, the Music Hall, filled up with 4,000 people each evening,
and hundreds were turned away.

In the spring of 1863, William and Catherine Booth, fresh from

[1] *Ibid.*, p. 9.   [2] *Ibid.*, p. 17.
[3] *The Nonconformist*, 21st September, 1859.
[4] Orr, J. Edwin, *The Second Evangelical Awakening in Britain*, pp. 81–91.
[5] *The Revival*, 25th February, 1860.
[6] Morgan, J. J., *op. cit.*, pp. 106–107.
[7] *The Revival*, 18th May, 22nd June, 1861.

revival meetings of great power in Cornwall, began preaching in Cardiff, and won 500 people to the faith.[1] Mrs. Booth preached with simplicity and modesty. So great was the interest in the Booth campaign that it became necessary to use a large circus building accommodating between 2,000 and 3,000 people. The effort was supported by Christians of every denomination. Quite a number of the converts of the Cardiff meetings were Cornish people, one couple having travelled by sea to Wales on account of conviction produced by the Revivalist in Cornwall. The Booths were followed by Richard Weaver on another visit, and crowds of 3,000 attended nightly, 500 professing faith.[2]

It should be emphasized that in all the Cardiff campaigns, English was the medium of preaching. The reports of revival in Cardiff during the earlier Welsh Revival movement were so scarce that it underlined the notion that Cardiff was looked on as a cosmopolitan city within Wales. That the English movements of the 1860s affected Cardiff so powerfully bears this out.

The Calvinistic Methodist Church of Wales (now the Presbyterian Church of Wales) reaped a rich harvest from the Revival of 1859. The number of converts who subsequently joined their churches was recorded as 36,190.[3]

The Congregationalists claimed a similar total of converts gained by their churches, about 36,000.[4] In a single county, Carnarvon, Congregationalists built a score of chapels to house the new recruits.

The Baptist churches gained about 14,000 new members from the converts.[5] The Rev. Thomas Thomas, Principal of the Baptist College at Pontypool, reported "tens of thousands" of additions, many new churches being formed for Welsh-speaking and English-speaking adherents. Double the usual number of students for the Baptist ministry began studies at Pontypool and Haverfordwest.

The Wesleyan Methodists gained 4,549 new members in 1859–60.[6] The Church of England in Wales supported the movement, but its gains had been estimated only, no reliable figures being available. The estimate suggested 20,000 new communicants.[7]

Principal Charles of Trevecca College outlined three main characteristics of the Welsh Revival thus:[8] firstly, an extraordinary spirit of prayer among the masses; secondly, a remarkable spirit of union among all denominations of Christians; and thirdly, a powerful missionary effort for the conversion of others. These

[1] Booth-Tucker, F., *Life of Catherine Booth*, p. 262.
[2] *The Revival*, 14th May, 1863.   [3] *Ibid.*, 19th January, 1865.
[4] *Ibid.*, 24th November, 1860.   [5] *Ibid.*, 19th January, 1865.
[6] *Ibid.*, 24th November, 1860.   [7] *The Freeman*, 26th October, 1859.
[8] *The Nonconformist*, 17th December, 1859.

three characteristics were displayed by the American, Irish and Scottish movements. Another remarkable affinity of movement is noticed in the fact that the Welsh Revival of 1859 was independent of great personalities—even David Morgan the Revivalist, who was used signally in the inception and spread of the revival, was a simple country pastor.

In what way did the Welsh movement differ from its contemporaries? There were fewer cases of physical prostration in Wales, but just as many evidences of intense conviction or agony of mind. In Ulster the physical prostrations were the stimulating incidents which created public interest; in Wales, the rapturous praise seemed to be the crisis point in each locality.

Take, for example, the outbreak of revival in a Carmarthenshire town, as recorded by the son of David Morgan.[1]

> One Sunday morning, an elder rose to speak, and his first remark was that the God they worshipped was without beginning and without end. "Amen!" exclaimed a young girl in the highest notes of a lovely voice. "Blessed be His name forever."
>
> This cry might be compared to the touch of the electric button that shivers a quarry into a thousand hurtling fragments. Scores leaped from their seats, and, gathering in the vacant space in the centre, they have vent to their pent-up emotions in outcries that were almost agonizing in their ardour and intensity.

Time and time again in the Morgan narrative one is struck with the recurrence of a purely oratorical stimulus which provoked a storm of praise, in which the already-converted half of the congregation indulged in unrestrained ejaculatory utterance and the unconverted half fell under the deepest conviction. The explanation must come from analysis of the Cymric *psyche*, the vehicle of the spiritual impulse.

[1] Morgan, J. J., *op. cit.*, pp. 82–83.

CHAPTER XVIII

DAYS OF POWER IN ENGLAND

THE PATTERN OF THE AWAKENING IN ENGLAND WAS NOTE-worthy, for it included full-scale Revival of the spontaneous and immediate type experienced in Ulster, Wales and Scotland; evangelistic movements in the metropolitan areas; and movements of delayed-action until the Revival produced the right atmosphere and leaders for evangelism.

North of the Tyne in Northumberland, late in the summer of 1859, there was an early stirring due to the visit of Dr. and Mrs. Walter C. Palmer.[1] The Palmers[2] had been witnesses of the original outbreak of revival in the city of Hamilton, 1857, in Ontario. Their ministry provided a fitting climax to twelve months of prayer meetings, a preparation going on in Newcastle from the time of the arrival of news of the American Revival.

The Times of London reported "A Religious 'Revival'" at Newcastle-on-Tyne in a headline:[3]

> this town has become the scene of a religious "Awakening" which bids fair to rival anything of the kind which has occurred either in America or the North of Ireland.

By October 1859 there seemed to be a more or less general awakening going on in the Tyneside city,[4] Anglican and Non-conformist clergymen and ministers conducting special services, in one of which the owner of a saloon who had invested in the brewery business created a sensation by renouncing all connexion with the liquor traffic. In the same month the Rev. Robert Young reported:[5]

> The Revival with which this town is favoured is advancing with increased power and glory. In Brunswick Place Chapel we hold a united prayer meeting from twelve o'clock to one; another meeting for exhortation and prayer, from three to five; and a similar service from seven to ten. Many seemed "filled with the Holy Ghost," and pray "as the Spirit gives them utterance." All attempts to proselytize

---

[1] *The Revival,* 17th September, 1st October, 1859.
[2] *Vide* Wheatley, R., *Life and Letters of Mrs. Phoebe Palmer,* and Hughes, G., *The Beloved Physician: Walter C. Palmer, passim.*
[3] *The Times,* 21st September, 1859.   [4] *The Record,* 21st September, 1859.
[5] *The Revival,* 1st, 22nd October, 1859.

are utterly repudiated: hence some designate the work "the Evangelical Alliance Revival." The meetings, though often crowding our spacious chapel, are orderly, and generally are marked by deep solemnity. It is true that, occasionally, there is the cry of the spirit-stricken sinner, and the bursting joy of the newly-emancipated captive, but that is music in our ears.

A month later, this Methodist minister stated that the Newcastle Awakening had accounted for 1,300 conversions in his church, all the converts being willing to publish their names. At the end of the year Mr. Young reported that there were 1,400 converts in Brunswick Chapel confirmed.[1]

Five years later in Newcastle, evangelism in church and public hall was still effective, going on "gloriously" among the working men.[2]

In the county of Durham, there was immediate response to the prayer challenge of 1859–60. In Sunderland, a meeting of ministers unanimously[3] resolved to commence prayer meetings, and in September 1859 these were held "morning, noon and night," well-attended by professing Christians and anxious inquirers. The first phase of Revival had begun. Later that year the ministers claimed that an extensive visitation had moved Sunderland. No less than 3,444 persons joined the Wesleyan Societies in a movement led by the Palmers.[4]

Another fruitful centre of revival evangelism in County Durham was the Tyneside city of Gateshead. The Palmers visited the city in May 1860, winning 500 or more converts.[5] A New Connexion (Methodist) Church there experienced a time of revival in 1859 under its pastor, William Booth. Four years later a circuit chapel reported that of the forty-nine professed conversions occurring within its walls that year thirty cases were known to have joined the society, of whom eleven were still in fellowship, another fourteen in fellowship elsewhere, and yet another three had just been restored from backsliding, showing a loss of only two out of the thirty.[6] In the second phase of the revival, 200 conversions were reported, in 1861, making a total in three years of 300 new members added to the New Connexion circuit. And so many sinners were brought to repentance that Bethesda Chapel earned the name of "the Converting Shop."[7]

It was during these revival times that Mrs. Catherine Booth (8th January, 1860) announced her intention of preaching—to the astonishment of her husband and his congregation.[8] Likewise, it

[1] *The Watchman*, 4th January, 1860.
[2] *The Revival*, 28th July, 1864; 21st December, 1865.
[3] *The Revival*, 17th September, 1859.   [4] *Wesleyan Times*, 11th May, 1863.
[5] *The Watchman*, 23rd May, 1860.   [6] *The Revival*, 26th March, 1863.
[7] Sandall, R., *History of the Salvation Army*, Vol. I, p. 8.   [8] *Ibid.*, pp. 8–9.

was during this revival that William and Catherine Booth began to preach the doctrine of Full Salvation, now an integral part of Salvationist teaching. The Booths conducted a preaching mission in Hartlepool, attracting up to 1,000 people, turning many away disappointed, and winning 250 converts.[1] In spite of this success, Methodist New Connexion Conference tried to set a limit on Booth's evangelism, leading to his resignation in 1862.[2]

Dr. and Mrs. Palmer campaigned in Carlisle in February 1860, their work being soon reported "the Revival of Carlisle."[3] A year later there was a further movement, attributed to the melting and subduing influence of the Holy Spirit, in which numbers of converted youths were found bringing in "the young heathen" from the streets. Throughout January 1861 this movement bore fruit in the conversion of young people chiefly; six months later the work of grace was still on the increase, supported by a united meeting of five churches for purposes of prayer, and effected by the hiring of a local theatre for purposes of preaching.

In the 1860s, evangelism continued in strength in Liverpool, with meetings of between 700 and 1,000 young men, many becoming converted. The American evangelist, E. Payson Hammond, was visiting Liverpool in the summer of 1861 and addressed large gatherings, following which hundreds of inquirers remained for conversation.[4] In the autumn, Reginald Radcliffe began Sunday evening meetings in the Concert Hall, which was overflowing. About the same time the Americans, Dr. and Mrs. Palmer, came to Liverpool for a rest from heavy labours, and were immediately caught up in "an extraordinary work of the Holy Spirit" not confined to any particular denomination, with converts numbered in the hundreds.

On Christmas Eve, 1859, Professor Finney arrived in Bolton with Mrs. Finney, and became a spearhead of a revival movement there among Congregationalists and Methodists.[5] The chapel was filled from the first meeting, and Professor Finney called for inquirers on the fourth night and found the vestry filled. The meetings were transferred to a larger Temperance Hall, and under Finney's direction the whole town was canvassed with happy results. Three months later more than 1,200 were attending the week-night services and hundreds were being turned away on Sundays.

In Manchester the religious revival appeared in full strength two years after the initial prayer meetings.[6] The work continued

[1] Booth-Tucker, F., *Life of Catherine Booth*, p. 216.
[2] Sandall, R., *op. cit.*, Vol. I, pp. 9–11.
[3] *The Watchman*, 22nd, 29th February, 1860.
[4] Orr, J. Edwin, *The Second Evangelical Awakening in Britain*, p. 157.
[5] Finney, C. G., *Memoirs of the Rev. Charles G. Finney*, pp. 458 ff.
[6] Cf. Orr, J. Edwin, *op. cit.*, pp. 159–160.

till the end of 1861, and there were strong testimonies to support the claim that the work was neither superficial nor evanescent. Finney's Manchester campaign was disapointing to him, but produced many converts.

One of the converts of the 1861 meetings was Henry Moorhouse, whose companions were as irreligious as himself. Moorhouse heard shouting and noise from within the Alhambra, buttoned up his coat ready for whatever fray was provided, and rushed in, only to be confronted by the sight of ex-pugilist Richard Weaver preaching the gospel in his inimitable style.[1] Before long Moorhouse and his companions had found the same salvation preached by Weaver, and Henry Moorhouse was set on his career as a remarkable evangelist of world-wide reputation.

Early in 1860 a London lady named Elizabeth Codner published anonymously in *The Revival*[2] a poem whose sentiments were so wistfully expressed that it became a well-known and much-used hymn for several generations, until its own sentimentality passed out of style in the period of the World Wars:

> Lord, I hear of showers of blessing
> Thou art scattering full and free.

Dr. Eugene Stock, the secretary of the Church Missionary Society and equally famed as a Deeper Life speaker in after years, declared in retrospect that the period under review was marked by a religious Revival of a kind unlike anything experienced in Britain since (with the exception of the localized Welsh Revival of 1905), adding that the most striking feature of the Revival of the 1860s was the phenomena of the prayer meetings.

> I can never forget 9th January, 1860, when, at nine o'clock on a bitterly cold morning, that hall was densely packed for nothing but simple prayer for the outpouring of the Holy Spirit.[3]

That hall was the huge Islington Agricultural Hall. The second week of January was devoted by multitudes of believers to special united prayer for an outpouring of the Holy Spirit all over the world.[4] This feature of the Revival originated in an appeal issued in 1853 by a group of American missionaries in Ludhiana, a small town in North-West India, asking all Christians throughout the world to set aside the second week of 1860 for united prayer.[5] The response of leaders and people to this call to prayer was as astonishing as it was spontaneous, for in London alone there were at least 200 united prayer-meetings.[6]

The effect of united prayer upon Christians of all denominations

[1] Pickering, H., *Chief Men among the Brethren*, pp. 167 ff.
[2] *The Revival*, 28th April, 1860.   [3] Stock, E., *My Recollections*, pp. 82–83.
[4] *The Freeman*, 25th January, 1860.   [5] *The Revival*, 3rd December, 1859.
[6] *Ibid.*, 21st January, 1860.

is always the same. Towards God their hearts are stirred with love that finds expression in a Christian unity transcending the artificial boundaries of race, people, class, and creed; towards outsiders their hearts are filled with love that sets out immediately, like the Good Shepherd, to bring the lost sheep into the fold.

The records of the movement in London are full of examples of the effect of prayer on worship, fellowship, and evangelism, all of which revived immeasurably. Awakened Christians in London soon found an opportunity of harnessing the flowing tides of Revival to generate sufficient power to carry the Light to the most darkened masses of the metropolis. The prime mover in the matter was that "Evangelical of the Evangelicals," the seventh Earl of Shaftesbury,[1] who helped begin a series of theatre meetings which he himself made possible by sponsoring the Religious Worship Act to remove all legal impediments.

On New Year's Day, 1860, the Britannia, the Garrick and Sadler's Wells theatres were thrown open for Sunday evening services for the people, attracting "overwhelming" and "immense" audiences to hear sermons by Established clergymen and Dissenting ministers.[2] Another two theatres were opened later that month, and a couple more in February, by which time all seven were catering for an aggregate attendance nightly of over 20,000.[3] Special services for upper- and middle-class people were held in St. Paul's Cathedral and Westminster Abbey, and also in St. James's and Exeter Halls in the West End.[4]

No numerical reports are available concerning aggregates of the vast but orderly crowds attending St. Paul's Cathedral for special services, led by the Bishop of London, "with his usual zeal";[5] neither are any estimates given of the total attendance at the very similar services in Westminster Abbey; on the basis of sitting space and the report of crowded gatherings, an estimate of 100,000 during the season would be modest.

The seasonal aggregate attendance at theatre services of the Shaftesbury United Committee appeared to be in excess of 250,000.[6] Likewise the Free Church theatre services held by Baptist, Congregationalist, Methodist and Presbyterian ministers in St. James's Hall, Piccadilly and the Britannia Theatre in the East End, attracted an aggregate of 250,000 each winter.[7]

Independently, services were begun in the Victoria Theatre, Waterloo, by Richard Weaver, and continued by William Carter. No less than 559 services were held in the first four winter seasons, with an aggregate of 865,100 people in attendance,[8] an average

---

[1] Hodder, E., *Life and Work of the Seventh Earl of Shaftesbury*, Vol. III, p. 3.
[2] *The Revival*, 7th January, 1860.   [3] Hodder, E., *loc. cit.*
[4] *The Revival*, 7th January, 1860.   [5] *The Freeman*, 4th January, 1860.
[6] *The Revival*, 27th July, 1861.   [7] Orr, J. Edwin, *op. cit.*, p. 99.   [8] *Ibid.*

seasonal aggregate of over 200,000 in a single theatre! Sunday
afternoon meetings for inquirers and converts were arranged, and
an observer reported more than 400 present, while the evening
meeting was "crammed to the roof." It is claimed that John
Pearce, who later founded the London chain of "J.P." Restaur-
ants, was converted in one of William Carter's meetings for the
"unwashed." In April 1862, the converts' meetings filled the
theatre, hundreds were turned away, and there were insufficient
workers to deal with the many penitents in the evening.

Yet another committee known as the Additional Theatre Services Committee commenced work in four theatres—the Maryle-
bone, Soho, Surrey, and City of London Theatres.[1] Usually
hundreds remained for prayer, inquiry or decision, among them
W. T. P. Wolston, afterwards the reputable Edinburgh physician.
No figures seem available, but it is not unreasonable to credit
these theatres with an aggregate attendance equal to the single
effort at the Victoria Theatre, 200,000 a season.

Services in the Garrick Theatre in Whitechapel were taken up
by the East London Special Services Committee, which arose
from a conference called together on 23rd January, 1861 by
Reginald Radcliffe in the Sussex Hall in Leadenhall Street to
discuss the need of the East End of London.[2] To some 200
Christians, Baptist Noel truly prophesied:

> If this work is done, we shall see some unknown Luthers and
> Whitefields excavated out of this dark mine, to spread the Gospel
> farther and wider than we have any idea. I believe we are on the eve
> of a greater work than England ever saw, and the East End of
> London is the right place to begin.

Out of this East End of London venture grew the Salvation
Army, a subject reserved for later treatment. No record of num-
bers reached by the East London Committee is available, at
Garrick or the City of London Theatres, or elsewhere.

In addition to all these organized, committee-controlled activities were "numberless special services in and around London."
On the basis of the known figures alone, it can be safely said that
a million aggregate of London's unchurched folk were reached
Sundays in theatre services.[3]

Nowhere in the stirring accounts of Revival in London was
there any evidence of prostration or hysteria. The work in London
seemed to have developed in a different way from that which
preceded it in Ulster, Wales or Scotland. The London Revival of
the early 1860s was one of preaching. All the evangelistic campaigns which were held throughout the metropolis in the Revival

---

[1] *Ibid.*   [2] *The Revival*, 2nd February, 1861.
[3] Cf. Orr, J. Edwin, *op. cit.*, p. 100.

years of the 1860s are too numerous to be chronicled. The results were manifold. In the Revival decade—prior to 1865—the Protestant churches of London added 200,000 seats to their total accommodation,[1] a 60 per cent increase which outstripped the fast-growing population of the metropolis by a small margin. In denominational reactions the impact of the 1859 Awakening on the life of London was felt in many ways and through many channels.

Bishop Handley Moule in later years recalled[2] his impressions of the rural Dorset revival in which both he and Evan Hopkins were converted:

> I must not close without a memory, however meagre, of one wonderful epoch in the parish. It was the Revival. The year was 1859, that "year of the right hand of the Most High" . . . Ulster was profoundly and lastingly moved and blessed. Here and there in England it was the same: and Fordington was one of the scenes of Divine Awakening. For surely it was Divine. No artificial means of excitement were dreamt of; my Father's whole genius was against it. No powerful personality, no Moody or Aitken, came to us. A city missionary and a London Bible-woman were the only helpers from a distance. But a power not of man brought souls to ask the old question: "What must I do to be saved?" Up and down the village the pastor, the pastoress and their faithful helpers, as they went on their daily rounds, found "the anxious". And the church was thronged to overflowing, and so was the spacious schoolroom, night by night throughout the whole week. The simplest means carried with them a heavenly power. The plain reading of a chapter often conveyed the call of God to men and women, and they "came to Jesus as they were."

The saintly Bishop affirmed that hundreds of people were awakened and continued in grace. A great social uplift followed. Shortly afterwards, Moule went up to Trinity College in Cambridge, where in 1867 he declared his faith.

Though instances of spontaneous Revival could be given in reports from all parts of Cornwall,[3] the most effective work developed through a visit of William and Catherine Booth from outside the county. The Revival movement began at Hayle in the middle of August. No actual conversions were noted on the first Sunday, so the evangelist used his opportunity on Monday to speak to believers. Nearly all present that evening stayed for prayer, and after a second message, a woman made her way to "the anxious seat," becoming in the hopes of the evangelist "the firstfruits of what I trust will be a glorious harvest."[4] Eighteen

---

[1] *The Nonconformist*, 15th November, 1865.
[2] Moule, H. C. G., *Memorials of a Vicarage*, pp. 48 ff.
[3] *Revival*, 21st April, 1861.   [4] *Ibid.*, 31st August, 1861.

months had passed and the convert in question had been followed by 7,000 others under the challenge of this evangelist and his ministering helpmeet.[1]

A survey of the Booth missions in Cornwall in 1861 and 1862 was given space in the *Wesleyan Times*, stressing the remarkable conversions of sinners, the awakening of slumbering churches, and the perseverance of the converts. It was said:[2]

> All the friends in every place unite in the delightful testimony that the results of the movement abide more generally than those of any other similar work in their past experience.

Yet this period of great fruitfulness in the lives of William and Catherine Booth is described as a "Wilderness" experience by General Booth's biographer, Harold Begbie.[3] William Booth was yet to do a greater work, but the period of these Cornish Revivals (1861–2) was one of profoundest import in the life of the founder of the Salvation Army.

How did Methodists show their appreciation of the Booths?[4] In June 1862, the Methodist New Connexion Conference at Dudley accepted Booth's resignation, disapproving his revivalism. Then the Primitive Methodist Conference at Sheffield aimed a blow at his calling in a resolution urging all its pastors "to avoid employing of revivalists, so-called." And the Wesleyan Conference in July at Camborne, in spite of their knowledge that the Booths had added 4,247 new members to Cornish Wesleyan churches, directed its superintendents not to sanction the use of their chapels for continuous services by outsiders. It is impossible to reject the opinion widely held in Cornwall that opposition to William Booth was caused by ministerial jealousy of a free-lance. Booth departed from Cornwall with the jeers of the incumbent Wesleyan President about "the perambulations of the male and female" ringing in his ears.

There were two phases of the Evangelical Awakening of 1859 in the middle belt of English counties, the first being the movement to prayer begun in summer 1859 and developed beyond all description after the second week of January in 1860, whereas the second was the evangelistic phase, sometimes following directly after the prayer movement but more often breaking out in the autumn of 1861 or later.

In the West Midlands the clergy of the great city of Birmingham convened a general prayer meeting late in 1859.[5] In early 1863 Dr. and Mrs. Palmer, with Methodist co-operation, began holding special services at noon-time and evening, a total of 133 inquirers

[1] Booth-Tucker, F., *op. cit.*, pp. 225 ff.   [2] *The Revival*, 12th March, 1863.
[3] Begbie, H., *The Life of William Booth*.   [4] Cf. Orr, J. Edwin, *op. cit.*, p. 116.
[5] *The Record*, 28th November, 1859.

recorded in the first six days.[1] The movement spread to all denominations and affected a number of neighbouring towns and villages. The pattern of the Awakening, prayer meetings and evangelistic services, was being repeated in the industrial heart of England.

The Palmers were followed in September 1863 by another pair who had been inspired by their joint ministry at Gateshead in 1859, none other than William and Catherine Booth, who enjoyed a successful time in the Moseley Street Chapel, 150 professed conversions recorded. The Booths were followed by their friend and patron, the Rev. James Caughey, who had deeply impressive meetings in Bath Street Chapel and the Alhambra Circus seating 3,000.[2] Thus it might be said that Birmingham was one of those English cities evangelized rather than revived by the Awakening.

In 1863, a religious Revival began in the Black Country, that intensely industrialized area to the north of Birmingham. Dr. and Mrs. Palmer, the lay evangelists, laboured for a month in Walsall, using the midday prayer meetings and evening preaching service technique.[3] As a result, 300 people made profession of conversion, including people as old as eighty years. Some converts requested prayer on behalf of their personal friends and had the joy of seeing them make decision too.

The Palmers' visit to Walsall (February 1863) was followed by that of the Booths, who laboured there until the summer.[4] One of William Booth's open-air meetings attracted about 5,000 people three-quarters of whom were men, and on these working men were turned loose a team of converted preachers, as Booth wrote, and revealed yet another factor in his future achievements:

> just of the stamp to grapple with this class, chiefly of their own order, talking to them in their own language, regarding themselves as illustrations of the power of the Gospel.

One had been a drunken, gambling, prize-fighting hooligan who had needed five or six policemen to take him to jail. Another had been a horse-racer, professional gambler and drunkard. Yet another was nicknamed "the Birmingham Rough," a wicked and abandoned character before his conversion. That evening the local chapel was crowded to hear Catherine Booth speak, and some forty decisions were recorded there. It is interesting to note that one of the converts of the Walsall Mission was a lad, Bramwell Booth, who (without parental urging) came under conviction and joined the penitents.[5]

---

[1] *The Revival*, 12th, 26th March, 1863.
[2] *Ibid.*, 8th October, 1863; cf. Smith, T. L., *Called Unto Holiness*, p. 23 (10,000 conversions in 1863).
[3] *Ibid.*, 5th March, 1863.   [4] *Ibid.*, 30th July, 1863.
[5] Booth-Tucker, F., *op. cit.*, p. 271.

In the autumn of 1863 William Booth was still labouring in the Black Country, and a letter to a friend described his experiences in Cradley Heath[1] (three miles from Dudley), population exceeding 20,000. The chapel was full on the first Sunday morning but too overcrowded for comfortable speaking or hearing at night. William Booth began by calling upon the leaders of the church to make a renewed consecration of themselves to God, so "a gracious melting and breaking up of heart followed, blessing a great number throughout the chapel." Conversions began to be declared in the days that followed.

William Booth's own account averred:

> At the commencement of the prayer meeting, a sturdy-looking man (who had been coming to the chapel every night but going away hardening his heart) jumped on to a form, and speaking out before all the people, said, "Do you know me?"
> The praying men answered, "Yes."
> "What am I then?" he said.
> They replied, "A backslider."
> "Well, then," said he, "I will be a backslider no longer; all of you come to Jesus with me"—and he fell in an agony of prayer for God to have mercy upon him; indeed the anguish and desire of his soul was too much for him, for he swooned away on the floor before us all. His wife was one of the first converted the previous week, and only that evening had sent up a request that God would save her husband, who was a poor miserable backslider. About thirty that night professed to obtain mercy.[2]

At Walsall,[3] William Booth's converts were announced to take part in the proceedings as the "Hallelujah Band." It was through their ministry that William Booth adopted as a lasting principle that the masses would be most effectively reached by their own kind. Indeed, a recent article written by an interested minister, the Rev. Joseph Pearce, claimed that the Walsall Revival Campaign had influenced William Booth much more than historians had admitted.[4]

William Booth was the guest of an ardent local-preacher, the drainage inspector of the New British Iron Company, Palmer by name. According to Mr. Pearce:[5]

> the Palmers had a spacious garden in which William Booth walked for hours in the deepest thought, with head on chest. This happened so frequently that one day Mr. Palmer had the temerity to say,
> "Excuse me, Mr. Booth, but I cannot help wondering what it is that engages your thoughts so frequently and protractedly as you pace the garden."

[1] *The Revival*, 5th November, 1863.   [2] *Ibid.*
[3] Sandall, R., *op. cit.*, Vol. I, pp. 16, 208.
[4] Cf. Orr, J. Edwin, *op. cit.*, pp. 138, 139.   [5] *Ibid.*

Mr. Booth, with face all a-shine, replied:

"My friend, I am thinking out a plan, which, when it is implemented, will mean blessing to the wide, wide world."

Not only was the industrial heart of Midland England moved by the Revival, but also the academic. The twin cultural capitals of England, the Universities of Oxford and Cambridge, were profoundly stirred by the prayer meeting movement. During the autumn of 1859 a Universities Prayer Union was begun, and an appeal was made for special prayer for Revival in Oxford and Cambridge.[1]

At that time Oxford University was anything but an evangelical stronghold. Wadham College was regarded as the evangelical college, and to Wadham came young Hay Aitken in 1861, fresh from a tour of evangelism in revived Scotland.[2]

Hay Aitken and his friend Freeman vowed to speak to every Wadham undergraduate about his spiritual welfare.[3] It seemed likely that both the ambitious evangelists extended their operations to the whole University:[4]

a sort of evangelical Revival among undergraduates had taken place, especially at Wadham, where W. Hay M. H. Aitken, afterwards the famous missioner, had been in residence.

Much the same sort of prayer meetings went on in Cambridge, where an observer reported:[5]

On Sunday evening I was in a prayer meeting at Cambridge, nothing but undergraduates crying to God for wholehearted consecration.

Into the Oxford prayer fellowships was thrust Francis James Chavasse, an aspiring Christian whose testimony against himself seems rather harsh: "proud, wilful, disobedient, selfish, black with sin, I need to be cleansed. . . ."[6]

Young Chavasse was confirmed in 1863, and grew in grace through his Oxford experience, attending prayer and evangelistic meetings. The "sort of evangelical Revival" in Oxford helped to shape his spiritual experience which made his life as Bishop of Liverpool what it was.

Into the Cambridge prayer fellowships was thrust Handley Carr Glyn Moule,[7] who succeeded Brooke Foss Westcott as Bishop of Durham in 1901. The Oxford and Cambridge meetings for prayer have continued until this day.

---

[1] *The Nonconformist*, 30th November, 1859.
[2] Wood, C. E., *Memoir and Letters of Canon Hay Aitken*, pp. 76 ff.
[3] Downer, A. C., *Century of Evangelical Religion in Oxford*, p. 58.
[4] Lancelot, J. B., *Francis James Chavasse*, p. 26.
[5] *The Revival*, 3rd March, 1863.   [6] Lancelot, J. B., *op. cit.*, p. 27.
[7] Harford, J. B., and Macdonald, F. C., *Handley Carr Glyn Moule*, p. 14.

CHAPTER XIX

AWAKENINGS FARTHER AFIELD

PROFESSOR GISLE JOHNSON WAS A WORN-OUT MAN BY THE
year 1860, but the mid-century revival in Norway continued
in strength[1] and received fresh vigour from an invasion of
Rosenius evangelists from Sweden. The two forces combined to
give Norway one of its most fruitful periods of growth.

In Sweden, the less stable leaders of revival "readers" faded
from sight and left Rosenius the undisputed director of the movement. News of the 1858 Awakening in America and the British
Revival added strength to Swedish Evangelicals. The National
Evangelical Foundation expanded. In 1858, Peter Paul Waldenström was converted. His public preaching commenced in Uppsala
in 1859, and within three years church pulpits had opened to him.
He rose to succeed Rosenius.[2]

Contacts with British and American leaders served to give
German Evangelical Christianity a new lease of life after the 1858–
59 Awakening. Theodor Christlieb served in a Lutheran Church
in London during the Awakening, and returned to Germany to
promote evangelism.[3] Robert Pearsall Smith, an erratic convert of
the 1858 Revival in the United States, visited Germany and
revived the circles of Pietists. Fervour was building up and broke
out in the days of Moody.[4]

Much the same relationship existed between the French-speaking Evangelicals and the Anglo-Saxons, there being an intimate
fellowship with Great Britain in particular.

It is noteworthy that the Anglican, Lutheran, Presbyterian and
Reformed Churches enjoyed a taken-for-granted fraternal fellowship during the eighteenth century. There were chaplaincies or
churches maintained by each in the other's own territory, but
only to serve its own members.

In the nineteenth century, however, Baptists and Methodists
began planting congregations of national adherents on the European Continent, to the outrage of the vested establishments.

Outstanding among Baptist pioneers in Europe was Johann

[1] Molland, E., *Church Life in Norway*, passim.
[2] Montgomery, M. W., *A Wind from the Holy Spirit in Sweden and Norway*, p. 58.
[3] Scharpff, P., *Geschichte der Evangelisation*, pp. 249 ff.   [4] *Ibid.*, pp. 239 ff.

Gerhard Oncken, born in Oldenburg in 1800.[1] He was converted in Britain and went to Hamburg in 1823 as a missionary of a British-founded mission, the Continental Society. Many were converted but the State Churches resisted. In 1834, Oncken sought believers' baptism, and became pastor of the first Baptist church which at last in 1858 was recognized officially by the Hamburg authorities. The steadily growing Baptist churches in Germany sent out missionaries to many other European countries, led by Oncken.

Methodists likewise began to preach in early decades of the nineteenth century in Germany—first English Wesleyan converts, then American Methodist Episcopal.[2]

Denmark was involved in political troubles at the mid-century, particularly involving Schleswig-Holstein and the rising nationalism of Germany, and in 1864, Prussia and Austria attacked, soon to defeat the Danes despite a spirited defence.

In 1865, Vilhelm Beck and Johannes Clausen engaged in ministry of revival and evangelism,[3] and enrolled their following in the Indremission. Meanwhile a religious awakening had begun on the isolated Danish island of Bornholm, far to the east in the Baltic. It was led by P. C. Trandberg, a powerful preacher of repentance and conversion, as was Beck. By 1863, Trandberg possessed an eager following of a thousand awakened believers.[4]

From Bornholm, closer to South Sweden than to Denmark, the Awakening spread to Copenhagen, through Zealand, Falster, Lolland and Jutland. In its outreach, the Awakening stirred up the strong opposition of High Churchmen, but it remained as the Luther Mission within the national Church.[5]

As in Sweden and Norway, at that time united under a single monarchy, the resurgence of the evangelical spirit created new movements within the predominant Lutheranism of the community, rather than creating new denominations outside. The Baptists and the Methodists entered all the Scandinavian countries through the conversion of individual nationals, but their total strength remained small, and the national life continued overwhelmingly Lutheran.

Baptist work in Scandinavia began with Oncken who founded two small congregations in the city of Copenhagen in 1840.[6] A Swedish sea captain was converted in a Methodist meeting in New Orleans in 1844 and in 1861 built the first Baptist church at

---

[1] Vedder, H. C., *Short History of the Baptists*. pp. 396 ff.
[2] Scharpff, P., *op. cit.*, pp. 131 ff.
[3] Andersen, J. O., *Survey of the History of the Church in Denmark*, pp. 60 ff.
[4] *Schaff-Herzog Encyclopedia*, on "Revivals."
[5] *Ibid.*   [6] Vedder, H. C., *op. cit.*, p. 405.

Göteborg. Captain Schroeder was preceded by Anders Wiberg, colleague of Rosenius, who had become a Baptist in 1852, becoming a colporteur of the American Baptist Publication Society in 1855.[1] In the 1860s, the Swedish Baptists extended their activities to Norway.[2] In all three kingdoms, they suffered persecution. At the same time, Finnish Baptist churches were begun.[3]

The Methodist denomination was planted also in Scandinavian countries and soon became truly indigenous.[4] Both Baptists and Methodists were wholly committed to the principles of evangelism demonstrated in the Awakenings.

Baptists and Methodists also entered French-speaking countries in the first half of the century but growth was doubled in the latter part. The McAll Mission to France was a spearhead of the evangelism of the mid-century Awakenings.[5]

The enterprising German Baptists entered the vast Russian Empire with an evangelical and evangelistic message.[6] Methodist influence was negligible. Not only was there revival in fullest measure in the 1860s in the Ukraine, but other movements of an evangelical type were affected and ultimately united with the Baptists.

The 1858 Awakening was extended to all six continents by the remarkable ministry of a very unusual Methodist, William Taylor, who proved to be one of the most versatile evangelists of all time, a follower of Wesley who made the world his parish in a way that few in history ever did.[7]

Taylor was born in Virginia in 1821, converted in 1841, and a year later began to work with the Baltimore Conference of the Methodist Episcopal Church. He served as an itinerant preacher until 1848. In 1849, Taylor followed the Gold Rush to California.[8] Lacking a church or a hall, he used a wooden box as a platform on the wharf at San Francisco, and soon gathered his congregation. Taylor became known up and down California as "the street preacher." He returned to Eastern States and Canada to engage in the aftermath of the 1858 Revival and a few years later heard a call to a world-wide ministry.[9]

In the 1860s, Taylor ministered in Australia and New Zealand, and then in South Africa.[10] This itineration he followed up with a visit to Britain. In the 1870s, he developed a remarkable ministry

[1] *Ibid.*, p. 401.   [2] Stiansen, P., *History of the Baptists in Norway*, pp. 140–144.
[3] Vedder, H. C., *op. cit.*, p. 404.
[4] Reid, J. M., *Missions and Missionary Society of the Methodist Episcopal Church*, Vol. II, pp. 204 ff.
[5] Vedder, H. C., *op. cit.*, p. 395.   [6] *Ibid.*, p. 406.
[7] Latourette, K. S., *A History of the Expansion of Christianity*, Vol. IV, p. 191.
[8] Taylor, W., *The Story of My Life*, 1895.
[9] *Ibid.*, pp. 73–75, 218–228.   [10] *Ibid.*, pp. 255 ff.

in Ceylon and India,[1] returned to United States to enlist missionaries, then toured Latin America.[2]

In the 1880s, the Methodist Episcopal Church appointed him
Bishop for Africa, where he set out to plant a chain of mission
stations across the width of equatorial Africa.[3] His energy until
his death was tremendous.

The effect of the 1858 Revival in America among the Indians is
seen in the happenings in Minnesota in the early 1860s.[4] Provoked
by the frauds practised on them, and led by medicine men, the
savage Sioux ravaged an area of about twenty thousand square
miles with torch and tomahawk, butchering six hundred people,
burning the mission and the homes of Christian Indians. The
revolt was suppressed by military force and scattered braves were
hunted down.

At Mankato, more than four hundred Indians were imprisoned
after thirty-eight of the worst offenders had been executed.
Williamson and Riggs of the American Board seized opportunity
to preach to the prisoners, teaching them also to read and write.
A deep work of grace began that winter among the braves, until
in the spring three hundred asked for baptism.[5]

At Fort Snelling, eighty miles away, families of the prisoners
camped in tents and tepees. A school was begun for them. When
Riggs came bringing letters from prisoners to families, he told of
the revival at the Mankato stockade. The camp was deeply moved,
and conviction stirred squaws to burn their idols.[6]

After four years, the prisoners and families were reunited in
Nebraska. By that time, four hundred church members constituted what they chose to call "the Pilgrim Church," and a work
of evangelism was extended round about.[7]

The period of the war between the States saw an increase of
Christian concern upon a larger scale than ever existed before in
United States.[8] Increased giving to Home Missions, to Bible and
Tract Societies, and to every charity was noted. In five years,
foreign missionary giving doubled although the war absorbed so
much energy.[9]

The 1858 Awakening carried over to the war between the
States, affecting both Federal and Confederate Armies. The War
Department in Washington appointed chaplains endorsed by the

[1] Taylor, W., *Four Years' Campaign in India*, *passim*.
[2] Taylor, W., *op. cit.*, p. 680.   [3] *Ibid.*, pp. 695 ff.
[4] Halliday, S. B., *The Church in America and Its Baptisms of Fire*, pp. 526 ff.
[5] *Ibid.*   [6] *Ibid.*   [7] *Ibid.*
[8] Beardsley, F. G., *A History of American Revivals*, pp. 240 ff.
[9] *Ibid.*

appropriate denominational authorities. William Warren Sweet has observed:[1]

> If the chaplain was an evangelical, a long stay in camp was likely to be improved by holding a revival meeting among the soldiers.

The records of the war are full of instances of such revival and evangelism in the theatre of war. In a New York regiment, an evangelistic campaign ran for thirty nights in succession in a tent furnished by the commanding general, and more than a hundred soldiers professed faith.[2] Supplementing the work of the chaplains was the United States Christian Commission, a part-ministerial, part-lay organization which served the troops by word of mouth and printed page, and by offering care and comfort.[3]

> We were taking a large number of wounded men down the Tennessee River after the battle of Pittsburg Landing. A number of young men of the Christian Commission were with me, and I told them that we must not let a man die on the boat that night without telling him of Christ and heaven . . . the cry of a wounded man is "Water! Water!" As we passed along from one to another giving them water, we told them of the water of life.'

The one reporting was D. L. Moody.[4] With the backing of the evangelistic Y.M.C.A. at home, he made frequent trips to the front to preach in the camps and minister on the battlefield. Nor did he forget the Confederate prisoners of war.

Religion in the armies of the Confederacy was even more conspicuous than among Union troops.[5] A major evangelical awakening occurred in the Army of Northern Virginia, supported by Baptist, Episcopalian, Methodist and Presbyterian clergy and ministers. A chaplain reported:[6]

> May 17, 1863, 10 a.m., I preached in the Presbyterian Church: house crowded with officers and soldiers; serious attention. At 3 p.m. I preached in Bates's brigade: a very good time, revival in the brigade. May 19, I preached in Johnson's brigade: thirty to forty mourners: glorious work in this command. May 20, I preached in General Polk's brigade: forty to fifty mourners; fifteen to twenty conversions. May 22, I spoke in General Riddle's brigade: a great work here; already more than one hundred conversions in this command.

Australia, of the order of the United States in size, possessed a very different type of colonial population.[7] By the time that emi-

[1] Sweet, W. W., *Story of Religion in America*, pp. 317 ff.
[2] *Ibid.*   [3] *Ibid.*
[4] Moody, W. R., *Life of Dwight L. Moody*, pp. 85–86.
[5] Bennett, W. W., *The Great Revival in the Southern Armies*, passim.
[6] Sweet, W. W., *op. cit.*, p. 318.
[7] Latourette, K. S., *op. cit.*, Vol. V, pp. 131 ff.

gration towards the Australian Colonies began, there was little or no persecution of dissenters for conscience's sake in Great Britain. Consequently, the bulk of the population possessed little or no motivation of a religious kind for emigrating. The Church of England predominated in numbers.[1]

The population of Australia in 1860 was about a million, occupying three million square miles. Consequently, there were but few big centres of population, Sydney and Melbourne competing in size. The news of the awakenings in Britain took time to reach Australia, and provoked prayer meetings for revival which was felt in measure.

In 1863, William Taylor of California reached Australia, and commenced evangelizing in the Methodist churches with considerable impact on other denominations.[2] Most of 1863 he gave to ministry in Victoria and Tasmania; 1864 to New South Wales and Queensland, with a side trip to New Zealand; and 1865 to South Australia. His evangelism was very fruitful, for more than six thousand converts were received by the circuits.[3]

The stirrings of the 1880s were reflected in Australia, British evangelists visiting the cities with enthusiastic new zeal. Australia produced its own evangelists, William George Taylor of the Central Hall in Sydney being prominent.[4]

In New Zealand, the 1860s were marked by bloody wars with the Maoris. Unlike their kin in Hawaii, the Maoris tended to develop native cults which combined Christianity and ancient notions.[5] In later decades, the Maoris adhered to the denominations introduced by the settlers, in particular to the Anglican.

Among white New Zealanders, the religious interest was much stronger than in Australia. In New Zealand, the largest city in South Island was founded by a colony of ardent Anglicans,[6] and the second largest by colonies of Scots Presbyterians.[7] In Anglicanism, the evangelical element was not inconsiderable; it was generally dominant in the Presbyterian Churches which derived ministers from evangelical sources. Methodism was also an evangelical constituency.[8]

The economy of New Zealand remained very dependent upon Great Britain, as also did its cultural and religious life. The revivals of the 1860s and 1880s were felt in turn in the country far to the south.

---

[1] *Ibid.*, p. 134.   [2] Taylor, W., *The Story of My Life*, pp. 255 ff.
[3] *Ibid.*   [4] Taylor, W. G., *The Life Story of an Australian Evangelist*, *passim*.
[5] Grace, T. S., *A Pioneer Missionary among the Maoris*, pp. 108 ff., pp. 134 ff.
[6] Harrop, A. J., *The Amazing Career of Edward Gibbon Wakefield*, pp. 150 ff.
[7] Ross, C. S., *The Story of the Otago Settlement*.
[8] Colwell, J., *A Century in the Pacific*, pp. 578 ff.

F

A far different condition prevailed in the other southern commonwealth, South Africa. Here the population was largely Dutch, followed by British settlers, confronting a continental mass of people of another colour and way of life. The deep piety of the Dutch settler set the standard for religious life in the sub-continent. In the nineteenth century, the Dutch ministry was strongly evangelical.

A conference of missionaries and ministers was held at Worcester, in the Cape Province of South Africa, during the month of April 1860, to hear first-hand reports of the Awakening in the United States and Great Britain.[1] It resulted in much prayer for revival in South Africa.[2]

At Pentecost that year, a revival movement commenced in quiet fashion without employment of any special agencies for rekindling the flame of spiritual life.[3] The revival became widespread, the most blessed awakening in South Africa.[4]

The minister of the Dutch Reformed Church in Worcester was the younger Andrew Murray, later renowned throughout the world as well as honoured in his own country. Shortly after the conference, a meeting of young people was held on church premises one Sunday evening. There a coloured girl asked is she might give out a hymn and offer prayer. While she was praying, those present "heard as it were a sound in the distance which came nearer and nearer, until the hall seemed to be shaken,"[5] whereupon the whole company began to pray both audibly and simultaneously. The minister was called.

Dominie Andrew Murray tried to silence the simultaneous prayer,[6] but had to give way to the strange phenomenon. The revival transformed life in the Worcester congregation and spread to towns and remote farms from the Cape to the Vaal. It moved the whole South African people.[7]

The movement made a lasting imprint upon the life of Andrew Murray.[8] Van der Lingen, a leader in the 1860 Revival, proposed to the Kerk that ten days between Ascension and Pentecost be thereafter devoted to prayer for revival and to evangelistic preaching.[9] The records of one hundred years demonstrate that these Pentecost services in the Dutch Reformed Churches have done more to evangelize the South African nation than any other agency.

[1] DuPlessis, J., *The Life of Andrew Murray*, .p. 195.
[2] *Die Kerkbode*, Capetown, August, 1859.
[3] DuPlessis, J., *op. cit.*, p. 193.   [4] *Ibid.*
[5] *Ibid.*, pp. 194-196, quoting Eerw. J. C. de Vries.   [6] *Ibid.*
[7] Retief, M. W., *Herlewings in ons Geskiedenis*, pp. 19 ff.
[8] Douglas, W., *Andrew Murray and His Message*.
[9] Retief, M. W., *op. cit.*, pp. 32 ff.

The English-speaking churches were likewise moved. About five years later, William Taylor of California arrived in Capetown and made his way around the coast to Durban, seldom staying more than a week in a place.[1] There was a revival in Grahamstown, King Williamstown, Queenstown, Port Elizabeth and Durban, affecting all classes of people, English-speaking and Dutch-speaking Europeans, Hottentots and Bantu. Seven thousand converts were placed in the care of the churches, of whom twelve hundred were Europeans.[2]

Baptists, Congregationalists, Presbyterians and others shared in the times of blessing, but the Anglican Communion was largely untouched by it, its bishop being an ardent Tractarian.[3] The Dutch Reformed and the Methodists, the people most stimulated by the Revival, continued to lead other denominations in growth. The Stellenbosch Seminary of the former, founded in 1859, tended to produce conservative and evangelical pastors.

In the Awakening of 1860, the manifestations of revival were confined more or less to people of European and mixed blood. But a decade later, shortly after the death of Moshesh, the king of the Basutos, a spiritual awakening began at the main station of the Paris Evangelical Missionary Society, spreading to almost all of Basutoland.[4]

The leaders of the Paris Evangelical Mission in Africa recognized that the work of French and Swiss Protestant Missions as a whole owed its being to the Haldanes and the evangelical forces they set in motion at the beginning of the century.[5] Coillard, an apostle to Southern Africa, himself was converted in a revival in the Jura in 1851.[6]

Many of the same factors played a part in the opening of the lower Congo to missionary work in the 1870s. Henry Richards witnessed a true movement of revival among his Bantu converts at Banza Manteke, described in records as the first "Pentecost on the Congo."[7]

But there were many missionaries who had seen the mighty power of God in revival in the homeland who waited in vain for the same in the land of their adoption and service. Theirs was the prospecting, the ploughing, the removal of obstacles, and sometimes the planting. Others who had not seen revival phenomena in the home land witnessed its advent on the mission field. Theirs

[1] Taylor, W., *Christian Adventures in South Africa*, pp. 522 ff.
[2] *Ibid.*, p. 527.
[3] Day, E. H., *Robert Gray, First Bishop of Cape Town, passim.*
[4] Thiessen, J. C., *Survey of World Missions*, p. 250.
[5] Mackintosh, C. W., *Coillard of the Zambesi*, pp. 3 ff.   [6] *Ibid.*
[7] Glover, R. H., *Progress of World Wide Missions*, p. 249.

was the satisfaction of knowing that such awakenings could occur among any people.

Bishop J. Wascom Pickett has produced an interesting study of *Christian Mass Movements in India*, many of which occurred at this time.

One may make a distinction between a mass movement into Christianity and an evangelical awakening. Sometimes, in such mass movements, there occurred the revival-typical outbreaks of prayer and confession of sin among the few. Christians, native or missionary. Other times there was simply a movement of an unprepared people seeking whatever Christianity had to offer.

South in Travancore, there was an ingathering of the Nadars in the 1860s, a startling movement.[1] About the same period, the Lutheran Mission at Chota Nagpur working among a primitive people enjoyed a mass movement, and by 1868 they had baptized ten thousand converts. In sixty years, their Christian community increased to nearly four hundred thousand people.[2]

There was a similar movement among the Chuhras in the Punjab that resulted in a revival among the lower castes and added multitudes to the churches in the 1870s.[3] Before 1860, there was an attempt to evangelize the Mazhabi Sikhs, a tribe of professional thieves. By 1881, these people were Christianized and transformed into useful citizenry.[4] In 1871, there arose a mass movement to Christianity among the caste of the Sweepers, and this added a quarter of a million to the churches. Other instances could be cited.

[1] Pickett, J. W., *Christian Mass Movements in India*, p. 42.
[2] *Ibid.*, pp. 45 ff.   [3] *Ibid.*, pp. 42 ff.   [4] *Ibid.*, pp. 51 ff.

CHAPTER XX

WORKING FORCES EXTENDED

THERE WERE THIRTY MILLION PEOPLE INHABITING THE United States of America in 1860. More than five million of this total were communicants of evangelical Protestant Churches, the aggressive Methodist and Baptist bodies claiming a total of three million members between them.

The historian, Bishop Warren C. Candler, has stated that fully a million people were converted in the American Revival of 1858.[1] Others have estimated between three hundred thousand and a million. The author has calculated the total accessions in the two-year period following the outbreak of revival as exceeding one million, a figure confirmed by 1855–65 statistics.[2]

The population of the United Kingdom at the same time exceeded twenty-seven million, of whom a third attended church services.

The Awakening beginning in Ulster in 1859 had affected all parts of Great Britain by 1865. There were a hundred thousand converts in the North of Ireland, a hundred thousand additions in Wales, three hundred thousand "impressed" in Scotland, and more than half a million converts in England, of whom 370,000 joined the Methodist, Baptist and Congregational Churches; more than a million were converted in the British Revival.[3]

Half-way through the nineteenth century, the Anglican Establishments of England, Wales and Ireland, with the Episcopalians in Scotland, the Colonies and the United States, comprised the largest of the Protestant denominations within the English-speaking world.

Most Anglican Churchmen in America[4] shared in the Awakening, as did those in Ireland[5] and in Wales;[6] Scottish Episcopalians of more traditional and less evangelical churchmanship were lukewarm towards it.[7] In England, some Bishops supported the movement, some were indifferent and some opposed.[8] Evangelical

---

[1] Candler, W. A., *Great Revivals and the Great Republic*, pp. 215–216.
[2] Orr, J. Edwin, *The Second Evangelical Awakening in America*, pp. 64–66.
[3] Orr, J. Edwin, *The Second Evangelical Awakening in Britain*, pp. 57, 77, 93, 201, 207.
[4] Orr, J. Edwin, *The Second Evangelical Awakening in America*, chapters i–vi.
[5] Orr, J. Edwin, *The Second Evangelical Awakening in Britain*, p. 184.
[6] *Ibid.*, p. 186.   [7] *Ibid.*, pp. 186–187.   [8] *Ibid.*, p. 186.

clergy co-operated with other Christians in the interdenominational prayer meetings and in evangelism. In certain dioceses, the revival meetings enjoyed episcopal blessing as well as divine favour, but in others only the divine favour.

The Tractarians were usually opposed to the Evangelical Revival,[1] the Evangelicals usually in favour. Indifferent Anglicans, unreached or unmoved or unhappy about a revival which seemed utterly alien to their easy-going religious way of life, reacted thus not because of convictions but because of the lack of them.

"I have always felt," recollected Eugene Stock[2] of the Church Missionary Society, "that if our clergy had more heartily welcomed the Revival, its effects within the Church of England would have been much greater."

The Baptists co-operated wholeheartedly in the 1858–59 Awakenings, in America, Ireland, Scotland, Wales and England.[3] Spurgeon built his Tabernacle on the crest of the Revival, and new Baptist churches rose everywhere to garner the increase, which numbered 300,000 baptisms.[4]

Likewise, the Congregationalists in America and Britain officially approved the Awakening and benefited greatly by it.[5] Less than 150,000 were added to the denomination, which possessed a numerical strength inferior to the Baptists.

The Methodists were the greatest gainers in the Awakening in America and Britain, 400,000 members being won in the respective periods of revival.[6] The most outstanding convert was Hugh Price Hughes. English Wesleyans limited their benefits by restrictive legislation on evangelists such as William Booth.

It is difficult to calculate Presbyterian gains, for in both Ulster and Scotland, membership in the church was considered a family affair, hence many converts were already known as members. It is possible that 400,000 converts continued in Presbyterian fellowship in America, Scotland, Ireland, England and Wales.[7]

The Lutherans of European stock in America showed a mixed reaction to the Awakening.[8] The Quakers[9] were deeply moved by it in Britain and America. The Christian Brethren gained converts[10] out of all proportion to their numbers.

The Awakenings in the Scandinavian countries, the Revival in Switzerland, France, Holland and Germany, added their quotas by the hundred thousands of converted men.

Most significant in the 1858–59 Awakenings was the rise of the

---

[1] *Ibid.*, pp. 187–188.   [2] Stock, E., *My Recollections*, pp. 82–83.
[3] Orr, J. Edwin, *op. cit.*, pp. 36, 190.
[4] *Ibid.*, pp. 190–191.   [5] *Ibid.*, pp. 36, 192.   [6] *Ibid.*, pp. 36, 193–198.
[7] *Ibid.*, pp. 36, 198–201.
[8] Wentz, A. R., *A Basic History of Lutheranism in America*, p. 92.
[9] Orr, J. Edwin, *op. cit.*, p. 203.   [10] *Ibid.*, p. 202.

laity to play a fuller part in the affairs of the churches. Bishop
Candler said:[1]

> The working forces of the churches were immeasurably increased.
> The revival of 1858 inaugurated in some sense the era of lay work in
> American Christianity. Wesley's system of class leaders, exhorters
> and local preachers had done much at an early date in the same
> direction but now the layman's day fully dawned on all the churches.
> No new doctrine was brought forward, but a new agency was
> brought to bear in spreading the old truth through the efforts of
> men who, if they could not interpret the scriptures with precision
> or train souls to perfection, could at least help inquiring sinners to
> find the Lord by relating how they themselves had found Him.

In both America and Britain, the organizers of the union prayer
meetings were business men, warmly supported by clergy who
were delighted to find the laymen willing. Another significant lay
development was the way in which meetings were provided by
Christian men for their associates in industry, the Services, the
colleges and the professions. G. E. Morgan commented:

> surveying the vast growth of Home Missions, the conviction gains
> force that the period following the Revival of 1859 was one of the
> most fruitful in the annals of Christianity in this country; and also
> that in these later days, when so many criticize and scepticize about
> Revival, it cannot be too strongly emphasized that the entire Home
> Mission Movement was not only inaugurated and manned, but
> financed by revival converts and sympathizers.[2]

As a natural corollary of the movement of the laity, the movement towards practical interdenominational unity developed rapidly.[3] Most lay movements are interdenominational, and most
revivals of religion also are interdenominational.[4] Further, in the
Awakening of 1858–59, the various denominations were so busy
trying to cater for an influx of new members that there was no
room for sectarian jealousy. With scarce an exception, the churches
were working together as one man. Arminian and Calvinist ignored their differences; Baptists and Paedobaptists were blessed
together, and everything was almost too good to be true. By
common consent, the doctrinal controversies were left alone, and
the idea worked well. At last the world was able to say without
irony, "Behold, how these Christians love one another!"

These factors held as true in Britain as in America, and their
influence was effective for a full generation.

The immediate outcome of the mid-nineteenth-century Awak-

[1] Candler, W. A., *op. cit.*, pp. 222–223.
[2] Morgan, G. E., *R. C. Morgan*, pp. 159–160.
[3] Orr, J. Edwin, *The Second Evangelical Awakening in Britain*, p. 223.
[4] Cf. Rouse and Neill, *A History of the Ecumenical Movement*, p. 253.

ening was the revival of many existing organizations and the creation of new ones. The Revival brought a flood of blessing down the old channels and broke through obstacles to form new rivers of Christian enterprise.[1]

The British and Foreign Bible Society had celebrated its jubilee in 1854. Five years later, the Awakening brought a host of helpers to the band of workers in the noble enterprise. Little credit is given by historians to the cause of the sudden expansion of the 1860s, but it is noted.[2]

The circulation of Scriptures among revived and converted multitudes in Ireland soared, and the Hibernian Bible Society became a contributor instead of a subsidiary of the parent society.[3] In 1861, the National Bible Society of Scotland was established.[4] The 1860s were years of expansion for the Welsh Bible auxiliaries.[5] Advances were made in every direction in England, and by 1863 "there was scarcely a city or town in England which had not its Bible-woman supported by local contributions.[6] At the same time, the circulation of the Scriptures at home and abroad exceeded two million, a 50 per cent gain over the Jubilee figures.

During the war between the States, the press of the American Bible Society was working at full pressure to keep up with the demand for Bibles, and these were supplied to both armies, while the financial responses increased in proportion.

The Open Air Mission, founded in 1853, gained strength in the 1860s through the ministry of the teams of evangelists under the direction of Gawin Kirkham.[7] Clergy of the Establishment[8] as well as ministers and laymen of other churches preached in the open air during the Revival, with crowds of twenty thousand reported in some places.

The Evangelization Society was founded by the supporters of the mid-century Awakening, and engaged in extensive evangelism throughout the length and breadth of Britain.[9] The City Missions entered into expanded evangelism in theatres, open-air meetings, slum visitation and the like.[10]

In 1860, William Pennefather, the son of an Irish nobleman, became the leader of a revival movement in Barnet. He opened a training home after the Fliedner model to prepare Church of England deaconesses whose ministry was soon greatly in demand in Evangelical parishes.[11] In 1864, Pennefather became vicar of

---

[1] Orr, J. Edwin, *op. cit.*, p. 208.   [2] *Ibid.*
[3] Canton, W., *History of the British and Foreign Bible Society*, Vol. III, p. 74.
[4] *Ibid.*, p. 75.   [5] *Ibid.*, p. 55.   [6] *Ibid.*, p. 16.
[7] Morgan, G. E., *op. cit.*, p. 159.
[8] Balleine, G. R., *History of the Evangelical Party in the Church of England*, p. 241.
[9] Morgan, G. E., *op. cit.*, p. 159.   [10] Orr, J. Edwin, *op. cit.*, p. 215.
[11] Balleine, G. R., *op. cit.*, p. 245.

St. Jude's in Mildmay, a North London suburb, and there he built a conference hall as a centre for home and foreign missions.

Hugh Price Hughes, the best-known convert of the Revival in Wales, founded the Sisterhood of the Methodist Church,[1] and with Collier and other pastor-evangelists he helped build the Central Hall movement which revitalized Methodism in the hearts of cities. Home Missions of the other denominations were likewise revived.

The most significant and the most fascinating home development of the 1858–59 Awakening was the birth of the Salvation Army.

The achievements of the husband-and-wife in shared evangelism, William and Catherine Booth, in the years of the Revival were notable.[2] Booth's experience in Cornwall taught him a connexion between holiness of Christian living and power in successful evangelism, for he preached one to achieve the other. His experience in the Black Country Awakening taught him that the masses could be most successfully reached by their own kind bearing witness. His frustration at the hands of unsympathetic denominational directors must have determined him to shape an organization of his own. He was an interdenominationalist, yet his Wesleyan convictions were strong; so his creation, the Salvation Army, became interdenominational in the support commanded from all sorts of Christians, yet denominational enough to be reckoned a convinced Arminian fellowship, more Wesleyan than the modern Methodists.

Prophetically, in the New Year of 1861, a conference was called in Sussex Hall, Leadenhall Street in the City of London to consider the appalling need of the slums of the East End.[3] The Hon. and Rev. Baptist Noël there predicted that some far-reaching work was about to begin, and so the East London Special Services Committee began its modest operation.

Six months later, William Booth visited London friends to seek employment in a Home Mission capacity, and was put into contact with leaders of the East London committee.[4] They invited him to become their evangelist, but four years of success in revival ministry elsewhere elapsed before Booth accepted their invitation. Into this opportunity for service, William Booth poured his passion for soul-winning and his experience of ministry in the Awakening. The committee became the Christian Revival Association; then the East London Christian Mission; then, as its

---

[1] *Minutes of the Methodist Conference*, 1903, pp. 128 ff.
[2] Orr, J. Edwin, *op. cit.*, pp. 215 ff.   [3] *Ibid.*, p. 100.
[4] Sandall, R., *History of the Salvation Army*, Vol. I, p. 22.

labours were extended, the Christian Mission, which was finally
renamed the Salvation Army.

The Salvation Army thus arose as a lasting extension of the
1858–59 Revival in its double ministry of evangelism and social
uplift. Many activities developed by Booth had already been
initiated by other workers of the Awakening—its evangelism,
indoor and outdoor, its mission to fallen women, to criminals, its
welfare work, and its missionary enterprise. While the Army bore
the indelible stamp of the personalities of William and Catherine
Booth, it was cast by them in the mould of the 1858–59 Revival.[1]

The Salvation Army entered the United States and soon
adapted itself to American conditions of urban life.[2] Its pioneers
entered country after country, becoming a world-wide movement
still committed to evangelism and social welfare.

The mid-nineteenth-century Awakening was primarily an urban
rather than a rural phenomenon. The English-speaking world was
fast becoming one of ever-enlarging cities, with huge concentra-
tions of population that for ever had left the influence of the rural
church behind.

It seemed that some new method was needed to reach the city
populations. While the United States was preoccupied with the
Civil War, the Revival in Britain produced a number of very
effective evangelists who achieved their greatest success, not in
rural Wales or Ulster or Scotland, but in industrial cities, particularly in England.[3]

Among these evangelists were Henry Grattan Guinness,
Brownlow North, Grant of Arndilly, Reginald Radcliffe, John
Hambledon and Gordon Forlong—all of them gentlemen. The
Awakening also produced working-men evangelists—Richard
Weaver, Duncan Matheson, James Turner and William Carter,
who likewise attracted the vast crowds. The ordained evangelists
were just as effective and numerous—Anglican, Presbyterian and
Free Church ministers.

Soon these British evangelists were crossing the Atlantic to
preach in the post-bellum United States. Men like Henry Moorhouse of Manchester made a profound impression upon D. L.
Moody in Chicago.[4] Moody, who had begun his evangelism in
the 1858 Revival there, was later to repay his debt to his highly
esteemed British colleagues.

With the Revival of 1858 came the successful introduction of
the Y.M.C.A. to American cities, and the flowering of the move-

---

[1] Orr, J. Edwin, *op. cit.*, p. 216.
[2] Sweet, W. W., *The Story of Religion in America*, pp. 374–375.
[3] Orr, J. Edwin, *op. cit.*, pp. 231 ff.   [4] *Ibid.*, p. 160.

ment in the United States.[1] The influx of converted young men into Christian churches found an excellent outlet in the evangelistic activities of the early Christian associations of young men.

From the beginning of the Revival in Britain, the Y.M.C.A. not only shared in the ingathering, but often sponsored the meetings which brought Christians together for united prayer and united evangelism. A conference of provincial and city Y.M.C.A. delegates met in London at the start of the Revival, and reiterated an early principle of the Y.M.C.A., binding it on all branches—a decided and authenticated conversion to God as the requirement for membership.[2] From that time forward, the Y.M.C.A. increased with the mid-century Awakening.

The lasting effect of the 1858–59 Revivals on the Y.M.C.A. is scarcely mentioned in standard histories of the subject. The year 1864, indeed, is officially recognized as "the turning point of the Y.M.C.A.," "the beginning of certain success."[3] The 1864 Edinburgh Conference of the Y.M.C.A. laid the foundations of the movement with its liberal provision for the all-round requirements of young men. The revived youth leaders of the Awakening of the 1860s had an excellent balance of spiritual and social aims and programmes.

The mid-nineteenth-century Revival brought expression to a concern for the evangelization of children, as distinct from their general welfare.

Edward Payson Hammond was born in 1831 in Connecticut,[4] converted about 1848, labouring in the 1858 Revival in America before proceeding to Edinburgh to study theology. In 1860, he was asked to preach in Musselburgh. Having left his greatcoat in the vestry, he proceeded there but found it locked. A very tiny girl opened it, and faltered that "a wheen o' us lassies" were praying. Hammond overheard a tiny tot offer so moving a prayer that tears spring to his eyes. His ideas were revolutionized. He became the children's evangelist.[5] Not long after, Spurgeon filled his Tabernacle with 8,000 children to hear Payson Hammond. Seventeen years later, Hammond returned to find a number of those child converts serving as Spurgeon's officers and workers.

Payson Hammond's lasting contribution to the religious life of the United States and the British countries was his insistent emphasis upon child conversion. Hammond used what were then considered novel methods to interest juveniles and stirred T. B.

---

[1] Sweet, W. W., *Revivalism in America*, p. 160.
[2] *The Revival*, 6th August, 1859.
[3] Hodder-Williams, *Life of Sir George Williams*, pp. 187, 203.
[4] Headley, P. C., *E. Payson Hammond: the Reaper and the Harvest*, *passim*.
[5] Orr, J. Edwin, *op. cit.*, p. 232.

Bishop and Josiah Spiers with the idea of child evangelism.[1] As a result of their application of his principles to their problems came the foundation of the C.S.S.M. (Children's Special Service Mission), an evangelistic agency whose influence in British life increased.

[1] *Ibid.*, p. 212.

CHAPTER XXI

POST-REVIVAL MISSIONS, I

THE MISSIONARY ZEAL CREATED BY THE REVIVALS AT THE beginning of the nineteenth century was denominational in its organization, although the denominations often worked together for a more successful prosecution of their objectives.

In the next generation, there was a reaction against the evangelical ecumenism of the Revival fellowship, leading to a resurgence of denominational exclusivism, in Tractarianism among the Anglicans, Confessionalism among the Lutherans and even Landmarkism among the Baptists in the regions of their great numerical strength. This exclusivism weakened the co-operation of various denominational societies, not so much by lack of co-operation on the mission field by missionaries, but by pressures from the home constituencies.

The great world-wide movement of the mid-nineteenth century brought a tremendous expansion of the operations of the existing societies, but it also brought into being a new type of foreign missionary endeavour, the interdenominational and non-denominational "faith" mission. In the Bible Societies and in specialized organizations, true interdenominationalism already existed, but it was confined to organizations with very limited objectives, never the founding of churches.

Every Revival of religion in the homelands is felt within a decade on the foreign mission fields. The records of missionary enterprise and pages of missionary biography following 1860 are full of the clearest evidence of the stimulating effect of the Revival throughout the world.[1]

Dr. Henry Grattan Guinness, one of the outstanding preachers of the 1859 Revival in the British Isles, carried his evangelistic passion from the Revival into foreign missionary work.[2] Founding a college in London for the training of missionaries, he systematically surveyed the neediest areas of the world, his work giving rise to the Regions Beyond Missionary Union with missions upon many continents.[3] Dr. Guinness's daughter, Geraldine,

---

[1] This volume was compiled before the appearance of Bishop Stephen C. Neill's scholarly and readable *History of Christian Missions*, which stresses many of the same points.

[2] Orr, J. Edwin, *The Second Evangelical Awakening in Britain*, p. 233.

[3] Latourette, K. S., *A History of the Expansion of Christianity*, Vol. V, pp. 111, 423.

married Howard Taylor of the China Inland Mission and became Dr. Hudson Taylor's biographer; Whitefield Guinness, his son, went to China also and built up the work of the China Inland Mission in Honan; his daughter, Lucy, married Karl Kumm, the founder of the Sudan United Mission.[1] In the third generation, many of Grattan Guinness's descendants were active in Christian work at home and abroad. Harry Guinness succeeded his father as principal of Harley College. Dr. Henry Grattan Guinness in his day not only won thousands of converts in the 1859 Revival but trained more than 1,300 eager volunteers for missionary service under thirty denominations in forty missionary societies![2]

The directors of the existing missions were challenged by the potentialities of the Awakening. A personal letter written by the unemotional and shrewd Church Missionary Society leader, Henry Venn, revealed his reaction to the Revival:[3]

> Yet I am so confident that we must either rise on the wave or be overwhelmed by it, that I shall propose on Monday to send a deputation to Ireland to the revival region to visit the great towns, and to obtain the prayers, sympathy, and hearts and hands, if possible, of some of the awakened servants of God. I am anxious thus to connect the Revival with missionary zeal for the sake of the Revivalists themselves as well as for our cause.

In 1860, the friends of the Revival convened at Liverpool a Conference on Missions.[4] Andrew Somerville, the Foreign Missions Secretary of the United Presbyterian Church in Scotland, told how the Revival was already making itself felt on foreign mission fields, and he declared that every recent letter he had received from foreign missionaries thanked God for the increase of intercession at home, and expected an increase of effectiveness abroad.[5] Arthur Tidman, Foreign Secretary of the far-ranging London Missionary Society, was quick to recognize another blessed benefit to missions, evident in the Awakenings. He related the spirit of Revival to the spirit of Christian unity:[6]

> They had heard of those blessed outpourings in America, in Sweden, in Ireland, in Scotland, in various parts of the metropolis, and other places . . . they had come together, knowing that God would bless them and be with them from day to day. . . . Let all differences be forgotten: let them not remember that they were Churchmen or Dissenters, Baptists or Wesleyans, Presbyterians or Episcopalians.

Lord Shaftesbury, chairman of a great public conference meeting in Liverpool's Philharmonic Hall, struck the same happy note,

---

[1] Morgan, G. E., *R. C. Morgan*, p. 130 n.   [2] *The Christian*, 7th July, 1910.
[3] Stock, E., *History of the Church Missionary Society*, Vol. II, pp. 32 ff.
[4] *Conference on Missions Held at Liverpool, 1860.*
[5] *Ibid.*, p. 52.   [6] *Ibid.*, p. 14.

claiming that "this union of all evangelical and orthodox denominations is a great sign of the times," greeting delegates and representatives as an "Ecumenical Council."[1] How prophetic were his remarks can be seen in the development of the Ecumenical Missionary Movement. Preceded by both trial conferences arranged by Dr. Alexander Duff in New York and in London in 1854,[2] the historic Liverpool Conference passed its responsibility to the Mildmay Conference of 1878,[3] followed by the London Conference of 1888,[4] crowned by the Ecumenical Missionary Conference in New York in 1900.[5] Thus the Revival of 1859 helped to lay the foundations of the modern international and interdenominational missionary structure.

The initiative for co-operation was evangelical impulse; the basis likewise was evangelical and the objectives were evangelistic.

The Awakening of 1858 occurred just before the outbreak of the war between the States which was fought over the issues of states' rights, but which deeply involved the institution of slavery. How did the Revival and the Emancipation affect the evangelization of the Negro?

At the beginning of the nineteenth century, a million Negroes inhabited the United States,[6] and about 70,000 were members of Christian bodies.[7] In 1860, there were four and a half million Negro people in the country, and of these half a million were members of churches.[8] The percentage of Negro and white population in church membership was the same in 1800, but in 1860 the percentage of Negroes was only half that of the whites.[9]

The startling changes in the status of Negroes after Emancipation was one for which neither they nor their white neighbours were prepared. Emancipation found the Negroes uneducated and untrained to fend for themselves, the Southern whites impoverished, inhibited and uncertain of the future. What followed was one of the great achievements of the Christian faith. Numerical gains of Protestant Christianity among American Negroes, 1815–1914, equalled the total made in all of Africa and Asia in the same period.[10] Never had a large body of depressed people made such gains in civilization in so few decades of opportunity, and it was

---

[1] *Ibid.*, p. 321.   [2] *Ibid.*, p. 374.
[3] *Proceedings of the General Conference on Foreign Missions, Mildmay Park, London, 1878.*
[4] *Centenary Conference on the Protestant Missions of the World, London,* 1888.
[5] *Ecumenical Missionary Conference, New York,* 1900.
[6] Negro population figures based on U.S. Census, *1800.*
[7] Church membership figures based on Latourette, *op. cit.,* Vol. IV, p. 341.
[8] *Ibid.*   [9] *Yearbook of the American Churches,* New York, 1933.
[10] Latourette, K. S., *op. cit.,* Vol. IV, p. 327.

the Christian message given to Negroes by Negroes that contributed most.[1]

Following Emancipation, the Negroes of their own volition tended to withdraw from the white churches into their own denominations.[2] Those in Methodist membership separated themselves into Negro Methodist denominations or conferences. Baptist churches rapidly arose, forming their own associations and conventions. From then on, the various Baptist churches took the lead until they claimed two-thirds of all Negro adherents. In fifty years, Negro church membership grew to four and a half million, to 22 per cent of the population of Negroes, a fourfold increase.[3]

Evangelism among Negroes was left to Negro preachers, but in education the white churches helped.[4] The main source of help came from an organization, the American Missionary Association, whose membership was open to all who supported "evangelical sentiments" and opposed slavery and other immoralities.[5]

Not only primary schools, but high schools and colleges were founded by Christians for the Negroes.[6] Then the Negroes themselves began to provide their own. Their outstanding educator after Emancipation was Booker T. Washington.[7]

Negro Christianity was an evangelical type. The Negroes adopted the "protracted meetings" of the revival movements, and added emotional fervour that surpassed their neighbours. Their support of missions to Negroes overseas was insignificant, perhaps because of poverty.[8]

The impact of the 1858–59 Revival was felt immediately in the British West Indies, among the emancipated slaves and their children. A spiritual decline had followed the first wave of blessing following Emancipation.

In 1859, a remarkable evangelical awakening began in a Moravian church and spread through the chapels of the island of Jamaica.[9] Beginning in the south, it moved Christian congregations throughout the island, in the central parishes, on the north and south coasts, from Spanish Town to Savanna-la-Mar, from Montego Bay to Ann's Bay.

Chapels became once more crowded. There was a widespread conviction of sin. Crime diminished. Ethical standards were raised. There was renewed generosity. Old superstitions which had reasserted themselves once more declined in power. As the movement spread, unhealthy excitement and religious hysteria showed them-

[1] *Ibid.*, p. 352.   [2] *Ibid.*
[3] U.S. Bureau of the Census, *Religious Bodies*, 1916.
[4] Latourette, K. S., *op. cit.*, Vol. IV, p. 356.
[5] Constitution, American Missionary Association, *Annual Report, 1865.*
[6] *Annual Report, 1865.*   [7] Washington, Booker T., *Up from Slavery.*
[8] Latourette, K. S., *op. cit.*, p. 364.
[9] Hamilton, J. T., *History of the Moravian Church*, p. 457.

selves in places, but the testimony of almost all observers, of whatever denomination, was that the Revival (a real blessing from God) did permanent good.[1]

The unhealthy excitement and religious hysteria cited by Dr. Ernest A. Payne were understandable in a population of recently liberated slaves. But so great was the improvement in Jamaica that the London Missionary Society in 1867 decided to withdraw from the field which it had come to regard as an evangelized country.[2]

The London Missionary Society withdrew from other West Indian islands. In the island of Trinidad, the Revival of 1859 rekindled the zeal of Negro Christians descended from the rebel slaves who were removed from the Carolinas by the British in the War of 1812.[3] In the following decade the churches began their missionary work among the East Indians working in the Trinidad estates, and East Indian churches were formed.[4]

European–African contact was greatest in the South African colonies. Dutch Reformed Church missions to non-Europeans had begun in 1826, but this outreach remained feeble until the 1860 Revival swept the Afrikaner churches, which at once increased their missionary concern.

The Methodists proved to be most aggressive in their missionary endeavours to reach Bantu peoples. The stirring 1860 Revival culminating in the mission of William Taylor in 1866 moved the European churches to evangelize the Bantu.[5]

Christina Forsyth, a convert of the Revival in Scotland, pioneered in Fingoland.[6] To Africa in 1861 came James Stewart, first a companion of Livingstone on the Zambesi, then explorer of the highlands of Nyasaland where Presbyterians in later years built a great mission, then back to the Lovedale Institution to become principal.[7]

Anglican missions to the Bantu arose from a plan made by Bishop Gray to appoint bishops and employ Anglo-Catholic orders to staff missions.[8] The controversial liberal Bishop Colenso left a successful Zulu Mission, continuing evangelical.[9]

Before and after the Revival, Livingstone was turning the light

[1] Payne, E. A. *Freedom in Jamaica*, pp. 88 ff.
[2] Lovett, R., *History of the London Missionary Society*, Vol. II, pp. 381 ff.
[3] The author visited in 1951 several Trinidadian Negro Baptist churches still using the quasi-military designations of the war of 1812 and the noisy worship of their Old South homes.
[4] *Canadian Presbyterian Mission to East Indians in Trinidad, passim.*
[5] Taylor, W., *Christian Adventures in South Africa*, pp. 522 ff.
[6] Livingstone, W. P., *Christina Forsyth of Fingoland.*
[7] Wells, J., *The Life of James Stewart, passim.*
[8] Pascoe, C. F., *Two Hundred Years of the S.P.G.*, p. 306.
[9] Hinchliff, P. B., *John William Colenso*, London, 1964.

of exploration and evangelization on the Continent of Africa. A lad who (during the Revival) heard him speak, decided to follow in his footsteps—F. S. Arnot, a true pioneer, accomplished a great work as a Brethren missionary,[1] making nine long pioneering journeys in Africa in thirty years or so of work before his death in 1914. He led out to Africa yet another pioneering missionary, Dan Crawford of "the long grass."[2] In 1858, the Universities' Mission to Central Africa was founded, following Livingstone's visit to the Cambridge colleges. It is now united with the S.P.G.

Missionaries began to move northwards, into the Rhodesias, Angola and the Congo. The cause in the Congo was aided greatly by the arrival of George Grenfell, a Baptist pioneer and mission director whose "earliest religious impressions of a serious kind date back to the early 'sixties, when the great wave of awakening that followed the Revival of 1859 was passing over the country."[3]

The 1859 Revival leader, H. Grattan Guinness, launched a work in the Congo in the 1870s, later transferred to the American Baptists.[4] Guinness in the 1880s sent out another mission, the Congo Balolo work.[5] The Swedish Mission Covenant, a product of the Revival in Sweden, commenced its Congo operations in the 1880s also.[6]

The death of Livingstone (1873) renewed the interest of many Christians in middle Africa in the 1870s. The Church Missionary Society entered Uganda in 1877.[7] Their great pioneer, Alexander Mackay, was a convert of the Revival.[8] Hannington, their first Anglican bishop, was murdered in 1885 on orders of Mwanga, the Baganda king, instituting a severe persecution of Christians.[9] Under a third bishop, Alfred R. Tucker, the Church Missionary Society made rapid gains, increasing in less than twenty years from two hundred to sixty thousand.[10] Other Protestant missions to neighbouring people were aided by Baganda converts.

In the Cameroons, a Baptist mission begun in 1848, extended by George Grenfell, was transferred to the Basel Mission when the Germans raised their flag in 1887.[11] A mass movement of the Bantu towards Christianity followed, in a quarter of a century building a church membership of fifteen thousand. In the 1880s, American Presbyterians expanded into the Cameroons.

[1] Baker, E., *Life and Explorations of F. S. Arnot.*
[2] Crawford, D., *Thinking Black.*
[3] Hawker, G., *The Life of George Grenfell, passim.*
[4] Guinness, Mrs. H. G., *The New World of Central Africa*, pp. 175 ff.
[5] *Ibid.*, pp. 461 ff.   [6] Lundahl, J. E., *Nils Westlind, passim.*
[7] Stock, E., *op. cit.*, Vol. III, pp. 95 ff.   [8] Mackay, *Mackay of Uganda*, p. 7.
[9] Stock, E., *op. cit.*, Vol. III, pp. 410 ff.
[10] Tucker, A. R., *Eighteen Years in Uganda and East Africa*, Vol. II, p. 359.
[11] Steiner, P., *Kamerun als Kolonie und Missionsfeld.*

The West African pioneer, Mary Slessor of Calabar, converted in Dundee during the Revival of the 1860s, joined the United Presbyterians in Nigerian work (founded in the 1840s), proving one of the most remarkable missionaries in Africa.[1]

In 1867, Samuel Adjai Crowther, a rescued slave educated in England, was consecrated as Anglican Bishop of the Niger territories, and a rapid spread of evangelical faith followed.[2]

There is no doubt that the nineteenth century Revivals opened up many countries of Africa to the gospel, the first providing societies and men, the second adding to them.

What then were the effects of the expansion of Evangelical Christianity throughout Africa in the latter part of the nineteenth century?

Missionaries reduced the languages of the natives to writing, prepared translations of the Scriptures, taught the people to read and write, opened schools for the young, established hospitals for the sick, introduced arts and crafts, and built up Christian communities.

Missionaries hastened the disintegration of native cultures. Polygamy was discouraged by most, marriage purchase by many, and initiation rites at puberty were discountenanced as being breeders of immorality. Missionaries struggled against murder and ritual killing and opposed the witch doctors. They undermined ancestor worship and animism.

Missionaries fought the exploitation of the Africans by the Europeans, and adamantly opposed slavery and the slave traffic, evangelicals being leaders in the opposition. They also encouraged their native charges to become self-reliant, in this way preparing for self-government to come. The governments of Roman Catholic background sometimes regarded Protestant missions as the breeding ground of democratic dissatisfaction.

[1] Livingstone, W. P., *Mary Slessor of Calabar*.
[2] Page, J., *The Black Bishop, Samuel Adjai Crowther*.

CHAPTER XXII

POST-REVIVAL MISSIONS, II

IN LATIN AMERICA, FOLLOWING THE REVOLUTIONS WHICH brought independence to many countries, the influence of the Roman Catholic Church in affairs political and spiritual declined. Bishops too often were foreigners; clergy were of poor quality; the "faithful" were often superstitious and ignorant. Alien philosophies increased.[1] The Catholicism encountered by Protestant visitors seemed to them to be not far removed from the aboriginal paganism. The failure of Catholicism (since acknowledged by Roman observers) called for an invasion by a revived Evangelicalism.

The Revival of 1858–59 onwards provided the enterprise and the volunteers for the invasion of the vast southern continent and its neighbours in the Caribbean. The High Church's parties were in favour still of respecting Rome's prior claim.[2]

In 1862, an Anglican Evangelical, W. H. Stirling, became the superintendent of the South American Missionary Society, and seven years later was consecrated Bishop of the Falkland Islands nearby.[3] Charles Darwin was greatly impressed with the success of the mission's labours among savages in Tierra del Fuego, whom he had declared to be hopelessly degraded, and he became a financial contributor to the work.[4]

Immigration opened the doors of the southern republics of South America. British colonists in Argentina were followed by chaplains.[5] Americans from the vanquished Confederacy emigrated to Brazil and were followed by Baptist, Methodist and Presbyterian ministers. German settlers in southern Brazil were followed by Lutheran clergy.[6] There were other Protestant immigrants.

In Chile, in 1855, a chaplain opened a church for American and British residents of Valparaiso.[7] In the 1860s, a liberal government

[1] Mackay, J. A., *The Other Spanish Christ*, pp. 167 ff.

[2] The World Missionary Conference at Edinburgh ignored Latin America as a mission field because of Anglo-Catholic insistence that the area was being cared for by the Roman Catholic Church.

[3] Macdonald, F. C., *Bishop Stirling of the Falklands.*   [4] *Ibid.*, pp. 68–70.

[5] Every, E. F., *Twenty-Five Years in South America*, p. 81.

[6] Braga and Grubb, *The Republic of Brazil*, pp. 50 ff., pp. 59 ff.

[7] Browning, Ritchie and Grubb, *West Coast Republics of South America*, pp. 27 ff.

came to power and the constitution was interpreted to sanction Protestant evangelism. In that decade, Spanish-speaking churches were organized in Valparaiso and Santiago. Italian Waldensians emigrated to Uruguay and Argentina and maintained churches.[1] The South American Missionary Society in the 1860s sent a chaplain to Callao, the port of Lima in Peru and began a Protestant work which was extended by a Bible Society agent, Penzotti, who suffered imprisonment on priestly instigation.[2]

William Taylor, who had been a Methodist evangelist in California during the Gold Rush, developed after the 1858 Revival a missionary burden for the world. In 1877, he began a tour of Latin America which focused the attention of the Methodist Episcopal Church upon the lands to their south.[3] Taylor developed a plan for self-supporting missions, and helped plant churches in several republics.

A Scottish physician, Robert Reid Kalley, who had shared in the movement among Madeirans, developed the interest in Brazil, where churches of Congregational organization were springing up after 1858.[4] The first missionary of Presbyterian affiliation arrived in Brazil in 1859, a presbytery being organized as early as 1865.[5] In 1867, the Methodists sent a pastor to Brazil, followed by Portuguese-speaking missionaries.[6] In 1879, the Southern Baptists supplied a pastor, followed by missionaries to the Brazilians.[7] From such small beginnings made after the 1858 Revival came the vast missionary enterprise which made Brazil the fastest-growing evangelical field in the world.[8]

It was not until the Revival of 1858 sent its impulses through the churches of United States that evangelical missions began to flourish in Mexico. The first Protestant communion was celebrated there in 1859. In 1860, the American Bible Society sent an agent to Mexico. He was followed by James Hickey, an Irish convert who gathered a congregation in Monterey.[9] Melinda Rankin, founder of a school for Mexicans on the Texas side of the border, moved to Monterey in 1865.[10] The Presbyterians, Baptists

---

[1] Mackay, J. A., *op. cit.*, p. 234.
[2] Browning, Ritchie and Grubb, *op. cit.*, pp. 79 ff.
[3] Taylor, W., *The Story of My Life*, p. 680.
[4] Braga and Grubb, *op. cit.*, pp. 54 ff.
[5] Gammon, S. R., *The Evangelical Invasion of Brazil*, pp. 111 ff.
[6] Braga and Grubb, *op. cit.*, pp. 61 ff.   [7] *Ibid.*, pp. 63 ff.
[8] The Presbyterian Churches of Brazil, in association with the Presbyterian Churches in the United States of America, in 1952 invited the author to help prepare a way for the celebration of the centenary of the arrival of the first evangelical missionaries. A result of the campaign, sponsored by Baptists, Congregationalists, Lutherans, Methodists and Presbyterians and other denominations, was a general awakening throughout Brazil in 1952—*vide* Bretones, Lauro, *Redemoinhos do Sul, A Year of Revival in Brazil with Dr. Edwin Orr*, or Appasamy, A. J., *Write the Vision! Edwin Orr's Thirty Years of Adventurous Service*. (ED.)
[9] Rankin, M., *Twenty Years among the Mexicans*, pp. 88 ff.   [10] *Ibid.*, pp. 120 ff.

and Methodists entered Mexico in the 1870s. These Protestant missionaries met with a fierce opposition from Roman priests. Converts were won from among the mestizo masses rather than the upper class Spanish élite or low-class Indian peasants.

The revived British churches found openings in Madagascar when the death of the persecuting Rànavàlona I relieved a secretly growing church of its worst sufferings. William Ellis brought a contingent of the London Missionary Society and a vigorous evangelistic-educational programme to the aid of the Christians in the 1860s.[1]

The Church Missionary Society entered the island of Madagascar in 1864[2] at the same time as the Society for the Propagation of the Gospel, of Anglo-Catholic conviction. Ten years later, the C.M.S. withdrew when the S.P.G. brought out a bishop consecrated by the Scottish Episcopal Church but opposed by the non-Anglican groups.[3]

In 1866, the Norwegian Missionary Society, a fellowship born of Revival in Norway, sent out a team of missionaries to labour in co-operation with the L.M.S. They concentrated effort on the Betsileo people.[4] Other Lutheran societies from the United States came to share responsibility.

From 1861 onward, the evangelical increase continued. In 1870, the L.M.S. alone had more than 260 churches, twenty thousand members and one hundred and thirty thousand adherents. By 1880, there were more than a thousand churches, seventy thousand members and two hundred and twenty-five thousand adherents.[5] Dispensaries and clinics were opened, and Malagasy given medical training. Schools were maintained in nearly every church building, and a teachers' college set up.

In Indonesia, the greatest growth of Christian churches occurred in the "Great East" cluster of islands, in mass movements[6] on Celebes, Ceram, Amboina, and other communities where native Christians began aggressive missionary work in nearby islands and extended the limits of the faith.[7] In Muslim Java, there were fewer converts.

In 1861, the Rhenish Missionary Society began work in Sumatra, where American missionaries had earlier been killed and

---

[1] Ellis, W., *The Martyr Church of Madagascar*, pp. 373 ff.
[2] Stock, E., *The History of the Church Missionary Society*, Vol. II, pp. 473 ff.
[3] *Ibid.*, pp. 478 ff.
[4] Burgess, A., *Zanahary in South Madagascar*, p. 132.
[5] Lovett, R., *The History of the London Missionary Society*, Vol. I, pp. 744 ff.
[6] Like Joseph Carel Kam, two other leaders in these awakenings, Riedel and Schwartz, were products of the post-Napoleonic Revival and graduates of Pfarrer Janicke's Berlin School.
[7] Rauws, J., *The Netherlands Indies*, pp. 53-54.

eaten. Under the keen leadership of Ludwig Nommensen,[1] the mission to the Bataks was eminently successful, a Christian community of 160,000 being gathered in fifty years.

In Inverary, in the highlands of Scotland, during the Revival of 1859, a high-spirited, unconverted lad attempted to disrupt a meeting led by two Irish laymen from the Ulster Revival. James Chalmers came under an intense conviction of sin, being brought in from the streets in the middle of the night.[2] He was trained for active service in the Glasgow City Mission and proceeded to the South Seas. Chalmers arrived in Raratonga in 1867 and spent ten years among the Christians there.

In 1871, the London Missionary Society began its work in New Guinea, a huge island difficult to penetrate. Missionaries and nationals from other Pacific islands made the initial landings, and in 1877 Chalmers joined them, soon becoming one of the greatest pioneers of the Pacific area. In 1901, he was martyred.[3]

In the 1880s, the north-east portion of the New Guinea territory came under German control and German missionaries entered.[4] In 1890, the L.M.S. divided the south-east portion with the Anglicans and Methodists of Australia.[5] The western part of New Guinea, under Dutch rule,[6] had been opened at the mid-century by the Gossner Mission.

In the 1860s, evangelical Polynesians carried the gospel to the remaining groups of islands in Polynesia till then unevangelized. In 1863, the American Board turned over its work in Hawaii to the Hawaiian Evangelical Association, which inaugurated missionary work in Micronesia.[7]

Grattan Guinness, George Pearse, and other leaders in the 1859 Revival in Britain joined in founding the North Africa Mission,[8] which sought a foothold in Morocco, Algeria and Tunis in the 1880s. It was difficult indeed to win converts from Islam in the Maghreb or Libya or Egypt.

In the 1860s, Protestant missionary work in the Sudan began, and during the same decade the Swedish Mission associated with the Rosenius Revival movement entered Ethiopia.[9]

In the 1860s, the American Board opened its colleges in Beirut

---

[1] Warneck, J., *Ludwig I. Nommensen, Ein Lebensbild.*
[2] Orr, J. Edwin, *The Second Evangelical Awakening in Britain,* p. 67.
[3] Lovett, R., *James Chalmers: Autobiography and Letters, passim.*
[4] Flierl, J., *Christ in New Guinea.*
[5] Brown, G., *Autobiography of George Brown, passim.*
[6] Rauws, J., *op. cit.,* p. 116.
[7] There was a remarkable revival in Pingelap, 1871; *vide* Halliday, S. B., *The Church in America and Its Baptisms of Fire,* p. 533.
[8] Rutherfurd and Glenny, *The Gospel in North Africa,* pp. 135 ff.
[9] *Vide* Beskow, G. E., *Den Svenska Missionen i Ost-Afrika, passim.*

(later known as the American University) and Istanbul (Robert College).[1] In the 1870s, the American Presbyterians and the Church Missionary Society opened work in Iran.[2] In the 1880s, a small beginning was made on the Arabian coast at Aden, under Ion Keith-Falconer.[3]

In 1858, a group of American missionaries in Ludhiana in north-west India asked all Christians[4] to set aside the second week of January 1860, for united prayer for divine blessing.[5] The response all over the world was phenomenal. In India, for years to come, there was unusual blessing.

The outstanding leader of the 1859 Revival in India was Dr. Alexander Duff, who affirmed:[6]

> In the face of myriads instantaneously saved under the mighty out-pourings of the Spirit of grace, I feel no disposition to enter into argument, discussion or controversy with anyone.

Dr. Alexander Duff sponsored united prayer meetings in Calcutta, sustained by Anglicans, Baptists, Congregationalists and Presbyterians.[7] Similar prayer meetings were begun in Madras, Bombay and other cities.[8] A great and increasing spirit of prayer prevailed among the Christians.

India had just emerged from the trying days of the Indian Mutiny. Among British garrisons were many outstanding Christians, and, thanks to the humanitarian and imperialist zeal of the Clapham Sect in London, there were also many ardent Christian men in the Indian Civil Service. There were local revivals among Europeans—as at Sialkot, where occurred striking conversions of officers and men and civilian residents.[9]

In 1860, Arulappan, the leader of a Brethren-style group of Tamils in the Tirunelveli district of South India, began declaiming against all sin. An extraordinary evangelical awakening ensued.[10]

> Old and young, men and women and children, suddenly seemed crushed by the agony of a deep conviction of sin, and then, as suddenly, seemed to believe in the forgiveness of sins.

The Anglicans reporting were astounded, for the movement among the nominal Christians and unevangelized heathen produced the same sort of prostrations and outcries noticed in the

---

[1] Hamlin, C., *My Life and Times, passim.*
[2] Anonymous, *A Century of Mission Work in Iran, 1834–1934.*
[3] Sinker, R., *Memorials of the Hon. Ion Keith-Falconer, passim.*
[4] *Vide* Chapter XVIII, p. 148.   [5] Ewing, J. W., *Goodly Fellowship,* p. 36.
[6] *The Revival,* 3rd November, 1860.
[7] Smith, G., *Life of Alexander Duff,* p. 301.
[8] *The Revival,* 29th October, 1859.   [9] *Ibid.,* 22nd September, 1859.
[10] Stock, E., *op. cit.,* Vol. II, p. 189; cf. Lang, G. H., *The History and Diaries of an Indian Christian.*

Revival of 1859 in Northern Ireland. There were thousands of lasting conversions.

In 1861, in Kerala, a remarkable family of the Brahman caste was converted, one Justus Joseph being ordained in 1865 by the Anglicans, and his brothers Matthew and Jacob forming an evangelistic team, one preaching and the other singing, the "Moody and Sankey of Travancore."[1]

In Kerala, the Malayalam-speaking section of India, the Reform Party of the Syrian Church (the Mar Thoma Church, as it later came to be known) was suffering ecclesiastical trouble in the 1870s.[2] In the 1830s, the Malayali leader, Abraham Malpan[3] of Maramon, had tried to effect a reformation in the Church, and, failing, had sent his nephew to Syria to seek full consecration as a bishop by the Jacobite patriarch, returning as the Metropolitan Mar Athanasius. Mar Athanasius had been a keen scholar in the C.M.S. college at Kottayam in the 1830s. He endeavoured to build up the Mar Thoma Church as an evangelical, catholic denomination.

Partly through the influence of the Josephs, a remarkable revival began in Kerala, in 1873; it commenced among the Syrian Christians though affecting also the Anglicans. It manifested the same strange physical accompaniments as seen in Ulster in 1859 and Tirunelveli in 1860.[4]

The Metropolitan Mar Athanasius acted very judiciously and sympathetically towards the movement, and freely gave the evangelists permission to preach in the Mar Thoma Churches. Much good was accomplished. Shortly afterwards, the Tamil leader, Arulappan, gained an entrance, and the people who followed him (among them the Joseph family) gave way to an extravagance, which was countered by wiser Evangelicals in both groups.[5]

The ubiquitous William Taylor of California arrived in India in 1870, and teamed up with a like-minded American Methodist, J. M. Thoburn, who had come to India following the 1858 Revival.[6] Not only in Lucknow, but throughout India there were evangelical awakenings under Taylor's exhortation, resulting in "an amazing growth."[7]

"We began 1869," stated John E. Clough of the American Baptist Telugu Mission,[8] "with a week of prayer." There followed a spontaneous revival that year, the beginning of a mass movement that brought 2,222 candidates for baptism in a single day in

[1] Stock, E., *op. cit.*, Vol. III, pp. 179 ff.   [2] *Ibid.*
[3] Cheriyan, P., *The Malabar Christians*, pp. 287 ff.
[4] Stock, E., *op. cit.*, Vol. III, pp. 179 ff.   [5] *Ibid.*
[6] Oldham, F. F., *Thoburn—Called of God, passim.*
[7] Taylor, W., *Four Years' Campaign in India.*
[8] Clough, J. E., *Social Christianity in the Orient*, p. 137.

1879, eight thousand in a week.[1] By 1882, the number of Baptist church members at Ongole had risen to twenty thousand.

In 1860, religious revival broke out among missionaries in Shanghai.[2] China, at that time, constituted the greatest missionary challenge and opportunity in the world. There were only 115 Protestant missionaries in the whole country, concentrated in coastal cities and river ports.[3]

Thanks to the Revival in America and Britain, the work of established societies revived and new societies were formed in the 1860s.[4] A mission-statesman of highest calibre, Timothy Richard, soon came out to China. He had been converted in the Welsh Revival of 1859. Joining the Baptist Missionary Society, he became its best-known missionary, famed for his educational ministry.[5]

In 1866, the missionary forces in China were increased by 25 per cent through the landing of the Lammermuir party of the newly-formed China Inland Mission under the direction of Dr. J. Hudson Taylor, justly described as one of the greatest missionaries of all time, whose programme in China was unprecedented.[6]

The founding of the China Inland Mission was epoch-making in a world sense as well as in its relation to China. The story of the call of James Hudson Taylor is well-known but his relation to the 1859 Revival and its relationship to the new Mission has only recently been stressed by a historian. This first organization of its type in missions was begotten in the 1859 Revival, both its founder's vision and its earliest candidates.[7]

While serving as a missionary of the Chinese Evangelization Society, Hudson Taylor had come under the influence of the revivalist, W. C. Burns. A letter (1860) from George Pearse: "You will be glad to know that the Revival has reached London and hundreds are being converted," thrilled him.[8] In need of physical, mental and spiritual recuperation, Hudson Taylor then returned to London.

Hudson Taylor devoted his spare time, especially his Sundays, to revival ministry in a fruitful training ground, the East End of London. In particular, he laboured in the Twig Folly Mission in Bethnal Green which carried on daily prayer meetings and

[1] Glover, R. H., *Progress of World Wide Missions*, p. 110.
[2] Stock, E., *History of the Church Missionary Society*, Vol. II, p. 34.
[3] Broomhall, M., *Hudson Taylor: the Man Who Believed God*, p. 103.
[4] Latourette, K. S., *History of Christian Missions in China*, pp. 357 ff.
[5] Soothill, W. E., *Timothy Richard of China, passim*.
[6] Latourette, K. S., *op. cit.*, p. 382.
[7] Orr, J. Edwin, *op. cit.*, pp. 226 ff.
[8] Taylor, H. and G., *Hudson Taylor in Early Years*, p. 499.

preaching services. A noted infidel was converted there, and many converts of the Revival were baptized as believers.[1]

The Revival then in progress (said Marshall Broomhall) was a revelation in the homeland of God's power to bless, while a million a month dying in China without God made its appalling contrast in the mind of the burdened missionary.[2] He was unable to shake off his deep impression.

While visiting George Pearse in Brighton in the afterglow of the wonderful Brighton Revival, Hudson Taylor faced his life's greatest crisis. On Sunday, 25th June, 1865, unable to bear the sight of a thousand Christian people rejoicing in their own security while multitudes perished for lack of knowledge, Hudson Taylor walked along the beach and made a great decision.[3]

The prayer life of British Christians had risen to record heights. George Müller's example in launching out by faith was being followed elsewhere. The need of China was appreciated by Hudson Taylor as by few others. So he applied the prayer and faith and action exemplified by the 1859 Awakening to the need of China, and the China Inland Mission became the extension of that great Revival into the evangelization of the world's most numerous people.[4]

The China Inland Mission[5] envisioned by Dr. Hudson Taylor was interdenominational rather than undenominational. Missionaries were sent to interior provinces of China where others of the same denomination laboured—Szechwan, for example, was an Anglican diocese. In due course, the China Inland Mission became the largest of all the missionary bodies, Protestant or Roman.

The example of the China Inland Mission had a profound effect on the world-wide missionary programme. Interdenominational Faith Missions and other interdenominational societies spread until they supplemented the work of the older denominational societies all over the world. Not all societies copied the China Inland Mission's constitution wholly, but few there were owing nothing to its principles and practice.

The 1860s were years of expansion for all the missions in China. Under Griffith John, the London Missionary Society reached out into the centre and north of China.[6] James Gilmour, a convert of the 1859 Revival, reached north into Mongolia, suffering privation and hardship.[7] In the 1860s, the American Board opened

[1] Orr, J. Edwin, *op. cit.*, p. 227.
[2] Broomhall, M., *op. cit.*, p. 113.
[3] *Ibid.*, p. 117.   [4] Orr, J. Edwin, *op. cit.*, p. 227.
[5] Taylor, H. and G., *Hudson Taylor and the China Inland Mission, passim.*
[6] John, Griffith, *A Voice from China*, pp. 187 ff.
[7] Lovett, R., *James Gilmour of Mongolia, passim.*

stations in the north.[1] In the same decade, the American Baptists entered the Swatow area.[2] The Southern Baptists maintained themselves in Shantung, in spite of the Civil War.[3] The American Episcopal Church moved up river.[4] The Church Missionary Society expanded its mid-China work.[5] American Presbyterians spread from Canton over the south.[6] Around Amoy, the English Presbyterians and the Reformed Church of the United States organized a presbytery, and the former opened a work in Formosa among the Chinese.[7] The Methodists of the United States spread from Foochow, opened a work up river on the Yangtze, and entered the north. Josiah Cox brought the British Methodist enterprise up river also.[8]

Kenneth Scott Latourette made the comment:

> Whatever the denomination, the large majority of the supporting constituencies and the missionaries were from those elements which had been most affected by the Evangelical awakening and kindred revivals. . . .[9]

In 1865, R. J. Thomas, a London missionary serving in China, went to Korea as an agent of the National Bible Society of Scotland.[10] Twenty years elapsed before Protestant missionaries were permitted to reside in the country.

In the 1860s came a development of Protestant missions in Japan, drawn chiefly from American denominations. The American Episcopal Church, the American Presbyterians, and the Reformed Church of America were first in the field.[11] The Japanese were still prejudiced against Christian teaching, but there was a desire to learn English and this provided contacts.

Up until 1872, only ten Japanese had been baptized by Protestant ministers. An unusual man, Neesima, smuggled himself out of Japan and was able to obtain an education in Christian schools in the United States, returning as a missionary to found the Doshisha University.[12] In 1872, the American Baptists sent in two missionaries, one of them a marine (Jonathan Goble) who had been with Commodore Perry in the opening of Japan by

---

[1] Blodgett and Baldwin, *Sketches of the Missions of the American Board in China*, pp. 43 ff.
[2] Ashmore, L. S., *The South China Mission of the American Baptist Foreign Mission*.
[3] McGillivray, D., *A Century of Protestant Missions in China*, p. 322.
[4] *Ibid.*, p. 297.   [5] *Ibid.*, pp. 23 ff.   [6] *Ibid.*, pp. 384 ff.
[7] Campbell, W., *Sketches from Formosa*.
[8] McGillivray, D., *op. cit.*, pp. 429 ff.
[9] Latourette, K. S., *A History of the Expansion of Christianity*, Vol. VI, p. 336.
[10] National Bible Society of Scotland, *Annual Report*, 1865.
[11] Cary, Otis, *A History of Christianity in Japan*, Vol. II, pp. 41 ff.
[12] Davis, J. D., *Life of Rev. Joseph Hardy Neesima*.

treaty.[1] The Canadian Methodists followed in 1873.[2] Then came the Bible Societies. By 1882, there were five thousand adult church members in Japanese Protestant churches.

As in China, the majority of these Christians were under the tutelage of evangelical teachers. Evangelicalism was the dynamic of the societies raised up in the denominations, for neo-Protestantism was still in its incubation stage. Apart from the zealous Roman Catholic missionaries, the missionary body in the Orient was an overwhelmingly evangelical invasion.

[1] American Baptist Missionary Union, *Annual Report*, 1873.
[2] Cary, Otis, *op. cit.*, p. 104.

CHAPTER XXIII

MOODYAN METHODS

As THE FIGURE OF CHARLES GRANDISON FINNEY DOMINATED American evangelism in the middle third of the nineteenth century, so the figure of Dwight Lyman Moody dominated the final third.

Finney was a well-educated scholar; Moody an uneducated countryman who never learned to spell or punctuate his pungent speech. This they had in common, that they were full of zeal to win men and women to Jesus Christ.

Family fortune scarcely suggested a career as a world evangelist for Moody.[1] His father had died when Dwight was four years old, leaving his mother and eight other children (including twins born posthumously) without provision. Nor did family religion suggest it. All the Moody children were baptized in the local Unitarian Church in Northfield, a village in rural Massachusetts.

It was as an eighteen-year-old in Boston that Dwight Moody was converted. It was a simple rather than a profound experience, for when he was examined for admission to church membership, he had so little to say that his candidacy was deferred until he had learned a little more.[2] A little over a year later, Moody moved to the frontier town of Chicago to better his fortune. It was here that his great career began.

The Revival of 1857–58 in Chicago made a profound impression on the life of the zealous young man from New England.[3] The churches of every denomination were packed to overflowing, yet the rapid growth of the town provided all the raw material for evangelism needed. In Chicago, Moody became interested in winning young folk to Christ through the Sunday School and through the Young Men's Christian Association.

Moody became an expert in "drumming up" scholars for Sunday School.[4] In 1858, he started a Sunday School of his own in a vacant saloon, and before long, it was the largest Sunday School in Chicago. All the while, he continued active in his business as a salesman.

[1] Moody, W. R., *The Life of Dwight L. Moody*.
[2] Pollock, J. C., *Moody: a Biographical Portrait*, pp. 14–15.
[3] Moody, W. R., *op. cit.*, p. 47. (The only satisfactory explanation of the date of Moody's letter is that he wrote it in the New Year of 1858.)   [4] *Ibid.*, pp. 55 ff.

Moody's Sunday School developed into a church. In 1860, Moody decided to give up his business income (then bringing him $5,000 a year) and to "live by faith" (which brought him $150 the first year). In 1864, the congregation occupied its own building on Illinois Street, and next year Moody was elected president of the Y.M.C.A. in Chicago. He remained a layman.

It was in 1867 that Moody made his first trip to Britain, seeking out leaders of the evangelical movement there, such as C. H. Spurgeon, George Müller, George Williams, Lord Shaftesbury, R. C. Morgan, Henry Varley, Harry Moorhouse, and those who seemed to Moody to have something to share with him in the work of the Lord.[1]

In 1868, the great Farwell Hall of the Y.M.C.A. was burned down. Harry Moorhouse, a product of the Revival in Manchester several years earlier, came to visit Moody, and was asked to preach—a mistake, everyone thought at first. Moorhouse preached for a week on the love of God, using the text, John 3 : 16. He profoundly moved D. L. Moody, whose preaching was never the same again, and who became a preacher of a new message, the Scripture in a new spirit.[2]

Moody had been married in 1862 to a young English-born girl. Emma Revell. In 1870, he met a helpmeet of a different kind, Ira D. Sankey, who became his soloist in his world ministry.[3] In 1871, the Great Fire destroyed the city of Chicago, reducing to ashes fifty churches and missions. In 1871, while visiting New York, Moody experienced a mighty enduement of the Holy Spirit.[4]

In 1872, Moody paid a second visit to Britain. After a night of prayer in Dublin, Henry Varley said to him: "Moody, the world has yet to see what God will do with a man fully consecrated to Him." That comment startled Moody.[5] His visit brought a local awakening in a North London Church and a number of invitations to return to Britain for a wider ministry followed. An Anglican Evangelical, William Pennefather, sent him an invitation by letter to America. Moody tried to settle again in Chicago, but he felt restless until he decided to return to Britain and win 10,000 souls to Christ.

In June 1873, the Moody and Sankey families arrived in Liverpool to learn that Pennefather had died.[6] Moody crossed to York and commenced meetings on short notice. The response was slow but definite. There was still no movement in the next campaign, in Sunderland. But in Newcastle-on-Tyne, the Moody and Sankey evangelism was more than successful.

[1] *Ibid.*, pp. 131 ff. [2] *Ibid.*, pp. 137 ff. [3] *Ibid.*, pp. 125 ff.
[4] *Ibid.*, p. 149. [5] *Ibid.*, pp. 134 ff. [6] *Ibid.*, pp. 152 ff.

The turning point in Moody's ministry came in his Edinburgh campaign.[1] Despite Calvinistic conservatism, the evangelist won the enthusiastic approval of the people, both inside and outside of the churches. The ministers studied the movement carefully, then began to back it without reserve. Moody introduced the noonday prayer meeting of the American 1858 Revival. His evening meetings were crowded, taxing the largest places.

After three weeks in Dundee, Moody began a work in Glasgow which made a lasting impact on the city.[2] Not only were thousands converted, but the United Evangelistic Committee transformed itself into the Glasgow Evangelistic Association and maintained a dozen subsidiary organizations of evangelism and relief.

The Belfast Mission of the Moody and Sankey team commenced in the autumn of 1874. A daily noonday prayer meeting was begun in a Donegall Square church. The evening meetings attracted an enormous attendance of young men. Anglican, Presbyterian and other ministers co-operated.[3]

In Dublin, the Roman Catholic majority noted Moody's avoidance of affront to their faith, and proved friendly, if not enthusiastic. Again there were several thousand professed conversions.[4]

The Manchester, Sheffield, Birmingham and Liverpool Missions followed, each with success.[5] They were moving towards a climax in London. Twenty thousand people nightly heard them in the Agricultural Hall in Islington. While William Taylor of California continued there, D. L. Moody preached in a tabernacle in Bow to the poor and in the opera house in the Haymarket to the rich each evening. The London meetings lasted nearly twenty weeks, and an aggregate of two and a half million people attended them.[6]

As in Scotland, Moody's work in England gave birth to many Christian enterprises besides giving a breath of revival to existent organizations. It made such an impact that Friedrich Engels, a collaborator with Karl Marx in his Communist propaganda, explained the whole business as a plot of the British *bourgeoisie* to import Yankee revivalism to keep the proletariat contented.[7]

Moody returned to the United States in August 1875 and commenced a campaign in Brooklyn in October, followed by a greater in Philadelphia in late November. Vast crowds attended, for news of success in Britain had filled the American church people with enthusiasm. In February 1876, Moody held a campaign in New York, where the New Yorkers attended in tens of thousands, many responding.

[1] *Ibid.*, pp. 182 ff. ·   [2] *Ibid.*, pp. 197 ff.   [3] *Ibid.*, pp. 207 ff.
[4] *Ibid.*, pp. 211 ff.   [5] *Ibid.*, pp. 215 ff.   [6] *Ibid.*, pp. 223 ff.
[7] Engels, F., *Socialism, Utopian and Scientific*, introduction.

Moody returned to Chicago to campaign in the winter of 1876, and received a hero's welcome from a city which claimed him as a son.[1] Early in 1877, he commenced ministry in Boston,[2] another city of his youth, but there he encountered opposition from both Roman and Unitarian sides. A year later, he was still campaigning in New England. Sankey parted from him to conduct a singing ministry in England, but failing there, returned to work with Moody as before. In 1880–81, together they ministered in cities across the country as far as the Pacific Coast.[3]

Moody's second British campaign[4] commenced in Newcastle-on-Tyne in October 1881, moving to Edinburgh for six weeks, then to Glasgow, in which neighbourhood he preached for five months. He then conducted short series of meetings in the Welsh cities and towns and in the provincial cities of England. In 1883, Moody conducted an eight-months' mission in London. Two large temporary structures were built, one in North London and the other in South London, and as soon as a three-weeks' mission had been completed in one, it was quickly transferred to another location on the same side of the river while the other building was being used across the river.

After 1884, Moody conducted his evangelistic campaigns in smaller American cities,[5] besides giving much of his time to educational promotion at Chicago and Northfield, and to conferences.

There has been endless confusion caused by the American use of the word "revival" to describe an organized campaign of evangelism as well as a great outpouring of the Spirit of God upon the churches.

The term "revival" for evangelical awakening has been used in the English-speaking countries outside North America to describe a renewed interest in religion after indifference or decline. In the United States, the word still carries this meaning, but more often it is understood to mean a series of evangelistic meetings.[6]

It seems to be appropriate to point out that Dwight Lyman Moody was an evangelist, and that his organized campaigns of evangelism were not necessarily "revivals" in the historic sense of the word, and that his calling cannot therefore be described as a revivalist, if such a word is also used to describe the ministry of men who have been privileged to stir the churches to revival. In modern times, Wesley and Whitefield were both revivalists and evangelists, as was Finney. But Evan Roberts of Wales was a

---

[1] Moody, W. R., *op. cit.*, pp. 263 ff.   [2] *Ibid.*, pp. 287 ff.
[3] *Ibid.*, pp. 291 ff.   [4] *Ibid.*, pp. 312 ff.   [5] *Ibid.*, pp. 297 ff.
[6] *Vide* chapter xxii, "The Burden of Revival," in *Write the Vision! Edwin Orr's Thirty Years of Adventurous Service,* by the Right Rev. A. J. Appasamy, D.Phil., Oxford, D.D., Serampore; Th.D., Marburg. (ED.)[1]

G

revivalist, and Gipsy Smith an evangelist. It often happens that there are elements of revival in an evangelistic campaign, and effects of evangelism in a revival movement. Evangelism is what dedicated men do for God, but revival is what God does to earnest men to bring them to a fuller dedication.

Like the President, Abraham Lincoln, Dwight Lyman Moody was physically far from being a glamorous figure.[1] He was not a great orator and his command of English was imperfect. His type of preaching was extremely simple, the use of the words of Scripture illustrated by homely stories and narrated in everyday language being standard in his homiletics.

Moody was not a theologian.[2] His theological convictions were strongly conservative, but he maintained cordial friendships with men of other points of view, and loyally stood by Henry Drummond in his disputed harmony of Science and Scripture.

Moody stirred up supercilious enemies among the classes who despised his homely ways, yet he also inspired loyalty and friendship among the best products of the universities of Edinburgh and Cambridge, far removed from his way of life.

A man is known by his associates or friends. Moody's co-workers were extremely able men. He made use of the musical talents of P. P. Bliss and George C. Stebbins, besides those of Ira D. Sankey. Associated with him in preaching were men like D. W. Whittle, Reuben A. Torrey, A. C. Dixon, and J. Wilbur Chapman, all Americans; and from Britain, Henry Varley, John McNeill, Henry Drummond, G. Campbell Morgan and F. B. Meyer. None of these men was a pale reflection of Moody. Each one exceeded him in talent though not in dedication of heart.

The distinguished historian, William Warren Sweet, wrote of Moody:[3]

The attempts of sociologists and psychologists to explain him seem trite and foolish.

In 1893, Moody conducted a great campaign at the World's Columbian Exposition in Chicago.[4] Approximately two million visitors attended this evangelistic series at the World's Fair, Moody sponsored with the help of his Bible Institute. Centres of preaching were chosen on the north-side, west-side and south-side of Chicago, and on Sunday mornings, Moody rented a huge circus tent near the lake front. To reach those speaking French, German, Polish and other languages of Europe, Moody invited Monod of Paris, Stoecker of Berlin, Pinder of Poland, and other European notables to conduct special meetings, and he also

[1] McLoughlin, W. G., *Modern Revivalism*, pp. 175 ff.   [2] *Ibid.*, pp. 210 ff.
[3] Sweet, W. W., *Revivalism in America*, p. 169.
[4] Moody, W. R., *op. cit.*, pp. 409 ff.

shared ministry with Thomas Spurgeon of New Zealand, Henry Varley of Australia, John McNeill of Scotland, famous English-speaking evangelists.

Moody's last campaign was held in Kansas City, Missouri, commencing in November 1899.[1] His committee was composed of Anglican, Baptist, Congregational, Disciples, Methodist and Presbyterian ministers. There were the usual great crowds, but Moody showed signs of exhaustion. He told his friends: "This is the first time in forty years of preaching that I have had to give up my meetings." He rushed home and lingered little, leaving his labours on 22nd December, 1899.[2]

An Australian, John Alexander Dowie, born in Edinburgh in 1847 but pastor of a Congregational Church in Melbourne, withdrew from his denomination to build up an independent congregation in Melbourne. He appeared at the World's Fair in Chicago in 1893, deciding to stay in the Illinois metropolis. By 1895, he had won a great following which met weekly in the Chicago Auditorium.[3]

In 1901, Dowie founded a Christian community on the shores of Lake Michigan forty miles north of Chicago, calling it Zion.[4] The sale of tobacco, liquor and drugs was prohibited and the use of pork banned. Every industry in town was under the control of the founder, John Alexander Dowie. His doctrines were generally evangelical, but he claimed to be Elijah the restorer, and he looked the part with his long white beard and benevolent appearance. The community thrived.

In 1903, Dowie proposed to take his gospel to the nation and the world, and began by renting the vast Madison Square Garden in New York City in October. Vast crowds attended, but the doubters heckled him in the press. Something snapped in his brain one night, and out of his mouth there flowed "a seething torrent of defiling invective."[5] The campaign was a huge failure, leaving Zion $300,000 in debt. Dowie died in delirium two years later, repudiated by his own denomination, later directed by Glenn Voliva,[6] who said that the earth was flat.

While Moody dominated the American scene in evangelism and conducted a great campaign in Toronto in 1834,[7] Canada produced its own effective evangelists in the Crossley-Hunter team in Canadian cities between 1887 and 1889. Crossley and

[1] *Ibid.*, pp. 545 ff.   [2] *Ibid.*, pp. 551 ff.
[3] Loud, G., *Evangelized America*, p. 290.   [4] *Ibid.*, pp. 291–292.
[5] *Ibid.*, p. 293.   [6] Sweet, W. W., *Story of Religion in America*, p. 378.
[7] Clark, S. D., *Church and Sect in Canada*, p. 401.

Hunter followed the Moody pattern.[1] A series in Ottawa was reported as "the most extraordinary revival" ever known in Canada.[2]

Many other evangelists arising in the United States copied Moody. The "Moody of the South" was Samuel Porter Jones of[3] Alabama, who was converted in 1872. It was not till 1884 that Jones attempted evangelism on a city-wide scale, his campaigns in Memphis and Nashville launching him to fame. His preaching was blunt to a point of coarseness and vulgarity, but his evangelism was much in demand in the Southern cities with occasional expeditions to other parts.

In 1887, B. Fay Mills[4] became an evangelist, specializing in district combination of churches. Within seven years, he veered away to a kind of social gospel preaching, his elementary gospel message being more and more muted until he was backed chiefly by Unitarians; and, in 1899, Mills abandoned evangelism—though in 1915 he resigned his Unitarian connexions and returned to Presbyterianism, disillusionment in the First World War having undermined his social notions.

In 1895, Moody designated J. Wilbur Chapman[5] as "the greatest evangelist in the country."

The movement under Moody in Great Britain was paralleled by a series of awakenings in the Scandinavian countries which were influenced by Anglo-Saxon Christianity more and more.

A great revival began in Norway in the 1880s, being particularly powerful in the town of Skien, but also effective over the western and southern parts of Norway.[6] This was the fourth awakening since the beginning of the century. Again it was mainly a lay movement, not sponsored by state church authorities.

Carl Olof Rosenius had died in Sweden in 1868, but his great work continued in strength within the state church. In 1876–77, yet another revival of evangelical Christianity occurred in Sweden.[7] One of the leaders of this movement was August Skogsbergh, who was called "the Swedish Moody."[8] Another was Paul Peter Waldenström, who had succeeded Rosenius as editor of *Pietisten*, the revival magazine founded by George Scott.[9]

Waldenström adopted an Anselmic view of the atonement of Christ, as a result of which those who followed him received

[1] Walsh, H. H., *The Christian Church in Canada*, p. 313.   [2] *Ibid.*
[3] Holcomb, W., *Sam Jones, passim.*
[4] Weigle, L. A., *Dictionary of American Biography.*
[5] McLoughlin, W. G., *op. cit.*, p. 377.
[6] Amdahl, E., *International Review of Missions*, Vol. XXIX, pp. 358 ff.
[7] Stephenson, G., *The Religious Aspects of Swedish Immigration*, pp. 103 ff.
[8] *Ibid.*, p. 104.
[9] Montgomery, M. W., *A Wind from the Holy Spirit in Sweden and Norway*, p. 58.

much criticism from the leaders of the Church of Sweden. They then formed in 1878 the Evangelical Mission Covenant (or *Svenska Missionsförbund*), retaining formal membership in the Church of Sweden but in fact operating a free church somewhat as did the Wesleyan movement before separating from the Church of England.[1]

Those of the Rosenius movement in Sweden who did not follow Waldenström continued their support of the Evangelical National Foundation, or *Evangeliska Fosterlands Stiftelsen*, begun in 1856.[2] It was equally evangelistic.

The Evangelical Mission Covenant in United States was formed of two revivalistic Lutheran synods in 1885.[3] It was entirely a free church of evangelistic low-church traditions, as also was the Augustana Synod which served the Lutherans from Sweden without the full approval of Swedish State Church authorities.

Frederick Franson, a Swedish-born emigrant, was converted in Nebraska and in 1875 came to Chicago to study the methods of D. L. Moody.[4] He became a member of the Moody Church, and went forth as an evangelist with its blessing.[5] In 1881, Franson crossed to Sweden, where he began to exercise a fruitful ministry in the chapels of the evangelistic sections of the Church.[6] He extended his ministry to Norway with striking success. In both countries, the clergy of the State Churches offered opposition to his ministry, and this was repeated in Denmark in a greater degree.[7] Yet in Copenhagen, in the New Year of 1884, Franson became the prophet of a great revival in the city. In 1885, Franson was arrested on false charges, imprisoned until influential Norwegians at court interceded with Danish royalty, and then finally banished from Denmark.[8]

Theodor Christlieb, who had ministered in a Lutheran Church in London as pastor during the mid-nineteenth-century awakening, returned to serve later as professor of Theology at Bonn,[9] supporting fully the evangelistic cause in all the German States. About the same time, Pearsall Smith (as noted in Chapter XIX) kindled interest in scriptural holiness and evangelism there.[10]

Elijah Schrenk, a German missionary from Africa, attended Moody's meetings in London and wrote home: "I want to become an evangelist."[11] Shortly thereafter, a German-American Y.M.C.A.

[1] Stephenson, G., *op. cit.*, p. 109.
[2] Gidland, M., *Kyrka och Väckelse*, 1849–1880, pp. 344 ff.
[3] Stephenson, G., *op. cit.*, pp. 278 ff.
[4] Grauer, O. C., *Fredrik Franson*, pp. 21 ff.
[5] *Ibid.*   [6] *Ibid.*, p. 34 ff.   [7] *Ibid.*, pp. 39 ff.   [8] *Ibid.*, pp. 47 ff.
[9] Scharpff, P., *Geschichte der Evangelisation*, pp. 249 ff.
[10] *Ibid.*, pp. 239 ff.   [11] *Ibid.*, pp. 262 ff.

secretary named Frederick von Schlümbach held evangelistic campaigns in Berlin and Hamburg, resulting in a revival and in the foundation of the first German Young Men's Christian Association.[1]

These and many other movements were soon brought together by Professor Christlieb, who founded the German Committee for Evangelism, and a seminary to train evangelists. He began at Gnadau in 1888 a series of conventions for both pastors and evangelists.[2] Thus the forces of the Revival in Germany developed an evangelistic drive and the movement went on for thirty years.

From this resulted the German Association for Evangelism and Christian Fellowship[3] which sent evangelists throughout the German lands, the most remarkable of whom were Samuel Keller and Elijah Schrenk, who had drawn inspiration from Moody. The movement waxed strong.

Historians claim that this movement began a Thirty Years' Revival in Germany, between 1880 and 1910, especially effective in the Established Church, and that several hundred thousand people were converted. The origins of this great German Awakening were mainly Anglo-American, though the movement soon became thoroughly Germanic in personnel and preaching.[4]

Protestantism in Poland, which had declined from its strength in early Reformation days, was mainly identified with Germans.[5] The same was true of Germanic landlords and their tenants in the Baltic States of Estonia and Latvia, where a peasant interest in Moravianism existed in spite of Russian imperial and German local tyranny.[6] In the Hapsburg dominions, where a reactionary Roman Catholicism obtained, there were minorities of Protestants suffering various disabilities.[7]

In Hungary, the rationalism of the Napoleonic period gave way to an evangelical awakening, in which the British and Foreign Bible Society took part by promoting the sale of the Kâroli Bible in Magyar.[8] With the revival came a strong Scottish influence through a mission in Budapest.[9] In 1849, full religious rights were granted Protestants, then rescinded, and renewed again in 1867.

[1] *Ibid.*, pp. 251 ff.   [2] *Ibid.*, pp. 257 ff.

[3] *Ibid.* Professor Scharpff and the author exchanged notes on German- and English-speaking evangelists in the nineteenth century at his home in Frankfurt, 1962.

[4] Scharpff, P., *op. cit.*

[5] Siegmund-Schultze, F., *Evangelische Kirche in Polen, passim.*

[6] Latourette, K. S., *The Nineteenth Century in Europe*, Vol. II, pp. 198–199.

[7] *Ibid.*, Vol. II, p. 202.

[8] Révész, Kovats and Ravasz, *Hungarian Protestantism.*

[9] Bucsay, M., *Geschichte des Protestantismus in Ungarn*, p. 185.

In the Moodyan period, Sunday Schools, Y.M. and Y.W.C.As., the Evangelical Alliance, the Student Christian Movement and the Christian Endeavour movement entered Hungary.[1]

It is strange that although the Protestants of Hungary equalled those of Denmark, Norway or Finland, and were more than half of those of the Netherlands or Sweden, there was less revival and less missionary activity.[2] In fact, Hungarian missionary activity did not even match that of the tiny French Protestant minority.

Lord Radstock, a product of the 1859 Revival in Britain, who had served against the Russians in the Crimean War, returned to Russia to witness to the upper classes in St. Petersburg in 1874 and again in 1877–78.[3] Among the converts within the aristocracy were Colonel Pashkov and Princess Natalia Lieven. Radstock was followed by Friederich Wilhelm Baedeker, German-born British subject, who travelled throughout the Russian Empire encouraging all the evangelical believers, including the Baptists, Mennonites, Stundists and other Protestant groups.[4] That the two British evangelists made an impression on the Russian intelligentsia is seen by the fact that Dostoievsky wrote about Radstock in his works, while Tolstoi referred to Baedeker.[5]

Among the humble peasants of the Ukraine, a revival had begun about 1860. Oncken, a Baptist leader from Germany, visited them in 1869.[6] In 1884, a twenty years' persecution began, hurting both nobles and peasants. Evangelicals continued to thrive. I. S. Prokhanov, converted in 1886, founded the All-Russia Evangelical Union.[7]

---

[1] Revesz, Kovats and Ravasz, *op. cit.*, p. 41–49.
[2] Latourette, K. S., *op. cit.*, p. 205.
[3] Latimer, R. S., *Liberty of Conscience under Three Tsars*, pp. 71–76.
[4] Latimer, R. S., *Dr. Baedeker and His Apostolic Work in Russia, passim.*
[5] Emhart, W. C., *Religion in the Soviet Union*, p. 284.   [6] *Ibid.*, p. 283.
[7] Casey, R. P., *Religion in Russia*, pp. 42 ff.

CHAPTER XXIV

DEDICATED VOLUNTEERS

"THERE NEVER WAS A PLACE," SAID MOODY, "THAT I AP-
proached with greater anxiety than Cambridge. Never
having had the privilege of a university education, I was
nervous about meeting university men."[1]

Well might Moody be anxious, for there were many high-
spirited students lying in wait for him. There were hoots and
cheers, fire-crackers and guffaws, but Moody kept his temper. His
student sponsors had heavy hearts that 5th November in 1882,
but next day a ringleader, Gerald Lander of Trinity, called to
apologize.[2]

Although seventeen hundred students had been counted in that
first meeting in the Corn Exchange, only a hundred attended the
second in a seated gymnasium, but they included Gerald Lander.
On Wednesday, before a larger crowd, Moody gave an evangelistic appeal and, after repeating it, saw more than fifty men
make their way to the inquiry room. One was Gerald Lander.
Throughout the week, conversions were professed by intellectuals and athletes, many of them proving to be deep and lasting.
The final meeting in the Corn Exchange brought eighteen hundred hearers, and concluded a mission which proved to be the
beginning of a world-wide movement.[3]

Next day, without the benefit of a Sunday start, Moody opened
his mission in the Corn Exchange in Oxford, which was filled to
overflowing. Bolder, he quenched attempts at rowdyism several
nights running and gained a hearing for his messages. The audience moved from the Clarendon Assembly Rooms to the Town
Hall, where Moody gathered inquirers in an after-meeting, and a
number made personal transactions with God.

Within a year of these two campaigns, Moody's converts were
preparing for foreign missionary work; others were helping in
Moody's evangelism at home. Two Studd brothers, of cricketing
fame, John Edward Kynaston and Charles Thomas, addressed one
of Moody's Stepney mission meetings, and a young man named
Wilfred Grenfell was converted.[4]

[1] Pollock, J. C., *Moody: A Biographical Portrait*, pp. 228 ff.
[2] *Ibid.*   [3] *Ibid.*   [4] *Ibid.*, pp. 249 ff.

Montagu Beauchamp, William Cassels, D. E. Hoste, Arthur and Cecil Polhill-Turner, Stanley Smith and C. T. Studd, all Moody's helpers and some his converts, offered themselves for work in China under the China Inland Mission. They first became a remarkable witness team named the Cambridge Seven, sailing for China in 1885.[1]

Meanwhile, in the United States and Canada, the Young Men's Christian Associations had become the main vehicles of religious life on the campuses of North American universities. The first Y.M.C.A.s for students were organized in the University of Michigan and the University of Virginia in 1858, during the Revival.[2] Within ten years, there were forty such associations; and an Inter-Collegiate Young Men's Christian Association was founded in 1877.[3]

Two years earlier, a young man named Luther Wishard moved to Princeton University and found fellowship in a local Philadelphian Society, which was a Christian union.[4] One of his friends therein was T. W. Wilson, known in class as Tommy, but afterwards better known as Woodrow Wilson who carried his Christian idealism to the Presidency of the United States of America.

Luther Wishard became the mainspring of the student Y.M.C.A.s, and within another ten years there were two hundred and fifty associations on campus with 12,000 members.[5] Another Princeton student leader, Robert Mateer, became the leader of the Inter-Seminary Missionary Alliance which held its first convention in 1880 with two hundred and fifty students from thirty or more seminaries present.[6] These student organizations both were strongly evangelical and evangelistic.

Luther Wishard, as organizer and evangelist of the Inter-Collegiate Y.M.C.A., had tried hard to interest Moody in collegiate ministry, but had been rebuffed by the modest Moody, conscious of academic deficiencies. In 1884, Wishard pleaded again with Moody, who consented to preach at a few colleges in 1885, including Dartmouth, Yale and Princeton. His college-slanted sermons, he knew, were few. He looked for help.

Meanwhile, Stanley Smith, the Cambridge oarsman, and C. T. Studd, the Cambridge cricketer, had visited Edinburgh University in 1884 to make an impact on the four thousand students.[7] Moody invited J. E. Kynaston Studd to spend the academic term in the autumn of 1885 in North American colleges, of which he visited twenty in thirteen weeks.[8] One of those challenged to a dedication

[1] *Ibid.*, pp. 252 ff.
[2] Shedd, C. P., *Two Centuries of Student Christian Movements*, p. 94.
[3] *Ibid.*, pp. 120 ff.   [4] *Ibid.*   [5] *Ibid.*
[6] *Ibid.*, p. 217.   [7] *Ibid.*, p. 281.   [8] *Ibid.*, p. 290.

of heart and life at Cornell University was John R. Mott, a law student who had been converted in a local revival in Postville, Iowa, at the age of 14.[1]

An outcome of Moody's growing interest in the student world was the convening of a college conference at Mount Hermon in Massachusetts in the summer of 1886, a noteworthy date.[2]

Two hundred and fifty students from a hundred colleges attended, and Moody was as popular as any eminent lecturer to collegians. One of the college delegates was Robert P. Wilder,[3] son of a missionary to India, who had already formed a student foreign missionary society at Princeton. The Wilder family, whose head had been one of the Williams College group of missionaries in the early 1800s, were praying that a thousand students from American universities might be enlisted for foreign missionary endeavour. To every student who would listen, Robert Wilder presented the call of missions. He persuaded Moody to set aside time for missionary talks, and this combination of prayer and presentation had its effect. One hundred delegates signed a declaration of willingness to serve overseas.

Robert Wilder and John Forman toured the universities and succeeded in enlisting about two thousand volunteers for missionary service. At first, Moody was cautious about the enthusiasm of the youngsters, but he continued to help them. The volunteers increased their own numbers to three thousand in the academic year, 1887–88.[4]

Moody's brilliant helper, Henry Drummond, visited the student conference at Northfield in the summer of 1887.[5] He had already been most successful in his ministry to British students, and he repeated his success with Americans in many colleges.[6] Drummond was attacked by his conservative brethren for his attempt to bring religion and science into harmony, and, though Moody lined up with the conservatives, he stood by Drummond as a great and zealous soul-winner.[7]

Luther Wishard returned the British visitors' calls by touring the universities of Cambridge, Oxford, Edinburgh and Glasgow in the spring of 1888. The summer he spent in Germany, France, Switzerland and Sweden. Wishard extended his journey around the world, reporting conversions from many places.[8]

James B. Reynolds, another student volunteer, crossed the Atlantic to Oslo University, arriving in the afterglow of a great

[1] *Ibid.*   [2] *Ibid.*, pp. 253 ff.
[3] Wilder, R. P., *The Great Commission, passim.*
[4] Shedd, C. P., *op. cit.*, p. 267.
[5] Smith, G. A., *Life of Henry Drummond*, pp. 368 ff.
[6] *Ibid.*   [7] *Ibid.*
[8] Shedd, C. P., *op. cit.*, pp. 282–285.

revival there.[1] He also visited Stockholm, Lund and Copenhagen in 1889.

In 1891, Robert Wilder visited the universities of Britain in the interests of foreign missions. In this endeavour, he enlisted three hundred British volunteers for the foreign field.[2]

In 1890 Henry Drummond sailed for Australia and spent a profitable time challenging students in the universities of the southern continent. His days were numbered, however, for he fell ill in 1894 and died in 1897.[3] John R. Mott organized the Student Volunteers in the universities of New Zealand and Australia just before Drummond died.[4]

The Student Volunteers sought to enlist every Christian in the objective of evangelizing all the world. Their watchword was "the evangelization of the world in this generation." Their methods were the recruitment of university students, and their dynamic was wholly evangelical.[5]

Latourette has declared his careful opinion that it was through the Student Volunteers in the various countries that a large proportion of the outstanding leaders in the world-wide spread of Protestant Christianity in the twentieth century were recruited.[6]

The same great historian has drawn attention to the fact that the decades in which evolutionary theory in science and higher criticism in religion were making headway were the same years in which the Student Volunteers were growing so rapidly.[7] Intellectuals were recruited for the evangelization of the pagan world.

Moody himself made provisions for training of students who felt called to home and foreign missionary service. In 1883, some of his personal friends in Chicago were praying that he might in proper time found an institute for the preparation of workers for world-wide missions.[8]

Once Moody was committed to the project, he announced his plans to his friends. Young Cyrus McCormick, a wealthy manufacturer, leaped up and offered fifty thousand dollars, which Moody calmly suggested he should make one hundred thousand dollars.[9]

C. T. Studd, on his twenty-fifth birthday, had inherited a share of his father's fortune, and he decided to give it away to Christian causes. He sent five thousand pounds to Moody for the Bible Institute, expressing a hope that he would use a part of it to

[1] *Ibid.*, p. 340.   [2] *Ibid.*, p. 348.
[3] Smith, G. A., *op. cit.*, pp. 386 ff.
[4] Mathews, B., *John R. Mott, World Citizen.*
[5] Latourette, K. S., *A History of the Expansion of Christianity*, Vol. IV, p. 97.
[6] *Ibid.*, p. 98.   [7] *Ibid.*, p. 436.
[8] Pollock, J. C., *op. cit.*, 261 ff.   [9] *Ibid.*, p. 262.

evangelize Indian people. Moody in turn promised it to train workers for missions.[1]

In 1889, the Bible Institute was opened, with Reuben Archer Torrey as its first superintendent. Torrey was a staunch evangelical,[2] but was a man of intellect, widely read and widely trained, not only a product of Yale, Leipzig and Erlangen, but capable of reading the New Testament in Greek for daily devotions.

"When I am gone," said Moody, "I shall leave some grand men and women behind." Certainly, this was true of his Bible Institute, producing its hundreds of workers annually.

Albert B. Simpson was born in Prince Edward Island in Maritime Canada at the end of 1843, and was converted near Chatham in Western Ontario shortly after the beginning of the 1858 Awakening which had first appeared in Hamilton, Ontario, the previous October. Simpson had been convicted under the pungent preaching of Grattan Guinness.[3]

In 1861, Simpson appeared before the London (Ontario) Presbytery and was approved for study at Knox College in Toronto.[4] He had already begun to preach, and continued to do so during college training.[5] He graduated in 1865, and became minister of Knox Church in Hamilton eight years after the world-wide Revival had begun there.[6]

Simpson's second pastorate was in Louisville in Kentucky, where he led the ministers of the city in sponsoring a campaign of evangelism with Major Whittle and P. P. Bliss.[7] He resigned after six years, and in 1879 moved to New York. After two years, he commenced a wider evangelistic ministry, opening in 1884 a Gospel Tabernacle, which took final shape and location in 1889.[8]

In 1886, A. B. Simpson organized a summer convention at Old Orchard, Maine, out of which came the Christian and Missionary Alliance,[9] at first interdenominational. Simpson laid emphasis upon Sanctification and Healing, but his primary motivation was the preaching of the gospel to all nations before the coming again of Jesus Christ. When he died in 1919, the Alliance was world-wide.

The Keswick Convention for the Deepening of the Spiritual Life, an evangelical movement with a truly world-wide influence, budded at gatherings in London, Oxford and Brighton in 1873–74–75.[10] and blossomed into early maturity at the Lake District

---

[1] *Ibid.*, p. 263.   [2] Davis, G. T. B., *Torrey and Alexander, passim.*
[3] Thompson, A. E., *The Life of A. B. Simpson*, p. 26.
[4] *Ibid.*, p. 27.   [5] *Ibid.*, pp. 31 ff.   [6] *Ibid.*, p. 42.
[7] *Ibid.*, pp. 53–62.   [8] *Ibid.*, pp. 82 ff.   [9] *Ibid.*, p. 128 ff.
[10] Pollock, J. C., *The Keswick Story*, pp. 23 ff.

resort in 1875; but the seed was sown in the great Revival of 1858–60 in the English-speaking world.[1]

William Edwin Boardman had published at the height of the Revival of 1858 a treatise upon *The Higher Christian Life*.[2] He was a zealous young Presbyterian business man when he started his search in the 1840s for a holier life.[3] This book was a huge success on both sides of the Atlantic, being published in Britain in 1860. A circulation of 200,000 copies was reported.

The year 1860 dated the conversion of a young English clergyman, Evan Hopkins, and it was not long before a copy of Boardman's treatise found its way into the hands of Hopkins,[4] then engaged in an engrossing revival ministry, not having found the time of reflection and retrospect that he needed to lead him into deeper blessing.

On 1st May, 1873, Evan Hopkins with fifteen other people met in Mayfair to discuss the subject of the deepening of the Christian life.[5] The convert and evangelist of the Revival entered a fuller experience so real that his wife was the first to follow him into it. Evan Hopkins became the outstanding leader of the Keswick Movement, making a contribution beyond estimation.

In July 1874, a conference was conducted at the Broadlands estate in Hampshire, the seat of Lord Mount Temple, the leaders being Mr. and Mrs. R. Pearsall Smith. Before he could participate in a conference announced for July 1875, Smith suffered a nervous breakdown brought about by charges of more serious import than the indiscretion which provoked them.[6] He retired from public life.

Also at Broadlands was Theodore Monod, the Frenchman who had been converted in 1858 in the United States.[7] Union Meetings for Promotion of Scriptural Holiness were begun in Oxford during August 1874, with the help of Canon Cristopher, an evangelical stalwart.[8]

Canon Harford-Battersby of the resort town of Keswick in Cumberland, who had been active in the diocese of Carlisle during the Awakening of 1860 when he formed an Evangelical Union to foster spiritual life,[9] had read Boardman's book and discussed the subject during an evangelistic mission with the Anglican evangelist, William Haslam.[10] Urged to attend the meetings in Oxford,

---

[1] Orr, J. Edwin, *The Second Evangelical Awakening in Britain*, pp. 218 ff.
[2] Smith, T. L., *Revivalism and Social Reform*, pp. 106–107.
[3] Boardman, M. M., *The Life and Labours of the Rev. W. E. Boardman*, *passim*.
[4] Harford-Battersby, *Memoir of T. D. Harford-Battersby*, p. 148.
[5] Sloan, W. B., *These Sixty Years*, pp. 9–10.
[6] Pollock, J. C., *op. cit.*, pp. 30 ff.
[7] Sloan, W. B., *op. cit.*, p. 12.   [8] *Ibid.*, p. 15.
[9] Harford-Battersby, *op. cit.*, p. 135.
[10] *Ibid.*, p. 152.

he heard Evan Hopkins there and himself entered into a deeper experience.

The Convention at Oxford was followed by a larger one at Brighton, begun on 29th May, 1875.[1] Henry Varley, of 1859 Revival fame, spoke there several times. D. L. Moody, closing his great Opera House meetings in London, sent the good will and prayers of eight thousand people.

The Vicar of St. John's, Keswick, invited his friends to the Lakeside town and thus began the series of Conventions for the Deepening of the Christian Life that gained for "Keswick" a unique place of leadership in the evangelical world. A majority of its leaders were evangelists or converts of the 1859 Revival, and quite a number of new speakers had a link therewith.[2]

Canon Harford Battersby continued to preside until his death; Evan Hopkins emerged as the leader; William Haslam ministered; Theodore Monod participated. After an address by Evan Hopkins, Handley C. G. Moule was stirred to stand publicly as a seeker after blessing, and as Principal of Ridley Hall, Cambridge, or (later) Bishop of Durham, he addressed Keswick thirteen times.[3]

Andrew Murray, leader of the Revival of 1860 in South Africa, entered into a deeper experience at Keswick in 1882, and became a mouthpiece of its message all over the world. In 1887, a new speaker was F. B. Meyer, converted during the Revival in the 1860s in London. Another convert was Charles Inwood, the Methodist evangelist.[4]

The Keswick Convention became a missionary force after Reginald Radcliffe in 1886 borrowed the tent for a missionary meeting. Hudson Taylor and Eugene Stock used the Keswick platform to enlist young people for the mission fields. Moody addressed the Keswick Convention in 1892.[5] The Keswick line of teaching was supported in the United States by such Evangelicals as Dwight L. Moody, Reuben A. Torrey, Adoniram J. Gordon, A. B. Simpson and J. Wilbur Chapman.[6] It never became the unifying force in America that it had become in Great Britain and the British countries of the eastern hemisphere.

Keswick borrowed its evangelical ecumenism, with its slogan, "All One in Christ Jesus," from the Revival of 1858-59 and the movements which followed it. Unlike certain other products of the Revival, the Keswick Convention maintained its evangelical and evangelistic character.

It is strange to notice that both the Keswick movement in

[1] Sloan, W. B., *op. cit.*, p. 19.   [2] Orr, J. Edwin, *op. cit.*, p. 219.
[3] *Ibid.*   [4] *Ibid.*, p. 220.   [5] *Ibid.*
[6] Smith, T. L., *Called Unto Holiness*, p. 25.

Britain and the Holiness movement in the United States owed much to the remarkable circulation of W. E. Boardman's book.[1]

Stemming from the same impulse in the same great awakening, how different were the two movements. Keswick became an evangelical-ecumenical force; the Holiness movement in the States led to division after division, as splinter denominations lacking a sense of revival unity were formed.

Timothy Smith has offered four reasons[2] why the Holiness Movement in America separated from the old, main-line denominations—the persistent opposition of ecclesiastical officials to Holiness associations; the recurrence of outbreaks of fanaticism in these Holiness associations; the attacks upon Holiness doctrine in the 1890s; and the increased activity of urban Holiness preachers.

The author of this treatise would add another reason—the intransigent American temperament developed by the existence of a western frontier which encouraged independence rather than conscientious compromise.

The pursuit of Scriptural Holiness took very different paths in Britain and America. Keswick doctrine represented a synthesis of Calvinistic and Arminian ideas, or rather a statement of the doctrine of holiness acceptable to more moderate Calvinists. Throughout its history, the Keswick movement[3] enlisted the support of Calvinists and Arminians—Anglicans, Baptists, Methodists and Presbyterians of either party without the dispute being ever heard of, except in rare instances in the case of hyper-Calvinists or hyper-Wesleyans and then only in the most cordial fraternity. But in the United States, the vehemence with which the doctrine was propounded, and the bitterness with which it was opposed, led to a severance of relations rather than a diffusion of influence. In American Holiness agitation, schism produced several major and many minor denominations—each stressing sanctification in its own Wesleyan terminology.

Methodists in America as in Britain had begun to lose their interest in their founder's doctrine of entire sanctification.[4] A majority of them was beginning to treat it as merely a credal statement, even though lip service was paid to the experience.

It was not that the major bodies of Methodists were left without witnesses to the doctrine of holiness. In the 1830s, Phoebe Palmer,[5] wife of a physician, Walter Palmer,[6] became a leader in

[1] *Ibid.*, p. 11.   [2] *Ibid.*, p. 27.
[3] Pollock, J. C., *The Keswick Story*, provides the most reliable account of the movement.
[4] Smith, T. L., *op. cit.*, pp. 114 ff.
[5] Wheatley, R., *Life and Letters of Mrs. Phoebe Palmer.*
[6] Hughes, G., *The Beloved Physician, Walter C. Palmer.* Cf. pp. 142, 145 ff., *supra.*

devotional meetings for women in New York City. In 1848, James Caughey returned from his tours of Britain, and kindled an enthusiasm for holy living among Canadian Methodists in 1852.[1] Five years later, in Hamilton, Ontario, the Palmers visited Caughey's Methodist contacts and were privileged to see the beginning of the world-wide 1858–59 Revival there.[2]

For four years during the 1860s, the Palmers visited Caughey's contacts in Britain, carrying the spirit of revival with them to the Methodists.[3] It was Walter and Phoebe Palmer, a husband-and-wife preaching team, who inspired William and Catherine Booth to follow suit. The comment of the bitter-tongued Wesleyan President upon "the perambulations of the male and female" hit the Booths and missed the Palmers.

When William Taylor, later the astonishing Methodist missionary bishop,[4] returned from his tour of duty in California, he renewed an earlier association with the Palmers and then toured the Eastern and Middle Western States between 1858 and 1860,[5] before taking off for his meteoric missions to the other five continents. Phoebe Palmer was the "Priscilla who taught many an Apollos the way of God more perfectly," Wesley-style.[6]

A sharp division in the Genesee Conference of western New York resulted in the organization of the Free Methodist Church[7] which claimed to uphold the standards of Wesleyanism. Wesleyan Methodists had already separated in 1843 from the major Methodist body over the slavery issue.[8] Their numbers increased in the Holiness camps.

In 1895, an organization named the Church of the Nazarene[9] appeared in California, and about the same time in New England an Association of Pentecostal Churches in America. In the decade following, these two Wesleyan-type organizations were joined by the Holiness Church of Texas to form the Pentecostal Church of the Nazarene, which, after a dozen years of confusion with the emerging Pentecostal denominations, dropped the word "Pentecostal" from their title.

The Nazarenes became the most vigorous of all the Holiness groups, growing from their union of ten thousand members to half a million in half a century of very rapid expansion. International headquarters were fixed in Kansas City, Missouri.

[1] Smith, T. L., *op. cit.*, p. 118.
[2] Orr, J. Edwin, *The Second Evangelical Awakening in Britain*, p. 147.
[3] *Ibid.*, indexed references.
[4] Taylor, W., *Seven Years' Street Preaching in San Francisco, passim.*
[5] Taylor, W., *The Story of my Life*, pp. 219–228.
[6] Smith, T. L., *op. cit.*, p. 122.
[7] Hogue, W. T., *A History of the Free Methodist Church.*
[8] Smith, T. L., *op. cit.*, p. 185.
[9] Redford, M. E., *The Rise of the Church of the Nazarene, passim.*

The agitation of the Holiness Movement also affected the Mennonites, being of Arminian theology. Boardman's views made an impression in Baptist circles and produced an evangelist, A. B. Earle,[1] outstanding until the rise of D. L. Moody. The gruff Baptist evangelist, Jacob Knapp, when he encountered Earle's "sanctified Baptists" in Boston, stated that holiness troubled him little.[2]

The effect of the American Holiness agitation was to make a powerful plea for holiness of life a sectarian appeal rather than an ecumenical one as in Britain. Where the subject was tenderly expounded in British countries, drawing together a cross-section of denominational membership, in the United States it was on occasion hotly debated at the expense of the spirit of tenderness.

The Holiness Movement in Germany proved to be ecumenical rather than sectarian. It produced the *Gemeinschaftsbewegung*,[3] or German Alliance for the Cultivation of Fellowship and Evangelism, often called the Gnadauer Band.[4]

Theodor Christlieb, revived in the Awakening in London in the 1860s, returned to Brighton for the Oxford and Brighton Conferences which had preceded the Keswick series.[5] Pearsall Smith in turn visited Germany,[6] where he exercised a very successful ministry despite his later aberration.

The cells of awakened believers within parish churches, existing from earlier Revivals, gave a fruitful opportunity for propagating the new ideas of evangelism and holy living. In 1888, the first conference for pastors and evangelists at Gnadau was eminently successful.[7]

The movement spread through the Germanic States, until 1898 the *Gemeinschsftsbewegung* was formed, remaining with the denominational organizations, maintaining 700 seminary trained preachers and 5,000 lay ministers and circles.[8]

In the winter of 1880–81, there was a time of revival in Williston Congregational Church, in Portland, Maine. Its pastor, Francis E. Clark, wishing to conserve the blessing, organized a Young People's Society of Christian Endeavour to call youth to greater dedication and service.[9] The idea caught on, became an organization to encourage young folk to participate in a church.

In 1886, one thousand delegates attended the first convention

[1] Earle, A. B., *Bringing in the Sheaves, passim.*
[2] Smith, T. L., *op. cit.*, p. 139.
[3] Scharpff, P., *Geschichte der Evangelisation*, pp. 220 ff.
[4] *Ibid.*, pp. 257 ff.   [5] *Ibid.*, p. 249.   [6] *Ibid.*, pp. 240 ff.   [7] *Ibid.*, p. 221.
[8] Bartels, Th., "Gemeinschaftsbewegung" in the *Twentieth Century Encyclopedia of Religious Knowledge.*
[9] Halliday, S. B., *The Church in America and Its Baptisms of Fire*, p. 347.

of Christian Endeavour held at Saratoga Springs, two thousand
the second one.[1] In 1888, five thousand Endeavourers attended
the convention in Chicago, and next year six thousand five hundred in Philadelphia, including overseas delegates. In 1890, eight
thousand attended the St. Louis convention, followed by fourteen
thousand in Minneapolis. In 1892, ten years after the foundation
of the first society, thirty-five thousand Christian Endeavourers
societies there, six years later a thousand.[2]

Denominational authorities adapted the idea, there being Baptist Young People's Unions of Christian Endeavour, and Epworth
Leagues of Christian Endeavour, etc. In 1888, Francis Clark
visited England, and three years later there were a hundred
societies there, six years later a thousand.[3]

In 1895, there were thirty-eight thousand C. E. Societies in the
world, with 2,225,000 members.[4] The movement was evangelical,
evangelistic and church-related, suited to the climate of the day,
which was evangelical and ecumenical concord.

[1] *Ibid.*, pp. 353 ff.   [2] *Ibid.*   [3] *Ibid.*   [4] *Ibid.*

CHAPTER XXV

MISSIONS REINFORCED

THE EVANGELICAL REVIVAL OF THE MID-CENTURY, WHICH
had produced the evangelism of Moody who in turn was
so much responsible for the recruitment of Christian students, had a striking effect upon the unevangelized parts of the
world.

At the time of the 1858–59 Revival, China had been scarcely
opened to the gospel. The China Inland Mission was organized to
carry the Word to inland China, and to begin this work the first
party had sailed for Shanghai in 1866.[1] In 1875, Hudson Taylor
prayed for eighteen missionary reinforcements to raise the mission
strength to about fifty; in 1875, he prayed for seventy; and in 1886,
he prayed for one hundred more. Where did Hudson Taylor find
his men? As in the case of the Cambridge Seven, he reached for
the best and often found them in the universities.[2] W. W. Cassels
became a missionary bishop in West China.[3] (Gerald Lander,
Moody's opponent converted at Cambridge, became a missionary
bishop in South China.[4]) Within thirty years, the China Inland
Mission numbered more than six hundred missionaries in two
hundred and sixty stations,[5] with nearly five hundred national
workers and more than five thousand communicants, though the
mission did not set out to build churches.

In the 1880s, the older missionary societies also moved into
new territories—the Baptists, Congregationalists, Lutherans,
Methodists and Presbyterians. Also, in 1888 the Christian and
Missionary Alliance began operations that were to extend all over
China.[6] And the Young Men's Christian Association organized in
China in the middle 1880s. The Y.M.C.A.s were evangelistic, and
enjoyed a rapid growth, stressing Chinese leadership which was
immediately forthcoming.[7] H. H. Kung, later Prime Minister of
China,[8] in the early days served as an officer, one among many

---

[1] Taylor, H. and G., *Hudson Taylor and the China Inland Mission, passim.*
[2] Pollock, J. C., *Moody: a Biographical Portrait*, pp. 252 ff.
[3] Broomhall, M., *W. W. Cassels, First Bishop in Western China, passim.*
[4] Pollock, J. C., *loc. cit.*   [5] *China's Millions*, 1906.
[6] Ekvall, R. B., *After Fifty Years (Christian and Missionary Alliance).*
[7] Latourette, K. S., *op. cit.*, Vol. VI, pp. 341–342.
[8] Orr, J. Edwin, *Through Blood and Fire in China*, pp. 140 ff.

professing Christians in the government of China—others being Sun Yat-sen, Chiang Kai-shek, etc.

The fact that almost all the missionaries in China were of revival-evangelistic background made it easy to convene them in missionary conferences to establish co-operation and comity.[1] In 1890, the second such conference sent out an appeal to the Protestant homelands to equip and send to China one thousand missionaries within five years. The number of Chinese comminicants then was about 50,000. It doubled within ten years and increased five-fold within twenty-five years.

The Evangelical design for China included an emphasis upon higher education, leading to the establishment of more than thirty universities and colleges and five hundred high schools. In this, Timothy Richard, a convert of the Revival of 1859 in Wales, made a great contribution.[2]

Evangelicals also erected hospitals, clinics and dispensaries, numbered in the hundreds. Patients treated rose in number from quarter of a million to a million in twenty years.

The work of evangelism had been proceeding slowly in Japan in the 1860s.[3] In 1872, the Week of Prayer sponsored by the World's Evangelical Alliance was held in Yokohama and there was an encouraging local revival.[4] In 1883, James Ballagh recalled the encouragement of the prayer times of the decade previous, and such was the effect on hearers that an intense revival ensued.[5]

A spirit of religious revival bringing times of refreshing from the presence of the Lord is spreading in Japan.[6]

The awakening spread to the Aoyama Gakuin in Tokyo, whose staff and students were deeply moved. In 1884, the Week of Prayer at Doshisha University could not be stopped but ran on until March, two hundred students being baptized. The revival spread to Sendai in 1886.[7]

There were intense emotional upheavals, much confession and restitution and many testimonies to the joy of new life in Christ.[8]

Otis Cary has titled the sixth chapter of his *History of Christianity in Japan* "Rapid Growth 1883–1888," when the Protestant enterprise in Japan experienced remarkable growth through[9] "the

---

[1] *Records of the General Conference of the Protestant Missionaries of China*, 1890.
[2] Soothill, W. E., *Timothy Richard of China, passim.*
[3] Cary, Otis, *A History of Christianity in Japan.*
[4] Iglehart, C. W., *A Century of Protestant Christianity in Japan*, p. 42.
[5] *Ibid.*, p. 72.
[6] Cary, Otis, *op. cit.*, p. 167, quoting Dr. Mackay, an American Methodist missionary.
[7] Iglehart, C. W., *op. cit.*, p. 73.   [8] *Ibid.*
[9] Cf. Iglehart, C. W., *op. cit.*, ch. iii, "Rapid Growth."

beginning of a series of remarkable revivals that exerted a power-ful influence upon Christians and through them upon un-believers."[1] Churches were crowded with eager listeners.[2] The word *rebaiburu* gained a place in Japanese Christian vocabulary.[3] There were "tears, sobbings and broken confessions of sin" among these stoics.[4]

Concurrently with revival, a dozen societies entered the coun-try.[5] Japanese denominational organizations were taking shape, such as Nippon Sei Ko Kwai, the Anglican Church of Japan.[6] In 1890, the foreign missionary staff numbered more than five hun-dred, with about three hundred organized churches and thirty thousand members.[7] In seven years, the adult membership in-creased from four to thirty thousand, evangelists from a hundred to four hundred, and self-support gained. "It was the springtime of Japan and the Church."[8]

Both Otis Cary (1909) and Iglehart (1959) in turn designated the decade following the period of Rapid Growth, the period of "Retarded Growth," and both attribute the decline to the theo-logical speculations that chilled the faith of the pastors.[9] In the 1890s, a wave of liberalism in theology caused some pastors to leave the ministry, and within ten years, theological students declined in numbers from three hundred to less than one hun-dred.[10] The optimistic predictions of the full conversion of the Empire to Christianity were not being fulfilled. The Christian faith was less influential in Japan than in China. Yet Christianity had ceased to be an alien way of life there.

It was in the 1880s that Evangelicals made an entrance to Korea.[11] American Presbyterians and Methodists bore the brunt of the invasion, though other nationalities and denominations participated. Not only was the background of the missionaries largely evangelical, but the methods advocated by them were evangelistic, encouraging the Koreans to evangelize the country themselves. In Korea, the ground was being prepared for an evangelical revival on a national scale.

In Burma, the Kachins and Chins were reached in the 1880s, through dedicated missionaries and Karen Christians using direct evangelism.[12]

In the north-eastern parts of India, as in Korea, a very evangeli-cal type of Protestantism began to take root through the efforts of

[1] Cary, Otis, *op. cit.*, ch. iv.
[2] *Ibid.*, p. 170. [3] *Ibid.* [4] *Ibid.*
[5] Latourette, K. S., *op. cit.*, p. 392. [6] *Ibid.*, p. 393.
[7] Iglehart, C. W., *op. cit.*, p. 75. [8] *Ibid.*
[9] Cary, Otis, *op. cit.*, p. 216. [10] *Ibid.*
[11] Latourette, K. S., *op. cit.*, Vol. VI, p. 420.
[12] Howard, R. L., *Baptists in Burma*, pp. 79 ff.

the Baptists and the Welsh Presbyterians.[1] Within a generation, these areas were to experience revival.

The Young Men's Christian Associations began their work in India in the 1880s, and had founded thirty-five Indian Y.M.C.A.s in a single decade.[2]

In the 1880s, the Salvation Army invaded India, and, under Booth-Tucker, adapted itself to Indian conditions very thoroughly.[3] The older missions were supplemented by newer organizations from Britain and the United States, from other parts of the British Empire and from Europe. A dozen societies in the second quarter became two dozen in the third quarter and doubled again to fifty in the fourth quarter of the nineteenth century.[4]

Thanks to the influence of the revivals in the Netherlands, the policies of exploitation of the Netherlands Indies (now Indonesia) began to give way to policies of uplift.[5] The revivals not only affected colonial administration but gave birth to new missionary societies, generally of more orthodox or more evangelistic motivation.[6] At the same time, in Indonesia, the missionary societies drew closer in co-operation and comity.[7]

American Methodists and Presbyterians entered the Philippines even before annexation (in 1898) by the United States.[8] They were followed by American Baptists and other denominations, and by the Christian and Missionary Alliance.[9]

At the same time, the long-smouldering anger of the Filipinos against their Spanish regular priests led to the schism of the Independent Catholic Church of the Philippines, with Aglipay[10] as its Archbishop. At first this church developed a Unitarian tendency, but afterwards swung into fellowship with the American Episcopal Church.

French imperial domination of Madagascar brought trouble to the missions operating there. Towards the end of the nineteenth century, a rebellion against French domination became an anti-Christian movement. Churches, schools and hospitals were destroyed, and many missions were left in ruins. It was a severe setback.[11]

A great revival began through a movement known as the

[1] Morris, J. H., *Story of Our Foreign Missions*, pp. 9 ff.
[2] McConaughy, D., *Pioneering With Christ*, pp. 26 ff.
[3] Mackenzie, F. A., *Booth-Tucker: Sadhu and Saint*.
[4] Glover, R. H., *Progress of World Wide Missions*, p. 109.
[5] Vandenbosch, A., *The Dutch East Indies*, pp. 48 ff.
[6] Rauws, J. *The Netherlands Indies*, pp. 56 ff.   [7] *Ibid.*, p. 74.
[8] Rodgers, J. B., *Forty Years in the Philippines*, p. 2.
[9] *World Statistics of Christian Missions*, 1916.
[10] Laubach, F., *The People of the Philippines*, pp. 137 ff.
[11] Sibree, J., *The Madagascar Mission*, pp. 77 ff.

Disciples of the Lord which arose from the conversion of an old Betsileo soldier, Rainisoalambo, who had dabbled in sorcery.[1]

The Disciples of the Lord multiplied so fast that in the space of a few years they were found in every part of the great island of Madagascar.[2] The revival, which was truly an indigenous work, emphasized the necessity of a personal experience of grace and the obligation of holy living. Belief in evil spirits played a large part in the revival, and exorcisms were practised. Yet the movement increased a desire for self-improvement, added an impetus to social reform, and gave encouragement to national evangelism.[3]

As a result of the Revival of 1880 in Norway, the Norwegian Mission Union was formed, later sending its missionaries to South Africa. Other missions from Scandinavia entered the country, fruits of revived missionary interest at home.[4]

In the late 1880s, Andrew Murray, famed as an advocate of evangelical revival and missions, helped form what later became the South Africa General Mission, to enter the Rhodesias and the neighbouring countries east and west.[5] The Paris Evangelical Missionary Society sent François Coillard to Barotseland, north of the Zambesi, and in 1887 he developed a mission there.[6] The older Protestant societies entered the Rhodesias in force with the British South Africa Company,[7] the South African Dutch Reformed Church included.

The redoubtable William Taylor, American revivalist and evangelist, was appointed Bishop for Africa by the American Methodist Episcopal Church, and landed at Loanda in 1885. Methodist work spread across the Continent, through Congo to Mozambique.[8] The Christian Brethren, stirred by F. S. Arnot, entered Angola in 1889, becoming the largest missionary organization there.[9]

The African Inland Mission was begun in 1895 by Peter C. Scott who revived Krapf's dream of planting a chain of mission stations across Africa.[10] It opened work in the Congo, Kenya and Tanganyika. In 1886, the Evangelical Missionary Society for East Africa was formed in Berlin. Its main sponsor was Pastor Friedrich von Bodelschwingh of the Inner Mission at Bielefeld.[11] It soon moved across the newly acquired German territory, and shared opportunities with older German societies.

---

[1] Burgess, A., *Zanahary in South Madagascar*, pp. 130 ff.
[2] *Ibid.*   [3] *Ibid.*
[4] *Christianity and the Natives of South Africa*, pp. 264 ff.   [5] *Ibid.*, pp. 242 ff.
[6] Mackintosh, C. W., *Coillard of the Zambesi, passim.*
[7] Richter, J., *Geschichte der evangelischen Mission in Africa*, p. 485.
[8] Springer, J. M., *The Heart of Central Africa*, pp. 19 ff.
[9] Baker, E., *Life and Explorations of F. S. Arnot*, pp. 238 ff.
[10] DuPlessis, J., *The Evangelization of Pagan Africa*, pp. 329-330.
[11] Richter, J., *op. cit.*, p. 581.

The Church Missionary Society extended its work in Kenya in the 1880s.[1] In 1891, a mission begun among the Kikuyu developed into a considerable enterprise under the Church of Scotland.[2]

In 1885, Simpson, founder of the Christian and Missionary Alliance, sent missionaries to the Congo.[3] In the 1880s, there arrived a Swedish Mission Covenant team,[4] which also entered the Equatorial African Congo, where the Paris Evangelical Mission shared the opportunity. Missions of various kinds, denominational and otherwise, spread throughout the whole Congo basin.

In 1887, a student under Grattan Guinness, Samuel A. Bill, entered the Qua Iboe area of Nigeria, backed by a strong board in Northern Ireland. The work, staunchly evangelical, grew to a Christian community of great proportions.[5]

In 1893, the Sudan Interior Mission entered Nigeria and spread its chain of mission stations across the full width of the Continent to Ethiopia.[6] Based on Canada, it became one of the largest interdenominational societies.

In the late 1880s, the North Africa Mission[7] extended its foothold in the cities of Morocco, Algeria and Tunis, and in 1888, its work was seconded in Morocco by the Southern Morocco Mission and in Algeria by the Algiers Mission Band which united with it three generations later. In the 1890s, it entered Tripoli in Libya.

From 1875 to 1895, the United Presbyterian Mission of North America increased its Egyptian membership ninefold, drawing many Copts.[8] In 1892, the North Africa Mission sent a scout to Egypt, but it was the Egypt General Mission,[9] a revival product with its base in Belfast, in the North of Ireland, that developed a considerable interdenominational work in the Nile kingdom.

The Church Missionary Society moved into the Sudan in the 1890s, as did the Presbyterian Mission in Egypt, but their greatest gains were in the south among the pagans, the Muslim resistance being as tenacious as before.[10]

The American Board missionaries reported an evangelical revival in Asia Minor in the year 1889 among the Armenians.[11] The evangelist of the movement was the Rev. Haratune Jenanian of

[1] Stock, F., *The History of the Church Missionary Society*, Vol. IV, pp. 428 ff.
[2] Philp, H. R. A., *A New Day in Kenya, passim.*
[3] Macaw, Mrs. A., *Congo, the First Alliance Mission Field, passim.*
[4] Lundahl, J. H., *Nils Westlind.*
[5] McKeown, R. K., *Twenty-Five Years in Qua Iboe*, pp. 52 ff.
[6] Hunter, J. H., *Flame of Fire: the Life and Work of Rowland V. Bingham, passim.*
[7] Rutherfurd and Glenny, *The Gospel in North Africa*, pp. 165–166.
[8] Watson, A., *The American Mission in Egypt, passim.*
[9] Roome, W. J. W., *"Blessed Be Egypt!" passim.*
[10] Watson, C. R., *Sorrow and Hope of the Egyptian Sudan, passim.*
[11] Halliday, S. B., *The Church in America and Its Baptisms of Fire*, p. 529.

Tarsus. There were three large Evangelical churches in Aintab, a town of 35,000. Response began in the smallest and spread to all three. Half the hearers were Gregorians. So great was the movement that missionaries and helpers around joined in the work. The attendances ranged from a thousand to two thousand, taxing all available space. Among the converts were gamblers and drunkards. In the accounting of several weeks, more than a thousand had professed conversion to God, 500 joinng the church on two Sundays.

The work of the American Board in Turkey was marked by a number of seasons of revival.[1] In the 1830s, the mission was begun in Istanbul in the face of great opposition. The first church was formed in the late 1840s. Forty years later there were more than a hundred and twenty-five churches with about 12,500 members and attendances weekly trebling that figure, served by nearly ninety ordained pastors and nearly nine hundred trained helpers.

As the years passed, the hostility of the old Gregorian Church towards Evangelicals passed, and not only were Evangelical pastors asked to preach in Gregorian churches but students were trained for Gregorian ministry by Evangelicals.[2]

In this period, medical missions were planted in Palestine. The work begun in Syria under Mrs. Bowen-Thompson[3] became the interdenominational British Syrian Mission, later Lebanon Evangelical Mission. In Baghdad in Iraq, Church Missionary Society work began in 1882, while Bishop Stewart of New Zealand reinforced the work in Iran.[4] The famed Islamic scholar and Christian missionary, Samuel Marinus Zwemer, arrived in Basra as a student volunteer in 1890.[5]

In the 1890s, the Regions Beyond Missionary Union, founded by the revivalist Grattan Guinness, entered Peru. The Help for Brazil Mission and the South American Evangelical Mission, working in other Latin countries, united with it to form the Evangelical Union of South America.[6]

Meanwhile, the Moravians at the mid-century had begun a mission on the Mosquito Coast, on the Caribbean side of Nicaragua. Originally an English buccaneering settlement, its population was Negro and Mulatto as well as Indian. In the year 1881, an extraordinary awakening began with confession of sins and restitution of wrongs which resulted in so many conversions that

---

[1] Barton, J. L., *Daybreak in Turkey*, *passim*.
[2] *Ibid.*, pp. 174–175.
[3] Pitman, E. R., *Missionary Heroines in Many Lands*.
[4] Stock, E., *The History of the Church Missionary Society*, Vol. III, p. 515.
[5] Wilson, J. C., *An Apostle to Islam: A Biography of Samuel M. Zwemer*, *passim*.
[6] The author preached in E.U.S.A. mission posts in both Brazil and Peru.

the church membership increased from a thousand or more to three thousand or more in a decade.[1]

In 1890, through C. I. Scofield, an associate of D. L. Moody, the Central American Mission was formed as an interdenominational society to carry the Gospel to the republics of Central America.[2]

The Christian and Missionary Alliance, at the first an interdenominational society, but afterwards a denomination in the United States, began its missionary enterprise in Latin America in the 1890s.[3] Its founder was Dr. A. B. Simpson, converted in Canada during the Awakening of '58 and a noted revival leader of Presbyterian stock.[4]

Each new invasion of Latin America by these forces of Evangelicalism followed an awakening. After the conclusion of the Spanish-American War, Protestant missions entered the islands of Cuba and Puerto Rico, gathering adherents very rapidly.[5] The character of these missions thus engaged was as usual, evangelical.

In most cases, a generation of pioneering and teaching passed before the infant churches were themselves to experience the phenomena of true revival. When these awakenings came in their courses, unparalleled advances were made in a vast territory which less evangelical societies were willing to leave to the Roman established Churches long moribund.[6] If ever an invasion of a territory were justified, the invasion of Latin America by Protestant missions was obviously a necessity.

[1] Hamilton, J. T., *History of the Moravian Church*, p. 530.
[2] Grubb, K. G., *Religion in Central America*.
[3] Thompson, A. E., *The Life of A. B. Simpson*, p. 228.
[4] *Ibid.*, pp. 17 ff.
[5] Grose, H. B., *Advance in the Antilles*, pp. 104, 208.
[6] As at the World Missionary Conference, Edinburgh.

CHAPTER XXVI

SOCIAL IMPACT OF REVIVAL, II

FOLLOWING THE MID-CENTURY AWAKENING, BRITAIN MAIN-
tained the lead it assumed fifty years earlier in initiating social
reform and relief.

It is an American historical opinion that the 1858 Revival had
little effect on the social welfare of the American people. Rather,
its effects were suspended while the nation's energies were being
consumed by the war between the States, a war with far-reaching
social after-effects.

During that war, Christians engaged in social action. The
United States Christian Commission brought spiritual good,
intellectual improvement, and social and spiritual welfare to the
troops of the Federal Government.[1] There were Christian organizations caring for the welfare of soldiers of the Confederate armies
also.[2] In the Union and the Confederate armies, Christian forces
both formal and informal tried to arrest the general moral disintegration caused by the brutality of war. Comforts were offered
prisoners of war, intelligence was sent to anxious relatives. The
Negroes were given as much protection as war permitted. Suddenly, in the course of hostilities, slavery was swept away.[3] What
Christians were striving for by peaceful agitation became manda-
tory almost overnight by military decree.

In post-war years, the American evangelicals found British
social enterprises ready to adopt.

The 1858–59 Evangelical Awakening, while primarily evangelistic, had developed a humane spirit as liberal as its theology
was conservative. Commenting on a single outcome of the Revival, G. M. Trevelyan[4] affirmed that it had "brought the enthusiasm
of 'conversion' after Wesley's original fashion to the army of the
homeless and unfed, to the drunkard, the criminal and the harlot,"
treating "social work and care for the material conditions of the
poor and outcast as being an essential part of the Christian mission

[1] Weigle, L. A., *American Idealism*, p. 188.
[2] Jones, J. W., *Christ in the Camp, passim.*
[3] Cf. Latourette, K. S., *A History of the Expansion of Christianity*, Vol. IV, pp.
346 ff.
[4] Trevelyan, G. M., *English Social History*, pp. 492 ff.

to the souls of men and women." These tributes belong to the 1858–59 Revival as a whole.

One of the first effects of the Awakening of 1858–59 was the creation of new and intense sympathy with the poor and suffering. "God has not ordained," protested Lord Shaftesbury, "that in a Christian country there should be an overwhelming mass of foul, helpless poverty."[1]

A revival school of Christian philanthropists arose, endeavouring to go straight to the heart of the slums with a practical Samaritanism, yet always ready to co-operate in all wide legislative improvements.[2] So, as the Revivals intensified the fervour of beliefs, denominational schemes, organizations, and committees were multiplied; numberless philanthropic institutions, homes, asylums, refuges, and schools were founded.[3]

As before, Lord Shaftesbury was spokesman for evangelical social reform. He initiated more Royal Commissions of social investigation than any parliamentarian in British history.[4] Had he achieved no more than the victory of the "'Ten Hours' Act," he could have rested with historical fame well-deserved. But he laboured to extend the benefits of the legislation of the first half of the century to all classes of working people.

During 1864 and 1867, the Industrial Extension Acts were passed, practically universalizing the provisions of labour protection.[5] In 1865, Lord Shaftesbury tackled the problem of Agricultural Gangs and relieved the children of the countryside from a bondage as brutal as that endured by their townsfellows in earlier decades.[6] In 1872, Shaftesbury worked for the abolition of abuse of child labour in brickyards.[7] His most striking victory was passing legislation forbidding the use of little boys to clean house and factory chimneys. In 1875 one of these boys, George Brewster, died of suffocation and with this and a hundred other illustrations of the horror of conditions among the chimney sweeps,[8] Shaftesbury awakened again the public conscience.

The seventh Earl of Shaftesbury was not without faults, of course. As an aristocrat of class-conscious times, he upheld the superiority of his order, detested trade unions,[9] was occasionally a narrow-minded diehard. He bitterly opposed the Salvation Army and refused to reconsider his attitude.[10]

There is an immediate connexion between an evangelical awakening and educational hunger, as seen in a report dated

---

[1] The Christian, 3rd June, 1909.   [2] Ibid.
[3] Canton, W., History of the British and Foreign Bible Society, Vol. III, pp. 1–2.
[4] Bready, J. W., Lord Shaftesbury and Social-Industrial Progress.
[5] Ibid., p. 313.   [6] Ibid., pp. 318 ff.   [7] Ibid., p. 326.   [8] Ibid., p. 333.
[9] Latourette, K. S., The Nineteenth Century in Europe, Vol. II, p. 376.
[10] Bready, J. W., op. cit., p. 402.

August 1859 from the district where the 1859 Revival first began:[1]

> Education is now become the principal object of concern among the
> uneducated class in this neighbourhood [Antrim], both of old and
> young. The present revival has created a thirsting desire for the Word
> of God, and it is their continual and increasing study to learn to read
> it for themselves. The spirit of inquiry is so great that we have been
> induced to open the school two evenings during the week, for the
> purpose of communicating instruction.

In Britain, there had been opposition to Sunday Schools. High
Church leaders suspected any lay influence in teaching; and upper-
class spokesmen deplored any thought of enlightening the masses.
These factors did not apply in America, where the Sunday School
programme in the churches became a factor in the growth of
membership in a way still unparalleled in Great Britain.

In Britain, things changed. From the time of 1859 onwards, the
Evangelical Awakening began to fill the Sunday Schools of the
three kingdoms with children eager to learn spiritual lessons. In
a seven-year period, denominations reported increases of thirty-
to fifty per cent.[2] They failed to maintain themselves in the
twentieth century in the way enjoyed in the United States.

In Great Britain, in 1815, elementary schools were entirely
private.[3] Two decades later, Lord Ashley (later the seventh Earl
of Shaftesbury) petitioned the Queen to provide for moral and
religious education for the working classes. The Government
proposed to do this by means of purely Anglican parish schools,
which provoked opposition from other Christians. Largely from
insistence by Evangelicals, the State contributed a measure of
support to elementary schools. In 1870, their recommendations
were fulfilled in the Education Act, setting up public day schools.[4]
A million or more were in attendance in England in 1870; two
million or more in 1885.[5]

Reference has already been made to the work of George Müller
among the orphans at Bristol.

During the 1859 Revival in Dublin, several members of a
brilliant family named Barnardo professed to accept Christ as
Saviour in the Metropolitan Hall series.[6] Two of the Barnardo
brothers endeavoured to persuade their younger brother Tom,
but he scoffed. Nevertheless, he attended the meetings and witnessed the striking demonstration of spiritual conviction. These
he explained away as emotional hysteria and psychological phenomena, yet, in spite of his subtle arguments, he was set to thinking.

---

[1] *The Revival*, 27th August, 1859.
[2] Orr, J. Edwin, *The Second Evangelical Awakening in Britain*, pp. 273 ff.
[3] Latourette, K. S., *op. cit.*, Vol. II, p. 355.
[4] *Ibid.*, pp. 356 ff.   [5] *Ibid.*
[6] Bready, J. W., *Dr. Barnardo: Physician, Pioneer, Prophet*, p. 50.

Later, Tom Barnardo attended a smaller meeting in the home of a devout Christian named William Fry. He remained cynical, in his own words "just as cheeky" as a young fellow could be. But an address by John Hambledon in the same place some weeks later caused him such conviction that long after midnight he sought, in great distress and with many tears, his brothers' help. He was converted on 26th May, 1862.[1] Tom Barnardo became attached to a Bible class run by Grattan Guinness, who invited young Hudson Taylor to address the group on the needs of China. There young Barnardo heard the call to missionary service and soon volunteered to go. Tragic discoveries in the dismal East End of London led him into his life-work, the founding of Dr. Barnardo's Homes, the world's largest private orphanage system.

In 1864, William Quarrier[2] of Glasgow started orphan homes in Scotland and shortly afterwards J. W. C. Fegan[3] of London organized his homes and orphanages in England. The British Revival thus raised up orphanage founders in Dublin and Glasgow and London. A similar work was done by Miss Annie MacPherson of Cambridge, as the idea spread throughout the country.

In 1884, a couple of unknown Christian men were introduced to Lord Shaftesbury, who paid rapt attention to their account of welfare work on behalf of children. He proposed the formation of a national society, and a meeting in the great Mansion House in London launched the project which in 1889 became the National Society for the Prevention of Cruelty to Children. Most of its early supporters were strong evangelicals.

Young and Ashton, in their volume describing *British Social Work in the Nineteenth Century*, have no hesitation in describing evangelicalism as "the greatest single urge" in humanitarianism.[4]

> The sentiment of human benevolence, and its practical expression, derived directly from religious influence. It came from the quickened knowledge, born of religious revivalism, that all men were the children of God and loved by Him.

A Christian man, John Augustus, a cobbler in Boston, offered in 1841 to bail out a drunkard. The Massachusetts Court agreed to the experiment, and in the next two decades, this single Christian man bailed out two thousand people who might otherwise have become criminals.[5]

---

[1] *Ibid.*   [2] *The Christian*, 22nd April, 1886.
[3] Morgan, G. E., *R. C. Morgan*, p. 144, 156.
[4] Young and Ashton, *British Social Work*, p. 41.
[5] *Encyclopaedia Britannica*, 1960, "Probation."

Due to the influence of Mary Carpenter[1] and Sarah Martin,[2] Christian women interested in the welfare of prisoners, care of people sentenced to prison in Britain increased. In 1854, the Youthful Offenders Act was passed in Britain.[3] In 1862, the Discharged Prisoners Act followed.[4]

The Probation of First Offenders became a law first in the State of Massachusetts in 1878. A similar law was passed by Parliament in 1887.[5] These and a hundred and one other measures originated in a saying eighteen centuries before: "I was in prison and ye visited me!" but it took the Awakenings of the eighteenth and nineteenth centuries to change the civic conscience.

Evangelical sentiment was expressed by Mrs. Barnardo: "The State should deal with it, but does not: the Church of Christ must!"[6] Individuals, not church bodies, initiated reform.

In the early months of the 1860 Revival in the city of London, attempts were made to reclaim the prostitutes who frequented the West End. A series of evangelistic meetings were held for prostitutes only, arranged at midnight or later. At the outset, many fallen girls burst into tears when addressed by the saintly Baptist Noël who talked very tenderly to them. The sponsors took a score of penitents to houses of rehabilitation. Foreign-born prostitutes were given the Good News in their own tongue. The Midnight Meeting Movement, as it was called, spread to other cities and towns of Great Britain, and a thousand women were reported to have been rescued in a year.[7]

The work was carried on by a rare champion. Josephine Elizabeth Grey was born in 1828, and married George Butler, an educator and churchman who became canon of Winchester. Her little girl tragically fell to her death in her own home. In her sorrow, Josephine Butler sought to share the greater pain of other unfortunates, and soon found her life work in social welfare.[8]

In 1864, almost secretly, Parliament passed its first Contagious Diseases Act, designed to curb and control prostitution in the neighbourhood of garrison towns. It, in fact, licensed the vice, and made prostitution a vested interest.[9]

In her visits to prisons, where she shared in the menial tasks of the women, Josephine Butler was confronted with the evil of state patronage and regulation of vice. She dedicated herself in righteous indignation to the abolition of the evil. "No other woman in history," affirmed the social reformer, Dame Millicent

[1] Carpenter, J. E., *Life and Work of Mary Carpenter.*
[2] Young and Ashton, *op. cit.,* p. 159.
[3] *Ibid.,* p. 165.   [4] *Ibid.,* p. 159.   [5] *Ibid.,* p. 174.
[6] Bourdillon, A. F. C., *Voluntary Social Services,* p. 45.
[7] Morgan, G. E., *op. cit.,* p. 145.   [8] Orr, J. Edwin, *op. cit.,* p. 214.
[9] Young and Ashton, *op. cit.,* pp. 205 ff.

Fawcett, "had such a far-reaching influence, or effected so wide-spread a change in public opinion."[1]

Concentrating upon the inequality of suspected women before the law, Josephine Butler worked for the repeal of the obnoxious legislation which made the government the official supervisor of iniquity.[2] In October 1869, the National Association for Repeal was formed.[3] Josephine Butler worked with might and main. Her life was threatened by the brutal opposition of interested pur-veyors of women's bodies, and on more than one occasion, she escaped over walls or through windows to save her life.[4] By 1877, more than eight hundred provincial and metropolitan committees had gathered eight thousand petitions with more than two million signatures, which were submitted to Parliament. A Royal Com-mission (1870–71) and a Select Committee of Parliament (1879 onward) investigated thoroughly the operation of the Acts. The report of the latter was antagonistic to the petitioners, so in 1883 Mrs. Butler rallied the Christian forces in prayer "so that the prayers of the people of God would be as the incense of Aaron, when he ran between the living and the dead . . . and the plague was stayed." The Acts were suspended in 1883 and repealed in 1886.

Josephine Butler influenced European public opinion against government supervision of vice. Victor Hugo in France and Gari-baldi in Italy were among her supporters. She revealed that the licensed brothel was the recruiting station for the nefarious white-slave traffic by which many an innocent girl was trapped into vice. She travelled widely in the United States in order to encourage American endeavours of like purpose. She died in 1906, but her work continued, for the League of Nations Convention for Sup-pression of the Traffic in Women and Children recognizably stemmed from her crusade.[5]

Josephine Butler encouraged Ellice Hopkins[6] and her sponsor, Bishop Lightfoot of Durham, in the formation of the White Cross Society (1883) that led to further victories for social decency. In 1885, Bramwell Booth of the Salvation Army and the journalist W. T. Stead, to expose white-slavery, purchased a thirteen-year-old girl for what could have been immoral purposes.[7] As a result, Stead went to prison for three months on technical charges, but his exposures of traffic in young girls created a great outcry throughout the country and led to the passing of a Criminal Law

[1] Fawcett, M., *Josephine Butler, passim.*
[2] Butler, J., *Personal Reminiscences of a Great Crusade, passim.*
[3] Morgan, G. E., *R. C. Morgan*, pp. 298 ff., quoting Mrs. Helen S. Dyer.
[4] *Ibid.*, p. 299 n.
[5] Fawcett, M., *op. cit.*
[6] Young and Ashton, *op. cit.*, pp. 221.   [7] *Ibid.*, pp. 209 ff.

Amendment Bill to end many abuses. This was a further triumph for evangelical action.[1]

In the year 1859, the young Swiss business man Henri Dunant followed the French Emperor Napoleon III to Northern Italy, hoping to arrange business contracts. Unwittingly, he found himself a spectator at the bloody battle of Solferino.

Henri Dunant was of a prominent evangelical family and was already active in the Young Men's Christian Association of Geneva.[2] Among those who had made a profound impression on his thinking were Elizabeth Fry, famed as a prison reformer, and Florence Nightingale, famed as a military nurse.[3]

Dunant was horrified by the suffering of the wounded and dying on the battlefield. He helped as best he could in the days that followed, noting the sincere if unskilled efforts of local people to alleviate the suffering. He wrote *A Memory of Solferino* and published it in 1862, sending it to statesmen and leaders throughout Europe. As a result, a Geneva Convention was held in 1864, and out from its findings and decisions came the Red Cross Movement.[4]

Not everyone expected to help proved willing. Some military leaders resented the intrusion of civilians on the battlefield. To Henri Dunant's sorrow, Florence Nightingale withheld her support,[5] saying that the succour of the wounded in war was a business of government. But enough help was forthcoming to speed the Red Cross on its errand of mercy, and it spread throughout the world.

Following the awakenings of the first part of the nineteenth century, evangelical Christians more and more advocated temperance in the use of spirituous liquors, and a number of societies carried the concern to churches and society. In Ireland, a devout Irish Roman Catholic priest—Father Theobald Mathew, who had been helped to his conviction by a Quaker—persuaded his own countrymen by the thousands to pledge a total abstinence, and won as many more in the United States and Great Britain.[6]

Awake to the dangers of alcoholic indulgence, the mid-century revivalists preached not only temperance but total abstinence. Converts with former drunken experience roamed the country-

---

[1] Stead, F. H., *The Story of Social Christianity.*
[2] Shedd, C. T., *History of the World's Alliance of Young Men's Christian Associations,* pp. 82 ff.
[3] Boardman, M. T., *Under the Red Cross Flag,* p. 32.
[4] Gumpert, M., *Dunant: the Story of the Red Cross.*
[5] Epstein, B. and S., *Henri Dunant,* p. 22.
[6] Stead, F. H., *op. cit.,* Vol. II, p. 199; *vide* Vol. IV, Cherrington, *Standard Encyclopedia of the Alcohol Problem.*

H

side of Britain, flaying verbally the vendors of liquor.[1] In 1862, the Church of England Temperance Society was founded, while other societies were strengthened.[2] But in the United States, the temperance cause was weakened by the heavy drinking during the Civil War, until in the year 1865, a national convention brought the existing temperance organizations together, the National Temperance Society emerging to usefulness.[3]

John Frederick Denison Maurice and Charles Kingsley, Broad Church English clergymen, in the earlier decades stirred up the interest of British Christians in a mild Christian Socialism, which, non-political in design, furthered the cause of the trade unions and the co-operative movement.[4]

The first Labour member to sit in the House of Commons was an evangelical Christian, Keir Hardie. He began his life of public service as a lay preacher in Glasgow's Evangelical Union.[5] Keir Hardie's religious convictions made him the first of a long line of Christians to serve the cause of the working people in political action. During the early days of trade unionism and the Labour Party alike, the Christian section of the party greatly exceeded the Marxist wing.

In 1856, Keir Hardie was born into a hard-working Scottish family, and at eight years of age he began to earn his living in Glasgow. He was raised an atheist, but in 1878 he was converted to Christ.[6] His evangelical conversion intensified his zeal for humanitarian reform. His outstanding labour tract bore the title: "Can a man be a Christian on a pound a week?" with his text taken from Proverbs, "Give me neither poverty nor riches."

Not all Evangelicals were sympathetic to the trade unions or to the Labour Party's objectives. William Wilberforce, the great Emancipator, had opposed trade unions, and Lord Shaftesbury was critical of socialism and chartism.[7] A majority of Anglican Evangelicals followed a *laissez-faire* policy towards the remaking of society as distinct from social amelioration. Middle-class Methodists gradually allied themselves with a progressive Liberalism in politics;[8] but Primitive Methodists showed strong sympathy with the Labour party.[9]

The sending of Keir Hardie to Europe to inform continental Socialists and trade unionists how deeply the British movement

---

[1] Orr, J. Edwin, *op. cit.*, p. 214.   [2] *Ibid.*
[3] Cherrington, *op. cit.*, Vol. IV, pp. 1863–1864.
[4] *Vide* Binyon, G. C., *The Christian Socialist Movement in England, passim.*
[5] Fleming, J. R., *The Church in Scotland, 1875–1929*, p. 163.
[6] Carswell, D., *Brother Scots*, pp. 155 ff.
[7] Binyon, G. C., *op. cit.*, pp. 24 ff.
[8] Taylor, E. R., *Methodism and Politics*, pp. 12 ff.
[9] Latourette, K. S., *op. cit.*, Vol. II, p. 376.

had drunk refreshing draughts from springs of Christianity[1] greatly impressed Ramsay Macdonald. The later Prime Minister noted that the continental trade unionists and socialists were generally opposed to the Church, but that they had been opposed to the Church long before they became social reformers; whereas the British Labour movement was totally different, having drawn strength from Christian leaders since the days of John Ball in the times of the Lollards.[2]

Seemingly, it was as natural for the British movement to draw inspiration and guidance from the Christian ethic as it was for the continental movement to deny its source or pass it by.

The attacks by leaders of the various labour movements in continental Europe upon Christian institutions and ideals made it inevitable that the Christians there would form their own parties. In Great Britain, Evangelical Christians never became identified with one political party; they supported the betterment of conditions through all parties. Some objectives for which the early Labour pioneers strove became acceptable not only to Liberals but Conservatives, and to both Democrats and Republicans in the United States and all parties in Commonwealth countries.

It is said that Hardie was more impressed by Moody's forthright evangelistic message, less with the philosophy of Moody's personal friends in British industry. Keir Hardie had collided with Lord Overtoun, the industrialist,[3] who as James Campbell White had been converted in the 1859 Awakening, and who supported Moody personally and financially in his evangelistic campaigns in Glasgow in 1874, 1882 and 1892. Lord Overtoun afterwards became a generous philanthropist. In Glasgow, one of his plants, for whose management he held no active responsibility, suffered a strike, aimed at ending conditions of exploitation.[4]

The tradition of active Christian men in high positions of leadership in Labour was continued by Arthur Henderson, born in 1863, who became chairman of the British Labour Party in 1908. He helped to keep the Labour Party clear of any relationship with the emerging Communist party. His was a long and useful life, crowned by being granted the Nobel Peace Prize. Henderson was converted in 1879 and he retained his status as a Methodist lay preacher throughout his career.[5]

But Labour held no monopoly. The two Prime Ministers who dominated the last third of their century in Britain were Salisbury and Gladstone, both devout Christian men. Throughout the last

[1] Bready, J. W., *This Freedom—Whence?* pp. 277–282, devotes many paragraphs to Hardie and Ramsay Macdonald.
[2] Trevelyan, G. M., *op. cit.*, pp. 13–14.
[3] Carswell, D., *op. cit.*, "Keir Hardie."   [4] *Ibid.*, "Lord Overtoun."
[5] *Dictionary of National Biography, 1931–1940.*

third, and (in fact) the latter half of the century, the welfare of the people was the dominant idea in many branches of Government.[1]

Timothy L. Smith, professor of the University of Minnesota, in his volume on *Revivalism and Social Reform*, made this pertinent observation concerning conditions in the United States at the same time:[2]

> The rapid growth of concern with purely social issues such as poverty, working men's rights, the liquor traffic, slum housing, and racial bitterness is the chief feature distinguishing American religion after 1865 from that of the first half of the nineteenth century.

Smith's volume has underscored the dynamic of the Christian gospel in transforming the face of the United States.[3] The United States was rapidly being industrialized as was Great Britain in earlier decades. The same situations prevailed in the United States, some industrialists being philanthropists while lacking sympathy with all organized labour.[4] On the other hand, organized labour in America adopted the strategy, tactics, weapons and warfare of their British confrères without experiencing the Christian dynamic. A number of ministers carried a social burden for something more than amelioration of conditions,[5] but the trade unions throughout the States seem less aware of their indebtedness to the gospel.

A Bishop of western New York State, Frederic Dan Huntington, spearheaded the social crusade in his denomination, the American Episcopalian, to build the kingdom of God in social justice.[6]

Washington Gladden,[7] a Congregationalist, and Walter Rauschenbusch,[8] a Baptist, emerged as the leaders of the advocates of the social gospel, but because their views were being supported by the advocates of a militant modernism in theology, there was a tendency on the part of evangelicals to shy away. There were ardent evangelicals as strongly burdened for the socially disinherited.

In America, Sam Jones and B. Fay Mills who shared evangelistic popularity with D. L. Moody had their emphasis on social reform. The former crusaded against sin and civic corruption.[9] The latter began preaching evangelistic sermons on Christianity and Socialism, and the Kingdom of Heaven on Earth, his post-millennial

---

[1] Latourette, K. S., *op. cit.*, p. 353.
[2] Smith, T. L., *Revivalism and Social Reform*, p. 148.
[3] *Ibid.*, chapter x.
[4] Sweet, W. W., *Story of Religion in America*, p. 348.
[5] Hopkins, C. H., *The Rise of the Social Gospel in American Protestantism, 1865–1915*.
[6] Smith, T. L., *op. cit.*, p. 159.
[7] *Dictionary of American Biography*, Vol. VIII.
[8] *Vide* Rauschenbusch, Walter, *Christianity and the Social Order*.
[9] Holcomb, W., *Life and Sayings of Sam Jones, passim*.

hope.[1] Not long afterwards, Mills deserted evangelism. His was not the message of the lineal successors of Moody in mass evangelism. Torrey and Chapman advocated social service, but neither was at all committed to the social gospel.

The post-millennial hope of the Kingdom of God on earth, which was encouraged by the sweeping success of the mid-century Revival,[2] waxed and waned before World War I. The American mass evangelists tended later to veer away from even the social amelioration programmes of Moody or his successors in favour of *laissez-faire* policy. An alliance between extreme right in politics and extreme right in religion was taking shape, even as there was an alliance of the extreme left.

The greatest achievements of the century—the abolition of the slave trade, reform of prisons, emancipation of slaves, care of the sick, education of the young, protection of workers and the like—were made, not by Churches as denominations or congregations, but by enlightened individuals and their voluntary supporters. Wilberforce did not wait for the help of the Convocations of the Church of England, nor did Fliedner enlist the support of Lutheran Synods, nor did the Tolpuddle Martyrs of the trade union movement appeal to the Methodist Conference. The work of the Lord was done by dedicated individuals nurtured in the faith and worship of evangelical fellowships. Churches and parliaments needed to be persuaded.

[1] Mills, B. F., *God's World, passim.*
[2] Thompson, C. L., *Times of Refreshing*, p. 90.

CHAPTER XXVII

AWAKENINGS OF 1905

IN 1903, F. B. MEYER, A CONVERT OF THE REVIVAL OF THE 1860s, ministered at the newly-organized Llandrindod Wells Convention; and a group of younger Welsh ministers were greatly blessed, so much so that they devoted themselves freely to prayer for another awakening in Wales.[1]

These pastors were increasingly blessed in their congregations, but it was a young layman who served to answer prayers for an awakening. Evan John Roberts was born on 8th July, 1878, at Bwlchymynydd, Loughor, Gorseinon. At the age of twelve, he took the place of his injured father in the coal-mines;[2] at twenty-six, he left as a candidate for the Presbyterian ministry. On 29th September, 1904, he faced a spiritual crisis.

In November 1904, the Reverend Seth Joshua commenced a series of revival meetings in the town of Blaenanerch. One day, he took with him a party of young people from Newquay, including the young theological student, Evan Roberts. At the conclusion of the meeting, Seth Joshua prayed "O Arglwydd, plyg ni!"[3] ("Bend us, O Lord!") and the words stuck in the mind of Evan Roberts, who at a meeting next day prayed: "Bend me, O Lord," while his tears flowed freely. He had realized a "Living Force" possessing him.

Evan Roberts returned to Newcastle Emlyn, and prayed for six others fully dedicated to God. When that prayer was answered, he realized a burden to return to his own people in the village of Loughor with the news of a free salvation.

During that time, one of the young ministers, R. B. Jones, commenced campaigning in Rhos in North Wales, and in due course experienced the unusual manifestations of revival.[4]

To his native place, Evan Roberts went and asked his pastor's permission to hold revival meetings in their chapel. The minister agreed, but predicted that he would find the ground hard and stony. At first this prediction seemed true.[5]

[1] Jones, R. B., *Rent Heavens*, chapter ii, "Origins."
[2] Shaw, S. B., *The Great Revival in Wales*, p. 122.
[3] Penn-Lewis, J., *The Awakening in Wales;* cf. Shaw, S. B., *op. cit.*, p. 62.
[4] Jones, R. B., *op. cit.*, chapter iii, November, 1904.
[5] Penn-Lewis, J., *op. cit.*

The young people waited upon God. Then six sinners repented of their sins, and a multitude of conversions followed. At six in the morning, the townsfolk were awakened by the sound of people flocking to early morning prayer meetings.

A local minister reported that the community had been converted into a praying multitude. The lives of hundreds of coalminers and tin-plate workers were transformed, men going straight from the mills and pit-heads to chapel, leaving the taverns practically empty.[1]

It was the same in North Wales, where local prayer meetings were so crowded that churches were unable to contain the intercessors. There was an extraordinary spiritual force gripping the townsfolk of Rhos also.[2]

On November 10th, the first public reference to these remarkable scenes was made, a newspaper devoting columns to the reports.[3] Other journals dispensed news paragraphs as the Revivalist (he was correctly designated) went to Trecynon and other towns and villages in Glamorganshire. A cleansing wave swept the blackened valleys.

At first people flocked to hear the passionate oratory of the young coal-miner, but in a short time the preaching gave way to scripture-based testimony. Churches began to be filled by eager crowds at all hours of the day, with neither the local pastor nor visiting evangelist in control.

Many were the evidences of the Spirit of God working in the country. Long-standing debts were paid, stolen goods returned. Pugilists, gamblers, tavern owners, drunkards were converted to God. Taverns were forsaken, and rowdiness changed to soberness.[4]

Cursing and profanity was so diminished that it was reported that a strike was provoked in the coal-mines—so many men gave up foul language that the pit-ponies dragging the coal trucks in the mine tunnels did not understand what was being said to them.

Even the children in the day schools became affected by the prevailing spirit. A kindergarten child raised his hand, gained attention, asked his teacher: "Do you love Jesus?" The arrow reached its mark; she went to India as a missionary.

Thirty years after the event, the writer was told by a renowned Baptist pastor of his visit to the scenes of the Welsh Revival.[5]

The Reverend H. J. Galley, later of Widcombe Chapel in Bath, then a student newly-graduated from Spurgeon's College in London, was reading in the London newspapers the accounts of

[1] *Ibid.*   [2] Jones, R. B., *loc. cit.*

[3] *Vide Western Mail*, consolidated reports entitled *The Religious Revival in Wales*.

[4] Jones, R. B., *op. cit.*, chapter v, "Immediate Practical Results."

[5] This is but one example of the accounts given to the author in person.

phenomenal activity in the Welsh Revival. He made up his mind to go, sent a telegram to a classmate, and in due course arrived at the little station in the valleys. His friend was there to meet him.

"Where is Even Roberts preaching?" asked the Englishman. "I don't know," replied the Welshman. "He may be in my church tonight or he may be a hundred miles away."

Evan Roberts avoided telling the people what times and places he would preach, to discourage sensation-seekers following him around. This word amazed Galley, who had come to hear the Revivalist, but he was even more amazed to find that his friend's church accommodated meetings each day from before breakfast until midnight, and that every other church and hall in town was likewise occupied, all of them being packed from 6 p.m. until midnight.

The veteran minister recalled that as they walked along, they passed two tavern-keepers on opposite sides of a street bewailing the lack of custom. Both taverns were closed up that week and converted to youth recreation halls.

The movement affected all Wales, all classes and all ages, and every denomination shared in the general awakening. Districts not visited by Roberts shared equally extraordinary stirrings.[1] Lists of converts were published in newspapers, 70,000 in two months and 85,000 in five months, and more than one hundred thousand professed conversions in the half-year of the awakening.[2]

Stocks of Welsh and English Bibles were sold out. Prayer meetings were held in coal-mines, in trains and trams and places of business. The works managers bore testimony of the change of behaviour of their employees. Magistrates were presented with white gloves in several places, signifying that there were no cases to try. The Miners' Associations declined to hold meetings on licensed premises, hitherto the custom.[3]

Of the one hundred thousand converted in the brief period of the Welsh Revival, six months, sixty thousand were still in the membership of the Welsh churches in 1910, in spite of heavy emigration to the English-speaking countries.[4]

Visitors flocked to Wales from the English-speaking countries and the Continent to observe. The immediate ethical results of the Awakening were astounding. A great wave of sobriety swept the country, causing severe financial losses to men in the liquor trade, and closing many of the taverns. There was a remarkable decrease in crime and a great improvement in public morals.[5]

Dr. G. Campbell Morgan, Westminster divine and Bible teacher

[1] Penn-Lewis, J., *op. cit., passim.*
[2] Jones, R. B., *op. cit.,* chapter v.   [3] *Ibid.*
[4] Morgan, J. V., *The Welsh Religious Revival,* p. 247.
[5] Penn-Lewis, J., *op. cit.*

famed in America and Britain, visited Wales and reported in London:[1]

> What is the character of this revival? It is a church revival. I do not mean by that merely a revival among church members. It is that, but it is held in church buildings. In Wales, the meetings are held in the chapels, all up and down the valleys, and it began among church members; and, when it touches the outside man, it makes him a church member at once. Within five weeks, twenty thousand have joined the churches in Wales—I think that more than that have been converted. It is a movement in the church and of the church, a movement in which the true functions and forces of the church are being exercised and fulfilled.

Evan Roberts bore a special burden for the Church: "Bend the church and save the world." Evan Roberts had no technique. He often made a test of the meeting on the following four points:[2]

> 1. The past must be made clear by confession of every known sin to God, and every wrong done to man must be put right.
> 2. Every doubtful thing in the believer's life must be put away.
> 3. Prompt and implicit obedience must be yielded to the Spirit of God.
> 4. Public confession of Christ must be made.

The observant Campbell Morgan commented upon the unusual meeting procedures in Revival:

> It was a meeting characterized by a perpetual series of interruptions and disorderliness. It was a meeting characterized by a great continuity and an absolute order.[3]

This is the paradox of all meetings typical of Evangelical Awakenings. Of the confessions of sin, Campbell Morgan reported:[4]

> The movement is characterized by the most remarkable confessions of sin, confessions that must be costly. I heard some of them, more rising who have been members of the church and officers of the church, confessing hidden sin in their hearts, impurity committed and condoned, and seeking prayer for its putting away.

Confession, according to J. Vyrnwy Morgan, was particular and specific.[5] Dr. Vyrnwy Morgan was one of those who deplored the influence of the secular press in reporting the Revival:

> That pure stream became impure under the hoof of the enemy—killed by the press of South Wales.[6]

[1] Sermon by G. Campbell Morgan, 25th December, 1904, quoted in Shaw, S. B., *op. cit.*, pp. 86 ff.
[2] Davis, G. T. B., *When the Fire Fell*, p. 79.
[3] Sermon by G. Campbell Morgan, 25th December, 1904, quoted in Shaw, S. B., *op. cit.*, p. 89.
[4] *Ibid.*, quoted in Davis, G. T. B., *op. cit.*, p. 95.
[5] Morgan, J. V., *op. cit.*, p. 228.   [6] *Ibid.*, p. 112.

There were many outstanding evangelists[1] in the Welsh Revival
—Joseph Jenkins, R. B. Jones, W. W. Lewis, Seth Joshua, W. S.
Jones, Keri Evans and of course Evan Roberts, who tended to
overshadow the others, even though he was the least known in
the beginning.

In 1904, Seth Joshua had prayed the Lord to raise up an evangelist from the coal-mine or the ploughed field, not a Cambridge
or Oxford man lest it minister to human pride.[2] Evan Roberts,
miner and mystic, was the answer. They said that he was clair-
voyant and clairaudient, or that he possessed the spiritual gift of
discernment described in the First Letter to the Corinthians.

Before the outbreak of revival, Evan Roberts was prone to
seeing visions and hearing voices.[3] His was such an unusual temperament that his detractors derided him as insane. During his
only preaching mission outside Wales proper (in 1905 in Liverpool) he submitted to a medical examination in which his exam-
iners unanimously affirmed his sanity.

In 1906, nevertheless, Evan Roberts suffered a complete nervous
breakdown. He was hidden from a prying public by the Penn-
Lewises, well known and wealthy Christian people who lived in
Leicester. For half his lifetime, the Revivalist adamantly refused
to take part in any ministry in public, refused callers, and lived the
life of a recluse, devoting his time to intercession.[4] His post-
Revival activity was regarded as a strange mystery by the Christian
public.[5]

The writer was privileged to enjoy the friendship and counsel
of Evan Roberts over a number of years, and found him mentally
alert, spiritually discerning, but physically indifferent in health.

While the phenomena of revival were confined to the principality of Wales, a wave of quickening went over all three kingdoms in the British Isles.[6] The records of the Keswick Convention
tell of an unusual moving of God that year,[7] in which a noted
industrialist-evangelist, A. Lindsay Glegg, was converted.[8] Joseph
Kemp, pastor of the Charlotte Chapel in Edinburgh, went to
Wales in 1905, and returned to Scotland 1906 to experience revival.
There were a thousand converts in this church.[9] There were
stirrings also in Ulster, but no great manifestation of divine
power as in 1859.

A generation later, travellers in Wales could notice testimonies

[1] Cf. Ellis, R., *Living Echoes, passim*.   [2] Penn-Lewis, J., *op. cit.*
[3] Bois, Henri, *Le Réveil au Pays de Galles, passim*.
[4] Personal knowledge.
[5] A. J. Russell, author of *For Sinners Only*, told the writer that when he called to
see Mr. Roberts, the door was kept chained.
[6] Shaw, S. B., *op. cit.*   [7] Pollock, J. C., *The Keswick Story*, pp. 123 ff.
[8] Personal knowledge.
[9] Kemp, W., *Joseph W. Kemp*, chapter v, "Revival."

in brick and stone across the country—churches and chapels with foundation-stones marked "Built 1860, enlarged 1905," citing the dates of the years following the Revivals.[1]

For decades, revival converts dominated life in the Church in Wales. The impact of the Welsh Revival was felt in Asia, where the missionaries from Wales laboured, but it was felt in lesser measure in the neighbouring British countries. It influenced the rise of Pentecostalism.

The First World War punctuated the period of the Welsh Revival, multitudes of young Welshmen dying on the field of battle. A generation that was ignorant of revival grew up to face the Great Depression that filled the valleys of Wales with unemployed miners who turned in utter despair to the gospel of Marxism.

At the time of the Welsh Revival, men justly asked: "Why Wales only?" In the British Isles, in Scandinavia and other parts of Europe, there was a proliferation of prayer groups and many continued in intercession for an awakening.[2]

Before the Welsh Revival, Reuben Archer Torrey, who had stepped into D. L. Moody's place when the evangelist collapsed, was visiting Britain in evangelistic campaigns. Assisted by Charles M. Alexander as singer, Torrey preached in cities with an aggregate population of fifteen millions, in Edinburgh, Aberdeen, Glasgow, and Dundee, in Belfast and Dublin, in Birmingham, Liverpool, Manchester and London. In each place, success was unprecedented since the days of Moody. In each city, large auditoriums seating many thousands were filled, and inquirers were registered in equally large numbers, about eight thousand in Birmingham, and fifteen thousand in London.[3]

A few years later, Alexander teamed up with Dr. J. Wilbur Chapman, a Presbyterian minister set aside for evangelism by General Assembly of the Presbyterian Church of the United States of America.[4] Chapman and Alexander also held Moody-style campaigns in Ireland, Scotland, Wales and England.[5]

When the answer to prayer came in Norway, it was remembered long in the minds of many notable Christians. Eivind Berggrav, the worthy Bishop of Oslo, in his home told the writer[6] that the most stirring awakening he had experienced was that of the 1905 Revival in Norway, particularly under the preaching of Albert Gustav Lunde, a mutual Norwegian Lutheran friend.

Albert Gustav Lunde was born in Norway in 1877 and died

[1] Orr, J. Edwin, *Can God—?* p. 82.   [2] Shaw, S. B., *op. cit.*, p. 156.
[3] Davis, G. T. B., *Torrey and Alexander*, p. 93 (75,000 claimed in three years).
[4] Ottman, F. C., *J. Wilbur Chapman*, pp. 222–236.   [5] *Ibid.*, pp. 258–272.
[6] In a social visit to Bispegård, at Gamlebyen, 1948.

there just before the outbreak of World War II. At the age of eighteen, he visited the United States and came under the influence of Dwight L. Moody. Moody's church in Chicago was situated on the north side where there was a Scandinavian population, ardently evangelical.[1]

Albert Lunde returned to Oslo, and in 1905 he preached, month after month, to great crowds in the Calmeyersgate Mission House, a capacious Lutheran Inner Mission auditorium. Later, what was called Albert Lundes Forsamling was built in Möllergaten in Oslo. Among other ministers touched by the movement was T. B. Barratt, an Englishman domiciled in Norway and eloquent in both languages.[2]

In Denmark, Sweden and Finland, awakenings were experienced in 1905. As in Norway, revival affected both the Lutherans and the Free Church bodies. Among the ministers stirred in Sweden was Lewi Pethrus.[3]

The movements in 1905 brought results also in Germany, renewing the zeal of those revived since the 1880s. The tide of blessing reached a number of European countries, including Russia where I. S. Prokhanov arose as an evangelist.[4]

In 1899, while in Los Angeles, Moody was presented with a petition signed by 15,831 people to visit New Zealand and Australia. He declined, so there were many Christian leaders regretting it.[5] The southern commonwealths had never experienced mass evangelism of the Moody type.

The invitation to Australia was not unfruitful. The work of Henri Bois[6] on *Le Réveil au Pays de Galles*, and the treatise by Mrs. Penn Lewis[7] on *The Awakening in Wales 1905* both have cited prayer meetings in the Moody Bible Institute in 1899, as well as those at the Keswick Convention in 1902, as factors in the Welsh Revival. They were also factors in a movement in Australasia. Dr. Reuben Archer Torrey was greatly moved by these prayer meetings in his Bible Institute.[8]

In 1901, Torrey and Alexander embarked for the island continent to conduct mass evangelistic campaigns in the major Australian cities. There were huge gatherings, much co-operation among the churches and twenty thousand conversions.[9]

A Melbourne Mission began in the Town Hall and concluded

[1] Welle, *Norges Kirkehistorie*, Vol. III, pp. 335 ff.; cf. *Norsk Riksmalsordbok* (Norse Encyclopedia).
[2] Albert Lunde and the writer were good friends.
[3] Frodsham, S. H., *With Signs Following*, pp. 77 ff.
[4] Bolshakoff, S., *The Christian Church and the Soviet State*.
[5] Alexander, H. C., *Charles M. Alexander*, p. 48.
[6] Bois, Henri, *op. cit.*, pp. 11, 19.   [7] Penn-Lewis, J., *op. cit.*, pp. 17 ff.
[8] Alexander, H. C., *op. cit.*, p. 48.   [9] *Ibid.*, pp. 50 ff.

in the vast Exhibition Building. It was a simultaneous campaign conducted by fifty missioners in fifty suburban centres.[1] Much real prayer had gone into the effort, for prayer circles of ministers had been in operation for the previous eleven years and there were 1,700 lay circles.[2]

From the metropolis, the missioners moved to the Victorian towns, thence to Tasmania. In August they tackled the metropolis of Sydney in New South Wales.[3] Late in August, the Torrey and Alexander party crossed the Tasman Sea to New Zealand and there campaigned in Christchurch, Dunedin and Wellington, leaving from Auckland.[4]

The news of the Welsh Revival quickened the Christians in both New Zealand and Australia. In 1909, Chapman and Alexander toured their cities in a well-organized campaign with great success. They commenced in the great Exhibition Hall in Melbourne, and continued in the largest halls in Sydney, Brisbane and Adelaide and smaller towns.[5] In 1912, Chapman and Alexander returned there, besides missioning in New Zealand centres from Invercargill in the south to Auckland in the north.[6]

Dr. J. Wilbur Chapman carried with him many younger men as associate evangelists, as did Torrey, but Chapman was the master of the city-wide simultaneous campaign.

Neither Moody nor Torrey nor Chapman ever visited South Africa, where half the Europeans spoke the vigorous Afrikaans language. The two most evangelistic denominations in South Africa were the Dutch Reformed Church, manifesting a warm evangelicalism in the style of Andrew Murray, and Methodism, which carried on evangelistic programmes since its earliest days in the country. Presbyterians, Lutherans, Baptists and Congregationalists, though smaller in numbers, were also evangelical and evangelistic.

At the turn of the century, the Anglo-Boer War was fought. The outnumbered Boers waged war cleverly and bravely, but they finally capitulated. In India, Ceylon, and the tiny island of St. Helena the commandos were held prisoners in military camps. The defeated Afrikaner soldiers turned to God for comfort in defeat and in hope for their country.[7] Chaplain A. P. Burger of Middelburg in the Transvaal, serving in the Republican Army, was sent to Shahjahanpur in India with about two thousand prisoners.[8] Other chaplains were held with Boer prisoners in

[1] Davis, G. T. B., op. cit., p. 76.
[2] Penn-Lewis, J., op. cit., p. 18; cf. Davis, G. T. B., p. 15 (2,000).
[3] Davis, G. T. B., op. cit., p. 57.   [4] Ibid., p. 58.
[5] Ottman, F. C., op. cit., pp. 146 ff.   [6] Ibid., pp. 237 ff.
[7] Retief, M. W., Herlewings in ons Geskiedenis, pp. 88 ff.
[8] Ibid., p. 90 ff.

Diatalawa in Ceylon.[1] In these camps, intense revivals of religion broke out, with lasting results. Chaplain A. F. Louw in St. Helena led a similar movement.[2]

The awakenings in the prisoner-of-war camps communicated themselves to the churches in the home land.[3] In the year 1905, awakenings were reported from various dorps in South Africa, in the Dutch Reformed churches.[4]

Gipsy Rodney Smith visited South Africa shortly after the war, and held great campaigns in the larger cities where the English-speaking and bilingual people resided. This post-war movement had much to do with healing the wounds of war, for both sides in the unhappy struggle shared similar religious traditions. In 1910, two colonies and two republics joined to form the Union. The bitterness of the war continued, but least of all in evangelical circles.

After his campaigns in the British countries, from Australia to Britain, in which one hundred thousand converts were reported, Torrey returned to the United States at the end of 1905, hailed as the successor to Moody,[5] whose Bible Institute in Chicago he directed. For six years, Torrey engaged in big city campaigns before his "retiring" to the Bible Institute of Los Angeles. He campaigned in Toronto and Ottawa, Philadelphia, Atlanta, San Francisco, Omaha, Cleveland, Nashville and Chicago and other cities. In Philadelphia, after two months of meetings there were about three thousand five hundred inquirers.

Charles Alexander, Torrey's song leader and deviser of the modern song-leading technique in evangelism, parted company with Torrey in 1908 and joined forces with Dr. Wilbur Chapman.[6] The latter had worked with both Moody and Mills and retained Moody's zeal and Mills's organizational techniques of simultaneous district meetings.

In 1908, Chapman conducted a campaign in Philadelphia, assisted by a score of evangelists and a score of singers in two-score districts of the city. Four hundred churches of the various denominations co-operated. The meetings lasted six weeks, and the attendances aggregated about a million and a half. If there had been about three thousand five hundred inquirers in Moody's and Torrey's Philadelphia campaigns, there were twice as many reported in Chapman's.[7]

[1] Ibid., pp. 92 ff.   [2] Ibid., pp. 95 ff.   [3] Ibid., p. 100.
[4] Cf. Grauer, E., Fredrik Franson, pp. 186 ff.
[5] Murray, H., Sixty Years an Evangelist: Gipsy Smith.
[6] Beardsley, F. G., A History of American Revivals, p. 320; cf. Davis, G. T. B., op. cit.
[7] Ottman, F. C., op. cit., pp. 109 ff.

Chapman tackled Boston in 1909, using thirty evangelists, holding nearly a thousand services in three weeks, with seven thousand inquirers.[1] Of a much more tolerant temper, Chapman won a wider support among ministers than Torrey.

Three years earlier, in 1906, under the auspices of the Boston Evangelical Alliance, Gipsy Rodney Smith conducted an evangelistic mission in Tremont Temple Baptist Church which in fifty meetings attracted more than a hundred thousand people.[2] Rodney Smith had been born in a gipsy encampment in England in 1860, was converted in 1876 during the Moody campaigns. For about five years, he worked in the Salvation Army; he then engaged in modest itinerant evangelism until his great success in Boston. Blessed with talent in singing, Gipsy Smith possessed rare winsomeness of personality and a remarkable command of language, even though he was without formal education. Gipsy Smith continued in evangelism of a wholesome character for seventy years.[3]

William E. Biederwolf was a graduate of the Princeton Graduate School and Seminary who (like Torrey) studied abroad, at the universities of Berlin and Paris. In 1906, after experience in evangelism with Mills and Chapman, he went out in his own campaigns. In 1913, Biederwolf was appointed secretary of the Commission on Evangelism of the Federal Council of Churches. He carried on the evangelical tradition.[4]

While a majority of Evangelical Christians in the United States had become conditioned to think of Revival in terms of promotion of mass evangelism, others scattered here and there realized that it meant the reviving and deepening of their spiritual life in God.

There is no record of a general awakening in the United States in the first decade of the twentieth century, but there are indications of widespread meetings of little groups of intercessors. It was from this minority and one of these that the modern Pentecostal movement arose.[5]

Between 1900 and 1905, there were sporadic manifestations of glossolalia (speaking in tongues) in cities like Topeka, Kansas and Houston, Texas.[6] It is usual however to trace the beginnings of the modern Pentecostal movement to a little meeting in Azusa

[1] *Ibid.*, p. 117; cf. Loetscher, L. A., *Presbyterianism and Revivals;* Ottman, F. C., *op. cit.*, pp. 128 ff.
[2] *Vide* Bayliss, E. F., *The Gipsy Smith Missions in America, passim.*
[3] Personal knowledge: *vide* Murray, H., *Gipsy Smith.*
[4] Schaeffer, C. E., *Brief History of the Department of Evangelism of the Federal Council of Churches*, pp. 5 ff.
[5] Frodsham, S. H., *With Signs Following*, gives instances of glossolalia from 1875 ff.
[6] *Ibid.*, pp. 19 ff.

Street in Los Angeles, where a humble Negro minister, W. J. Seymour, and others with him spoke in tongues.[1] That was April 1906. The same year, there were glossolalic outbreaks in Toronto,[2] and in 1907 such manifestations were occurring in Western Canada also.

Some Pentecostal leaders talk of the start of a "Pentecostal Revival" in 1906. It would be more accurate to say that glossolalia appeared after a widespread evangelical awakening among people of many denominations, with the exception of odd outbreaks in several mission fields.

Reports of Pentecostal experiences intrigued T. B. Barratt, a Methodist minister in Norway.[3] While visiting the United States in 1906 to raise funds to build a central mission in Oslo, Barratt attested a profound experience of the anointing of the Holy Spirit, speaking and singing in tongues. He returned to preach with great power in Oslo, his following gradually separating itself from the other denominations to become an assembly of Pentecostal believers, the forerunner of a great denomination in Scandinavia. Tongues occurred in other denominations without causing schism.

Soon after hearing of Barratt's experience, a Baptist minister in Stockholm, Lewi Pethrus, in turn sought the same for himself.[4] He was called to a church which soon became Pentecostalist in character, separating from the Baptists in 1913, and becoming the mother church of no less than eight hundred Swedish Pentecostal assemblies with a hundred thousand members enrolled.

From Sweden, the movement spread to nearby Finland, where also it had been preceded by general awakening in all the churches.[5] In 1907, it appeared in the Netherlands, where a lady in Amsterdam had heard of the movement in the United States.[6] At the same time, assemblies of Pentecostals began in Germany.[7] Manifestations occurred in the Baltic States also, and soon the movement was general in Europe, beginning in most cases with individuals or small groups.

In 1906, an Anglican clergyman in Sunderland (the Rev. A. A. Boddy) shared with his prayer-meeting group the news of the happenings in Los Angeles.[8] Early in 1907, Boddy crossed to Oslo to see the work of Barratt for himself, and in September Barratt visited Sunderland to preach in Boddy's All Saints' Parish Church. Evensong was followed by a prayer meeting that continued till 4 a.m., and the Pentecostal movement began in the British Isles.

---

[1] *Ibid.*, p. 31.   [2] Kulbeck, G. C., *What God Hath Wrought*, p. 29.
[3] Lange, S. Barratt, *T. B. Barratt*, pp. 171 ff.
[4] Frodsham, S. H., *op. cit.*, pp. 77 ff.
[5] Gee, Donald, *The Pentecostal Movement*, p. 26.
[6] *Ibid.*, p. 27.   [7] *Ibid.*, p. 42.   [8] *Ibid.*, pp. 15, 20 ff.

Boddy, after a glossolalic experience, entered the Pentecostal fellowship.

It was among a minority of "the children of the Revival" in Wales that Pentecostalism appeared. An American missionary who had shared in the Los Angeles beginnings visited Wales in 1907. Out of his mission came the ministry of George Jeffreys and Stephen Jeffreys, who were to become vigorous evangelists in later decades, the former being the founder of the Elim Pentecostal churches.[1] Donald Gee, a convert of Seth Joshua, became an outstanding leader in the Assemblies of God.[2] In Wales, the Apostolic Church gained strength.

In 1908, the Pentecostal movement made its appearance in Australia, starting in Melbourne, Ballarat and Bendigo.[3] That year, glossolalia was manifested in South Africa, spreading out from Johannesburg, gathering English and Afrikaans-speaking followers, the latter chiefly within the Apostolic Faith Mission.[4] The movement in few years had become world-wide.

There was widespread opposition to the new manifestations.[5] The most violent attacks came from some of the most spiritual sections and leaders of the Evangelicals. Pentecostalism had produced no John Wesley to guide by wisdom or recommend by acknowledged scholarship. There were extremes and extravagances that the later Pentecostal leaders deplored. There was a tendency among unconvinced denominationalists to talk of counterfeits and satanic motivation. As the opposition increased, Pentecostals began to withdraw membership from other denominations and form Pentecostal congregations.

As Pentecostalism drew its adherents from the Anglican, Baptist, Lutheran, Methodist, and Presbyterian fellowships, it borrowed various forms of church government and polity, giving birth to denominations within itself at variance with one another in minor matters.

The largest Pentecostalist organization in the United States was formed in 1914, taking the name Assemblies of God,[6] uniting seven thousand congregations in a fast-growing membership, with headquarters in Springfield, Missouri. It was only one of many denominations using the designation, Pentecostal.

Numerically weaker Pentecostal denominations in other countries taking the lead, a World Conference of Pentecostal Churches convened to strengthen the world-wide movement.

---

[1] Ibid., pp. 34 ff.   [2] Personal knowledge.
[3] Frodsham, S. H., op. cit., p. 155.   [4] Gee, Donald, op. cit., pp. 71 ff.
[5] Ibid., pp. 16 ff., "The Problem of Opposition."
[6] Ibid., p. 87; cf. Frodsham, op. cit.

CHAPTER XXVIII

AWAKENINGS FARTHEST AFIELD

IT IS ONE OF THE MYSTERIES OF REVIVAL THAT THE AWAKENING which so profoundly moved a people on the Celtic fringe of Britain should pass over neighbouring countries to revive Scandinavia on the northern fringe of Europe, then animate a people on the farther skirts of the African continent, then move the tribes on the farther side of India, then stir a nation on the farther skirts of Asia, Korea, and then inspire a movement on the farthest tip of America, Chile.

In the latter part of the eighteenth century, evangelical Malagasy had suffered for the faith because of the notion propagated by enemies in Madagascar that to be Protestant was to be pro-English, to be Roman Catholic was to be French.[1]

At the time of the 1905 Revival, the Republic in France became anti-clerical and established a separation of church and state. A new French Governor-General was appointed who showed his anti-clericalism by curbing the churches and the missions while encouraging the old native cults. Churches were made the property of the State, and holding schools therein was forbidden. The Christian Endeavour Societies and Young Men's Christian Associations were proscribed, being suspected as nurseries of Malagasy nationalism.[2]

The first movement of revival at the end of the eighteenth century, Disciples of the Lord, was followed by another which broke out a few years later, provoked by the news of the Welsh Revival of 1904. Again it began in the Betsileo area, at the mission station of Mme Rowlands of the London Missionary Society.[3] It repeated certain features of the earlier revival, bearing heavily upon the *mpisikidy*, diviners and sorcerers.

A Malagasy woman named Ravelonjanahary[4] led the movement in 1905 as it further destroyed witchcraft. There were meetings in which more than eighty people approached the Communion Table to surrender their amulets and make a profession of following Jesus Christ.

[1] Mondain, G., *Un Siècle de Mission Protestante à Madagascar*, p. 311.
[2] Sibree, J., *Fifty Years in Madagascar*, pp. 288–298.
[3] Chapus and Bothun, *Au Souffle de l'Esprit*, pp. 172–173.
[4] Sibree, J., *op. cit.*, pp. 6–8.

Ravelonjanahary was a woman little educated, but she possessed a transparent love for her neighbours, an ardent desire to do good and to assuage human misery. Again a purely indigenous movement succeeded. The awakening spread throughout the great island, thousands of people making confession of sin and seeking salvation.[1]

Norwegian missionaries through their contact with the Scandinavian movements of 1905 as well as Congregationalists in the London Missionary Society through contacts with the Welsh Revival rejoiced in the Malagasy Awakening. A pattern of revival was established. Within twenty years evangelicals numbered half a million adherents and church membership was a hundred thousand.

There was immediate contact also between Wales and India, for there were many Welsh missionaries labouring in the hills of Assam.

Early in 1903, a church at Mawphlang in the Khasia Hills of eastern India announced Monday evening prayer meetings to seek an outpouring of the Holy Spirit throughout Khasia and all the world. In 1904, the prayer meetings became more fervent in spirit, as by the end of the year news from Wales created a heartfelt hunger.[2]

The General Assembly of the Khasia Presbyterian Churches was held at Cherrapoonjee in 1905, and proved to be a remarkable one indeed. The delegates returned to their villages with an increased faith and intensified longing.[3]

On the first Sunday in March, at Mawphlang, when their Bible lesson dealt with the baptism of the Holy Spirit, an unusual manifestation of fervour filled the congregation with prayer and weeping and praise.[4]

A Presbytery meeting at Pariong broke the pattern of their usual procedure, when the chairman invited one or two by name to lead in prayer, others also stood up to lead the congregation in intercession. It became impossible to close the usual service the following Sunday, simultaneous prayer and praise and weeping, and even fainting moving the congregation. These manifestations accompanied the extension of the awakening into other parts, and continued for eighteen months.[5]

The Khasia tribespeople were head-hunters, with human sacrifice persisting in obscure cults. It is therefore interesting to note how the impact of the Welsh Revival affected them.

---

[1] Chapus and Bothun, *op. cit.*, pp. 6–8.
[2] Roberts, Mrs. John, *The Revival in the Khasia Hills, passim.*
[3] *Ibid.*   [4] *Ibid.*   [5] *Ibid.*

The awakening brought an intense conviction of sin in March
1905, but in June a wave of rejoicing. In a united presbytery meeting of fifteen hundred, singing overwhelmed the preaching, and
many of these primitive people danced for joy, their arms out-
stretched, their faces radiant.[1] Missionaries were astounded to see
principal men and elder leaders jump for joy. At first some
missionaries disapproved, but changed their minds as the revival
transformed Christians and won hundreds of non-Christians to
the fellowship.

There were setbacks in some quarters when spurious signs and
prophecies appeared, but the Khasia Christians quickly learned to
distinguish between the true and false, and noted the way of life
of those deceived by other impulses.[2]

The Assam Revival powerfully affected other tribes, the Lushai,
the Nagas and nearby people.[3] The effect of the Revival within a
generation was to make head-hunting people into predominantly
Christian people, the Khasias becoming overwhelmingly Presbyterian, the Nagas Baptist and the Lushai partly Presbyterian, partly
Baptist.[4] In due course, the hills of Assam became India's most
evangelically Christian territory. Theirs was a transformation of
life.

The hill tribes speak non-Aryan languages, as do the Dravidian
peoples of Andhra, Tamilnad, Kerala and Kannara. The awakening touched all four linguistic provinces.

On the western side of the Bay of Bengal, the awakening
appeared among the Telugus of Andhra in prayer meetings, the
missionaries having had contact with the prayers for revival at
Chicago Moody Church and the Keswick Convention.[5] In that
part of India, there had been famine in 1904 and there were
epidemics in 1906.

Canadian and American missionaries reported awakenings
among Telugu Christians in 1905 and by 1906 Andhra had become
"one of the great storm centres of Revival" in India.[6]

At Kurnool, there was a great awakening in 1906—"a burning,
cleansing, quickening, transforming," a mighty spiritual upheaval
such as had never been seen before.[7] It was marked by deep conviction of sin. It was without human leaders. There were stirring
meetings at Nellore, and at Ongole.[8] In the awakening at Akidu
in 1906 there was much confession of sin. The meetings lasted

[1] *Ibid.*   [2] *Ibid.*   [3] Dyer, H. S., *Revival in India*, pp. 127 ff.
[4] Morris, J. H., *The Story of Our Foreign Mission*, and Sword, V. H., *Baptists in Assam.*
[5] Craig, J., *Forty Years among the Telugus*, p. 149.
[6] Dyer, H. S., *op. cit.*, pp. 140 ff., 134 ff.; cf. *Students and the Missionary Crusade*, p. 380.
[7] Stanton, W. A., *The Awakening of India*, pp. 60, 64.
[8] Craig, J., *op. cit.*, pp. 154 ff.

between five and ten hours, and yet no one became tired, physically or mentally.[1]

The results of the awakening were seen in increased attendances at prayer meetings and worship services, by transformation of Christian behaviour, and in a concern for the salvation of friends and neighbours.

Many in Madras were praying for an outpouring of the Holy Spirit in 1905.[2] Anglicans were in various places deeply moved, while Methodists and other denominations experienced blessings aplenty. As in Madras, so in Coimbatore:

God has come to Coimbatore and we are like them that dream.
Our mouth literally is filled with laughter, our tongue with singing.[3]

At a long-established mission station, a sermon was preached on the subject of true and false foundations. Suddenly the whole congregation broke out in loud cries and confessions of sins. The heathen rushed in on all sides and remained awestruck. Instead of closing at noon, the meeting continued into the night. The next four days brought "indescribable scenes" to the place.[4]

Other revivals in the Tamil country began in increased exercise of prayer, continued in confession of sin, resulted in restitution and amendment of ways, followed by concern for the souls of friends and neighbours.

Near the tip of South India there resided the saintly Amy Carmichael, an Ulster woman from County Down, whose mother and pastor had been "impressed" in the Ulster Revival of 1859.[5] Amy Carmichael had devoted her life to the rescue of devadasis, little temple prostitutes, and around her mission house in Dohnavur had grown up a numerous Christian colony of workers with the boy and girl "orphans."

On 22nd October, 1905, to quote one of the tiny girls, "Jesus came to Dohnavur." In the daily devotional meeting, Amy Carmichael was obliged to stop speaking, utterly overcome. A wonderful time of refreshing ensued in which the workers were thoroughly revived, backsliders among the helpers were restored, and many young people were converted.[6]

Some extravagance was reported in revivals in Kerala,[7] but a steadying influence was found in the work of Walker of Tirunelveli, the Anglican Evangelical missioner who performed such useful services in Tamil and Malayalam-speaking areas.[8] In his series of missions in Kerala, supported by the Anglicans and other

[1] *Ibid.*, pp. 152 ff.   [2] Dyer, H. S., *op. cit.*, pp. 147 ff.
[3] *Ibid.*, p. 114, quoting Handley Bird.   [4] *Ibid.*, pp. 114–115.
[5] Houghton, F., *Amy Carmichael of Dohnavur*, p. 5.   [6] *Ibid.*, pp. 147 ff.
[7] Stock, E., *The History of the Church Missionary Society*, Vol. IV, p. 254.
[8] *Ibid.*

Protestants and the Mar Thoma Church and other Syrians, there were tens of thousands in attendance and many conversions.

In Kannara, the awakening began with prayers for the reviving of the Cannarese churches.[1] The answers came in the usual way, conviction and confession of sin, followed by conversions.

The awakening powerfully affected the Aryan-speaking districts as well. In Central India, an awakening began at Yeotmal, another at Khudawandpur, another at Hoshangabad.[2] Walker, the Anglican missioner, preached at Lucknow, Agra, Jabalpur, Allahabad, Poona and Nasik.[3] In April, 1906 a sweeping revival stirred Aurangabad in spite of a temperature of 109 degrees Fahrenheit. The movement spread from there to the churches of Bombay.[4]

In Marathi country, news of the Welsh Revival stirred the heart of Pandita Ramabai in Mukti, and by June 1905 there were five hundred or more meeting twice daily there for revival intercession. The answer came suddenly, manifesting itself in spontaneity of prayer, in confession of sins, and in bitter weeping; there was speaking in tongues. The movement influenced the people powerfully for more than a year.[5] Poona and other cities in the area were greatly influenced.[6]

In the shadow of the Himalayas, a local work of awakening stirred the community at Pilibhit. The Anglican community at Meerut was moved by divine power in October 1905. Awakenings occurred in other parts of Uttar Pradesh.[7]

Missionaries reported a great awakening in the Gujerati-speaking area. There was unusual quickening in 1906 among Indian workers. In the schools, there were visions and trances.[8]

Another "storm centre" of the Revival was in north-west India. An American student volunteer, John Hyde, went to India in 1892 as a missionary but more and more devoted himself to intercessory prayer. Praying Hyde, as he was called, with a group of friends spent days and nights in prayer for an awakening throughout India.[9]

Their prayers were answered in a series of outpourings of the Spirit in north-western India, beginning in 1904 at Sialkot. A decided spiritual upheaval occurred in a girls' school directed by Mary Campbell, resulting in confession of sins and repentance towards God.[10] The revival spirit next touched a theological seminary, but missed a boys' school where the directors were afraid of the dynamic movement.

[1] *Ibid.*, pp. 61 ff.   [2] Dyer, H. S., *op. cit.*, p. 115.
[3] *Ibid.*, p. 64.   [4] *Ibid.*, p. 89.
[5] *Ibid.*, pp. 41 ff.; cf. Frodsham, S. H., *With Signs Following*, p. 105.
[6] Dyer, H. S., *op. cit.*, pp. 48 ff.   [7] *Ibid.*, pp. 59 ff.
[8] *Ibid.*, pp. 109 ff.   [9] Miller, B., *Praying Hyde*, pp. 47 ff.   [10] *Ibid.*, p. 47.

A new principal, Dr. W. B. Anderson, called for united prayer meetings.[1] Missionaries and nationals were stirred and the results were seen in a deepening of spiritual life among Christians, followed by a widening outreach of evangelism among non-Christians.[2]

In August 1905, Pengwern Jones of the Welsh Khasia Hills Mission addressed the convention. Time came to close the meeting, but instead the whole congregation fell before God. Confessions of sin were made that often shocked hearers but later were found hard to remember.[3]

These Sialkot Conventions continued year by year, with a fresh outpouring each year that was felt in widening circles throughout India.[4] Hyde remained a praying force behind the scenes; in 1911 he returned home, dying of cancer in 1912.

A pupil in one of the American Presbyterian Mission schools was a young Sikh named Sundar Singh. On 18th December, 1904, Sundar Singh had a vision of Jesus Christ and was converted.[5] He became a Christian Sadhu, engaging from 1905 onwards in an itinerant evangelism in India and Tibet, into which he disappeared without trace a quarter of a century later. Sadhu Sundar Singh was one of the most unusual evangelical mystics.

It may be asked, why were such awakenings not experienced until the beginning of the twentieth century when evangelization had begun so much earlier? A possible clue to the answer may be found in a statement made by the Reverend W. T. A. Barber, of the Wesleyan Missionary Society, at the Ecumenical Missionary Conference held in New York in 1900:[6]

> Now, as far as my knowledge goes, ordinarily the Holy Spirit does not move on heathen populations—at any rate, in Eastern lands—in this wondrous way. He does mightily save men in every heathen land, but a revival in the sense that we have learned to associate the term with the labour of such men as Moody does not occur among unprepared Chinese or Hindus. The remarkable thing is that such revivals do occur amidst the generations that have been leavened by the influence of Christian schools. When, a year or two ago, the Reverend Thomas Cook, one of our most successful English evangelists, made a special campaign in Ceylon, he found that many were brought to conversion, but, with scarcely an exception, every convert had been educated in mission High Schools.

There is a certain "coming of age" in Revival. The Awakenings of 1905 in India were indigenous, and the period was marked by a rising of Indian ministers and laymen to fuller responsibility.

[1] Ibid., p. 48.   [2] Dyer, H. S., op. cit., pp. 97 ff.
[3] Miller, B., op. cit., pp. 63 ff.   [4] Ibid., p. 96.
[5] Appasamy, A. J., Sundar Singh: a Biography.
[6] Ecumenical Missionary Conference, Vol. II, p. 116.

The several revivals which have moved the Christian Church in Korea have been related to the national affairs of the peninsular country in every case.

In 1905, the Empire of Japan defeated Russia and gained control of Korea as the spoils of war. National indignation affected the Christians, and many looked to the Church to provide organized resistance. The missionaries and many church leaders preached forbearance and forgiveness, hence the angrier agitators tried to undermine their work in the churches.[1]

Half the missionaries in Korea were Presbyterians, from the United States, Australia and Canada, and they were moved by the news of the Welsh Revival influencing the Presbyterians in Assam. In August 1906, these missionaries at Pyong-Yang met for a week of prayer and Bible study. They had a deep concern for the need of the country in its time of humiliation.[2] They studied the First Epistle of John, which afterwards became their textbook in revival work. Refreshed themselves, they planned intensive Bible study for the Korean Church. They gave themselves so much to their task that during the winter, social and recreational affairs lost their appeal.

It was customary for representatives of area churches to come from far and wide at the New Year for Bible study.[3] In spite of opposition, a strange new spirit entered the meeting of fifteen hundred men. So many men wanted to pray that the leader told the whole audience: "If you want to pray like that, all pray." The effect was beyond description—not confusion, but a vast harmony of sound and spirit, like the noise of the surf in an ocean of prayer. As the prayer continued, an intense conviction of sin settled on the meeting, giving way to bitter weeping for sin. Man after man arose, confessed his sins, broke down and wept in intense conviction. There were those who beat their fists on the earthen floor. The meeting went on until two o'clock in the morning.[4]

The following evening, according to accounts by Lord William Cecil in the London *Times*,[5] an elder arose and confessed a grudge against his missionary colleague and asked for forgiveness. The missionary stood to pray but reached only the address to Deity: "Apa-ge, Father" when a rush of power seemed to take hold of the meeting. Some threw themselves on the floor; others stood with arms uplifted. The meeting went on from eight in the evening until five o'clock in the morning. An observer described the phenomena of the occasion as "terrifying."[6]

In meetings following, conviction of sin and reconciliation of

---

[1] Blair, W. N., *The Korea Pentecost, passim.*
[2] *Ibid.*   [3] *Ibid.*   [4] *Ibid.*
[5] Paik, L. G., *History of Protestant Missions in Korea*, p. 357.   *Ibid.*

enemies continued. The heathen Koreans were astounded, and a powerful impulse of evangelism was felt. Not only was there deep confession, but much restitution. The movement went on for days. Ninety per cent of the students in Union Christian College professed conversion.[1]

The delegates to the Winter Bible Class went back to their homes, and carried the revival to their various churches. Everywhere phenomena were the same. There was deep conviction of sin, followed by confession and restitution, a notable feature of all gatherings being the audible prayer in unison, a mode of intercession entirely new.[2]

Practically every evangelical church in all of Korea received blessing. Missionaries claimed that the effects were uniformly wholesome, save where believers resisted the Spirit or deceived the brethren.[3] The work could not be gainsaid.

An elder struggled with his conviction night after night, but received no peace. He gradually lost interest and was removed from office. The confession of a woman exposed his immorality. He sank lower and became a brothel owner.[4]

The Korean Presbyterian Church was set up in the 1907 revival period, a Board of Foreign Missions being organized. Intense efforts were made to evangelize not only the people of Korea but also those Koreans living in Russian Siberia and Chinese Manchuria and overseas.[5] Thus far the movement was Korean.

With the big evangelistic campaigns of the United States in mind, some zealous promoters persuaded the Koreans to embark on a Million Souls Movement, aimed at enlisting a million new converts.[6] The objective, which appeared to be of human origin, was not realized, for by that time (1910) the Revival had run its course.

Korean church membership quadrupled in a decade, and continued to rise, giving to the one per cent Christians in the population an influence far beyond their numbers. Within thirty years, the Korean Protestants numbered three hundred thousand. This nation moved by revival rapidly became the most evangelized part of the Orient.[7]

William Blair has speculated upon what might have happened in Korea had the Christian Church yielded to the temptation of resisting the Japanese by carnal rather than by spiritual methods. The country wanted a leader, and the Christian Church was the most influential single organization in Korea. The Koreans would have flocked behind the banner of the Cross, and some Constantine

---

[1] *Ibid.*, p. 359.   [2] *Ibid.*, p. 358.   [3] Blair, W. N., *op. cit.*   [4] *Ibid.*
[5] *Ibid.*   [6] Clark, C. A., *The Korean Church and the Nevius Methods*, p. 155.
[7] As in Brazil, percentage Evangelical growth has exceeded population growth per cent.

might have arisen to use such a banner. But the result would have been a worldly church.[1]

Instead, the Korean Church retained its zeal for God while maintaining its loyalty to country. The Korean Church became self-supporting in a way unknown in the Orient. The Korean church members became enthusiastic in witnessing and generous in giving.[2] More than thirty years went by with the Japanese military power in control of their country, but their faith never dimmed. In Korea, a persecuted Church provided the spiritual backbone for a nation.

It has been noticed that the period of revival in Japanese evangelical churches in the 1880s was followed by a period of death and decline in the 1890s, due to anti-evangelical liberalism in ecclesiastical high places.

There came a recovery at the beginning of the twentieth century, leading to great conferences of prayer in Tokyo in October of 1900.[3] A spirit of prayer fell upon the Christians of Japan.

The Student Volunteer Movement, meeting in conference in Toronto in 1902, reported that

> this great spiritual awakening followed after a period of great spiritual depression in the Japanese churches.[4]

The 1900 movement of prayer was followed by a united evangelistic campaign in May–June of 1901.[5] It was undergirded by faithful prayer and armed by scriptural preaching.

The greatest benefits were reaped by little suburban churches, which received more eager inquirers than they could handle. Some pastors came to the committee to say: "We have enough, so please don't help us any more. Our houses will not hold the people."[6]

Indeed they were overwhelmed, for no less than 17,939 converts were added in a short time to their churches. The Protestant forces, which had declined from 45,000 to 40,000, added a full 25,000 in twelve months.[7] None could say that a spiritual awakening ill-suited the Japanese.

In the last decade of the nineteenth century, the Empire of China suffered humiliation after humiliation at the hands of foreign powers, and even of the neighbouring "upstarts."

It was hard for Chinese patriots to distinguish between the foreigners who brought them helpful services and those who exploited the weakness of the great country. The rising anti-

[1] Blair, W. N., *op. cit.*   [2] Clark, C. A., *op. cit.*, pp. 73–74.
[3] *World Wide Evangelization*, pp. 390 ff.
[4] *Ibid.*   [5] *Ibid.*   [6] *Ibid.*   [7] *Ibid.*

foreign feeling directed itself against the missionaries as well as the foreign diplomats and traders.[1]

In 1900 came the Boxer movement. It cannot be described as "the Boxer Rebellion," seeing that it was encouraged by the Imperial Government of China. The village train-bands were revived and became known as I Ho Chuan, Righteous Harmony Fists, hence the Western name, the Boxers.[2]

In the autumn of 1899, the wrath of the Boxers was directed against the missionaries, and on the last day of the year, a British missionary was murdered. In mid-1900, the Empress Dowager gave orders to slaughter all foreigners.

A blood bath ensued, in which a hundred or so missionaries and thousands of Chinese Christians were done to death.[3] The Western Powers intervened with strong military forces and captured Peking in August. The old order was doomed.

The Chinese Christians had acquitted themselves bravely in their hour of martyrdom and persecution. Much curiosity was aroused in the hearts of their neighbours. In 1904, a visiting bishop found all the churches crowded to capacity. With the increased opportunity of preaching came movements of revival all over China.[4]

For example, in 1905 there was an outbreak of revival at Foochow College. The movement rose through the ministry of a Chinese evangelist and spread through all the churches of Foochow district.[5] There was a similar revival in Soochow.

These awakenings of 1905 onwards spread to other parts of China, continuing effective till the upheavals of 1911, when revolution swept the Middle Kingdom. There was a notable increase in baptisms. One large society, which had baptized only 700 in all its field in 1895, baptized in 1905 about 2,500 and in 1914 about 4,500. Converts in some areas were multiplying so quickly that missionaries could not deal with them adequately.

The most remarkable movement undoubtedly was the awakening in the Manchurian provinces. From the 1887 awakenings in the colleges of Canada was thrust forth a remarkable missioner, Jonathan Goforth.[6] Proceeding to China under the Canadian Presbyterian Board, Goforth became a leading missionary in Manchuria.[7]

Jonathan Goforth was deeply moved by the news of the Welsh

[1] Smith, A. H., *China in Convulsion, passim.*

[2] *Encyclopaedia Britannica*, 1960, "China," History.

[3] *Vide* Glover, A. E., *A Thousand Miles of Miracle in China*, and Broomhall, M., *Martyred Missionaries of the China Inland Mission.*

[4] Varg, P. A., *Missionaries, Chinese and Diplomats*, p. 86.

[5] *Students and the Missionary Crusade*, p. 337.

[6] Goforth, R., *Goforth of China, passim.*

[7] Goforth, Jonathan, *"By My Spirit," passim.*

Revival of 1904. A few years later, the Korean Revival of 1907 impressed him first-hand with the boundless possibilities of the revival method. He urged his colleagues to pray and revival resulted.[1]

The Manchurian Revival began in 1908, and demonstrated its power at Changte.[2] The meetings were often marked by public confession of sins and extremes of emotional behaviour. Yet it was conceded by critics that permanent moral and spiritual transformations resulted.[3] Some of the converts relapsed, observers claiming that the most lasting results stemmed from the least demonstrative manifestations of conviction. The Presbyterians reported about thirteen thousand baptisms in the five years of the awakening.[4]

There had been stirrings in Manchuria in the year 1906, set in motion by the awakenings within China proper.[5] Now the Manchurian Revival sent a second wave of blessing over China. The churches continued to grow.

The Revolution of 1911, although directed by Dr. Sun Yat-sen, who was a Christian, marked the beginning of a reaction against Christianity. The popularity of the Church decreased as the strength of nationalism grew. The churches also were weakened as education took the place of a vigorous evangelism, until more than half the missionary force was engaged in education.[6]

The Revival in China in these years proved the beginning of a true indigenous spirit in the Chinese churches. In spite of opposition, a way was being prepared for the coming of greater awakenings among the Chinese Christians in all the provinces of the vast sub-continent.

There was another unexpected awakening in a far-off country in the early 1900s, in Chile, in the farthest reaches of the South American continent.

A colleague of Pandita Ramabai in Mukti in India sent a report of the awakening there to her classmate of missionary training days, now the wife of the Methodist Episcopal minister in the city of Valparaiso in Chile.[7]

The congregation in Valparaiso set aside time for prayer for more than a year. In the beginning of 1909, an unusual meeting heralded a startling awakening in Chile.[8] It was marked by audible,

[1] *Ibid.*, pp. 33 ff.   [2] *Ibid.*, pp. 74 ff.
[3] Webster, J., *The Revival in Manchuria, passim.*
[4] Latourette, K. S., *A History of the Expansion of Christianity*, Vol. VI, p. 344.
[5] Goforth, R., *op. cit.*, p. 181.
[6] Latourette, K. S., *History of Christian Missions in China*, pp. 441 ff.
[7] Gee, Donald. *The Pentecostal Movement*, p. 57.
[8] Frodsham, S. H., *With Signs Following*, p. 176.

simultaneous congregational praying typical of other awakenings. There were manifestations and dreams, and, after six months, glossolalic utterances. The latter caused dissension within the missionary body, and the congregation led by its pastor, W. C. Hoover, separated to form a new denomination.

The newspapers printed serious, satirical or lurid reports. Attendances increased from about a hundred and fifty to nine hundred. The pastor was haled into court to answer charges of giving people a beverage called "the blood of the Lamb" but the case was dropped.[1]

Within a generation, indigenous Pentecostal churches had outstripped all other Protestants, gathering a constituency of half a million, one Chilean in eight being a professed Evangelical, three out of four Evangelicals being Pentecostal.

[1] Gee, Donald, *loc. cit.*

CHAPTER XXIX

CONTEMPORARY MOVEMENTS

THE EVANGELICAL AWAKENINGS, WHICH OCCURRED IN SIX main movements between the first decade of the nineteenth century and the first decade of the twentieth, affected the Anglican, Baptist, Congregationalist, Lutheran, Methodist, and Presbyterian denominations in many countries, and gave rise to Christian Brethren, Disciples, the Salvation Army, Nazarene and Pentecostal denominations and several smaller evangelical bodies. It is worth noting that there is no record of any of these movements visibly affecting the Roman Catholic Church. Roman Catholic people generally remained untouched by the praying or preaching that marked these great Awakenings.

This does not mean that the nineteenth century registered no spiritual renewal or advance in the Roman Catholic communion. But it means that there have been missing certain elements in Roman Catholicism needful for a communication of the spiritual manifestations of the Evangelical Revivals. Two most significant Roman defaults concerned the priesthood of all believers, active in every Revival in the participation of the laity, and the authority of Holy Scripture, evident in the preaching of the evangelists, whether in the State or Free Protestant Churches.

The writer once asked the librarian of a great Roman Catholic university what records there were of spiritual revivals in the Roman Catholic communion that seemed similar or parallel to the world-wide Protestant Awakenings. The genial scholar was nonplussed for a moment. Then he took his guest to a shelf of volumes dealing with the saints and the orders—cloistered individuals and organizations in every case, even though at work in the civic community. It did not compare with the general movements which were known to have affected whole citizenries of Protestants. There is no record of a Roman Catholic revival to compare with the Revivals of 1858 in America, of 1859 in Ulster and Scotland, or of 1905 either in Wales or Scandinavia. Nor did any of these movements at all affect the congregations of the Roman Church, other than to convert individuals.

Much the same thing could be said of the Greek Orthodox communion. Evangelical Awakenings stirred the congregations of certain Churches of the East, such as the Armenian Gregorian[1] or the Indian Jacobite,[2] but this usually occurred through the presence of "a mission of help" manned by an Evangelical Society, and resulted in the formation of an evangelical organization as well as in the leavening of the less-evangelical ancient church. It may be said in general terms that the spiritual movements known as Revivals were phenomena peculiar to wholly evangelical communities.

Revivals in the Roman Catholic Church meant something quite different to awakenings in other denominations in the Evangelical community. In the Latin Church, traditionally, revivals usually expressed themselves through new sodalities, communities which took the time-honoured vows of poverty, chastity and obedience, and monastic orders buttressing the secular priesthood.

The scepticism of the eighteenth century and the upsurge of revolutionary political activity injured Roman Catholicism more severely than its separated brethren. Revolution had triumphed in France rather than in Italy, Spain or Portugal, yet it was in France that the marked revival of Roman Catholic fervour and activity occurred.

The awakening in the Roman Catholic Church manifested itself in the emergence of new orders and in the renewal of older orders.[3] In a hundred years after Waterloo, a greater number of new orders, of vocations for the ministry and of volunteers for service were registered than in any previous century in Roman Catholic history. A score of new orders and a number of teaching brotherhoods came into being.[4]

It was significant that the most militant of the Roman orders was revived, the Society of Jesus regaining its full legal existence in 1814.[5] It was also significant that a greater number of the new orders were manned by devout womenfolk, who specialized in the care of the sick, the orphaned and the poor, as well as in teaching.[6]

The revival of piety in the Roman Catholic Church led to missionary activity. The larger number of Roman Catholic missionaries were celibate, some regular and some secular, some priestly and some lay. Not only did the Jesuits extend their mission fields; other orders were founded to meet the need of foreign missions.[7]

In the nineteenth century, Roman Catholics of France under-

[1] Anderson, R., *The History of the Mission of the American Board to the Oriental Churches.*

[2] Cheriyan, P., *The Malabar Churches and the Church Missionary Society.*

[3] Latourette, K. S., *A History of the Expansion of Christianity*, Vol. IV, p. 26.

[4] *Ibid.*   [5] Nippold, F., *The Papacy in the Nineteenth Century*, pp. 31 ff.

[6] Latourette, K. S., *op. cit.*, pp. 26–27.   [7] *Ibid.*, Vol. IV, p. 53.

took a larger part of the staffing and supporting of foreign missions.[1] No longer had Spain and Portugal the place of prominence, even though they remained more intransigently Roman Catholic in their national life. Irish Roman Catholics had but a small share in the missions, for the Irish priesthood was concerned with providing spiritual care for Irish emigrants to the United States, Canada, Australia and New Zealand.[2]

There was no drawing together of Protestant and Roman Catholic either in the homelands or in the mission fields. In the exclusively Roman Catholic countries, the entrance of Protestant missionaries was bitterly opposed, even to the death. The Roman Catholic authorities did not hesitate to appeal to the secular government to expel the intruders. Of course, this did not in any way hinder Roman Catholic missionaries in entering the territories of tolerant Protestant powers. Antipathy was not only organizational but theological. The declaration of the Infallibility of the Pope offended Protestants more than ever.

In Protestant countries, the Roman Catholic minorities usually increased in the nineteenth century, generally by immigration. In Britain approximately 120,000 Roman Catholics resided in 1800; a century later, there were two million.[3] This increase was chiefly due to the immigration of hundreds of thousands of Irishmen to the cities where the industrial revolution provided jobs. In the Netherlands, Roman Catholics increased from one-third of a million to two million in a century, largely through their higher birth rate.[4] But in Scandinavia, though penalties against them were removed, their numbers remained tiny.[5] At the close of the Revolution in the United States, there were just 24,000 Roman Catholics; in 1910, there were sixteen million, thanks largely to a heavy immigration from Southern and Eastern Europe.[6] Irish immigration and a high birth rate gave the increase to Australian Roman Catholicism. One-fifth of the Australian population in 1910 made a claim to Roman Catholicism in the census,[7] but the numbers of practising Roman Catholics was very much smaller. The same applied to Roman Catholicism in New Zealand. In Canada, in 1910 there were two million French Roman Catholics and substantial groups of other language.[8] Forty per cent of all Canadian church members were claimed by Rome, but it must be remembered that what a Protestant denomination would list as

[1] *Vide* Schwager, F., *Katholische Heidenmission*, pp. 36 ff.
[2] American Catholic Historical Association, *Catholic Church in Contemporary Europe*, Vol. II, pp. 160–161.
[3] *Histoire Générale Comparée des Missions*, p. 533.
[4] *Ibid.*, p. 534.   [5] *Ibid.*, p. 535.
[6] Sweet, W. W., *Story of Religion in America*, pp. 202, 379.
[7] *Vide Australasian Catholic Directory*, p. 193.
[8] *Vide Canada Year Book*, 1912, p. 23.

adherents would be regarded as unqualified membership by Roman Catholic diocesans.

Conversions of Protestants to Roman Catholic affiliation have often occurred through marriage in which a promise has been made to bring up the children in the Roman faith. Conversions of the Roman Catholics to Protestantism have occurred by the thousands in mass evangelism.

During the nineteenth century, very little was done in missionary work by the Greek Orthodox Churches.[1] In various Levantine countries, the Orthodox churchmen were busy maintaining the life of their national communities, not trying to evangelize the non-Christians.

Protestant missionaries to Greek Orthodox countries tried at first to infuse new vigour into the older congregations, but those influenced by them were often subjected to persecution by the hierarchy, making it necessary to organize new evangelical churches.[2]

In the nineteenth century, Russian Orthodox authorities maintained their own missions in the fast-expanding Russian Empire and to Russians emigrating overseas, especially to the United States.[3] In Russia, the Orthodox Church was little more than a long arm of the Imperial Russian Government, and its departments of extension could not be compared to either Roman Catholic or Protestant missionary societies. Dissenters were persecuted, but grew rapidly after 1905, the Baptists and kindred groups multiplying.[4]

The two great indigenous American religious systems, the Church of Jesus Christ of Latter Day Saints[5] and the Church of Christ, Scientist,[6] much better known as Mormonism and Christian Science, emerged in the aftermath of evangelical awakenings, though neither was evangelical, one appearing about 1825 and the other about 1875.

It was in the western parts of New York State, the "burnt-over" district of the revivals of the beginning of the nineteenth century, that Joseph Smith claimed the visions and experiences that led to the founding of his great ecclesiastical organization.[7] The Smith family obviously had many contacts with the evangelistic denominations of the frontier, but none claimed them as members. The

---

[1] Latourette, K. S., *op. cit.*, Vol. IV, p. 42.　　[2] *Ibid.*, p. 130.
[3] *Ibid.*, p. 129.　　[4] Vedder, H. C., *Short History of the Baptists*, p. 408.
[5] *Vide* Roberts, B. H., *Comprehensive History of the Church of Jesus Christ of Latter Day Saints* (official history).
[6] *Vide* Wilbur, Sybil, *Life of Mary Baker Eddy*.
[7] Sweet, W. W., *op. cit.*, pp. 275 ff.

I

first fervour of the Second Great Awakening and some of its manifestations were carried over into Mormonism, though not the evangelical doctrine of authority, limited to the Christian Scriptures.

At the age of fifteen, Joseph Smith began to see visions and hear voices, including one which told him that no existing churches were of divine recognition, and that he was to restore the true church. He also averred that an angel had told him that Scriptures of the Western Hemisphere lay buried in the hill Cumora nearby, and that he must wait for permission to dig for them. A few years later, in 1827, Smith dug up a stone box in which was found a book made of thin golden plates inscribed in "Reformed Egyptian" writing. With the plates, the prophet found two stones by the aid of which he was able to read the strange characters. For three years, Smith was engaged in translating this book, and in 1830 the Book of Mormon was printed at Palmyra, New York.

Non-Mormons have found the Book of Mormon baffling, its original script unknown to linguistic science, and its translation into English a matter of strained incredulity.[1] One thing is certain, the religious following built up by the prophet Smith and his extraordinary revelation had departed at its point of origin from the evangelical position.

The first Mormon church was formed in 1830.[2] In 1836, head-quarters were removed to Kirtland, Ohio, from which the Mormon saints moved to Missouri, from which they were driven out as a body fifteen thousand strong to Illinois. Mormons built up the town of Nauvoo, in which they were maintaining a university and a well-equipped private militia, until it had become the largest town in the State. In 1843, Joseph Smith received a revelation authorizing polygamy that stirred up local opposition, resulting in riots in which the Illinois Militia intervened, disarmed the Mormon Legion and placed the prophet and his brother in prison, where on 27th June, 1844 a mob with the evident collusion of the militia brutally murdered them.[3] The Mormon trek in covered wagons to a new home in Utah was an epic adventure.

Not all the followers of Joseph Smith in the Middle West trekked west with Brigham Young. A number remained with the son of the founder of Mormonism, Joseph Smith, Junior, who not only opposed polygamy but denied that his father had ever practised it.[4] Brigham Young,[5] who led the majority west to the

[1] *Vide* Linn, W. A., *Story of the Mormons*, 1901.
[2] Latourette, K. S., *op. cit.*, Vol. IV, p. 202.
[3] Sweet, W. W., *op. cit.*, p. 277.
[4] *Vide Dictionary of American Biography*, Vol. XVII.
[5] *Vide* Hunter, M. R., *Brigham Young, the Colonizer*.

Salt Lake Basin, was an able administrator who frowned upon the earlier prophetic utterances and speaking with tongues. He built up the Mormon Church as a co-operative society which steadily grew in numbers until it passed the million mark in membership. In many ways, the Church of Latter Day Saints took on the appearance of a Protestant denomination, but its theology was as exotic as its mores were puritan.

In 1847, again in western New York State, a series of strange occurrences focused national attention upon the activities of the Fox Sisters.[1] A considerable following of people congregated to delve in spiritist manifestations. In Britain, a Society for Psychical Research was founded in the 1870s to investigate psychic phenomena. Spiritism, misnamed Spiritualism,[2] remained a nebulous body of occult believers, increasing in strength after each great war. Outstanding men such as Sir Arthur Conan Doyle were attracted to the movement, which was anti-evangelical in faith and practice.

In 1875, a bizarre Russian noblewoman with a dubious past, Helen Blavatsky, arrived in the United States to found Theosophy, which was to preserve the ancient wisdom of the East. In 1878, she left for Great Britain and India, founding her pantheistic Theosophical Societies.[3]

In 1875, Mary Baker Eddy published *Science and Health with a Key to the Scriptures*.[4] She had been afflicted with a strange nervous sickness in childhood, and was cured by a "faith healer" who had no evangelical connexions. Christian Science, which based its peculiar doctrines upon neither the plain teachings of Christ nor the findings of modern science, taught that neither matter nor evil nor sickness nor sin nor death has any real existence. Mind may overcome all these things only as it works in harmony with Divine Mind. It is impossible for an orthodox Christian, whether a Roman Catholic or Protestant, to discuss such matters with a Christian Scientist, because of an extraordinary divergence in semantic value.

It is difficult to find any connexion between evangelical Christianity and Christian Science, either theologically, or historically, or psychologically. Christian Science has been described as the religion of the comfortable, an outgrowth of a prosperous society.

[1] Sweet, W. W., *op. cit.*, pp. 279–280.
[2] *Vide* Doyle, A. Conan, *History of Spiritualism*.
[3] Sweet, W. W., *op. cit.*, p. 371.
[4] *Ibid.*, p. 376.

In place of an evangelistic concern for the individual and for society, it substituted therapeutic psychology. Christian Science denied the Christian concept of God, of man, of sin, of salvation, and substituted other meanings for these elementary Christian terms.

In 1872, Charles Taze Russell of Pittsburgh[1] founded the International Bible Students, named later Jehovah's Witnesses. The doctrine of the Trinity he repudiated; Roman Catholic and Protestant Churches he regarded as satanic. In spite of serious charges of sexual and financial irregularity, he gathered twelve hundred congregations.

Russell was succeeded by Joseph F. Rutherford, whose organizational genius built the movement.[2] The Watchtower Bible and Tract Society printed magazines and books by the millions, enlisting fanatical followers as publishers (part-time) or pioneers (full-time) directed locally by company servants, with regional and zone servants under the rigid control of the Society in Brooklyn.[3] Its totalitarian dictatorship foreshadowed a future triumph when "error" was to be purged. Not only totalitarian but democratic governments declared the Witnesses subversive.

At first, the Jehovah's Witnesses declared that their numbers were to constitute the mystic 144,000 mentioned in the Revelation. When that target was reached, two kinds of citizenship were propounded, one heavenly and the other earthly.

Rutherford died in 1942 and was succeeded by Nathan Knorr.[4] By an indefatigable proselytizing, the Witnesses raised their numbers up to half a million in eighty countries. By witnessing, they moved heaven and earth to make one proselyte, often wrecking family and civic integrity.

Arnold Toynbee has described Communism as a Christian heresy, and certainly it sprang out of the Christian social conscience rather than out of Islam or Buddhism, even thought it reacted quite bitterly against basic Christian beliefs.

The founding father of Communism,[5] the anti-Christian Karl Heinrich Marx, was of the purest Jewish stock, but his father became a Protestant proselyte who had him baptized in infancy.[6]

Karl Marx was not ignorant of Christianity of the evangelical emphasis. He was born at the onset of the post-Napoleonic

[1] Martin and Klann, *Jehovah of the Watchtower*, pp. 11 ff.
[2] *Twentieth Century Encyclopedia of Religious Knowledge:* "Jehovah's Witnesses."
[3] Schnell, W. J., *Thirty Years a Watchtower Slave.*
[4] *Twentieth Century Encyclopedia of Religious Knowledge, loc. cit.*
[5] Berdyaev, N., *The Origin of Russian Communism*, p. 192.
[6] Spargo, J., *Karl Marx: His Life and Work*, pp. 121 ff.

Revival in Germany, and raised during its extension throughout Lower Rhineland when his sister-in-law was active in it.[1] The social conscience of the Revival was manifested in social reforms all around him. He knew of the nineteenth-century expectation that society could be perfected through the gospel.

Marx was in London during the great Revival of 1860 onward.[2] Marx founded his International in 1864 and stayed in its company or at the desks of the British Museum. He was a contemporary of Lord Shaftesbury and his reforming friends, and he was still a resident of London when D. L. Moody came to preach. He derided the Moody campaigns, if his friend Engels be accepted as a reliable indicator.[3] Marx became so obsessed with his dogma that he learned to hate Christians for doing good and so delaying the day of violence. He was impatient with evolutionary methods.

As Marx had rebelled against Christianity and its ethics and methods, he did not understand the Acts of the Apostles who turned their world "upside down" by persuasion rather than by resort to violence. Christian meekness he considered cowardice and Christian humility he considered self-contempt; Christian steadfastness he put down as abasement and Christian obedience he put down as subjection; while Christian kindness he called obsequiousness. For the rule of God in society he substituted a war of the classes; for love, he substituted hatred. He denied God.

It was interesting that Marx published in 1859 (the Year of Grace) a trial volume of what was afterwards rewritten as *Das Kapital*, published eight years later.

Communism was little more than a nuisance movement until well into the twentieth century. After the Russian Revolution, it took upon itself the fervour and trappings of a cult, calling for wholehearted dedication of life and purpose. Its atheistic character remained unmodified despite expediences of propaganda and policy.

Not only did Communism have the trappings and fervour of a cult, but it gained through the Russian and subsequent Revolutions the means for practising power politics on a world scale. Not only was Marx influenced by the Christian ideal and presented a secularized transformation of the same, but his followers mimicked historic Evangelical Christianity so that the Communist Orthodox possessed their Canonical Scriptures (the writings of Marx and Lenin), their Way of Salvation (class warfare and the dictatorship of the proletariat), and their eschatological goal (the classless society). The secular parody of Evangelical Christianity

---

[1] Krummacher, F. W., *Gottfried Daniel Krummacher*, pp. 222 ff.
[2] *Vide* Spargo, J., *op. cit.*
[3] Engels, F., *Socialism, Utopian and Scientific*, introduction.

was carried further in the mid-twentieth century in China with the use of the techniques of mass evangelism, chorus singing, rallies, testimonies, and confessions.

Christian socialists found the Marxist spirit very different to their own temper and motives. They disagreed with Marx about God, about the nature of man, about the Christian morality and the purpose of life, about so many things that it was obvious that they agreed in only a few points, the need of reform of society and its regulation.

There is little doubt that Christianity never before faced an opponent as thorough as World Communism. In the past, Evangelical Christianity survived group persecution, military force, moral sabotage, philosophical assault and antipathetic division, in turn. In Communism, all of these weapons are used at once, together with a deadly new one, brain-washing.

CHAPTER XXX

CENTURY OF PROGRESS

WRITING THE HISTORY OF A CENTURY IS LIKE CLIMBING A lofty mountain and surveying the ranges and their intermediate valleys. A perspective can be gained that is not permitted the observer who stays on the valley floor.

A geographical surveyor may trace the start of a stream in a single spring, and trace its long course through the tangled uplands out into the wider valley where it broadens but loses its impetus. The effect of obstacles may be noted and diversions accounted for, and a scientific consideration of the known facts may follow.

But are there patterns in history? Are there laws? Is there purpose? Secular historians such as Arnold Toynbee profess to find patterns and church historians such as Latourette present interpretations. Obviously, the historian must bring a presupposed philosophy to bear upon his facts before he can interpret them.

Many historians believe that men and movements are partly or wholly guided by preceding events and sequences. Some would limit their philosophies to nothing but a time relationship. Others think that history occurs in cycles, and some insist that progress is predetermined by dialectic. Is there a major Christian principle? The words of the Apostle Paul in the Epistle to the Ephesians supply a key:

> For God has allowed us to know the secret of His plan, and it is this: He purposes in His sovereign will that all human history shall be consummated in Christ, that everything that exists in heaven or earth shall find its perfection or fulfilment in Him.

Christians variously interpret the purpose of God in history. Some, seeing nothing but depravity in man, are inclined to think of history as a record of utter confusion following the rejection of the gospel by the majority of mankind. Others, seeing everything as progress, are inclined to view history as a proof of the coming of the Kingdom by the inevitable co-operation of man with God.

There is truth in both these points of view. A study of history shows renewal and reaction, renewal and reaction, with progress being made, yet alternatives of good and evil remaining.

For the Christian, the focal point of history is the invasion of human affairs by God in the person of Jesus Christ. The Man of History committed His message to a group of men who received from Him dynamic in the Holy Spirit and carried His gospel from country to country and generation to generation.

The first three centuries of progress were followed by a millennium of changed direction, when the Church was united with the State and political force compelled the consciences of men. These centuries have therefore been called the Dark Ages, though they were not entirely without light.

Before the fifteenth century, a change began. From the time of John Wycliffe and the Lollards onwards, the impact of Evangelical Revivals or Awakenings was felt in the realm of personal liberty—knowing the truth made men free, and made them wish for freedom for all. The Social Rising of 1381 advocated a programme of freedom for all men, rooted in an evangelical conviction. Its daughter movement in Bohemia maintained a measure of freedom against the forces of tyranny for more than a century. The Reformation in Germany caused such a ferment in men's minds that a rising became inevitable—but it was only crushed because some of those responsible for the hunger for freedom betrayed it. The hunger for righteousness of the early Puritans brought about another attempt to establish freedom under the law, and, like the endeavours before it, the Commonwealth failed because its proponents in the main had not learned that force was not the method of the Spirit—rather it was persuasion.

In the eighteenth, nineteenth and twentieth centuries, the revived Evangelicals learned a different method. New Testament counsels began to prevail, helping to persuade freethinkers and Christians, traditionalists and Evangelicals, that freedom was God's intent for every man.

The movements of the fifteenth, sixteenth and seventeenth centuries were Awakenings in the exact sense of the word—discoveries of truth. The movements of the eighteenth, nineteenth and twentieth centuries were Revivals. They were used by the Spirit of God to change the shape of things on earth as well as to win souls to heaven.

Thus the nineteenth century became in itself the century of Christian Action carrying the Good News into every quarter of the world, into every part of life. Those whose hearts the Spirit had touched became the great initiators of reform and welfare and even tuned the conscience of unregenerate men to a sense of divine harmony in society.

The upheavals of the late eighteenth century, especially the American and French Revolutions, were followed by a decline in Christian witness so serious that, in the judgment of Kenneth Scott Latourette, "it seemed as though Christianity were a waning influence, about to be ushered out of the affairs of men." Even in the dynamic society of the United States, the moral breakdown and the plight of the churches were so desperate that an Episcopal Bishop considered the situation hopeless and simply ceased to function.

In despair, Christian leaders began to pray for divine intervention. The answer came in a series of six great waves of evangelical renewal and advance which made the nineteenth century up till 1914 the "Great Century" of evangelism.

An Evangelical Awakening is a movement of the Holy Spirit in the Church of Christ bringing about a revival of New Testament Christianity. Such an awakening may, of course, change in a significant way an individual only; or it may affect a larger group of people; or it may move a congregation, or the churches of a city or a district, or the whole body of believers throughout a country or continent; or indeed the larger body of believers throughout the world. Such an awakening may run its course briefly, or it may last a whole lifetime. Such Awakenings come about in various ways, but there is a pattern which is common to all.

The main effect of an Evangelical Awakening is always the repetition of the phenomena of the Acts of the Apostles, which narrative gives one a simple account of an Evangelical Awakening, one that revived believers, then converted sinners to God.

In this way, an Evangelical Awakening may be said to effect the revitalizing of the lives of nominal Christians, and of bringing outsiders into vital touch with the divine dynamic causing every such Awakening—the Spirit of God. The surest evidence of the divine origin of any such quickening is its presentation of the evangelical message declared in the New Testament and its re-enactment of the phenomena evidenced in the same Sacred Literature.

From the study of Evangelical Revivals or Awakenings in cities and districts, countries and continents, and generations and centuries, it is possible to trace a pattern of action and discover a progression of achievement which establish in the minds of those who accept the New Testament as recorded history an undoubted conclusion that the same Spirit of God who moved the apostles has wrought His mighty works in the centuries preceding our own with the same results but with greater general effects than those of which the apostles dreamed in their day.

Although the records are scarce, there were Evangelical Awakenings in the centuries before the rise of John Wycliffe, the Oxford reformer. But such movements in mediaeval times seemed very limited in their scope, or abortive in their effects. What was achieved in the days of John Wycliffe—the dissemination of the Scriptures in the language of the people—has never been lost— nor has the doctrine of Scriptural Authority. Thus the Lollard Revival led to the Reformation which would have been impossible without it, and the principle of appeal to the Word of God in the matter of reform has likewise never been lost. The Reformation led to the Puritan movement in which the essentials of evangelical theology were refined; and the Puritan movement prepared the way for the eighteenth-, nineteenth- and twentieth-century Awakenings.

A student of Church History in general and of the Great Awakenings in particular must surely be impressed with the remarkable continuity of doctrine as well as the continuity of action. Any one could begin reading the story of the Gospels, continue on into the narrative of the Acts of the Apostles, then without any sense of interruption begin reading the story of Wycliffe's preachers, or the Covenanters, or Wesleyan circuit riders, or Hans Nielson Hauge in Norway, or Judson in Burma. It is the same kind of Christianity.

Not only so, but the student of such movements would find in the preaching of the Awakenings and Revivals the same message preached and the same doctrines taught in the days of the apostles. Non-evangelical Christianity, with its accretions of dogma and use of worldly power, would seem to be a system utterly alien to that of the Church of the Apostles, resembling much more the forces both ecclesiastical and secular that had opposed New Testament Christianity.

The reader of the Acts of the Apostles must surely notice that the Church began to spread by extraordinary praying and preaching. So too the "upper-room" type of praying and pentecostal sort of preaching together with the irrepressible kind of personal witness find their place in the Great Awakenings rather than in less evangelical ecclesiastical patterns. Undoubtedly, these are revivals of First-Century Christianity.

The writer long ago rejected the designation "the Frontier Revivals" commonly given to the awakenings of the early nineteenth century in the United States, along with the idea that such Revivals are "frontier phenomena." The Revivals originated not on the frontiers of the westering nation but in the colleges of settled communities. They were paralleled in Europe by like revivals among the Swiss, Norse, Scots and others hardly inhabiting "frontiers." "Le Réveil," which moved the Reformed

Churches of Switzerland, France and the Netherlands, began among students in Geneva in 1816. Even in recording the revivals among the illiterate frontiersmen of Kentucky or Tennessee—as William Warren Sweet stated—there was "entirely too much stress placed upon the emotional excesses of camp meetings and all too little upon the routine work of the frontier churches and preachers." Finally, it is fallacious to consider "Revivals" as "frontier phenomena" when the most widespread and effective of all such movements, the Awakening of 1858–59 around the world, started in cities such as New York, Philadelphia, Belfast, Glasgow, London and Birmingham. The conclusion that because the American frontier has closed, evangelical awakenings are now impossible is contradicted by facts and logic. The Revivals of 1905 began in urban Wales, Norway and other countries in big cities as well as rural communities.

When John Wesley died, Evangelical Christendom was confined to Great Britain, Scandinavia, parts of Germany, Holland and Switzerland, minorities in France and Hungary, and territory east of the Alleghenies in North America, while Latin America was closed by the intransigent governments of Spain and Portugal. Africa was unexplored, Islam was hostile to the gospel, the East India Company made missionaries unwelcome in India, and none resided in China, Japan or Korea. South Seas islanders were savages.

The evangelical denominations were without Sunday Schools, Bible Societies, Home Missions, and Foreign Missions—apart from Moravians.

The "turn-of-the-century" awakenings sent off pioneer missionaries to the South Seas, to Latin America, to Black Africa, to India and China. Denominational missionary societies such as the Baptist Missionary Society, the American Board and other national missions arose. The British and Foreign Bible Society was founded, followed by other national Bible Societies.

The awakenings raised up able evangelists on the American frontier, sent the Haldanes up and down to revive Scotland, produced Hans Nielsen Hauge to transform Norway, and provoked revival and evangelism in England, Germany, Holland and other European countries. Sunday Schools and a host of evangelistic and philanthropic agencies arose to reach and deal with home problems.

Granted freedom under law, social reforms were bound to follow. It was the Evangelicals of the Revival who, in the main, brought about the emancipation of the slaves, then tackled social injustice, supported the modern trade union and legislated reform of labouring conditions. None of this was accomplished by force —all by verbal persuasion against which the reactionaries could not stand. Along with the prevention of social injustice came a multitude of agencies created to care for the unfortunate, until at last the very State itself, the still unregenerate society, began adopting the programme of the New Testament as the norm of civilization, so that even the anti-Christian revolutions began to adopt Christian idealism, though they too fell into temptation to legislate righteousness by force.

William Wilberforce mobilized evangelical and political opinion in Great Britain to secure an abolition of the Slave Trade and the Emancipation of the slaves throughout the British Empire, an achievement not won for another thirty years in the United States. John Howard pioneered prison reform, which was carried on by Elizabeth Fry in London. Theodore Fliedner adopted the same ideas in Germany, building homes and hospitals, training deaconesses and nurses, his most famous pupil being Florence Nightingale, who in turn influenced Henri Dunant, as ardent an evangelical as Fliedner, in founding the Red Cross.

The connexion between the great Evangelical Awakenings and popular education is not hard to establish. The Lollards and the Reformers were led by scholars who were ready to share all the blessings of education with their followers. The Puritans established universities and colleges where none previously existed. The Revivalists of the eighteenth century founded schools and colleges as a matter of course. The nineteenth-century awakenings led to the foundation of numerous schools, high schools and colleges both in the United States and Europe and elsewhere, extending general education until the State took over a fully-fledged popular programme.

Great Britain was the first of the world's countries to be industrialized, and its workers were caught in a treadmill of competitive labour which kept them straining for sixteen hours a day. Evangelical leaders, including Shaftesbury and members of the "Clapham Sect," brought an end to much of the sorry exploitation, and promoted all sorts of social improvements. No less an authority than Prime Minister Lloyd George credited to the Evangelical Revival "the movement which improved the condition of the working classes, in wages, hours of labour and otherwise." This was paralleled in the United States by what have been called "the Sentimental Years," when organized good works and betterment flourished on a scale never before known.

The years between 1792 and 1842 produced continuous revivals in the United States, with an interruption due to the War of 1812. In its second phase, the outstanding figure Charles Grandison

Finney dominated the middle third of the century as Dwight L. Moody dominated the final third. At the same time, James Caughey reaped thousands of converts in Great Britain and the United States, William Booth being one among many impressed by his ministry.

The leaders of the Awakening in Scotland were Robert and James Haldane, who were succeeded by William C. Burns in the next generation. At this time, Charles Simeon was building up the Evangelical clergy of the Church of England into its dominant force and a wave of revival produced the Primitive Methodist evangelists under whom Spurgeon was converted.

Converts of "Le Réveil" won by Robert Haldane in Geneva extended the work all over France and it spread to the Netherlands, a parallel revival in Germany being led by great evangelists such as the Krummachers. Revival continued in Norway and a great movement began in Sweden under George Scott and Carl Olof Rosenius. In the far Ukraine, a revival begun among German settlers of Pietist and Mennonite affiliation developed into the Stundist movement among the Russians themselves, a movement encouraged by Bible-reading following popular distribution.

This second wave of Revival reinforced the foreign missionary invasion of all the continents, and continued its social impact upon the sending countries. Captain Allen Gardiner pioneered in the wilds of South America and died tragically. David Livingstone explored African territories. Missionaries reconnoitred the citadels of Islam. William Carey was followed by societies ready to evangelize India. Robert Morrison opened a way for missionaries to settle in the treaty ports of China. Evangelism in Oceania was followed by extensive awakenings in Hawaii and other Polynesian kingdoms. There were setbacks also.

Missionary pioneers opened up Madagascar to the gospel and completed a translation of the Old and New Testaments before a violent persecution compelled them in 1836 to abandon a couple of hundred converts to the fury of their enemies. A quarter of a century elapsed before re-contact.

Evangelical Christianity faced other setbacks throughout the world in the second third of the nineteenth century. Tractarianism arose in the Church of England, an Anglo-Catholic revival, to challenge the leadership of Evangelical Church clergy. High Church Parties rose among Lutherans in Germany to challenge a new Rationalism. There was similar dissension in the Reformed Churches. The Church of Scotland was rent by the Disruption, which, thanks to the early nineteenth-century Revival, strengthened evangelism.

Among Baptists in the area of their greatest numerical strength in the United States, another exclusive movement (Landmarkism) arose and isolated Baptists from other Evangelicals. The extravagances of eschatalogical interpretation caused dissension and decline in the Unites Stated as the churches began to lose more members than they were gaining by immigration. And a gross materialism grew among Americans as political unrest gripped Europe at the mid-century.

In the autumn of 1857, there were signs of an awakening—success in revival and evangelism in Canada, and an extraordinary movement of men to prayer in New York City which spread from city to city throughout the United States and over the world. Churches, halls and theatres were filled at noon for prayer, and the overflow filled churches of all denominations at night in a truly remarkable turning of a whole nation towards God.

The same movement also affected the United Kingdom, beginning in 1859 in Ulster, the most northerly province in Ireland. Approximately ten per cent of the population professed conversion in Wales and Scotland as well, and a great awakening continued in England for years. Repercussions were felt in many other European countries.

The phenomena of Revival were reported in parts of India, Africa and the West Indies. The missionaries returning to Madagascar found that two hundred converts had increased to 20,000.

Out of the 1859 Awakening in Britain arose a phalanx of famous evangelists—aristocrats and working men. Spurgeon built his Tabernacle on the crest of the movement. The intervention of the war between the States (in which there was extraordinary revival and evangelism in every theatre of war) delayed the emergence of great American evangelists from the 1858 Awakening.

The 1858–59 Awakenings extended the working forces of Evangelical Christendom. Not only were a million converted in both the United States and the United Kingdom, but existing evangelistic and philanthropic organizations were revived and new vehicles of endeavour created. The Bible Societies flourished as never before. Home Missions were founded, and the Salvation Army arose to extend the evangelistic-social ministry of the Revival in countries around the world. The impact upon the youthful Y.M.C.A. organization was tremendous.

The mid-century Awakenings revived all the existing missionary societies and enable them to enter other fields. The practical evangelical ecumenism of the Revival was embodied in the China Inland Mission founded by Hudson Taylor in the aftermath of the British Awakening, the first of the interdenominational "faith missions." As in the first half of the century, practically every missionary invasion was launched by men revived or converted in the Awakenings in the various sending countries.

For example, the first permanent missions in Brazil followed the 1858-59 Awakenings. In Indonesia and India, mass movements to Christianity followed. China was penetrated by the converts of the Revival from many countries. The missionary occupation of Africa was rapid, and the liberated Negro in the Anglo-American territories was thoroughly evangelized.

In the 1870s, Dwight L. Moody rose to fame as a world evangelist. Beginning quietly in York in 1873, Moody progressed through Sunderland, Newcastle, Edinburgh, Dundee, Glasgow, Belfast, Dublin, Manchester, Sheffield, Birmingham and Liverpool, using methods of the 1858 Revival in prayer and preaching. About 2,500,000 people aggregate heard him in twenty weeks in London.

In 1875, Moody returned to his native land a national figure, campaigning equally successfully in Brooklyn, Philadelphia, New York, Chicago, Boston and other cities. From then onwards, he ministered in cities on both sides of the Atlantic. A flock of successful evangelists was associated with him. Perhaps his greatest campaign was conducted at the World's Exposition in Chicago in 1893. Moody died in action in 1899.

In the Moody period, another awakening began in Sweden, extending the work of the National Evangelical Foundation (EFS) and an offshoot, the Evangelical Mission Covenant (SMF). Revivals continued in Norway and Denmark and Finland.

As a result of the impact of Anglo-American Revivalists— including Moody—a Thirty Years' Revival began in Germany, from 1880 until 1910. Outstanding leaders were Dr. Theodor Christlieb (who founded the German Committee for Evangelism and the Gemeinschaftsbewegung) and Elijah Schrenk and Samuel Keller.

In the same period, there was both revival in the Ukrainian peasantry and evangelism among Russian upper classes, the latter begun by British gentlemen, Radstock and Baedeker. Prokhanov, converted in 1886, founded the All-Russia Evangelical Union which in the next century united in denominational organization with the Baptists.

It is curious to notice that Charles Darwin's most significant publication (1859) occurred at the time of the Awakening in Great Britain and the United States. It heralded a clash between sceptics who interpreted many new scientific conclusions as anti-theistic and traditional theologians who too readily agreed with all their interpretations.

Yet far from antagonizing the academic world, the Awakening

resulted in the most extraordinary invasion of the universities and colleges by the Christian message and the most successful recruitment of university-trained personnel in the history of higher education and evangelism.

In the 1858 Awakening in the United States, revivals among students, resulted in formation of the College Y.M.C.A.s, and in the following year, prayer meetings at Oxford and Cambridge gave rise to local Christian Unions which later united to form the Inter-Varsity Fellowship. In the local student fellowship at Princeton in 1875 were several outstanding young men—Robert Mateer, who became leader of the Inter-Seminary Missionary Alliance; T. W. Wilson, who became president of Princeton University and later (as T. Woodrow Wilson) the President of the United States, and Luther Wishard, who as organizer and evangelist of the Inter-Collegiate Y.M.C.A., pleaded with a reluctant Moody to minister to a sincerely interested student constituency.

In 1882, Moody was persuaded to campaign in Cambridge University, where at first he stirred up scornful opposition. Out of the awakening, the Cambridge Seven (C. T. Studd and other first-rank varsity men) stirred the student world and proceeded to China as missionaries.

Thus encouraged, Moody acceded to Wishard's promptings to arrange a conference for students at Mount Hermon, in his home state. A youthful delegate, Robert Wilder, presented the claims of the mission fields, and a hundred of the 250 present responded; within an academic year, two thousand from American universities and colleges had offered. Thus was born the Student Volunteer Movement with a watchword to "evangelize the world in this generation." Under the direction of men like John R. Mott, Volunteers multiplied on every continent.

Out of the 1859 Awakening arose the Keswick Movement for the Deepening of the Spiritual Life (1875). In the eastern hemisphere, it became a unifying force in Evangelicalism, a missionary recruitment centre of the highest quality. Out of the same agitation in America, the organizations in the Holiness Movement resulted in splintering, giving birth to vigorous denominations.

Christian Endeavour, a movement for training young people in church-related activity, began in a local revival in Maine in 1881, under Francis E. Clark. Within fifteen years, there were more than two million members in forty thousand local societies. They were ecumenical and evangelical. A number of denominations promoted equivalent young people's organizations.

The 1880s witnessed advances in the evangelization of China, as well as a remarkable seven years' revival in Japan, but the years of rapid growth in the island empire were followed by a decline caused by an onslaught of a rationalist theology among national pastors.

The awakenings in sending countries caused an extension of missionary enterprise on every continent. Albert B. Simpson, a convert of the 1858 Revival in Canada, founded the Christian and Missionary Alliance in 1886, at first as an interdenominational organization but later itself becoming a denomination as missionary-minded as the Moravians.

In the social impact of mid-century Revivals, greater effects were seen in the industrialized United Kingdom. Lord Shaftesbury continued his extraordinary parliamentary programme for the betterment of humanity. Great orphanages were begun. A Society was formed for the Prevention of Cruelty to Children (1889), while Josephine Butler rallied evangelical opinion to abolish the licensing of prostitution in Great Britain (1886). The evangelical interest motivated much of the agitation for the betterment of conditions for the labouring people, many leaders in the Labour Party itself being avowed evangelical Christians. In the United States, there also was a growing concern with purely social issues such as rights of the working man, poverty, the liquor trade, slum housing and racial bitterness.

To achieve all this reform, the crusaders of the Evangelical Awakenings did not stoop to any form of class warfare. Rather, under the guidance of the Spirit, they enlisted the privileged in the service of the poor. The seventh Earl of Shaftesbury single-handed accomplished as much in a lifetime as has been achieved by any party in any parliament—yet he remained an aristocrat.

Out of this evangelical concern grew a liberal social gospel whose advocates became indifferent by degrees to the dynamic of the Christian gospel, the transforming of individual lives by the power of Jesus Christ, evangelism initiating reform.

Prayer meetings were held in the Moody Bible Institute and elsewhere at the turn of the twentieth century for another awakening. Traceable to this intercession were the Welsh and other Revivals in 1904–5 onwards, as well as the world-girdling evangelistic campaigns of Torrey and Alexander and Chapman and Alexander, who succeeded D. L. Moody in mass evangelism.

A 26-year-old student, Evan Roberts, was the chief instrument in a remarkable outpouring of the Spirit upon the Churches of Wales in 1904, in which fully 100,000 were converted. There was a similar awakening in Scandinavia in 1905, and repercussions in Germany and Russia. In Boer prisoner-of-war camps, a revival of evangelical fervour communicated itself to the churches of South Africa.

Awakenings were reported from 1905 onwards in Madagascar,

K

Assam and all parts of India, Korea, Manchuria and parts of China, Chile and parts of Latin America. The Chilean movement brought forth glossolalic manifestations and gave rise to an indigenous Pentecostal denomination which soon became a dominant force in evangelical life there.

Just as the early nineteenth century revivals added the Christian Brethren and the Disciples of Christ to the Protestant constituency, so the early twentieth century revivals produced the Pentecostal movement. Even before the early 1900s, glossolalia was reported in United States. From an occurrence in Los Angeles in 1906, the modern Pentecostal movement grew. Converts of the Welsh and Scandinavian Awakenings came into touch with this interest, each giving rise to vigorous Pentecostal denominations in British and Scandinavian countries, while similar fellowships such as the Assemblies of God arose in the United States and elsewhere. There was widespread opposition to the movement, especially in the historic evangelical constituency, but the new effluence of evangelical Christianity outlived its initial extravagances and developed a programme of dynamic evangelism at home and abroad.

In the life of the Church in the Great Century, the contributions of the Evangelical Awakenings were tremendous. They gave opportunity to the evangelists to reach millions of people with the simple gospel message. They produced mission societies, denominational or interdenominational, and sent out the world's greatest missionaries. And the mission fields to which the phenomena of the Great Revivals were exported became the countries in which New Testament Christianity reached its greatest strength of numbers and influence—Brazil, Korea, Madagascar and parts of Polynesia serving as examples from each of the major areas of the world, the Evangelical cause there outstripping that of many sending countries. Not only so, the Awakenings made a contribution to social progress second to none.

The nineteenth century was marked by great advances in Science. Man's knowledge grew in astronomy, biology, botany, chemistry, geology, geography, physics and physiology. Knowledge struck a blow at superstition, but encouraged an enlightened people to seek Truth.

The increase of knowledge was matched by a profitable application of its gains to living. The invention of machines increased the supply of food, the production of clothing, the building of houses, the development of transportation, and the extension of communications.

Factories, shops, stores, trains, steamships, roads and telegraphs added to man's mastery of nature and enabled him to travel far and wide. It was significant that this development occurred in the countries committed to the sending forth of the Good News of the Christian faith.

The factory system led to the building of great cities which dwarfed anything hitherto known. In spite of serious inequalities of distribution, the wealth of nations increased. Capitalism lavishly produced the goods, and its supporting middle class found the wealth to finance the proclamation of the gospel and all its works.

The revolutions which marked the beginning of the century encouraged the growth of nationalism. Some nations struggled for independence while others extended their imperial control of more backward peoples.

The nineteenth century was largely a period of peace. Europe suffered a few brief wars and Latin America a number of revolutions. There were colonial conquests and revolts, and a Civil War distressed but did not destroy the United States.

The Pax Britannica, from Waterloo in 1815 till the First World War in 1914, coincided with this "great century" of evangelical renewal and advance. It was the period in which Great Britain led the world in industrialization, when British commerce penetrated the Seven Seas, when the Royal Navy was supreme, when the British Empire outgrew all its predecessors in an imperialism whose benefits outweighed its injustices.

It is impossible to escape the conclusion that this imperialism facilitated the growth of missions in its territories and in the territories of neighbours. German, Scandinavian, and the British missionaries followed the flag.

This factor, together with the independence of the United States and its Monroe Doctrine, led to the remarkable growth of Evangelical Christianity in the Americas. Likewise, the building of schools and hospitals in the missionary penetration of Africa followed imperialism.

Even the Opium Wars in China, which were in fact opposed by the missionaries, resulted in an opening of China to the gospel and the founding of schools, orphanages, leprosaria, hospitals, colleges and universities.

The nineteenth century proved to be a time of evangelical renewal and advance, in which shone widely the Light of the Nations. The phenomena of the Great Awakenings brought blessing untold to the Christian believer, to the congregation, to the Christian community, to the Church at large, to the labouring man, to the world of women, to the welfare of children, to the care of the sick, to the shelter of the insane, to the protection of the unfortunate, to the education of the young, to the guaranteeing of liberty, to the granting of freedom, to the administration of justice, to the evolution of self-government, to the crusade for peace among the nations—in fact, in the nineteenth century, the Evangelical Awakenings may be shown to be the foremost method of an Almighty God to promote the betterment of all mankind and His chiefest instrument to win men to transforming faith in Himself.

The world is now in another age of revolution like the one which preceded the century herein described. Again, a flood of immorality and a wave of lawlessness has enveloped the earth. In some countries, it is said that Christianity has become a waning influence, about to be ushered out of the affairs of men. How long must it take for despair to drive the Christians to prayer for another Revival of New Testament Christianity?

The Author would welcome any information regarding Evangelical Awakenings and their direct and indirect results in any country whatsoever during the Twentieth Century. Most useful would be reports with details of publication or authority. The Paternoster Press, 3 Mount Radford Crescent, Exeter, Devon, England.

BIBLIOGRAPHY

Acts of the General Assembly of the Church of Scotland, Edinburgh, 1859–1865.

Adams, D., *The Revival at Ahoghill*, Belfast, 1859.

Alexander, H. C., *Charles M. Alexander*, London, 1920.

Allen, W. O. B., and McClure, E., *Two Hundred Years of the S.P.C.K.*, London, 1898.

Andersen, J. O., *Survey of the History of the Church in Denmark*, Copenhagen, 1930.

Anderson, R., *The History of the Mission of the American Board to the Oriental Churches*, Vols. I–II, Boston, 1872.

Anderson, R., *The Hawaiian Islands: Missionary Labors*, Boston, 1865.

Anderson, R., *History of the Sandwich Islands Mission*, Boston, 1870.

Appasamy, A. J., *Sundar Singh: a Biography*, London, 1958.

Armstrong, M. W., *The Great Awakening in Nova Scotia, 1776–1809*, Hartford, 1948.

Arthur, W., *The Revival in Ballymena and Coleraine*, London, 1859.

Ashmore, L. S., *The South China Mission of the American Baptist Foreign Mission Society*, Shanghai, 1920.

Aulard, A., *Christianity and the French Revolution*, London, 1927.

The Australasian Catholic Directory, Sydney, 1910.

Babcock, R., *Memoir of John Mason Peck*, Philadelphia, 1864.

Baillie, J., *The Revival, or What I Saw in Ireland*, London, 1860.

Baird, Robert, *The State and Prospects of Religion in America*, London, 1855.

Baker, E., *The Life and Explorations of F. S. Arnot*, London, 1921.

Balfour, R. G., *Presbyterianism in the Colonies*, Edinburgh, 1899.

Balleine, G. R., *A History of the Evangelical Party in the Church of England*, London, 1908.

Barnes, G. H., *The Anti-Slavery Impulse, 1830–1844*, New York, 1933.

Barton, J. L., *Daybreak in Turkey*, Boston, 1908.

Bayliss, E. F., *The Gipsy Smith Missions in America*, Boston, 1907.

Bayne, P., *The Free Church of Scotland*, Edinburgh, 1894.

Beardsley. F. G., *A History of American Revivals*, New York, 1912.

Begbie, H., *The Life of William Booth*, London, 1926.

Bennett, W. W., *The Great Revival in the Southern Armies*, Philadelphia, 1877.

Bill, I. E., *Fifty Years with the Baptist Ministers and Churches of the Maritime Provinces*, Saint John, 1880.

Bingham, H., *A Residence of Twenty-One Years in Hawaii*, Hartford, 1848.

Binns, L. E., *The Evangelical Movement in the English Church*, London, 1928.

Binyon, G. C., *The Christian Socialist Movement in England*, London, 1931.

Blodgett and Baldwin, *The Missions of the American Board in China*, Boston, 1896.

Boardman, M. M., *Life and Labours of the Rev. W. E. Boardman*, New York, 1887.

Boardman, M. T., *Under the Red Cross Flag*, Philadelphia, 1915.

Boardman, W. E., *The Higher Christian Life*, Boston, 1858.

Bois, Henri, *Le Réveil au Pays de Galles*, Toulouse, 1905.

Bolshakoff, S., *The Christian Church and the Soviet State*, London, 1942.

Bonar, A., *Memoirs of Robert Murray McCheyne*, Chicago, 1948.

Booth-Tucker, F., *The Life of Catherine Booth*, London, 1924.

Bourdillon, A. F. C., *Voluntary Social Services*, London, 1945.

Braga, E., and Grubb, K. G., *The Republic of Brazil*, London, 1932.

Brain, B. M., *The Transformation of Hawaii*, New York, 1898.

Branch, E. D., *The Sentimental Years: 1836–1860*, New York, 1934.

Bready, J. W., *England Before and After Wesley—the Evangelical Revival and Social Reform*, New York, 1938.

Bready, J. W., *Dr. Barnardo: Physician, Pioneer, Prophet*, London, 1930.

Bready, J. W., *Lord Shaftesbury and Social-Industrial Progress*, London, 1926.

Bready, J. W., *This Freedom—Whence?* London, 1942.

Broadbent, E. H., *The Pilgrim Church*, London, 1931.

Broomhall, M., *Hudson Taylor: the Man Who Believed God*, London, 1929.

Brown, A. J., *One Hundred Years: a History of the Foreign Missionary Work of the Presbyterian Church*, New York, 1937.

Brown, G., *Autiography of George Brown* (S.W. Pacific), London, 1908.

Brown, P. A., *The French Revolution in English History*, London, 1920.

Browning, W. E., Ritchie, J., Grubb, K. G., *The West Coast Republics of South America*, London, 1930.

Bucsay, M., *Geschichte des Protestantismus in Ungarn*, Stuttgart, 1959.

Burgess, A., *Unkulunkulu in Zululand*, Minneapolis, 1934.

Burgess, A., *Zanahary in South Madagascar*, Minneapolis, 1932.

Butler, Josephine, *Personal Reminiscences of a Great Crusade*, London, 1913.

Cameron, J., *Centenary History of the Presbyterian Church in New South Wales*, Sydney, 1905.

Candler, W. A., *Great Revivals and the Great Republic*, Nashville, 1904.

Canton, W., *A History of the British and Foreign Bible Society*, Vols. I–V., London, 1904–10.

Carey, S. Pearce, *William Carey, Fellow of the Linnean Society*, New York, 1923.

Carpenter, J. E., *The Life and Work of Mary Carpenter*, London, 1881.

Carson, J. T., *God's River in Spate*, Belfast, 1958.

Carswell, D., *Brother Scots*, London, 1927.

Cartwright, P., *The Autobiography of Peter Cartwright*, New York, 1856.

Cary, Otis, *A History of Christianity in Japan*, Vols. I–II, New York, 1909.

Casey, R. P., *Religion in Russia*, New York, 1946.

Caughey, J., *Methodism in Earnest*, Richmond, 1852.

Caughey, J., *Showers of Blessing*, Boston, 1857.

Centenary Conference on the Protestant Missions of the World, London, 1888.

Chamberlain, Mrs. M. E., *Fifty Years in Foreign Fields* (Reformed Church), New York, 1925.

Chambers, T. W., *The Noon Prayer Meeting*, New York, 1858.

Chapus, G. S., and Bothun, F., *Au Souffle de l'Esprit*, Tananarive, 1951.

Cheriyan, P., *The Malabar Christians and the C.M.S.*, Kottayam, 1935.

Cherrington, E. H., *Standard Encyclopedia of the Alcohol Problem*, Westerville, 1930.

Christianity and the Natives of South Africa, Lovedale, n.d.

Clark, C. A., *The Korean Church and the Nevius Methods*, New York, 1930.

Clark, Elmer T., *The Small Sects in America*, Nashville, 1937.

Clark, S. D., *Church and Sect in Canada*, Toronto, 1948.

Claus, W. B., *Dr. Ludwig Krapf*, Basel, n.d.

Cleveland, C. C., *The Great Revival in the West*, Chicago, 1916.

Clough, E. R., *Social Christianity in the Orient*, New York, 1914.

Cole, C. C., *The Social Ideas of the Northern Evangelists*, New York, 1954.

Colquhoun, J. C., *Wilberforce: His Friends and His Times*, London, 1867.

Colwell, J., *A Century in the Pacific*, London, 1914.

Conant, W. C., *Narratives of Remarkable Conversions*, New York, 1858.

Conference on Missions Held at Liverpool, London, 1860.

Conrad, A. Z., *Boston's Awakening*, Boston, 1909.

Conybeare, F. C., *Russian Dissenters*, New York, 1962.

Cook, Sir Edward, *The Life of Florence Nightingale*, Vols. I–II, London, 1913.

Cornish, G. H., *Cyclopedia of Methodism in Canada*, Toronto, 1881.

Craig, J., *Forty Years among the Telugus*, Toronto, 1908.

Davies, G. C. B., *The First Evangelical Bishop*, London, 1958.

Davis, G. T. B., *Torrey and Alexander*, New York, 1905.

Day, E. H., *Robert Gray, First Bishop of Cape Town*, London, 1930.

Descamps, Baron (ed.), *Histoire Générale Comparée des Missions*, Paris, 1932.

Douglas, W. M., *Andrew Murray and His Message*, London, 1926.

Downer, A. C., *A Century of Evangelical Religion in Oxford*, London, 1938.

Drach, G., *The Foreign Missions of the Lutheran Church*, Philadelphia, 1926.

Drach, G., and Kuder, C. F., *Telugu Mission of the Evangelical Lutheran Church*, Philadelphia, 1914.

Drury, A. W., *A History of the United Brethren*, Dayton, 1931.

DuBois, W. E. B., *The Negro Church*, Atlanta, 1903.

DuPlessis, J., *The Evangelization of Pagan Africa*, Capetown, 1930.

DuPlessis, J., *A History of Christian Missions in South Africa*, London, 1911.

DuPlessis, J., *The Life of Andrew Murray*, London, 1919.

Dwight, E. W., *Memoirs of Henry Obookiah*, New Haven, 1818.

Dwight, H. O., *Centennial History of the American Bible Society*, New York, 1916.

Dyer, H. S., *Revival in India*, London, 1907.

Earle, A. B., *Bringing in the Sheaves*, Boston, 1868.

E. M. C., *Ecumenical Missionary Conference in New York*, New York, 1900.

Edwards, J., *Memoirs of David Brainerd*, Boston, 1749.

Ekvall, R. B., *After Fifty Years—Christian and Missionary Alliance*, Harrisburg, 1939.

Elder, J. R., *The Letters and Journals of Samuel Marsden*, Dunedin, 1932.

Ellis, J. B., *The Diocese of Jamaica*, London, 1913.

Ellis, R., *Living Echoes of the Welsh Revival*, London, 1951.

Ellis, W., *History of Madagascar*, Vols. I–II, London, 1939.

Ellis, W., *The Martyr Church—in Madagascar*, London, 1870.

Ellis, W., *Polynesian Researches*, London, 1831.

Emhart, W. C., *Religion in the Soviet Union*, New York, 1961.

Encyclopaedia Britannica, 1960, Chicago, 1960

Engels, F., *Socialism, Utopian and Scientific*, Introduction, New York, 1935.

Engels, F., *The Condition of the Working Class in England, 1844*, London, 1892.

Epstein, B. and S., *Henri Dunant*, New York, 1963.

Evans, Eifion, *When He Is Come*, London, 1959.

Every, E. F., *Twenty Five Years in South America*, London, 1929.

Ewing, J. W., *Goodly Fellowship* (Evangelical Alliance), London, 1946.

Farrer, J. A., *Crimes and Punishment* (English translation of Beccaria's *Dei Delitti e Delle Pene*), London, 1880.

Farndale, W. E., *The Secret of Mow Cop*, London, 1950.

Findlay and Holdsworth, *A History of the Wesleyan Methodist Missionary Society*, Vols. I–V, London, 1924.

Finney, C. G., *The Memoirs of Charles G. Finney*, New York, 1908.

Finney, C. G., *Revivals of Religion*, 3rd edition, London, 1928.

Fitch, E. R., *The Baptists of Canada*, Toronto, 1911.

Fleming, J. R., *A History of the Church in Scotland, 1843–1874*, Edinburgh, 1927.

Fleming, J. R., *A History of the Church in Scotland, 1875–1929*, Edinburgh, 1933.

Frodsham, S. H., *With Signs Following*, Springfield, Mo., 1946.

Fullerton, W. Y., *C. H. Spurgeon: a Biography*, London, 1920.

Gammon, S. R., *The Evangelical Invasion of Brazil*, Richmond, 1910.

Garrison, W. E., *Religion Follows the Frontier: a History of the Disciples of Christ*, New York, 1931.

Gee, Donald, *The Pentecostal Movement*, London, 1949.

Gewehr, W. M., *The Great Awakening in Virginia*, Durham, N. C., 1930.

Gibson, W., *The Year of Grace*, Jubilee edition, Edinburgh, 1909.

Gidland, M., *Kyrka och Väckelse, 1840–1880*, Uppsala, 1955.

Glover, R. H., *The Progress of World Wide Missions*, New York, 1925.

Goforth, Jonathan, *By My Spirit* (Revival in China), London, n.d.

Goforth, Rosalind, *Goforth of China*, London, n.d.

Gordon, A., *Our India Mission* (United Presbyterian Church of North America), Philadelphia, 1888.

Grace, T. S., *A Pioneer Missionary among the Maoris, 1850–79*, Palmerstone North, n.d.

Grauer, O. C., *Fredrik Franson*, Chicago, 1940.

Grose, H. B., *Advance in the Antilles*, New York, 1910.

Grubb, K. G., *Religion in Central America*, London, 1937.

Guinness, Mrs. H. G., *The New World of Central Africa*, New York, 1890.

Gulick, O. H., *The Pilgrims of Hawaii*, New York, 1918.

Gützlaff, Karl, *Journal of Three Voyages (along the China Coast)*, London, 1834.

Haldane, A., *Lives of Robert and James Alexander Haldane*, New York, 1854.

Halliday, S. B., *The Church in America and Its Baptisms of Fire*, New York, 1896.

Hamilton, J. T., *A History of the Moravian Church*, Bethlehem, Pa., 1900.

Hamlin, Cyrus, *My Life and Times*, Boston, 1893.

Hammond, J. L. & B., *The Town Labourer, 1760–1832*, London, 1917.

Hardy, A. S., *Life and Letters of Rev. Joseph Hardy Neesima*, Boston, 1892.

Harford-Battersby, *Memoir of T. D. Harford-Battersby*, London, 1890.

Harford, J. B., and Macdonald, F. C., *Handley Carr Glyn Moule, Bishop of Durham*, London, 1922.

Harris, J., *A Century of Emancipation*, London, 1933.

Harrop, A. J., *The Amazing Career of Edward Gibbon Wakefield*, London, 1928.

Haslam, W., *From Death Unto Life*, London, 1880.

Hawker, G., *The Life of George Grenfell*, London, 1909.

Headley, P. C., *E. Payson Hammond, the Reaper and the Harvest*, London, 1885.

Heuss, T., *Friedrich Naumann*, Berlin, 1937.

Hinchliff, P. B., *The Anglican Church in South Africa*, London, 1963.

Hinchliff, P. B., *John William Colenso*, London, 1964.

Hinton, J. H., *A Memoir of William Knibb*, London, 1847.

Hodder, E., *Life and Work of the Seventh Earl of Shaftesbury*, London, 1887.

Hodder-Williams, J. E., *The Life of Sir George Williams*, London, 1906.

Hogue, W. T., *A History of the Free Methodist Church*, Chicago, 1915.

Holcomb, W., *The Life and Sayings of Sam Jones*, Atlanta, 1906.

Hole, C., *Early History of the Church Missionary Society*, London, 1896.

Holmqvist, H., *Fran Romantiken till Första Världskriget*, Vol. III: *Handbok i Svensk Kyrkehistoria*, Stockholm, 1952.

Hopkins, C. H., *The Rise of the Social Gospel in American Protestantism, 1865–1915*, New Haven, 1940.

Hopkins, Samuel, *The Works of Samuel Hopkins*, Boston, 1852.

Houghton, F., *Amy Carmichael of Dohnavur*, London, 1954.

Howard, R. L., *The Baptists in Burma*, Philadelphia, 1931.

Hughes, G., *The Beloved Physician: Walter C. Palmer*, New York, 1884.

Hunter, J. H., *Flame of Fire: the Life of Rowland V. Bingham*, Toronto, 1961.

Iglehart, C. W., *A Century of Protestant Christianity in Japan*, Tokyo, 1959.

Inglis, K. S., *Churches and the Working Classes*, London, 1963.

International Review of Missions, London, 1912 ff.

Ironside, H. A., *A Historical Sketch of the Brethren Movement*, Grand Rapids, 1942.

Jeffrey, R., *Indian Mission of the Irish Presbyterian Church*, London, 1890.

Johnson, C. A., *The Frontier Camp Meeting*, Dallas, 1955.

Jones, J. W., *Christ in the Camp* (Civil War Revivals), Richmond, 1887.

Karsten, H., *Geschichte der Leipziger Mission*, Leipzig, 1893.

Kelsey, R. W., *Friends and the Indians, 1655–1917*, Philadelphia, 1917.

Kemp, W., *Joseph W. Kemp*, London, 1934.

Kesson, J., *The Cross and the Dragon*, London, 1854.

Kluit, M. E., *Het Reveil in Nederland*, Amsterdam, 1950.

Kruijf, E. F., *Geschiedenis van het Nederlandsche Zendinggenootschap*, Groningen, 1894.

Koch, H., *Danmarks Kirke gjennem Tiderne*, Copenhagen.

Koch, H., *Grundtvig* (translated by Llewellyn Jones), Copenhagen.

Krummacher, F. W., *Gottfried Daniel Krummacher*, Berlin, 1935.

Kulbeck, G. C., *What God Hath Wrought*, Toronto, 1958.

Lacy, B. R., *Revivals in the Midst of the Years*, Richmond, 1943.

Lancelot, J. B., *Francis James Chavasse*, London, 1929.

Lang, G. H., *Anthony Norris Groves: Saint and Pioneer*, London, 1939.

Lang, G. H., *The History and Diaries of an Indian Christian*, London, 1939.

Latimer, R. S., *Dr. Baedeker and His Apostolic Work in Russia*, London, 1907.

Latimer, R. S., *Under Three Tsars, Liberty of Conscience in Russia, 1856–1909*, London, 1909.

Latourette, K. S., *Christianity in a Revolutionary Age*, Vol. II, *the Nineteenth Century in Europe*, New York, 1950.

Latourette, K. S., *A History of Christian Missions in China*, London, 1929.

Latourette, K. S., *A History of the Expansion of Christianity*, Vols. IV, V and VI: *The Great Century*, London, 1938–45.

Latourette, K. S., *A History of the Expansion of Christianity*, Vol. VII, London, 1947.

Laubach, F., *The People of the Philippines*, New York, 1925.

Lecky, W. E. H., *A History of England in the Eighteenth Century*, Vols. I–VII, London, 1892.

Livingstone, W. P., *Christina Forsyth of Fingoland*, London, 1919.

Livingstone, W. P., *Mary Slessor of Calabar*, London, 1916.

Loetscher, L. A., *Presbyterianism and Revivals*, Philadelphia, 1944.

Loud, G. C., *Evangelized America*, New York, 1928.

Lovett, R., *James Chalmers: Autobiography and Letters*, London, 1902.

Lovett, R., *James Gilmour of Mongolia*, London, 1935.

Lovett, R., *The History of the London Missionary Society*, Vols. I–II, London, 1899.

Lundahl, J. E., *Nils Westlind* (Congo Pioneer), Stockholm, 1915.

Macdonald, F. C., *Bishop Stirling of the Falklands*, London, 1929.

McFarland, G. B., *A Historical Sketch of the Protestant Mission in Siam, 1828–1928*, Bangkok, 1929.

McGillivray, D., *A Century of Protestant Mission in China, 1807–1907*, Shanghai, 1907.

Mackay, A. M. *Mackay, Pioneer Missionary to Uganda*, London, 1890.

Mackay, J. A., *The Other Spanish Christ*, London, 1932.

Mackay, R. W., *The Tübingen School and Its Antecedents*, London, 1863.

McKeown, R. L., *Twenty Five Years in Qua Iboe*, London, 1912.

Mackichan, D., *The Missionary Ideal in the Scottish Churches*, London, 1927.

Mackintosh, C. W., *Coillard of the Zambesi*, London, 1907.

McLoughlin, W. G., *Modern Revivalism*, New York, 1959.

MacRae, A., *Revivals in the Highlands and Islands in the Nineteenth Century*, Stirling, 1906.

Manross, W. W., *The Episcopal Church in the United States, 1800–1840*, New York, 1935.

Marsh, J. W., and Stirling, W. H., *The Story of Captain Allen Gardiner*, London, 1868.

Marshman, J. C., *The Life and Times of Carey, Marshman and Ward*, Vols. I–II, London, 1859.

Martin, A. D., *Doctor Vanderkemp*, London, n.d.

Martin, W. R., and Klann, N. H., *Jehovah of the Watchtower*, London, 1953.

Mason, F., *The Karen Apostle—Ko Thah Byu*, Boston, 1843.

Massie, J. W., *Revivals in Ireland*, London, 1860.

Mathews, Basil, *John R. Mott, World Citizen*, New York, 1934.

Mays, B. E., and Nicholson, J. W., *The Negroes' Church*, New York, 1933.

Milne, W., *A Retrospect of the First Ten Years of the Protestant Mission to China*, Malacca, 1820.

Minutes, General Assembly of the Presbyterian Church in Ireland, 1859, Belfast, 1859.

The Minutes of the Methodist Conference, 1903, London, 1903.

Moffat, J. S., *The Lives of Robert and Mary Moffat*, London, 1886.

Mondain, G., *Un Siècle de Mission Protestante à Madagascar*, Paris, 1920.

Montgomery, M. W., *A Wind from the Holy Spirit in Sweden and Norway*, New York, 1884.

Moody, W. R., *The Life of Dwight L. Moody*, New York, 1900.

Moorhouse, H., *Recollections of Henry Moorhouse*, Chicago, 1881.

Morgan, G. Campbell, *Sermon in Westminster Chapel, 25th December, 1904*, London, 1904.

Morgan, G. E., *R. C. Morgan: His Life and Times*, London, 1909.

Morgan, J. J., *The '59 Revival in Wales*, Mold, 1909.

Morgan, J. V., *The Welsh Religious Revival*, London, 1909.

Morris, J. H., *The Story of Our Foreign Mission*, Presbyterian Church of Wales, Liverpool, 1930.

Moule, Handley C. G., *Memorials of a Vicarage*, London, 1920.

Mours, S., *Un Siècle d'Evangelisation en France, 1815–1914*, Paris, 1963.

Müller, G., *The Autobiography of George Müller*, 3rd edition, London, 1905.

Murray, H., *Sixty Years an Evangelist. Gipsy Smith*, London, 1937.

Mullins, J. D., *Our Beginnings. Colonial and Continental Society*, London, n.d.

Neill, S. C., *A History of Christian Missions*, London, 1964.

Newcomb, H., *The Harvest and the Reapers*, Boston, 1858.

Newman, A. H., *A Manual of Church History*, Vols. I–II, Philadelphia, 1931.

Nippold, F., *The Papacy in the Nineteenth Century*, New York, 1900.

Noble, W. F. P., *A Century of Gospel Work*, Philadelphia, 1876.

Northcott, C., *Robert Moffat, Pioneer in Africa*, London, 1961.

Nyman, H., *Paavo Ruotsalainen, Den Bidande Tron*, Helsinki, 1949.

Oldham, F. F., *Thoburn—Called of God*, New York, 1918.

Olsen, M. E., *A History of the Origin and Progress of Seventh-Day Adventists*, Washington, 1932.

Orr, J. Edwin, *Can God—?* London, 1934.

Orr, J. Edwin, *I Saw No Tears*, London, 1946.

Orr, J. Edwin, *The Second Evangelical Awakening in America*, London, 1953.

Orr, J. Edwin, *The Second Evangelical Awakening in Britain*, London, 1949.

Orr, John, *English Deism: Its Roots and Fruits*, Grand Rapids, 1934.

Ottman, F. C., *J. Wilbur Chapman*, New York, 1920.

Overton, J. H., *The Evangelical Revival in the Eighteenth Century*, London, 1886.

Page, J., *The Black Bishop, Samuel Adjai Crowther*, New York, n.d.

Paik, L. G., *A History of Protestant Missions in Korea*, Pyungyang, 1929.

Pascoe, C. F., *Two Hundred Years of the S.P.G.*, London, 1901.

Payne, E. A., *Freedom in Jamaica*, London, 1946.

Penn-Lewis, J., *The Awakening in Wales*, New York, 1905.

Phillips, W. A., *A History of the Church of Ireland*, Vols. I–III, London, 1931.

Philp, H. R. A., *A New Day in Kenya*, London, 1936.

Pickering, H., *Chief Men Among the Brethren*, London, 1931.

Pickett, J. W., *Christian Mass Movements in India*, New York, 1933.

Pierson, A. T., *George Müller of Bristol*, New York, 1905.

Pitman, E. R., *Missionary Heroines in Many Lands*, London, n.d.

Pitts, H., *The Australian Aboriginal and the Christian Church*, London, 1914.

Pollock, J. C., *The Keswick Story*, London, 1964.

Pollock, J. C., *Moody: A Biographical Portrait*, New York, 1963.

Proceedings and Debates of the General Assembly of the Free Church of Scotland, 1860: Proceedings of the General Assembly on Revival, Edinburgh, 1860.

Proceedings of the General Conference on Foreign Missions, Mildmay Park, London, 1878, London, 1878.

Rankin, M., *Twenty Years among the Mexicans*, Cincinnati, 1875.

Rauws, J., and others, *The Netherlands Indies*, London, 1935.

Rauschenbusch, W., *Christianity and the Social Crisis*, London, 1909.
Rauschenbusch, W., *Christianizing the Social Order*, New York, 1919.
Records of the General Conference of the Protestant Missionaries of China, 1890, Shanghai, 1890.
Redford, M. E., *The Rise of the Church of the Nazarene*, Kansas City, 1951.
Reid, J. M., *Missions and Missionary Society of the Methodist Episcopal Church*, Vol. I, New York, 1895–96.
Reid, J. S., *A History of the Presbyterian Church in Ireland*, Belfast, 1867.
Reid, W., *Authentic Records of Revival*, London, 1860.
Retief, M. W., *Herlewings in Ons Geskiedenis*, Capetown, 1951.
Révész, Kovats and Ravasz, *Hungarian Protestantism*, Cleveland.
Rice, E. W., *The Sunday School Movement*, Philadelphia, 1917.
Richards, T. C., *Samuel J. Mills*, Boston, 1906.
Richardson, R., *Memoirs of Alexander Campbell*, New York, 1868.
Richter, J., *Geschichte der Evangelischen Mission in Afrika*, Gütersloh, 1922.
Roberts, B. H., *Comprehensive History of the Church of Jesus Christ of the Latter Day Saints*, Salt Lake City, 1930.
Roberts, Mrs. John, *The Revival in the Khasia Hills*, London, 1909.
Rodgers, J. B., *Forty Years in the Philippines*, New York, 1940.
Roome, W. J. W., *"Blessed Be Egypt!"* London, 1898.
Root, H. I., *A Century in Ceylon: a History of the American Board in Ceylon, 1816–1916*, Boston, 1916.
Rosenqvist, G. O., *Finlands Kyrka*, The Church of Finland, Lund, 1946.
Ross, C. S., *The Story of the Otago Church and Settlement*, Dunedin, 1887.
Rouse, R., and Neill, S. C., *A History of the Ecumenical Movement*, Philadelphia, 1954.
Rutherford, J., and Glenny, E. H., *The Gospel in North Africa*, London, 1900.
Sandall, R., *History of the Salvation Army*, Vol. I, London, 1947.
Sanderson, J. E., *First Century of Methodism in Canada*, Vols. I–II, Toronto, 1908.
Sargant, W., *Battle for the Mind*, London, 1957.
Schaeffer, C. E., *A Brief History of the Department of Evangelism of the Federal Council of Churches*, New York, 1951.
Schaff-Herzog, *The New Schaff-Herzog Encyclopedia*, London, 1908–45.
Scharpff, P., *Geschichte der Evangelisation*, Giessen, 1964.
Schlatter, W., *Geschichte der Basler Mission, 1815–1915*, Basel, 1916.
Schnell, W. J., *Thirty Years a Watchtower Slave*, Grand Rapids, 1956.
Schwager, F., *Die Katholische Heidenmission*, Steyl, 1907.
Sellers, C. C., *Lorenzo Dow*, New York, 1928.
Shaw, J., *Twelve Years in America*, London, 1867.
Shaw, J. M., *Pulpit under the Sky*, Hans Nilsen Hauge, Minneapolis.
Shaw, P. E., *The Catholic Apostolic Church*, London, 1946.
Shaw, S. B., *The Great Revival in Wales*, Chicago, 1905.
Shaw, W., *Story of My Mission in S. E. Africa*, London, 1860.
Shearer, J., *Old Time Revivals*, London, n.d.
Shedd, C. T., *History of the World's Alliance of Young Men's Christian Associations*, New York.

Shedd, C. P., *Two Centuries of Student Christian Movements*, New York, 1934.

Shepherd, R. H. W., *Lovedale, South Africa, 1841–1941*, Lovedale, 1941.

Sibree, J., *Fifty Years in Madagascar*, London, 1924.

Sibree, J., *The Madagascar Mission*, London, 1907.

Siegmund-Schultze, F., *Evangelische Kirche in Polen*, Barmen.

Simon, J. S., *The Revival of Religion in the Eighteenth Century* (Fernley Lectures), London, 1907.

Sinker, R., *Memorials of the Hon. Ion Keith-Falconer*, Cambridge, 1888.

Sissons, C. B., *Egerton Ryerson, His Life and Letters*, Toronto, 1937.

Sloan, W. B., *These Sixty Years*, The Keswick Movement, London, 1935.

Smith, A. H., *China in Convulsion*, Vols. I–II, Chicago, 1901.

Smith, C. Henry, *The Story of the Mennonites*, Newton, Kansas, 1950.

Smith, G., *Henry Martyn*, London, 1892.

Smith, G., *The Life of Alexander Duff*, London, 1899.

Smith, G., *The Life of John Wilson*, London, 1879.

Smith, G., *Stephen Hislop, Pioneer Missionary*, London, 1879.

Smith, G. A., *The Life of Henry Drummond*, London, 1898.

Smith, T. L., *Called Unto Holiness*, Kansas City, 1962.

Smith, T. L., *Revivalism and Social Reform*, New York, 1957.

Soothill, W. E., *Timothy Richard of China*, London, 1924.

Spargo, J., *Karl Marx: His Life and Work*, New York, 1910.

Spring, G., *Memoirs of the Rev. Samuel J. Mills*, New York, 1820.

Springer, J. M., *The Heart of Central Africa*, Cincinnati, 1909.

Stanton, W. A., *The Awakening of India*, Portland, Maine, 1910.

Stead, F. H., *The Story of Social Christianity*, London, n.d.

Steiner, P., *Kamerun als Kolonie und Missionsfeld*, Basel, 1909.

Stephen, Sir Leslie, *English Thought in the Eighteenth Century*, London, 1881.

Stephenson, G., *The Religious Aspects of Swedish Immigration*, Minneapolis, 1932.

Stiansen, P., *A History of the Baptists in Norway*, Chicago, 1933.

Stock, E., *History of the Church Missionary Society*, Vols. I–IV, London, 1899–1916.

Stock, E., *My Recollections*, London, 1909.

Strachan, A., *A Life of the Rev. Samuel Leigh*, London, 1870.

Strickland, A. B., *The Great American Revival*, Cincinnati, 1934.

Strong, W. E., *The Story of the American Board*, Boston, 1910.

S. V. M., *Students and the Missionary Crusade*, Nashville, New York, 1906.

Sundkler, B., *Svenska Missionssälskapet*, Stockholm, 1937.

Sutton, A., *Orissa and Its Evangelization*, Derby, 1850.

Sweet, W. W., *Revivalism in America*, New York, 1945.

Sweet, W. W., *The Story of Religion in America*, New York, 1950.

Sword, V. H., *Baptists in Assam, 1836–1936*, Chicago, 1935.

Taylor, E. R., *Methodism and Politics, 1791–1851*, London, 1935.

Taylor, H. and G., *Hudson Taylor in Early Years*, London, 1911.

Taylor, H. and G., *Hudson Taylor and the China Inland Mission*, London, 1918.

Taylor, W., *Christian Adventures in South Africa*, London, 1867.

Taylor, W., *Four Years' Campaign in India*, London, 1876.

Taylor, W., *Seven Years' Street Preaching in San Francisco*, New York, 1857.

Taylor, W., *The Story of My Life*, London, 1897.

Taylor, W. G., *The Life Story of an Australian Evangelist*, London, 1920.

Tewkesbury, D. G., *Colleges and Universities before the Civil War*, New York, 1932.

Thiessen, J. C., *A Survey of World Missions*, Chicago, 1955.

Thomas, D. Y., *One Hundred Years of the Monroe Doctrine*, New York, 1923.

Thomas, N. W., *The Natives of Australia*, London, 1906.

Thompson, A. E., *The Life of A. B. Simpson*, New York, 1920.

Thompson, C. L., *Times of Refreshing*, Chicago, 1877.

Thomson, B., *The Fijians*, London, 1908.

Torbet, R. G., *A History of the Baptists*, Philadelphia, 1952.

Townsend, Leah, *South Carolina Baptists, 1670–1805*, Florence, S. C., 1935.

Townsend, W. J., Workman, H. B., and Eayrs, G., *A New History of Methodism*, Vols. I–II, London, 1909.

Tracy, J., *History of the American Board of Commissioners for Foreign Missions*, New York, 1842.

Trevelyan, G. M., *English Social History*, London, 1944.

Tucker, A. R., *Eighteen Years in Uganda and East Africa*, Vols. I–II, London, 1908.

Turner, G., *Nineteen Years in Polynesia*, London, 1861.

Loetscher, L. A. (ed.), *Twentieth Century Encyclopaedia of Religious Knowledge*, Vols. I and II, Grand Rapids, 1955.

Tyler, B., *Memoir of the Life of Asahel Nettleton*, Hartford, 1844.

U.S. Bureau of the Census, *Religious Bodies, 1916*, Washington, 1916.

Vandenbosch, A., *The Dutch East Indies*, Grand Rapids, 1933.

Varg, P. A., *Missionaries, Chinese and Diplomats*, Princeton, 1958.

Vedder, H. C., *A Short History of the Baptists*, Philadelphia, 1907.

Walker, F. D., *The Call of the West Indies*, London, n.d.

Walsh, H. H., *The Christian Church in Canada*, Toronto, 1956.

Warneck, G., *Geschichte der Protestantischen Missionen*, Berlin, 1913.

Warneck, J., *Ludwig I. Nommensen, Ein Lebensbild*, Barmen, 1928.

Warre-Cornish, F., *The English Church in the Nineteenth Century*, London, 1910.

Washington, Booker T., *Up from Slavery: an Autobiography*, New York, 1901.

Watson, A., *The American Mission in Egypt, 1854–1896*, Pittsburgh, 1904.

Watson, C. R., *The Sorrow and Hope of the Egyptian Sudan*, Philadelphia, 1913.

Watt, H., *Thomas Chalmers and the Disruption*, Edinburgh, 1943.

Wayland, F., *Memoir of Adoniram Judson*, Boston, 1853.

Webb, Sidney and Beatrice, *A History of Trade Unionism*, London, 1894.

Webster, J., *The Revival in Manchuria*, London, 1910.

Weigle, L. A., *American Idealism*, New Haven, 1928.

Weir, J., *The Ulster Awakening*, London, 1860.

Welle, I., *Norges Kirkehistorie*, Vol. I–III, Oslo, 1948.

Wells, J., *The Life of James Stewart*, London, 1909.

Wentz, A. R., *A Basic History of Lutheranism in America*, Philadelphia, 1955.

Wentz, A. R., *Fliedner, the Faithful*, Philadelphia, 1936.

Wentz, A. R., *The Lutheran Church in American History*, Philadelphia, 1933.

Western Mail, The Religious Revival in Wales, reports, Cardiff, 1905.

Westin, Gunnar, *George Scott och Hans Verksamhet i Sverige*, Stockholm, 1927.

Westin, Gunnar, *Den Kristna Friförsamlingen i Norden* (English translation by Virgil Olson, Nashville, 1958), Stockholm, 1956.

Wheatley, R., *The Life and Letters of Mrs. Phoebe Palmer*, New York, 1876.

Whiteside, J., *A History of the Wesleyan Methodist Church in South Africa*, London, 1906.

Whitney, J., *Elizabeth Fry, Quaker Heroine*, Boston, 1936.

Wilbur, Sybil, *The Life of Mary Baker Eddy*, Boston, 1907.

Wilder, R. P., *The Great Commission, the Missionary Response*, London, 1936.

Wilson, J. C., *An Apostle to Islam: Samuel M. Zwemer*, Grand Rapids, 1952.

Winkel, W. F. A., *Leven en Arbeid van Dr. Kuyper*, Amsterdam, 1921.

Wolff, Christian, *Eigene Lebensbeschreibung*, Berlin, 1841.

Wolff, J., *Travels and Adventures of the Rev. Joseph Wolff*, London, 1861.

Wood, A. S., *The Inextinguishable Blaze*, London, 1960.

Wood, C. E., *Memoir and Letters of Canon Hay Aitken*, London, 1928.

Wordsworth, J., *The National Church of Sweden*, London, 1911.

World Statistics of Christian Missions, New York, 1916.

World Wide Evangelization, Toronto, 1902, New York, 1902.

Wright, G. F., *Charles Grandison Finney*, Boston, 1893.

The Yearbook of the American Churches, New York, 1933.

F.C.C., *The Yearbook of the American Churches*, New York, 1933.

Young, A. F., and Ashton, E. T., *British Social Work in the Nineteenth Century*, London, 1956.

INDEX